Meşad Ḥashavyahu

Tel Mor

Makmish
Tell Kudadi

Tell Judeideh
Lachish

Maresha

Mamre

Lod

'Ein el-Jedide
Bir el-Qutt
Siyar el-Ghanam
Kh. Jahzam
Kh. el-Makhrum
Khan el-Ahmar
Givat Ram
Kh. Abu Ghunneim

Tell en-Naṣbeh

Khirbet el-Mafjer
Na'aran

Kh. el-Maḥruq

Mount Nebo

Medeba

Sea

Meṣer

Tel Mevorakh

Kebara Cave

Naḥal Oren

Tel Megadim

Shaʿar ha-ʿAliyah

Nazareth

Tel Kedesh
(Tell Abu-Qudeis)

Megiddo
Beth ha-Shittah

Horvat Minha
Sde Naḥum
Tell Basul

Kinneret

Nahariya

Montfort

Tell Keisan

Khirbet el-Minya
Tel Kinneret

Kursi

Kefar Birʿam
Kefar Neburaya
Meiron

Jisr Banat Yaʿaqub

Kefar Gilʿadi

GALILEE

UPPER

GALILEE

GOLAN

ENCYCLOPEDIA
OF ARCHAEOLOGICAL
EXCAVATIONS
IN THE HOLY LAND

ENCYCLOPEDIA OF ARCHAEOLOGICAL EXCAVATIONS IN THE HOLY LAND

VOLUME III

Editors, English Edition

Michael Avi-Yonah

Ephraim Stern

Oxford University Press

ISBN 0–19–647929–0

Simultaneously published in the United States and Canada by
Prentice-Hall, Inc., Englewood Cliffs, N.J.

PRINTED IN ISRAEL by Peli Printing Works Ltd.

EDITORS, ENGLISH EDITION:
The late Michael Avi-Yonah
Ephraim Stern

EDITORIAL DIRECTOR:
Joseph Aviram

ASSISTANT EDITOR:
Essa Cindorf

ILLUSTRATIONS EDITOR:
Joseph S. Schweig

EDITORIAL BOARD
OF THE HEBREW EDITION

EDITOR-IN-CHIEF:
Benjamin Mazar

EDITORS:
the late Yohanan Aharoni
Nahman Avigad
the late Michael Avi-Yonah
the late Moshe Stekelis
Yigael Yadin

EDITORIAL DIRECTOR:
Joseph Aviram

SCIENTIFIC SECRETARY:
Magen Broshi

ILLUSTRATIONS EDITOR:
Joseph S. Schweig

VOLUME THREE — LIST OF CONTRIBUTORS

PROF. YOHANAN AHARONI (deceased), Tel Aviv University — *Judean Desert Caves (Naḥal Ḥever Caves), Tel Kinneret, Lachish, Megiddo*

PROF. RUTH AMIRAN, Israel Museum, Jerusalem — *Tel Nagila*

PROF. SHIMON APPLEBAUM, Tel Aviv University — *Mamre, Marwa*

PROF. NAHMAN AVIGAD, Hebrew University, Jerusalem — *Judean Desert Caves (Naḥal David Caves), Kefar Bir'am, Kefar Neburaya, Tell Kudadi, Makmish*

MR. JOSEPH AVIRAM, Hebrew University, Jerusalem — *Judean Desert Caves*

PROF. MICHAEL AVI-YONAH (deceased), Hebrew University, Jerusalem — *Mareshah, Medeba, Na'aran, Nessana*

FR. BELLARMINO BAGATTI, O.F.M., Jerusalem — *Nazareth, Mount Nebo*

MR. PESAH BAR-ADON, Department of Antiquities and Museums, Jerusalem — *Judean Desert Caves (Naḥal Mishmar Caves)*

DR. DAN BARAG, Hebrew University, Jerusalem — *Ma'on, Meiron*

PROF. OFER BAR-YOSEF, Hebrew University, Jerusalem — *Kebara Cave*

PIERRE BENOIT, O.P., Ecole Biblique et Archéologique Française, Jerusalem — *Tell Keisan*

MR. MERON BENVENISTI, Jerusalem — *Montfort*

MR. MAGEN BROSHI, Israel Museum, Jerusalem — *Tell Judeideh, Tel Megadim, Tell en-Naṣbeh*

MR. RUDOLF COHEN, Department of Antiquities and Museums, Jerusalem — *Monasteries*

M. HENRI DE CONTENSON, Centre National de la Recherche Scientifique, Paris — *Central Jordan Valley*

PROF. MOSHE DOTHAN, Haifa University — *Kadesh-Barnea, Meṣer, Tel Mor, Nahariya*

MR. ABRAHAM EITAN, Department of Antiquities and Museums, Jerusalem — *Tel Nagila*

DR. DAVID GILEAD (deceased), Tel Aviv University — *Jisr Banat Ya'aqub, Judean Desert Caves (Prehistoric Sites)*

PROF. NELSON GLUECK (deceased), Hebrew Union College — *Tell el-Kheleifeh*

PROF. OLEG GRABAR, University of Michigan — *Khirbet el-Minya*

MR. ROBERT W. HAMILTON, F.S.A., British Academy — *Khirbet al-Mafjar*

DR. JACOB KAPLAN, Museum of Antiquities, Tel Aviv–Jaffa — *Kefar Gil'adi, Lod*

DR. AHARON KEMPINSKI, Tel Aviv University — *Tel Masos*

MR. AMOS KLONER, Department of Antiquities and Museums, Jerusalem — *Mareshah*

PROF. BENJAMIN MAZAR, Hebrew University, Jerusalem — *Kinneret*

DR. ERIC M. MEYERS, University of North Carolina — *Meiron*

PROF. JOSEPH NAVEH, Hebrew University, Jerusalem — *Meṣad Ḥashvayahu*

PROF. ABRAHAM NEGEV, Hebrew University, Jerusalem — *Kurnub*

DR. TAMAR NOY, Israel Museum, Jerusalem — *Naḥal Oren*

M. JEAN PERROT, French Archaeological Mission, Jerusalem — *Ḥorvat Minḥa*

PROF. MOSHE STEKELIS (deceased), Hebrew University, Jerusalem — *Megalithic Monuments*

DR. EPHRAIM STERN, Hebrew University, Jerusalem — *Judean Desert Caves (Wadi Murabba'at), Tel Kedesh, Tel Mevorakh*

MISS OLGA TUFNELL, Archaeological Institute, University of London — *Lachish*

MR. NEHEMIAH TZORI, Department of Antiquities and Museums, Jerusalem — *Ḥorvat Minḥa*

DR. DAVID USSISHKIN, Tel Aviv University — *Lachish*

PROF. YIGAEL YADIN, Hebrew University, Jerusalem — *Judean Desert Caves (Cave of the Letters), Masada, Megiddo*

DR. ZEEV YEIVIN, Department of Antiquities and Museums, Jerusalem — *Khirbet el-Maḥruq*

LIST OF ABBREVIATIONS

Abel, GP. F. M. Abel, Géographie de la Palestine 1–2, Paris 1933–1938

Aharoni, LB. Aharoni, Y: The Land of the Bible, London 1966

Alt, KSch. A. Alt, Kleine Schriften zur Geschichte des Volkes Israel 1–3, München 1953–1959

Avi-Yonah, HL. Avi-Yonah, M.: The Holy Land, Grand Rapids 1966

Benoit et alii, Discoveries 2. P. Benoit — J. T. Milik — R. de Vaux, Discoveries in the Judaean Desert 2 (Les Grottes de Murabba'at), Oxford 1961

Bliss — Macalister, Excavations. F. J. Bliss — R. A. S. Macalister, Excavations in Palestine during the Years 1898–1900, London 1902

Brünnow — Domaszewski, Die Provincia Arabia. R.E. Brünnow — A. V. Domaszewski, Die Provincia Arabia 1–3, Strassburg 1904–1909

Clermont-Ganneau, ARP. C. Clermont-Ganneau, Archaeological Researches in Palestine 1–2, London 1896–1899

Clermont-Ganneau, RAO. C. Clermont-Ganneau, Recueil d'archéologie orientale 1–8, Paris 1888 ss.

Conder-Kitchener, SWP. C. R. Conder–H. H. Kitchener, Survey of Western Palestine, Memoirs 1–3, London 1881–1883

Crowfoot, Early Churches J. W. Crowfoot, Early Churches in Palestine, London 1941

EI. Eretz-Israel, Jerusalem 1950 ff.

Enc. Miqr. Encyclopaedia Biblica, 6 vols, Jerusalem 1955 ff.

Frey, Corpus. J. B. Frey, Corpus Inscriptionum Iudaicarum 2, Roma 1952

Goodenough, Jewish Symbols. E. R. Goodenough, Jewish Symbols in the Greco-Roman Period 1–12, New York 1953–1965

Guérin, Galilée. V. Guérin, Description géographique, historique et archéologique de la Palestine, Galilée, Paris 1868–1880

Guérin, Galilée. V. Guérin, Description géographique historique et archéologique de la Palestine, Judée, Paris 1868–1869

Hill, BMC. G. F. Hill, Catalogue of the Greek Coins in the British Museum, Palestine, London 1914

Klein, Corpus. S. Klein, Jüdisch-palästinisches Corpus Inscriptionum, Wien-Berlin 1920

Kohl-Watzinger, Synagogen. H. Kohl — C. Watzinger, Antike Synagogen in Galilea, Leipzig 1916

Lidzbarski, Ephemeris. M. Lidzbarski, Ephemeris für semitische Epigraphik 1–3, Giessen 1902–1915

Musil, Arabia Petraea. A. Musil, Arabia Petraea 1–3, Wien 1907–1908

Pritchard, ANET. J. B. Pritchard (ed.) Ancient Near Eastern Texts Relating to the Old Testament, Princeton 1950

Robinson, Biblical Researches. E. Robinson, Biblical Researches in Palestine, London 1841

Saller-Bagatti, Town of Nebo. S. J. Saller — B. Bagatti, The Town of Nebo, Jerusalem 1949

Schürer, GJV2. E. Schürer, Geschichte des jüdischen Volkes im Zeitalter Jesu Christi, Leipzig 1907

Stern, Material Culture. E. Stern, The Material Culture of the Land of the Bible in the Persian Period, Jerusalem 1973 (Hebrew)

Sukenik, Ancient Synagogues. E. L. Sukenik, Ancient Synagogues in Palestine and Greece, London 1934

Vincent-Abel, Jérusalem Nouvelle. L. H. Vincent —F. M. Abel, Jérusalem nouvelle 1–2, Paris 1912–1926

Vincent-Steve, Jérusalem. L. H. Vincent — M. A. Steve, Jérusalem de l'Ancien Testament 1–4, Paris 1954–1956

Watzinger, DP. K. Watzinger, Denkmäler Palästinas 1–2, Leipzig 1933–1935

Wilson-Kitchener, Special Papers. Ch. Wilson — H. H. Kitchener, The Survey of Western Palestine, Special Papers, London 1881

AAA	Annals of Archaeology and Anthropology
AASOR	Annual of the American Schools of Oriental Research
ADAJ	Annual of the Department of Antiquities of Jordan
AJA	American Journal of Archaeology
AJSLL	American Journal of Semitic Languages and Literatures
'Alon	Bulletin of the Israel Department of Antiquities
APEF	Annual of the Palestine Exploration Fund
'Atiqot	Journal of the Israel Department of Antiquities
BA	Biblical Archaeologist
BASOR	Bulletin of the American Schools of Oriental Research
BBSAJ	Bulletin, British School of Archaeology in Jerusalem
BIAL	Bulletin, Institute of Archaeology, London
BIES	Bulletin of the Israel Exploration Society (1951–1962), continuing
BJPES	Bulletin of the Jewish Palestine Exploration Society
BMB	Bulletin du musée de Beyrouth
BPM	Bulletin of the Palestine Museum
BS	Bibliotheca Sacra
BZ	Biblische Zeitschrift
CRAIBL	Comptes-rendus Academie des inscriptions et belles-lettres
HUCA	Hebrew Union College Annual
IEJ	Israel Exploration Journal
ILN	The Illustrated London News
JAOS	Journal of the American Oriental Society
JBL	Journal of Biblical Literature
JCS	Journal of Cuneiform Studies
JEA	Journal of Egyptian Archaeology
JNES	Journal of Near Eastern Studies
JPOS	Journal of the Palestine Oriental Society
JRAI	Journal of the Royal Anthropological Institute
JRAS	Journal of the Royal Asiatic Society
JRS	Journal of Roman Studies
MDOG	Mitteilungen der deutschen orientalischen Gesellschaft
MUSJ	Mélanges de l'Université Saint Joseph de Beyrouth
OLZ	Orientalistische Literaturzeitung
PEFA	Palestine Exploration Fund, Annual
PEFQSt	Palestine Exploration Fund, Quarterly Statement
PEQ	Palestine Exploration Quarterly
PJB	Palästina-Jahrbuch
QDAP	Quarterly of the Department of Antiquities in Palestine
RAr	Revue Archéologique
RB	Revue biblique
RHR	Revue de l'histoire des religions
TLZ	Theologische Literaturzeitung
VT	Vetus Testamentum
Yediot	Continuation of BIES (1962–1968)
ZAW	Zeitschrift für die alttestamentliche Wissenchaft
ZDPV	Zeitschrift des deutschen Palästina-Vereins

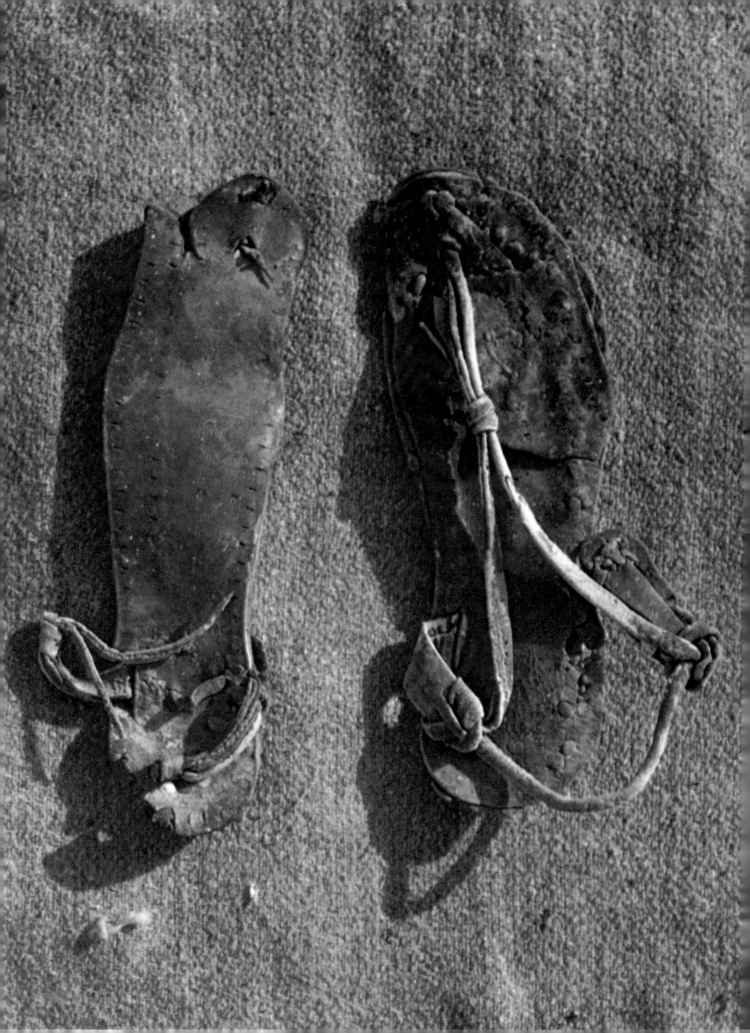

JISR BANAT YAʿAQUB

IDENTIFICATION. Near the Banat Yaʿaqub Bridge (in Hebrew, **Gesher Benot Yaʿakov**) on the banks of the Jordan River, about 4 kilometers (2.5 miles) south of Lake Ḥuleh (prior to its drainage), Pleistocene deposits were uncovered containing stone implements and animal remains. In the 1930's and 1950's, the Jordan River bed was widened, and in the course of the work, archaeological material was collected by M. Stekelis, who conducted surveys and soundings at the site.

EXCAVATIONS

The surveys revealed concentrations of flint and basalt artifacts as well as fauna to the north and south of the bridge. In 1937, a sounding (4 by 7 meters) was made on the right bank of the Jordan River, about 20 meters south of the bridge, uncovering several layers. In 1951, the Jordan River bed was again widened and additional layers came to light to complete the stratigraphy established from the 1937 investigation. Since the site encroached upon the Syro-Israeli border, a thorough examination was difficult, and some questions could not be resolved.

The following stratigraphy was established (from top to botton):

LAYER I (0–.42 meter): gravel with unabraded flint implements of Levallois technique covered with black patina.

LAYER II (.42–.6 meter): yellow clay with unabraded handaxes, made of gray flint and covered with black patina.

LAYER III (.6–.9 meter): green with unabraded flakes and handaxes made of gray flint.

LAYER IV (.9–1.7 meters): a thick bed of black soil with unabraded handaxes made of gray flint and covered with black patina; also three rolled handaxes made of basalt. Abundant mollusca *(Melanopsis viviparus)* and one tusk (1.75 meters in length) of an elephant *(Elephas trogontherii)*.

LAYER V (1.7–3.4 meters): hardened black soil with rich unabraded basalt industry of handaxes and cleavers. Abundant mollusca and mammal bones.

LAYER VI (3.4–5.5 meters): a thick layer of pebbles and boulders with heavily rolled basalt handaxes and cleavers.

THE LITHIC INDUSTRY

The implements in layers I–IV were made of flint,

Woman's sandals from the time of Bar Kokhba, found in the Cave of the Letters, Judean Desert.

whereas basalt was the material used in layer V. In layer I, the toolkit—points, flakes, and cores—was made by the Levallois technique. Layer II yielded small and elongated amygdaloid bifaces, several reminiscent of Micoquian bifaces. Acheulian bifaces and flakes were found in layers III–IV. Layer V contained forty-seven bifaces, twenty-eight cleavers, and twenty rough flakes, all made of basalt. They were produced by the block-on-block technique. Bifaces (130–298 millimeters in length) are trimmed on both faces with two cutting edges and a pointed end. Some of them have retained their natural cortex on the butt. Cleavers (120–175 millimeters in length) were shaped from large basalt flakes. They are rectangular or U-shaped, and the majority have broad and thick striking platforms and secondary flaking on the sides.

FAUNA

The animal remains were studied by D. A. Hooijer, who distinguished nine species:

LAYER II. Elephant *(Elephas trogonotherii* Pohlig), deer *(Dama,* cf. *Mesopotamica* Brooke), horse *(Equus,* cf. *caballus* L.).

LAYER III. Elephant *(Elephas trogontherii* Pohlig), rhinoceros *(Dicerorhinus merckii* [Jaeger]).

LAYER IV. Elephant *(Elephas trogontherii* Pohlig).

LAYER V. Stegodon *(Stegodon mediterraneus* Hooijer), bison (cf. *Bison priscus* [Bojanus]); also pig *(Sus* cf. *scrofa* L.) and stag *(Cervus* cf. elaphus L.) but not clearly identified.

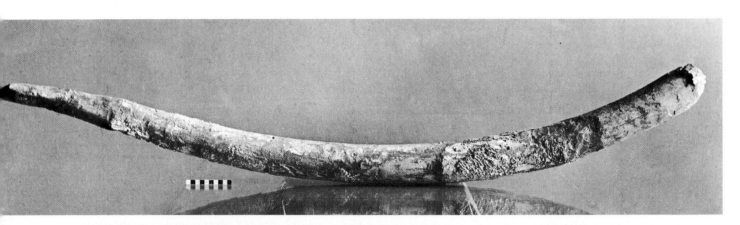

In the opinion of Hooijer, the fauna can be dated to the Mindel-Riss Interglacial, i.e., the Middle Pleistocene.

GEOLOGY

The above deposits, which are up to 8 meters thick, lie in unconformity on layers of the Villafranchian period. Between the upper and the lower strata is a 4-meter-thick deposit containing layers II-V. L. Picard attributed the lower part, layers IV–V, to the Middle Pleistocene and the upper part, layers II-III, to the Middle and Upper Pleistocene. Ecologically, Picard considered that layers IV-V were formed in a swampy environment whereas layers II-III were of lacustrine origin.

CONCLUSION

The study of the Pleistocene deposits of Jisr Banat Ya'aqub, although not yet completed, have contributed greatly to the study of the prehistory of Israel and the Near East. Here for the first time stone implements and fossil animal remains hitherto unknown were found in Israel, in a stratigraphic and geological relationship, thus adding a further dimension to the prehistoric cultures of Israel. Once the geological stratigraphy of the site is clearly established, it will help to clarify the relative chronology of the Pleistocene of the Jordan Valley. The geological and prehistoric chronology of the Jordan Valley is important in that almost every prehistoric culture is represented there, from the Developed Oldowan and Early Acheulian (see 'Ubeidiya) through the Acheulian and Mousterian cultures to the Neolithic (see Sha'ar ha-Golan). Geological, paleontological, and palynological data will, it is hoped, make it possible to set up a chronological framework for the Jordan Valley. Within it, Jisr Banat Ya'aqub will be an important link.

As to the relative chronology, it can already be stated that from the archaeological, geological, and paleontological evidence, the lower layers IV-V can be related to the Middle Pleistocene and layers I-III to the Middle and Upper Pleistocene. According to the European Alpine chronology of the Pleistocene, the early Jisr Banat Ya'aqub deposits extend from the Mindel to the Riss Glaciation and the upper layers from the Riss-Würm Interglacial to the Early Würm Glaciation.   D. GILEAD

BIBLIOGRAPHY

M. Stekelis–L. Picard, *QDAP* 6 (1937), 214–15; 7 (1938), 45 • M. Stekelis, *IV Congress Inter. de Cièncìas Prehist. y Protohist. Cronica*, Madrid, 1954, 391–94 • D. A. Hooijer, *Bull. Research Council of Israel* 8G (1959), 177–99; 9G (1960), 104–8 • M. Stekelis, *ibid.*, 61–90 • L. Picard, *The Israel Academy of Sciences and Humanities*, 1, 4, 1–34 • E. de Vaumas, *IEJ* 13 (1963), 195–206 • D. Gilead, *World Archaeology* 2:1–11 (1970); *idem, Qadmoniot* 3 (1970), 88–90 (Hebrew).

Opposite page, top: Tusk of an elephant; Bottom: Fragments of a tusk, tooth and vertebra of a prehistoric elephant (Elephas trogontherii); This page: Handstones.

JORDAN VALLEY

EXPLORATION. In 1953, a survey was conducted in the Jordan Valley between the Yarmuk and the plains of Moab, by J. Mellaart and H. de Contenson, who examined hundreds of sites, especially sites exposed to damage during work on the diversion of the Yarmuk. Two of the sites excavated in this survey will be dealt with here, Tell Abu Ḥabil and Tell esh-Shunah. Three other sites, among others, were recently excavated in the Jordan Valley—Tell Delhamiyah, Ḥorvat Minḥa (q.v.) and Neve Ur (see bibliography).

Tell Abu Ḥabil. This mound is situated on the east bank of the Jordan, east of Tell Abu es-Ṣuf, about 15 kilometers (9 miles) southeast of Beth-Shean (map reference 20451972). N. Glueck, who discovered the site, dated most of the pottery collected on the surface to the Chalcolithic period and a small quantity to the Neolithic.

Mellaart and de Contenson dug two trial trenches on the mound. The deposit was found to be 2 meters thick, consisting of a series of superimposed dwelling pits similar to those discovered at Beersheba and at Jericho in the Pottery Neolithic period. Settlement at Tell Abu Ḥabil commenced in the early part of the Chalcolithic period, contemporary with Tell esh-Shunah I and Beth-Shean XVIII (Glueck's "Neolithic" finds are to be ascribed to this period) and continued almost up to the Ghassulian phase. A similar variant of the Ghassulian phase is found at other Jordan Valley sites as well, as for example at Tell Fendi opposite Beth-Shean, Tell es-Saʿidiyeh et-Taḥta on the southern bank of Wadi Kafrinjeh, and others.

Tell esh-Shunah. This mound lies on the border between the Jordan Valley and Gilead (map reference 207224) about 4 kilometers (2.5 miles) southeast of the confluence of the Yarmuk and the Jordan River and about 3 kilometers (2 miles) east of the Jordan ford Mahaṣat Umm es-Sisan. The mound rises about 10 meters above the surroundings, and is about 1 kilometer long. Today two villages, Khirbet esh-Shunah and Sheikh Hasin, stand on the mound.

The site was discovered during the 1953 survey by de Contenson, who sank a trial trench in the mound. A second was dug by Mellaart. The following strata were distinguished in the trenches, from bottom to top:

I Early Chalcolithic period
II Late Chalcolithic period
III Early Bronze Age I
IV Early Bronze Age II
V Early Bronze Age III
VI Arab period

STRATUM I, EARLY CHALCOLITHIC. In one of the trial trenches, virgin soil was reached at a depth of 2.8 meters below surface level. The first settlement on the site was established at the foot of the hills, on a terrace built of sand mixed with pebbles. Above the layer of sand was a layer of red clay (.3 meter thick), and above this was the occupation layer (also .3 meter thick) comprising a floor made of beaten earth, pebbles, and ashes. Fireplaces were found in this layer as was a pit dug into the clay and the sandy layer. The pit, 1 meter deep, with a diameter 1.5 meters, resembles a silo with a flat base. The pottery and flints found in the pit are similar to those found on the floor. The pit has parallels in Beth-Shean below stratum XVIII, and also has analogies with structures of the Chalcolithic strata at Tell el-Farʿa (North) and the Pottery Neolithic strata at Jericho (strata VIII-IX of Garstang).

Although pottery formed the major part of the finds, there were also several "Canaanite" flint blades with abrupt retouch, fragments of limestone and basalt implements, broken grindstones, and in the pits, bone awls. The pottery is handmade of gritty buff clay, and is usually covered with a red slip applied in horizontal bands, and in some cases over the whole surface of the vessel. Burnish is rare. Some pottery in this layer was painted in mat zigzag patterns or decorated with bands in relief. Only a few types of vessels occur, among which are simple bowls, hole-mouth jars, high-footed bowls, and middle-sized stone jars. Also appearing here are the store jars characteristic of this period, with bow rims, two flat loop handles widening near the point of attachment to the vessel, and spiral-shaped mat impressions on their flat base.

The assemblage of stratum I, especially the pottery, closely resembles that of Beth-Shean XVIII, and the assemblage from the pits beneath stratum I is similar to the earliest Chalcolithic complex at

Tell el-Far'a (called Middle Chalcolithic by R. de Vaux, who later, however, also inclined to consider this complex Early Chalcolithic), Jericho VIII of Garstang and Pottery Neolithic B of Kathleen Kenyon. Similar pottery is also found at other sites in the Jordan Valley. This stratum is contemporary to the Late Neolithic at Byblos and to the Halafian culture in Northern Syria (Ugarit IV$_2$–III$_1$, and Amuq D).

The culture represented in this stratum apparently appears in the Jordan Valley between the Neolithic of Jericho IX and the Chalcolithic Ghassulian culture. It should be considered a variant of the Early Chalcolithic, like the other variants such as The Yarmukian, the Wadi-Rabah phase, and the early stage of the Beersheba culture.

STRATUM II, LATE CHALCOLITHIC. In this stratum two occupation levels were discovered, separated from each other and from the earlier level by layers of clayey soil. In the upper level a straight wall was found. The pottery of this level consists of three types: gray-burnished ware, red-burnished ware, and ordinary pottery. The gray-burnished carinated bowls are characteristic of Esdraelon Ware. The red-burnished ware (group A according to the classification of Kathleen Kenyon) is of the same type that appears in the north together with the gray-burnished ware. The ordinary pottery resembles that of Ghassul IV and the lowest level at Tell 'Umm Hamad esh-Shariqi, which are contemporary with Tulul Abu el-'Alaiq (see Jericho), the upper Chalcolithic layer at Tell el-Far'a (North) (q.v.), and Beth-Shean XVII. The ordinary ware at Tell esh-Shunah is similar to that of Meṣer II and of Beth-Shean XVI, whereas the preceding layer corresponds, as mentioned above, to Beth-Shean XVIII. It can therefore be assumed that the settlement at Tell esh-Shunah was interrupted for a short time.

Judging from their finds, these sites belong to a proto-Urban stage and the culture of stratum II represents the Late Chalcolithic of the north.

STRATUM III, EARLY BRONZE AGE I. Three floors with brown earth between them were discovered. The intermediate floor belongs to an apsidal structure. This stratum, which contained pottery decorated with band slip, is contemporary with Beth-Shean XV–XIV.

STRATUM IV, EARLY BRONZE AGE II. Two floors and a straight wall were uncovered here. Band-slip

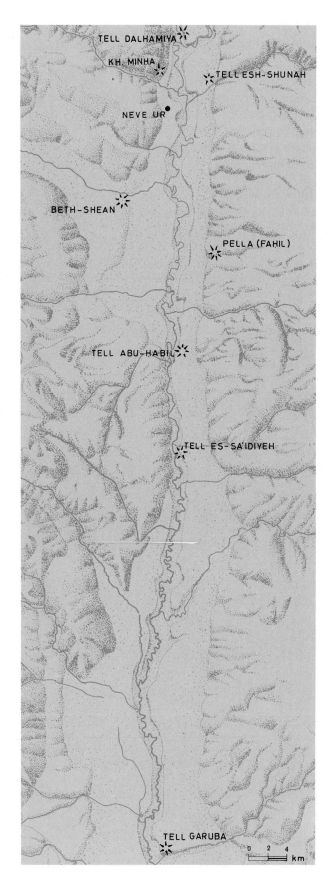

decoration is still common, but ordinary burnish and pattern burnishing also appear. This stratum parallels Beth-Shean XIV–XIII.

STRATUM V, EARLY BRONZE AGE III. This stratum contained pottery of Khirbet Kerak ware, many sherds of which were scattered all over the area of the mound.

STRATUM VI, ARAB PERIOD. Glazed and painted pottery was found. H. DE CONTENSON

BIBLIOGRAPHY

Tell Abu Ḥabil: N. Glueck, *AASOR* 25–28 (1945/9), 275–76, 432, 435 • H. de Contenson, *ADAJ* 4–5 (1960), 12–98, *idem*, *MUSJ* 37 (1961), 60, n. 5 • J. Mellaart, *ADAJ* 6–7 (1962), 137–38.
Tell esh-Shunah: H. de Contenson, *ADAJ* 4–5 (1960); *idem*, *RB* 68 (1961), 546–56 • J. Mellaart, *ADAJ* 6–7 (1962), 131–33 • H. de Contenson, *ibid.*, 8–9 (1964), 30 ff.
Neve Ur: J. Perrot, et al, *IEJ* 17 (1967), 201–32 (includes bibliography).
Ḥorvat Minḥa: *ibid.*, for bibliography, *idem*, *Qadmoniot* 2 (1969), 52–56 (Hebrew).
Tell Delhamiyeh: M. Stekelis, *EI* 8 (1967), 88 94 (Hebrew).

Judean Desert. Map of prehistoric sites.

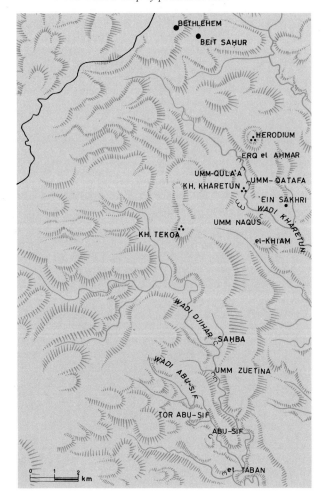

JUDEAN DESERT CAVES — Prehistoric Sites

IDENTIFICATION. The prehistoric sites of the Judean Desert are situated southeast of Bethlehem, in Wadi Kharetun, Wadi Djihar, Wadi Abu-Sif, and their vicinity. Between the years 1928 and 1949, they were explored by R. Neuville on behalf of the Institute de Paléontologie Humaine in Paris. In 1962, J. G. Echegaray resumed the excavation of one of the sites, the el-Khiam terrace, on behalf of Spanish institutions. H. Vallois studied the human remains, R. Vaufrey, G. Haas, and E. Tchernov examined the fauna. This group of sites comprises eight caves: Umm-Qatafa, Abu-Sif, Sahba, Umm-Naqus, et-Taban, Umm-Zuetina, 'Ein-Sakhri and Umm-Qala'a; two rock shelters: Erq el-Ahmar and el-Quseir; and two terrace deposits: Tor Abu-Sif and el-Khiam.

The excavations showed a continuous occupation of the area from the Lower Palaeolithic to the Pre-Pottery Neolithic period. After an interruption, occupation was resumed during the Chalcolithic period.

The faunal and geological studies enabled R. Neuville to establish a geo-chronological framework, and to trace the prehistoric past of Palestine by comparing his finds with the material from the Carmel Caves (q.v.).

The Umm-Qatafa Cave consists of one main chamber from which a long and narrow gallery leads into a second cave whose vault had collapsed. In the center of the main chamber, water had seeped in and carved out a channel which formed three linked pits. Part of the cave and almost the whole of the main chamber were excavated to a depth of 3.5 meters. The cave was later dug to a depth of about 5 meters and 8 meters in the main chamber. Bedrock was reached in the pits at a depth of 12.11 meters.

A complete section was exposed in pits I–II where Neuville distinguished thirteen strata, labeled A-J. Three of them were subdivided: E into three stages, and D and G into two. Strata B, C, H–J were sterile. Stratum A contained Ghassulian remains; stratum D, Upper Acheulian (D_2), and Micoquian (D_1); strata E_1 and E_2 are Middle Acheulian, E_3–G_2

Tayacian. Pit III lacked remains of the three upper strata. It contained seven strata, as follows: strata D and E, which are apparently identical with D_1 and E_1 of pits I–II; strata F and F_1 are identical with E_2; F_2 is identical with E_3; G is identical with G, and H is identical with H. In the second cave Neuville distinguished nine strata. All of them were sterile, with the exception of stratum A which contained Ghassulian remains.

From the shape of the cave and from the examination of the deposits and the fauna, Neuville inferred that the cave and its pits were formed during a period of great humidity and intense karstic activity. At the end of this period, the deposits of stratum J were covered with stagnant water. Strata G–I consist of travertine deposited in a dry climate (but still humid by comparison with present conditions). The same applies to strata B–D, though strata B and C were deposited in a colder and more humid climate. Strata E and F were formed in a warm and humid climate. The stalagmites of strata E_{1-2} bear witness to the high degree of humidity. From these observations, Neuville concluded that the karstic activity which produced the cave and the humid climate in which the stalagmites were formed coincide with two pluvials, whereas the cold climate inferred from strata B and C heralded the approach of a third pluvial. Comparing those pluvials with L. Picard's A–B–C, he correlated C with the Würm Glaciation and B with the Riss Glaciation.

The difference between the Tayacian industry of strata G (pit III), G_1 and G_2 (pits I–II) and that of F_2 (pit III), E_3–F (pits I–II) is quantitative and lies in a varying proportion of tools of the same type obtained by identical techniques.

The stone industry is mainly represented by flakes and some retouched flakes or blades with discontinuous retouch. Most flakes have a plain striking platform. A few show a faceted striking platform, the angle between the latter and the back of the flake being always obtuse. The flakes are obtained from simple cores. In strata E_3, F, and F_2 there is an increasing proportion of retouched tools and flakes with a faceted striking platform (from 5 to 15 percent for the former, from 17 to 25 percent for the latter).

The difference between the assemblage of strata F, F_1 (pit III), E_1, E_2 (pits I–II) and that of D_1 and D_2 (pits I–II), which were attributed to the Middle, the

Upper, and the final Acheulian (Micoquian), is to be found either in the types of flaked implements and their quatitative relationship or in the varying types and dimensions of the handaxes. Those characteristic of the Middle Acheulian are oval, lanceolate, and almond shaped. They are accompanied by flakes obtained by a technique similar to that used in the earlier levels. The Upper Acheulian is represented by broad ovate, discoidal, and cordiform handaxes and an increased number of burins. Characteristic of the final (Micoquian) stage are small handaxes, mostly pointed, but also heart-shaped, triangular, discoidal, narrow and

Abu Sif Cave. Plan and Section.
1. Black soil, hearths; sterile. 2. Light-brown porous dolomite travertine deposit, slightly clayey, hearths, remains of fauna, and numerous Mousterian artifacts.
3. Light-brown porous clayey travertine with limestone boulders, little fauna, many Mousterian artifacts. 4. Reddish chalky clay, little fauna, many artifacts. 5. Light-brown porous clayey travertine with yellow boulders, little fauna, many Mousterian artifacts. 6. Clay soil with phosphate, hearths, rare fauna, many artifacts. 7. Gravel disintegrating into white chalk, no fauna or artifacts. 8. Compact light-gray travertine, angular gravel, no fauna, hand axes. 9. Chalky earth layer.

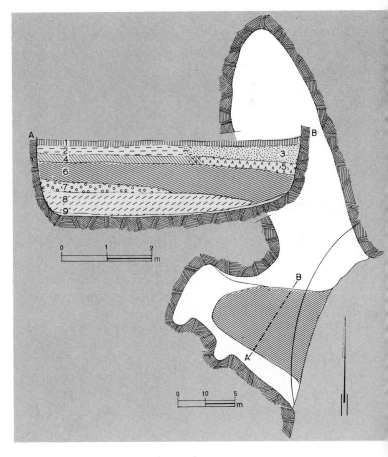

Below: Umm Zuetina Cave, animal figurine of limestone; Bottom: Saḥba Cave. Plan and Section.
1. Black soil, remains of hearths and late potsherds.
2. Dark-brown travertine deposit, slightly clayey, remains of hearths and fauna, numerous Mousterian artifacts.
3. Compact brown phosphatic chalky clay, remains of fauna, many Mousterian artifacts.
4. Fallen gravel crumbled into chalk.

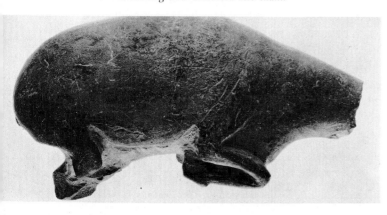

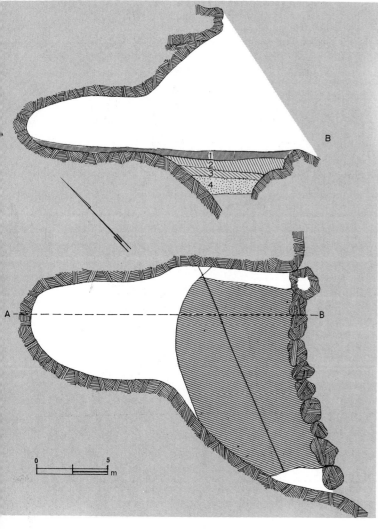

broad oval. They are accompanied by a few scrapers and burins. The site was subsequently abandoned for a long period, during which strata B and C (pits I–II) were deposited.

Occupation of the site was resumed in the Ghassulian period (stratum A). Three dwelling pits (I–III) were found. The sides of one pit were apparently lined with stones. The industry collected in the pits consists of flint, bones, basalt, limestone, and pottery. The flint implements include sickle blades, awls, fan scrapers, adzes, and one arrowhead. Sickle blades are the majority, with awls second in quantity. Among the stone implements are one piriform mace-head, grinding stones, a fragment of a basalt pedestal, and a few basalt bowls. The rims of the latter bear an incised decoration of triangles filled with parallel incisions. The pedestal fragment is decorated on one side with an incised herringbone pattern, and on the other side with chevrons.

The pottery consists of sherds of cornets, churns, cups, basins, bowls, hole-mouth jars, and jars with short or long necks, The handles include lug handles, knob handles, and plain short ledge handles. The decoration is mainly a thumb-indented rope motif or painted parallel bands, zigzags, or triangles. An ossuary fragment (later published separately by J. Perrot) was also found. The dwelling pits lined with stones and the vessels — the churn, decorated basalt bowls, and pedestal fragment — are typically Ghassulian. However, some of the sherds, e.g., those of a flat bowl, are dated to the Early Bronze Age.

The Abu-Sif Cave consists of two chambers but only the southern chamber and the terrace in front of it yielded archaeological deposists, and the excavation was thus confined to that area.

Bedrock was reached at a depth of 1.62 meters; six layers (A–F) were differentiated in section. Three layers, A, D, and F, were sterile. Mousterian artifacts were found in strata B and C and stratum E yielded remains belonging to the final stage of the Acheulian. On the basis of the travertine deposits mixed with gravel, Neuville correlated stratum E with stratum C at Umm-Qatafa and the sterile stratum D with the sterile stratum B there. The final Acheulian industry (stratum E) is represented by eight small handaxes and several flakes. The Mousterian assemblage contains retouched points, Levallois blades or flakes with faceted or plain striking platforms. The most frequent type, the point, is generally long and narrow, and sometimes straight or curved. Side scrapers and burins are rare. The cores are all Levallois; blades and flakes are numerous. The industries of the two Mousterian strata differ in that the upper stratum (B) shows an increase in the number of tools with a plain striking platform and in the number of blades, which resemble Upper Paleolithic blades, and also of curved points obtained from them.

The Sahba Cave was found empty of ancient deposits, and therefore excavation was carried out on the terrace in front of the cave and at the entrance. It was interrupted at a depth of 2.3 meters without reaching bedrock. Four strata, A–D, were uncovered. Stratum D was sterile and strata B–C contained traces of hearths and Mousterian artifacts.

The Mousterian industry at Sahba resembles that of Abu-Sif.

The et-Taban Cave was found empty of ancient deposits; the excavations were therefore concentrated in the terrace. Bedrock was reached at a depth of 1.7 meters and four strata, A–D, were distinguished in section. Stratum D was sterile. Stratum C contained hearths and Mousterian remains, and stratum B, hearths and Upper Paleolithic artifacts. A few sherds were found in stratum A, some belonging to the Early Bronze Age. In stratum C, the tools were made of Levallois flakes, most of which have a faceted striking platform. Here again, the most common type is the broad point, generally retouched on both edges, and the side scraper. Neuville dated this layer at et-Taban later than stratum B at Abu-Sif.

End scrapers predominate in stratum B. Other tools include burins. Châtelperronian points, knives retouched by flaking, and some truncated blades. Cores are prismatic. Mousterian-type tools are rare. One Emireh point and two bone points were also found.

The Umm-Naqus Cave. An area of 48 square meters was excavated inside this cave and on the terrace in front of it. At a depth of 2 meters, the dig was concentrated in a small sounding, where bedrock was reached at a depth of 3 meters. Four strata, labeled A–D, were distinguished. Stratum D was sterile. Stratum C contained traces of hearths and Mousterian artifacts, and stratum B yielded some Upper Paleolithic remains. Traces of hearths and pottery from various periods appeared in

stratum A. Neuville established that stratum C was later than Abu-Sif B and C. Stratum C tools are fashioned from Levallois flakes or blades. The main types are points and side scrapers, most of them thin (points outnumber scrapers). Among the points, some are elongated, straight or curved, or triangular, elongated or short, with one or both edges retouched, or without retouch.

In stratum B, end scrapers predominate. Dihedral and angle burins, retouched blades, and one broken Gravettian blade were also found. Because of the small number of implements, it was impossible to correlate it with a definite stage of the Upper Paleolithic.

The 'Erq el-Ahmar Shelter is located in Wadi Kharetun. This is a very large site, about 30 meters long and 6 meters wide. An area of about 50 square meters was excavated in its southern part. The thickness of deposits above bedrock is 2–3 meters. Mousterian, Upper Paleolithic (stages I–IV), and Lower Natufian artifacts were brought to light. This site is most important because of its long unbroken stratigraphic sequence.

The stratigraphy from bedrock upward is as follows: STRATUM H. A layer of black clay (.2–1 meter) separated from bedrock by a thin (about .2 meter) sterile bed of reddish-brown earth. Flint implements are abundant and consist of numerous flakes and blades made in the Levallois technique; 85 percent display a faceted striking platform. Most of the implements themselves are not retouched. Some show partial retouches, and only one side scraper was carefully retouched on both edges. Abundant fauna was collected.

Neuville called this industry Levallois, but these assemblages are now known as Mousterian of Levallois facies. The stratigraphic position of stratum H in the sequence of Mousterian cultures in Palestine indicates that it apparently belongs to an early stage of the Mousterian.

STRATUM G. Dark-brown clay with stones at the base, .4 meter thick. This sterile bed separates the preceding Mousterian layer from the overlying Upper Paleolithic, stage II, deposit.

STRATA E–F. .4 meter and .2 meter thick, respectively, they have the same composition as strata B–D, i.e., dark-brown clay. In stratum E, animal remains were abundant whereas none appeared in stratum F.

The industry is similar in both strata. Scrapers

make up about half of the tools, mostly fashioned from flakes. Points, the second largest group, are made of blades of medium size and retouched on one edge. Among the other tools are small prismatic and discoidal cores and thin, broad, and generally short blades. It should be noted that in these strata, and to a lesser extent also in strata B–D, discoidal cores and cores prepared for the production of flakes and blades are still in use, indicating the persistence of Mousterian techniques.

The Emireh point is absent in this industry, the proportion of end scrapers on blades is relatively high, and points are more developed than in industries from stage I. Therefore, Neuville assigned these two strata to stage II of the Upper Paleolithic.

STRATUM D. .1–.45 meter thick, with abundant fauna and more than 150 flint implements. The most common and characteristic tool (over one third of those recorded) is a medium-sized, narrow point with careful retouch on one edge, the other edge retouched only toward the ends. Such points are the so-called Font-Yves or Krems type. Points similar to those of the preceding strata were also found. Scrapers appear in the same proportion as points. Carinated scrapers are rare. Burins, though less common than scrapers, are more typical and varied than in earlier layers. Among them are dihedral burins and burins on truncation.

This is chiefly a blade industry but discoidal Levallois cores and prepared striking platforms are still in use. On the basis of these groups of tools, especially the points which are the hallmark of the stratum, the industry was attributed to stage III of the Upper Paleolithic.

STRATUM C. .3–.4 meter thick, containing only a small number of tools which did not permit a classification more precise than the Upper Paleolithic.

STRATUM B. .4–.65 meter thick, with some fauna, a few hearths, and more than 160 flint implements. The majority are scrapers, half of them end scrapers on blades or flakes, one fifth are carinated, and one fifth are beaked. Burins and points are rare, less frequent in this layer than in the preceding stratum. Prepared striking platforms are rare.

Neuville assigned this industry to stage IV of the Upper Paleolithic.

STRATUM A_2. A .2-meter-thick deposit of gray chalky travertine containing fauna, flint implements, and a burial. Tools include lunates, half of them with the Helwan-type retouch, backed bladelets mostly with truncated ends, some displaying a Helwan-type retouch, and some with a gloss that designates them as sickle blades. Awls and burins are scare. Only one micro-burin was found. Various types of scrapers and a few atypical, notched implements were recovered. Bone tools consist chiefly of polished awls and points and also beads and a fragment of a harpoon. The pestles include a beautifully carved basalt specimen. Stones with V-shaped hollows were apparently mortars, and others, with an incision, were probably whetstones. The many red ocher fragments and *Dentalium* shells found, probably served as ornaments. This assemblage is typical of the Natufian culture, and since the Helwan-type retouch is frequent and the micro-burin extremely rare, Neuville assigned the industry to the first stage of the Natufian culture.

A rectangular burial pit (.5 meter deep) paved with flat stone slabs (1 by 1.9 meters) contained the remains of seven individuals, four adults and three children. Only one skeleton, that of a twenty- to thirty-year-old woman, was more or less complete and adorned with a necklace of bones and teeth. Of the other bodies, only the skulls had been buried. A horse tooth was found next to each skull. We thus have here a collective burial accompanied by funerary offerings.

El-Khiam. This is an open site, situated on the terrace of Wadi Kharetun. It was investigated by Neuville in 1933 in two sounding pits, one in the center of the terrace and one to the west of it. In 1951, J. Perrot published the material from this excavation. In 1962, J. G. Echegaray resumed work in an area of 6 by 6 meters next to Neuville's pit I. The thickness of the archaeological deposits reaches 6 meters. Echegaray recognized fifteen strata. His stratigraphy and quantitative data will be used hereafter. Perrot differentiated ten strata, labeled A–J. The relationship between the two stratigraphies is roughly the following: 1–3 = A, 4 = B, 5 = C, 6–8 = D, 9–10 = E–F.

Because of the thickness of the archaeological deposits and its continuous occupation over a long period as an open site, el-Khiam is a site of major importance.

The stratigraphy, bottom upwards is as follows:

STRATA 11 d–c. Two layers (.3 meter and .5 meter thick) containing a rich flint industry (about 850 implements) to which finds from the upper part of stratum 12—a sterile layer with intrusive tools—should be added. Scrapers are typical of this stratum. They are plentiful, mainly carinated, with some nosed scrapers and end scrapers. Side scrapers and a few Mousterian-type points are also present. Burins are rare. A few awls fashioned from blades were also collected. Echegaray classified this industry as Lower Aurignacian (Aurinaciense Primitiv).

STRATA 11 a–b. 1 meter thick. The flint industry comprises more than 3,000 implements with a large proportion of scrapers—carinated, end scrapers on flakes and blades—burins and awls, backed blades, atypical Gravettian points, a few retouched bladelets, and several triangular ones. Echegaray classified this industry as Middle Aurignacian.

STRATUM 10. .95 meter thick with a total of 2,800 tools. Flint implements are for the most part typologically the same as in the preceding layers, but the number of burins with concave truncation and of geometric microliths increases and the blunted-back points are scarce. Echegaray calls this industry Upper Aurignacian (Aurinciense Reciente). Strata 11 and 10 correspond approximately to Neuville's Upper Paleolithic IV.

STRATUM 9. .7 meter thick; 1,500 flint implements were collected. Scrapers are numerous, but unlike the preceding layers, there is a decrease in carinated scrapers in comparison with scrapers fashioned from blades. Burins are less common and most are on truncation. Awls are frequent. There is an increase in microliths, among them blunted-back bladelets, geometric microliths, and micro-burins. Echegaray attributes the industry to the Atlitian culture, i.e., to the Upper Paleolithic V of Neuville.

STRATA 8–6. .13 meter, .18 meter, and .2 meter thick respectively. Three stages of the Kebaran culture are represented here. Echegaray dates the Kebaran to the Mesolithic, whereas Neuville and Perrot classify it in the Upper Paleolithic VI, its final stage. The industry includes many backed bladelets, some with a concave back, some with oblique truncature. They are numerous in stratum 6. Scalene triangles occur in stratum 8 and become rare in the other strata. Micro-burins are found in stratum 6 and their number increases toward stratum 8. Lunates, common in stratum 6, make their first appearance in stratum 8 where their shape is closer to a triangle. The micro-Gravettian-type point is present in all the layers. Some points found in strata 8–7 may be regarded as the predecessors of the Natufian arrowheads. There are also awls fashioned from bladelets and burins, including burins on truncation. End scrapers and carinated round scrapers are also found.

This industry is called Kebaran essentially because it is placed between the Natufian and the Atlitian cultures. Although it has some affinities with the Kebaran assemblage found in the Kebara Cave itself, it nevertheless shows some differences. Echegaray subdivided the Kebaran at el-Khiam into three phases, I–III, corresponding to the three strata.

STRATA 5–4. Each Stratum is .3 meter thick. The flint industry found in these strata was called Natufian by Perrot and Khiamian by Echegaray. The flint assemblage includes lunates, numerous micro-burins, and awls, also small arrowheads with two notches next to the concave base, dihedral burins, burins on truncation, and various types of scrapers. No tools have Helwan-type retouch. Snails and perforated shells served as ornaments. Mortars and pestles are common, and a fragment of a stone vessel was found.

This assemblage corresponds to the Natufian industry and according to the former subdivision of the Natufian, the abundance of micro-burins, the presence of simple arrowheads, the absence of Helwan-type retouch, the bone industry and art objects place stratum 5 in the second stage of the Natufian and stratum 4 in the late stage. Part of the finds dated by Perrot to the Natufian stage IV were assigned by Echegaray to the beginning of the next cultural stage, which he called proto-Tahunian. The first stage of the Natufian is not represented here as it is known from other sites, e.g., Erq el-Ahmar (see above), el-Wad (see Carmel Caves), and the Kebara Cave (q.v.). In the opinion of Echegaray, however, there is an uninterrupted evolution at el-Khiam from the Kebaran of stratum 6 to the industry of stratum 5. Since the evolution is different at other sites, Echegaray preferred not to call the industry of strata 5–4 Natufian, but Khiamian. Although the industry resembles Natufian industries in other sites, it evolved somewhat differently. When the results of excavations in the Natufian layers of Eynan (q.v.), Naḥal Oren (q.v.), and Jericho (q.v.) are published, it will be possible to trace more clearly the evolution of the Mesolithic industries in Palestine.

STRATA 3–2. Each stratum is .2 meter thick. They contain a transitional flint industry extending from the Lower Khiamian to the Upper Tahunian of stratum 1. Lunates are still present, though in smaller numbers. Also found are micro-burins and small arrowheads with a concave base and two notches near it. New types appear: leaf-shaped tanged arrowheads with pressure flaking, tanged and notched arrowheads, and arrowheads with wings and tangs. A few sickle blades, awls, burins, and scrapers were also found. This industry was assigned by Perrot to the Natufian IV, but according to Echegaray it was the precursor of the Tahunian culture, and he therefore named it proto-Tahunian.

STRATUM 1. .6 meter thick. Only the lower two thirds of this stratum are undisturbed. Traces of structures — stone walls and round stone hearths — were unearthed. The flint industry included many microlithic lunates, blunted-back bladelets, some pointed and some with an oblique truncature, a few sickle blades, small arrowheads retouched by pressure, some with tangs and some with tangs and wings, also, awls, burins, and scrapers. Several axes were recovered by Neuville as well as hoes and picks. None, however, were found in the later excavations. This stratum is assigned to the Tahunian culture of the Neolithic period.

The el-Quseir Shelter. It is located at the confluence of Wadi Makhta-el-Djaf and Wadi Murabba'at. One of Neuville's former workers undertook the excavation, and Perrot published the finds. Two strata (C and D) containing flint implements and fauna were distinguished.

STRATUM D. .56 meter thick. It contained 665 pieces of flint, of which only thirty-five are tools. Scrapers, among them end scrapers and carinated scrapers, account for one half of the tools. There are also burins, blunted-back bladelets, a few cores, and many blades and bladelets. Some blades and flakes have a prepared striking platform.

The most interesting find is a bone point with a split base. It is 38 millimeters long, 5–7 millimeters in diameter and has an oval section. This small tool, which is reminiscent of tools of the Aurignacian

culture in France, is the only one of its kind so far found in Israel.

STRATUM C. 1.4 meters thick. The flint industry numbers 270 implements, the majority are scrapers of various types, chiefly carinated and beaked scrapers. Burins are not numerous. There are also retouched and obliquely truncated blades, denticulated pieces, and numerous tools of Mousterian type with a double patina, probably in secondary usage. This assemblage can be assigned to the Upper Paleolithic stage IV. The industry from stratum D appears to be somewhat older.

Masrak e-Naaj is located in Wadi Taamreh. The lithic assemblage, which was scanty and recovered by unsystematic excavation, was published by Perrot. Scrapers make up half of the tools. Burins are rare, blunted-back bladelets are relatively numerous. This industry probably belongs to stages III–IV of the Upper Paleolithic.

The 'Ein Sakhri Cave. A small cave which has not been excavated. The main finds were collected during the cleaning of the cave by its owner. Several flint implements were found — lunates, a rectangular blade of the sickle-blade type, and blunted-back bladelets, etc. However, the main importance of the finds is the discovery of some tools and objects which seldom occur in similar industries: a fragment of a bone harpoon with unilateral barbs, which resembles others found in Natufian deposits at Kebara (q.v.) and el-Wad (see Carmel Caves), a basalt pestle decorated at the end, which seems to have a phallic connotation, and, most striking of all, a small calcite figurine, whose features are partially schematic, almost certainly representing a man and a woman in an erotic seated posture.

The Umm-Zuetina Cave. A large cave almost emptied of ancient finds. Only at the entrance was an archaeological deposit (.6 meter thick) left undisturbed. The finds were attributed by Neuville to the first phase of the Natufian culture.

About one hundred flint implements were collected: lunates, of which only a few display the Helwan-type retouch and one still attached to a fragment of a bone handle; scrapers; a few awls; tiny micro-burins; and trapezoid bladelets. The relatively rich bone industry comprises awls, fragments of sickle blade handles, and various polished fragments.

Besides flint and bone, this cave yielded one of the

most outstanding finds in Natufian art: an almost complete limestone figurine, carefully carved with a burin, which left marks on it. It depicts a ruminant, stag or gazelle, grazing in a crouched position with its neck bent forward. The head is missing. Traces of paint bear witness to the red color which apparently covered the whole figurine, which in its present state has a length of 15 centimeters. Some archaeologists have compared it with West European Magdalenian works of art. (The Magdalenian culture flourished at a considerable geographic distance but was broadly contemporaneous with the Natufian).

Tor Abu Sif. On the terrace of the Tor Abu Sif a deposit of .65 meter was discovered containing traces of a hearth, bones, fauna, and flint implements.

Many small lunates (average length, 19 millimeters) were found of which 7 percent only have the Helwan-type retouch; also many rectangular bladelets with blunted back and retouched ends— most of them showing a gloss from use on the working edge. Only a few of them display the Helwan-type retouch; many blades and bladelets are truncated and pointed. Some notched pieces, borers, tiny awls, micro-burins, scrapers and cores, mainly pyramidal, were also found.

In view of the presence of micro-burins, truncated blades, and scrapers, and the scarcity of the Helwan-type retouch, Neuville placed this industry in the second phase of the Natufian.

The Umm-Qula'a Cave is located in Wadi Kharetun. It was explored by Neuville who dug some sounding pits. The finds were only partially published and include a number of cornets and sherds, mostly of the Ghassulian Chalcolithic culture. A 32-centimeter-long dagger or knife made of tabular flint and carefully worked can be dated to the same period.   D. GILEAD

BIBLIOGRAPHY

R. Neuville–A. Mallon, *Syria* 12 (1931), 24–47 • R. Neuville–R. Vaufrey, *L'Anthropologie* 41 (1931), 13–51, 249–63 • R. Neuville, *ibid.*, 43 (1933), 580–60; H. Vallois, *ibid.*, 46 (1936), 529–39 • R. Neuville, *Le Paléolithique et le Mésolithique du Désert de Judée*, Paris, 1951 • J. Perrot, *Bull. Soc. Prehist. Fr.* 52 (1955), 493–506 • E. Tchernov, *Paleolithic Avifauna in Palestine, Bull. Res. Council of Israel,* 11b (1962), 95–131; *idem, Succession of Rodent Faunas during the Later Quaternary of Israel* (unpublished thesis) • J. G. Echegaray, *RB* 70 (1963), 94–119; *idem, Excavaciones en la terraza de El Khiam* 1 (Biblioteca praehistorica hispana, Madrid) 1, 1964; 2, 1966; *idem, ADAJ* 8–9 (1964), 93–94.

JUDEAN DESERT CAVES

EXPLORATION. The archaeological expedition to the Judean Desert was carried out in three stages. In January, 1960, a ten-day survey of the caves in Naḥal Ṣeelim was conducted under the direction of Y. Aharoni. Fragments of papyri and scrolls and various vessels were found. In the light of the great interest aroused by these discoveries, it was decided to undertake more extensive explorations, as well as excavations, in all the valleys between En-Gedi and Masada. For this purpose a joint expedition was formed by the Hebrew University, the Israel Exploration Society, and the Department of Antiquities. The Israel Defense Forces provided men and equipment, erected the camp sites, and furnished all supplies.

The area to be explored between Masada and En-

Naḥal David.

Gedi was divided into four sectors, in each of which a separate camp was set up. Camp A, headed by N. Avigad, was located on the southern bank of Naḥal Ṣeelim and toward the end of the survey moved to Naḥal David. Camp B, headed by Y. Aharoni, was set up on the northern bank of Naḥal Ṣeelim. Camp C, headed by P. Bar-Adon, was at Naḥal Mishmar and Naḥal 'Asahel. Camp D. headed by Y. Yadin, was set up on the northern bank of Naḥal Ḥever, J. Aviram acted as organizer of the survey. This campaign extended from March 23 to April 6, 1960. Some eighty soldiers and one hundred civilian volunteers took part.

The third stage took place from March 14 to March 27, 1961, with the same participants but in different sectors. Camp A was now at En-Gedi and explored Naḥal David; Camp B moved to the southern bank of Naḥal Ḥever and worked in the

This page: Judean Desert Caves, map of the caves and expedition's camps; Opposite page: Naḥal Ṣeelim.

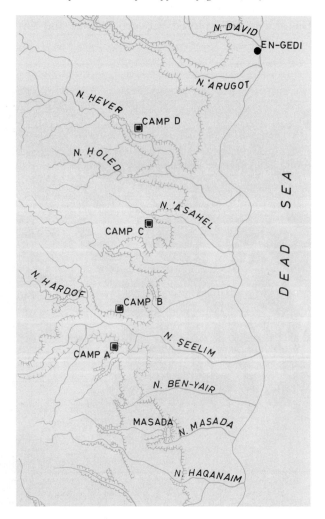

Cave of Horror; Camp C remained at Naḥal Mishmar but explored the area above the Cave of the Treasure; Camp D continued working in the Cave of the Letters in Naḥal Ḥever. One hundred soldiers and three hundred volunteers took part in this campaign.

J. AVIRAM

BIBLIOGRAPHY

J. Aviram, *IEJ* 11 (1961), 3–5; 12 (1962), 167–68.

THE NAḤAL DAVID CAVES

Expedition A of the Judean Desert Campaign of 1960–61 explored the southern cliff of Naḥal Ṣeelim and Naḥal David under the direction of N. Avigad. Scores of openings which could be reached only with great difficulty were located in the steep southern cliff of Naḥal Ṣeelim. On investigation, however, it was found that these were merely openings of recesses and cavities and small caves that served as shelters for mountain goats and birds of prey. Only in two caves in the middle of the valley were sherds found, providing evidence of human occupation in the Chalcolithic period.

After exploring Naḥal Ṣeelim, the expedition moved to Naḥal David, near En-Gedi, which was then the northernmost valley within Israel territory draining into the Dead Sea. The caves of this valley had been surveyed and examined many times by archaeologists and various explorers, but no excavations had ever been carried out in them. Expedition A excavated in two main sites — the Cave of the Pool in the west and a group of tomb caves in the east.

The Cave of the Pool was examined for the first time by the engineer, G. D. Sandel in 1905, and again in 1956 by Y. Aharoni. The cave is located at the western end of Naḥal David, in the northern cliff of the high canyon, north of the dry waterfall. The entrance, facing east, is hidden from sight by a bulge in the rock. Access to the cave was extremely difficult and arduous, for it could be reached only by a climb of about 150 meters up from the riverbed. The opening of the cave is about 2.5 meters wide, and to its left, a smaller opening, leading to a cavity in the rock, connected to the cave. The cave, a natural one irregular in shape, measures about 33 meters in length, and 6–7 meters in width in the front and 3–4 meters in the rear.

Most of its floor was covered by fallen stones and by a thick layer of light earth and bats' droppings. Accumulations of ash and the soot-blackened ceiling indicate that bonfires had been lighted there. The excavation of the cave showed that, like the other Judean Desert caves, it too had served as a refuge in various periods.

CHALCOLITHIC PERIOD. The cave was first inhabited in the Chalcolithic period, in about the last third of the fourth millennium B.C. Only a small number of objects of this period were found. These include typical sherds of the period, a few flint, stone, and bone implements, and fragments of mats and nets, the products of very fine weaving art.

ISRAELITE PERIOD. After the Chalcolithic period, the cave was not used again for human habitation until about the seventh century B.C., at which time nearby En-Gedi was the site of a prosperous settle-ment. Among the few remains of this period are pottery bowls, fragments of cooking pots, juglets, a pottery lamp with a thick raised base, perforated clay balls, a red stone weight, a long iron needle, etc.

ROMAN PERIOD. The cave was inhabited for the third time in the second century A.D., during the Bar Kokhba War, as is attested by the discovery in the cave of two bronze coins. One is a coin of Bar Kokhba with the inscriptions "Shimon" and "For the freedom of Jerusalem." The second is a Tyrian coin dated to the year 253 of the era of Tyre (i.e., A.D. 127/28).

The majority of the finds in the cave date to this period. They are identical for the most part with the objects from the Bar Kokhba period discovered in the other Judean Desert caves. Many sherds of storage jars were found, particularly of large hand-

made pithoi, used for storing food, cooking pots with thin ribbed sides, fragments of "Herodian" lamps in use until the mid-second century A.D., and fragments of assorted glass vessels. Two bronze arrowheads and shafts were also among the finds, together with wooden combs, wooden spindles, remains of plain woven material, and baskets and ropes of wickerwork. Food remains in the cave included date pits, several whole dates still with their fire-blackened flesh, and pomegranate rind. Carobs were found in smaller quantity, as were the shells of walnuts and almonds and fruit of the Egyptian dom palm and olive pits. The cave also contained the bones of animals and birds eaten by the occupants.

The pool, which gave the cave its modern name, is located near the entrance to the cave. The pool was partly hewn out of the rock, and partly constructed. It was completely coated with a plaster of excellent quality. The type of plaster enabled the excavators to date the pool to the Roman period, i.e., the Bar Kokhba era. The pool measures 5 meters in length and 1.2 meters in width, and has a capacity of about 12 cubic meters. Rainwater entered the pool from above, through a vertical gutter, part of which is still preserved.

The construction of such a pool in the desert must have entailed considerable expense. It seems therefore that it was constructed by prominent citizens of nearby En-Gedi, who had prepared it in advance for the emergency of a possible siege, and took refuge in it when the time came. These people escaped the fate of their brethren who fled to the caves of Naḥal Ḥever and met their death there. Since no human skeletons or any objects of value or written documents were found in the Cave of the Pool, it seems that the pool saved the occupants from death by thirst, and they remained in the cave until the danger was past. When they could finally leave in safety, they apparently took with them all their valuables.

Burial Caves. The expedition examined several caves and cavities in the white-chalk cliff near the lower part of Naḥal David, east of the waterfall. The small caves were found to have been used for burials, both primary and secondary. The brittle and porous rock allowed the water to seep through, so that the dryness prevailing in the other caves of the Judean Desert was not found here, and the organic material was damaged by the dampness.

Following, are the main caves cleared and explored:
1. A burial cave consisting of four chambers. Burials were discovered in situ in the third chamber only, which also has a rock pillar left in its center. Four wooden coffins were found covered with a white sediment. Each coffin was made of only four planks, which had completely rotted away. Nearly all of the bones had also distintegrated.
2. A small chamber hewn below tomb 1. This chamber held a disorderly collection of bones together with offerings, such as juglets, lamps, a bronze ladle, two wooden bowls, etc.
3. A cave located left of the above chamber. It consisted of a single chamber (2.5 by 4.4 meters) with a square pit in its center (measuring 1 by 2.7 meters). This cave also served as a depository for bones. About one hundred skulls, some arranged in groups, and piles of bones were found, as well as various vessels, such as spindle-shaped bottles, juglets, pottery lamps, two bronze ladles, etc.
4. A cave situated in the ravine, west of the above group of caves. It measures 3.3 by 3.5 meters and contained remains of wooden coffins that had been destroyed by fallen rocks and partly rotted as a result of the dampness. The coffins were used for regular burials. Later, other skeletons were placed in the cave in no particular order. One coffin contained seven skulls, and skulls and bones were scattered all over the floor. One coffin is of special interest. Topped with a gabled lid, it is decorated with inlays made of bone and wood in a pattern of circles, rosettes, and pomegranates. One coffin, in which bones had been deposited, contained traces of food that had been provided for the dead. In one coffin was found a complete skeleton, wrapped in a shroud (found completely disintegrated) with leather shoes on the feet.
5. A cave (3.1 by 3.15 meters) near cave 4. Because of a collapsed roof, it was impossible to clear it completely. A few skulls, a group of cooking pots, and a glass bottle were found in it.
6. A very small cave west of the above caves. Only a few sherds were found, including a fragment of an alabaster bowl.

Judging by the pottery and other finds, these burial caves were used by the inhabitants of En-Gedi in the first century B.C., i.e., at the end of the Hasmonaean period.

Part of "Genesis Apocryphon", one of the scrolls, found in the Judean Desert Caves.

Another burial cave was found north of Naḥal David on the side of the Dead Sea and excavated under the direction of Y. Yadin. It contained remnants of wooden coffins as well as a large number of bones and skulls gathered together in piles, apparently in a hasty collective burial. It was dated by the pottery to the Herodian period, and it is perhaps contemporary with the caves described above.

N. AVIGAD

BIBLIOGRAPHY

G. D. Sandel, *ZDPV* 30 (1907), 79–84 • Y. Aharoni, *BIES* 22 (1958), 40–44 (Hebrew) • N. Avigad, *IEJ* 11 (1961), 6–10; 12 (1962), 169–83 • D. V. Zaitschek, *ibid.*, 184–85.

THE NAḤAL ḤEVER CAVES

Naḥal Ḥever, one of the deepest canyons in the Judean Desert, drains into the Dead Sea about 7 kilometers (4 miles) south of En-Gedi. The caves in Naḥal Ḥever were first explored at the end of 1953 by an expedition sponsored by the Department of Antiquities, and directed by Y. Aharoni. The same expedition examined the southern cave, the Cave of Horror, in the spring of 1955. The excavation of these caves was resumed in 1960–61 as part of the joint archaeological expedition to the Judean Desert. The northern cave in Naḥal Ḥever (Cave of the Letters) was excavated by Y. Yadin during both years and that of the southern cave (Cave of Horror) by Y. Aharoni in 1961.

The Naḥal Ḥever caves proved to have been occupied in two periods: as dwelling caves in the Chalcolithic period, and as refuges in the Bar Kokhba period.

CHALCOLITHIC PERIOD. Chalcolithic sherds were found in nearly all the caves examined. The most interesting finds came from the Cave of Horror. Despite its difficulty of access, it contained an occupation level from the Chalcolithic period. The pottery included the rim of a hole-mouth jar, incised below the rim with a double herringbone design. The most important find was a burial in the center of the cave, beneath a thick burned

Left: Naḥal Ḥever, Cave of Horror; Below: Naḥal Ḥever, burial in the Cave of Horror — Bar Kokhba period.

layer of a later period. The skeleton had been laid bent on its side. Beneath the skeleton was a charred mat, but it seems that the fire did not occur at the same time as the burial, but later, and burned through the level of dung covering the grave. Carbon-14 tests of the mat yielded a date of 5,460 $\pm$ 125 B.P., i.e., about 3500 B.C. (between 3624 and 3374 B.C.). Although this date is slightly earlier than that received for similar material from Naḥal Mishmar, a date in the thirty-fourth century seems reasonable.

BAR KOKHBA PERIOD. Evidence of one of the most dramatic chapters in the history of the Bar Kokhba War was discovred in the cliffs of Naḥal Ḥever—the Roman siege on a group of Jewish fighters who had sought refuge in the deep caves on the two sides of the valley.

Roman Camps. Two Roman camps were discovered on the cliffs on either side of the valley. The larger camp (A), situated on the northern cliff above the Cave of the Letters, was about 50 meters long and was surrounded on three sides by a rectangular wall (about 1 meter thick) with rounded corners. No wall was needed on the southern side, the cliff's precipice providing adequate defense. The single entrance (2 meters wide) was located in the middle of the northern wall, and was defended by a projecting semicircular wall *(clavicula)*. The foundations of tents are visible on either side of the entrance, eight on each side, as in the small camps at Masada. Other walls are seen on the west side. The command post (praetorium), consisting of three large rooms, was constructed opposite the gate between the two groups of tents. A rectangular structure (about 6 meters long) on the east may have been a storehouse for food, as suggested by Y. Yadin. There were several ovens among the various structures. In the center of the camp was a semicircular construction, apparently to hold the unit's standard.

The southern camp (B), situated above the Cave of Horror, was less well protected, and was apparently slightly smaller than camp A. It was also built above the precipice and surrounded by a wall on its other sides. Like camp A, this one also was 50 meters long and had a single entrance, protected by a *clavicula*. A guardroom was built at the gate opposite the entrance. Within the area of the camp, only the foundations of three structures to the right of the gate were preserved. Each contained

Below: Fragments of parchments with Hebrew script, from the Cave of Horror; Bottom: Hebrew ostracon inscribed "Saul son of Saul, Shalom", found near burial in the Cave of Horror.

two rooms with one external opening. Another room was built between the western structure and the wall. No other foundations can be distinguished in the area of the camp, the tent foundations having all been completely erased. Outside the wall in the north, on the other hand, the remains of three rooms were discovered. Nearby was a fragment of a small wall, perhaps the wall enclosing the other structures. These remains indicate that the camp was later enlarged to the north, as in the south the cliff tapers to a mere point.

The mouths of both caves in the valley are situated 80 to 100 meters beneath the top of the cliff. It is thus obvious that the Roman camps were established in order to lay siege to the cave below them and at the same time to observe the cave opposite.

The Cave of Horror. Access to this cave was the most difficult of the caves so far examined. It is situated in a precipitous cliff, 80 meters below the top. The mouth of the cave is square, 3 meters wide and 2.5 meters high. From a corridor, with approximately the same measurements, continues to a depth of about 65 meters and opens into a wide chamber at a slightly higher level. The cave is a natural one, and there are only scattered traces of rock cutting and straightening. A small recess had a built wall.

Before the excavation, Bedouins had looted the cave, especially the inner part, greatly disturbing the original position of the finds. The front section of the cave had served as the living quarters, and contained only a few fallen stones. Under an upper layer of dung was an occupation level from the Bar Kokhba period. Its date was established by four coins of Bar Kokhba, three with the inscription "The Second Year of the freedom of Israel" and the fourth with the inscription "For the freedom of Jerusalem." Apart from the ordinary pottery vessels, there were other household articles such as baskets, ropes (some tied to jar handles), wooden and stone whorls, parts of wooden boxes with colored leather covers and iron joints, wooden combs, gaming counters, needles, awls, nails, an iron knife, and remains of clothes and leather sandals. There were also food remains —olives, dates, wheat, and barley. Some of the vessels were found in a thick layer of ash in the center of the cave, where they seem to have been deliberately smashed and burned. Some fragments of glass vessels were also found, warped by the fire. Several small fragments of papyri were uncovered, on which a few isolated Aramaic-Hebrew letters had been saved from the flames.

The inner part of the cave was filled with large fallen rocks. It had been used for burials and as a refuge. It contained a large number of human skulls and skeletons, which had been disturbed by the Bedouins. At least forty skeletons of men and women of various ages were uncovered, as well as those of children and infants. They were scattered about the cave, and some of those who had died in the siege were buried in the inner recesses of the cave. This is illustrated by the grave of a man buried in a cavity between the rocks. The body was laid on the left side, and the face pointed to the northwest, toward Jerusalem. Beneath the head near the forehead were the remains of khaki-colored material, tied in a knot. Near the grave several ostraca were found one with the inscription "Saul son of Saul, Shalom."

Remains of parchments and papyri were also found in the inner part of the cave. They include 1. a fragment of parchment in Hebrew-Aramaic script. In the nine lines preserved, the words "on Thy people, Israel" could be deciphered; 2. a Greek papyrus, with ten preserved rows of writing, apparently part of a letter, but the contents are extremely fragmentary; 3. nine fragments of a fine parchment scroll written in small and beautiful Greek letters. These are a Greek translation of the Twelve Minor Prophets. B. Lifshitz has identified them with portions of the Books of Hosea, Amos, Joel, Jonah, Nahum, and Zachariah.

A comparison of these texts with the Greek translation of the Twelve Minor Prophets, published in 1953 by D. Barthélemy, shows without any doubt that they belong to one and the same scroll. The text of the scroll shows it to be a Hebrew recension of the Septuagint, in a style more faithful to the Hebrew version. The Tetragrammaton is written in early Hebrew script.

A lamp from the Arab period was found in the deepest recesses of the cave, indicating that in that period the cave was still visited and perhaps even searched.

Because of the terrifying sight of the skeletons in the cave it was given the name "The Cave of Horror." The finds bear witness to the desperate fight of the last of Bar Kokhba's fighters. Once the Romans had found their place of hiding and set up

Above: Arrowheads from the Bar Kokhba Revolt, found in Naḥal Ṣeelim (Reconstructed); Right: Naḥal Ṣeelim.

their camps above them, there was no longer any hope for the besieged fugitives, for it was impossible to descend the sheer cliffs. It was sufficient for the Romans to lay siege on the cave's entrances from above in order to achieve the death of the cave's occupants by starvation and thirst. The finds nevertheless indicate that the siege continued for a long time, the warriors preferring death to falling prisoner to the Romans. These events, which have left their echo in Jewish legends, have now been confirmed by archaeology.

THE NAḤAL ṢEELIM CAVES

Naḥal Ṣeelim is one of the longest canyons in the Judean Desert, flowing into the Dead Sea 5 kilometers (3 miles) north of Masada. The caves were explored in the spring of 1960 by an expedition headed by Y. Aharoni, and yielded the first inscriptions found on the Israel side of the Judean Desert. After this discovery two larger expeditions were organized.

Finds from three periods—the Chalcolithic, Israelite, and Bar Kokhba periods—were uncovered in the vicinity of Naḥal Ṣeelim and in the caves.

CHALCOLITHIC PERIOD. Remains from this period occurred in almost every cave examined. In addition, a few structures were found on the plateau above the caves. The most interesting Chalcolithic finds came from the following two sites:

1. Two small caves (numbers 45 and 49) near the Ṣefirah Pool with a Chalcolithic occupation level and remains of hearths. The occupants of the caves no doubt obtained their water from this pool. Apart from pottery and fragments of cloth, ropes, and baskets, there were four mace-heads, two of hematite and two of copper, which were similar in form and composition to those found in the Cave of the Treasure in Naḥal Mishmar. The front part of a copper ax lay next to them. A group of bone, shell, and ivory plaques decorated in geometric designs and perforated for hanging were also discovered. Similar pieces are known from the Beersheba culture.

2. The main cave above 'Ein Namer (the Cave of the Skulls, number 32). A rich Chalcolithic occupation level was discovered below the Bar Kokhba level. Two cloth bags tied together were found in one of the corners in the depths of the cave. They held a large number of beads strung on thread. Nearby lay the remains of a purse also made of strung beads sewn together, with white and green beads arranged in a geometric design.

ISRAELITE PERIOD. Two forts from the Iron Age II were discovered in the area of Naḥal Ṣeelim, one in the west, on Mount Haṣron (Rajm el-Baqara, map reference 17220871) and the second in the north, near Mount Itay (Khashm el-Atar, map reference 17910880). Two Israelite houses were situated

nearby. These forts indicate that a road descended from the Hebron area through Naḥal Ṣeelim to the shore of the Dead Sea.

BAR KOKHBA PERIOD. Several Roman forts were discovered on the plateau above Naḥal Ṣeelim near 'En 'Anevah. These forts guarded the desert routes and served the Roman forces in their efforts to secure control over the desert.

Four caves used as hideouts by the Bar Kokhba warriors were discovered on the banks of Naḥal Ṣeelim and Naḥal Hardof, which drains into it. One of the caves (number 40) is situated on the southern bank of Naḥal Hardof and is called the Miqve Cave, because of its water pool (with a capacity of at least 2.6 cubic meters). The pool is plastered like the one in the Cave of the Pool in Naḥal David. No outstanding finds were discovered in the cave. These pools attest to the careful preparation of the caves so that they would be ready to serve as refuges in times of emergency.

The three main caves were discovered on the northern bank of Naḥal Ṣeelim, opposite 'Ein Namer, near the Ascent of the Warriors:

Cave 32 (the Cave of the Skulls), the largest, was the main hideout and dwelling place of the fugitives hiding in these three caves. It had been thoroughly dug up by Bedouins. A secondary burial of seven skulls and skeletons was discovered in one of the innermost crevices.

Cave 31 (the Cave of the Arrows), a small cave, difficult of access and thus escaped searches by

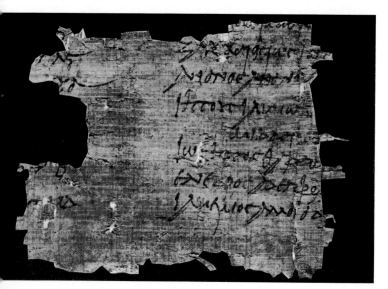

Bedouins. Various sherds and food remains were found, as well as a coin of Trajan. The most interesting find was an arsenal of arrows belonging to the Bar Kokhba fighters, consisting of eleven iron arrowheads and a large number of shafts, upper part made of wood and lower part of cane. The end of the shaft was painted red and black and notched for the bowstring.

Cave 34 (the Cave of the Scrolls), a small cave, well hidden and difficult to reach. It too was overlooked by the Bedouins. A vulture's nest lay across a large part of the cave, above most of the main finds. Aside from the usual finds, there were also fragments of papyri and parchments and two coins, one of Elagabalus (A.D. 218–222) and one of Alexander Severus (A.D. 222–235), i.e., dating from about one hundred years after the Bar Kokhba Revolt.

The written material includes 1. two very thin strips of parchment, containing two portions of the phylactery prayers from Exodus 13:1–16; the text is identical with the Masoretic Text apart from a single variant also appearing in the Septuagint תאכלו instead of תאכל; Exodus 13:16); 2. the edge of a leather scroll containing single Hebrew-Aramaic letters; 3. fragments of Aramaic and Greek papyri. The Greek papyri, deciphered by B. Lifshitz, were in a more complete state of preservation. They contain writing in columns: names and numbers. Most of the names are typically Jewish, such as ''Zakkai the son of Joseph,'' ''Ḥanan the son of Ḥanan,'' ''Jeshu the son of Jacob,'' ''Jeshu the son of Levi,'' etc. To most names was added the appellative ''brother'' ἀδελφός, which apparently signified either a rank or a title common among the Bar Kokhba fighters. These papyri were undoubtedly official documents kept in the archives of the warriors.

The various finds show that these caves too served as a refuge for a group of fighters at the end of the Bar Kokhba War. The late coins indicate that the caves were visited for at least a hundred years after the war. Y. AHARONI

BIBLIOGRAPHY

Y. Aharoni, 'Atiqot 3 (1961), 148–62 • M. Levin and S. Horowitz, ibid., 163–64 • H. Nathan, ibid., 165–75 • Y. Aharoni, IEJ 11 (1961), 11–24 • B. Lifshitz, ibid., 53–58 • L. Y. Rahmani, ibid., 63–64 • Y. Aharoni, IEJ 12 (1962), 186–99 • L. Y. Rahmani, ibid., 200 • B. Lifshitz, ibid., 201–07 • D. Barag, ibid., 208–14.

THE CAVE OF THE LETTERS

The Cave of the Letters was excavated by Expedition D, under the direction of Y. Yadin, in two seasons — the spring of 1960 and of 1961. At the same time, the Roman camp above the cave was surveyed and partly cleared, and the entire area on the southern bank of Naḥal 'Arugot, the eastern cliff between Naḥal 'Arugot and Naḥal Ḥever, the northern bank, and part of the southern bank of Naḥal Ḥever were thoroughly explored.

The Cave of the Letters is situated some 100 meters below the Roman camp, and slightly to the west, and about 200 meters above the wadi bed. The descent to the cave is from the north, down to a ledge some 10 meters below the cave opening, which was reached by means of rope ladders.

The cave is about 150 meters deep. It has two openings, one on the west and the other on the east, about 7 meters apart. These lead to three successive large, natural chambers which are connected by natural corridors. Hall A measures 18 by 31 meters; hall B, 15 by 26 meters; hall C, 23 by 52 meters. The floors in all three chambers were found covered with considerable rock debris, most of which had fallen from the ceiling before the occupation of the cave in the time of Bar Kokhba. The finds were discovered for the most part in their original hiding places. It can be assumed that during the Bar Kokhba War, the occupants of the cave buried their possessions while planning their flight from the cave in which they were besieged by the Romans. Some of the occupants did not succeed in escaping, for in one of the niches (locus 2) in the inner chamber (hall C) the skeletons of seventeen persons (three men, eight women, and six children) were found. Most of the skulls were found deposited in baskets, while the other bones had been wrapped in mats and placed in baskets. Several skeletons had been wrapped in pieces of cloth.

The finds, including the documents, were found hidden beneath stones in various niches and crevices throughout the cave. The major caches include the following:

Locus 57, about 10 meters from the entrance of hall A. A mine detector uncovered a basket containing nineteen carefully packed utensils of metal, mostly bronze. They included two large bowls, three incense shovels, a patera, and thirteen jugs, all of which were manufactured in Italy. It appears that Bar Kokhba's soldiers (from En-Gedi, see below) either acquired them before the Revolt or took them as booty from a Roman unit at the beginning of the war. All representations of human faces had been deliberately effaced from the vessels, so that they could be used by Jews. This is the largest group of objects of this Type found in Israel or neighboring countries. The vessels are dated between the second half of the first century A.D. and 135.

Locus 61, a narrow crevice near the entrance to hall C. It had been carefully blocked with stone slabs after the objects were deposited. Some of the finds were found scattered on the floor, though most had been placed in waterskins and a basket.

The finds here included 1. several metal utensils — jugs and an incense shovel like those found in locus 57, knives and a sickle; 2. numerous wooden objects — several complete bowls, a painted jewelry box and a mirror; 3. leather objects — a pair of sandals, several purses, and three waterskins; 4. an exceptionally well-preserved woven basket; 5. fragments of clothing and sacking (of special interest was a bundle of balls of flax); 6. documents (described below), some found in a leather purse placed inside a waterskin, others were scattered on the floor. One of the Aramaic documents was found rolled up in a hollow reed. A roll of blank parchment was found tied with a string, evidently prepared for use.

Locus 64, in hall C, contained a large, folded net and two cooking pots, one of which bore no traces of use.

Locus 65, near the entrance to hall C, contained six keys of various sizes.

Locus 66, hall C. Beneath a rock were found three glass plates packed in palm fibers. The largest one is unique in the ancient East, both in form and manufacture, and in its excellent state of preservation.

Below: Bronze vessels: bowls, jugs, censers, and a key. Opposite page: Bronze incense shovel and patera with a relief of Thetis riding a Sea Centaur.

*Left: The archive of Babata, as found;
Below: Document No. 12 from Babata's
archive (the lower part): Before seven
witnesses, Babata proposes an
arrangement to the two guardians for
managing the finances of her orphan
son — A.D. 125.*

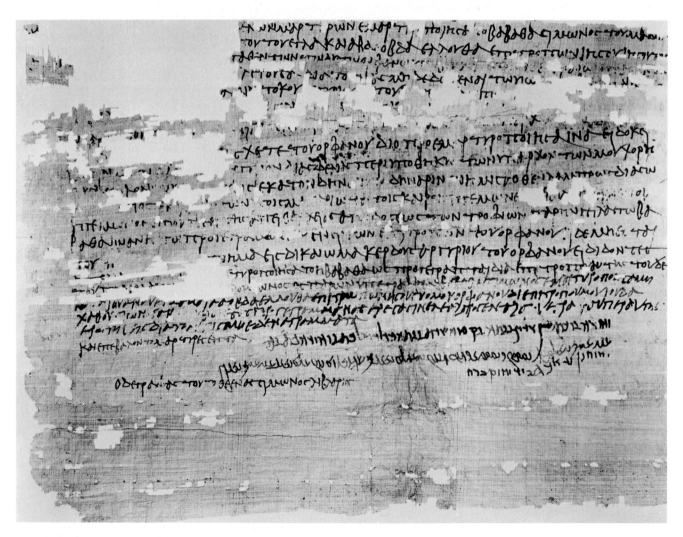

Locus 7, near the northern end of hall C. On the floor of this cavity was a waterskin containing various possessions of a woman — jewelry, purses, a miror, cosmetic utensils of glass, wood, and bone, several balls of dyed spun wool, and a bundle of unspun wool dyed purple, intended for the fringes of the outer garment (tallith), as well as several such finished fringes.

At the bottom of the waterskin was hidden the most important find in this locus — fifteen documents, separately folded and tied together in a bundle. All were letters from Simeon Bar Kokhba to the leaders of the revolt in the En-Gedi region. The modern name of the cave derives from these letters, which were found in the first campaign in 1960.

THE DOCUMENTS

Most of the documents were discovered in loci 61 and 7. Several fragments of scrolls and individual documents were also found near the entrance of the cave, in hall A and in the corridor leading from hall B to hall C.

A. The Biblical Scrolls. 1. PSALMS. In hall A, a small fragment of a scroll of the Book of Psalms was found, containing several verses of Psalms 15–16; the text is basically identical with the Masoretic Text. The scroll can be dated to the end of the first century A.D. This fragment was apparently dropped by the Bedouins who looted the cave in the 1950's.

2. NUMBERS. A tiny fragment, containing verses 7–8 of chapter 20, was found in the eastern entrance, and may also have been dropped by Bedouins.

B. The Archive of Babata. The largest group of documents was found in locus 61. It is now known as the Archive of Babata, after the name of its owner, Babata daughter of Simeon. In one of the waterskins found in this locus was a leather purse containing many papyri, folded and arranged in bundles according to subject matter. In the purse were thirty-five documents of various dates (from A.D. 93 to 132), written in several languages and scripts; six were in Nabataean, three in Aramaic, seventeen in Greek, and nine in Greek with subscriptions in Aramaic or Nabataean, or in both.

The group included documents concerning the family affairs of Babata, her property, and legal suits in which she was involved in matters of her property and that of her family. Among these are

Below, top to bottom: Letter of Simeon ben Kosiba to the En-Gedites (first few lines); Waterskin containing the letters of Bar Kokhba (90 cm. long); The net, as found.

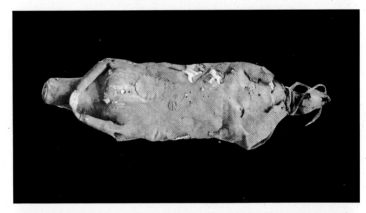

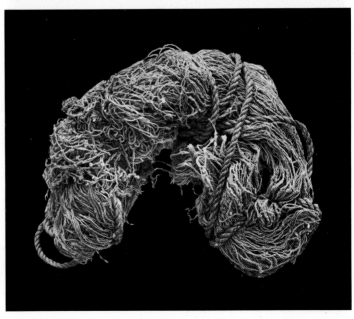

several personal documents, such as a marriage deed and a ketubah. The documents reveal an interesting series of events in the life of this woman.

THE NABATAEAN DOCUMENTS. The earliest of the group were written in the reign of the last Nabataean king, Rabel II, at the end of the first century A.D. They deal with the ownership and sale of palm groves, which had been bought by Babata's father in his native village Maḥoza, near Zoar at the southern end of the Dead Sea. The documents contain many important details concerning the distribution of the Jewish population within the Nabataean kingdom, as well as data on agricultural practices in that period.

DOCUMENT NUMBER 6 is a gift-deed written in Aramaic and drawn by Babata's father in favor of Miriam, her mother. It can be definitely dated by the names of the Roman consuls and the year of the Provincia Arabia to July 13, 120. This is the only gift-deed preserved from the Mishnaic period.

DOCUMENT NUMBER 7 is Babata's ketubah from her marriage to her second husband, Judah son of Eleazar, of En-Gedi. The ketubah is written in Aramaic and resembles the text of the Jerusalemite ketubah. It opens with the phrase "According to the law of Moses and the Jews."

The other documents deal with Babata's claims against the guardians appointed by the authorities at Petra for her orphaned son, Joshua, by her first husband (also named Joshua), and also deal with property claimed from her by the families of her first and second husbands.

These legal documents contain precise dates and provide new details about the Roman governors of the Provincia Arabia, several of whom were previously unknown: Julius Julianus (A.D. 125); T. Aninius Sextius Florentinus (A.D. 127), whose tomb has been discovered at Petra; (T.) Haterius Nepos (A.D. 130). The documents mention administrative centers in the south and in Transjordan, such as "Petra the Metropolis of Arabia," Rabbat-Moab and Mezra'a at the northern end of the Tongue of the Dead Sea. Of interest for the history of En-Gedi is a document from A.D. 124, which mentions a sum of money borrowed by Babata's second husband from a centurion of the Cohors I Militaria Thracum, then stationed at En-Gedi.

Most of these deeds (including the Nabataean and Aramaic ones) are of the "tied" type, i.e., the text of the deed was written twice: on the upper part (interior) and on the lower part (exterior). The top part was then rolled and tied with a string which ran, at several places, through the papyrus, and the witnesses signed on the reverse side, opposite the knots sealing this upper, and thus "interior" part. These deeds, found while still closed, can shed light upon the Talmudic descriptions of drafting and tying deeds.

This page: Sickle with iron blade and wooden handle (the handle is 13.2 cm. long); Opposite page: Glass bowl.

Below: Bronze jug. At the base of the handle, a figure, which was deliberately effaced, can be seen; Bottom: Basket with bronze vessels, as found.

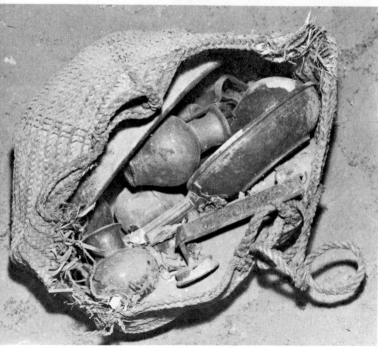

Babata's family was large and ramified, and most of it lived, at one time or another, at En-Gedi. It should be noted that her second husband, Judah son of Eleazar, had another wife as well — Miriam daughter of Be'ayan — who caused Babata much trouble, as can be learned from a document dated A.D. 131, i.e., at the start of the Bar Kokhba Revolt. This may further serve to explain how, at the end of the revolt, Babata came to be in this cave in Naḥal Ḥever, in which the leaders of the revolt from En-Gedi had taken refuge, for they were headed by Jonathan son of Be'ayan (see below).

C. The Archive of the En-Gedites. Near the water-skin containing Babata's archive, a bundle of six documents was found scattered on the floor. It has no direct connection with Babata. All were documents connected with the Bar Kokhba Revolt and had been written at En-Gedi. Most of them are written in rich Mishnaic Hebrew; several are in Aramaic. All deal with administrative affairs concerning the lease of state-owned lands and related matters. The documents are dated according to the years of the Bar Kokhba era: "On the first day of Iyyar, in the first year of the redemption of Israel by Simeon bar Kosiba, Prince of Israel;" "On the fifth day of Elul, in the first year of Simeon bar Kosiba;" "On the twenty-eighth day of Marḥeshvan in the third year of Simeon ben Kosiba, Prince of Israel;" "On the second day of Kislev, in the third year of Simeon ben Kosiba, Prince of Israel;" and "On the twenty-fourth day of Tebet, in the third year of Simeon bar Kosiba, Prince of Israel."
These documents contain much information on the administrative organization of the government under Bar Kokhba, for the state-owned lands at En-Gedi were leased by "Jonathan the son of MḤNYM, the administrator of Simeon ben Kosiba, Prince of Israel, at En-Gedi."

D. The Bar Kokhba Letters. This bundle of fifteen documents was found hidden in a waterskin in locus 7 (see above). With the documents were two clay seal impressions (bullae) with their strings. All the documents were written on papyrus, except one which was written on a wooden slat. The letters are in the three languages current among the Jewish inhabitants of that period: Aramaic, Hebrew, and Greek. Almost all are written in the first person singular, and though their scripts indicate that they had been dictated to different scribes, no two letters are in the same hand. The two Greek letters were written by two of Bar Kokhba's non-Jewish subordinates.

One document opens with the characteristic phrases "Simeon bar Kosiba to Jonathan son of Be'ayan and Masabala son of Simeon..." All the letters are addressed to these same two persons (or to one of them — Jonathan), who were the commanders in the En-Gedi region and the heads of the government there. The letters mainly contain instructions concerning supplies (grain, salt), including lulabs, ethrogs, myrtles, and willows for the Festival of Tabernacles (Sukkot). Several contain orders to detain persons from En-Gedi and Tekoa, on the charge of not having complied with Bar Kokhba's instructions. One Hebrew letter indicates that the supply situation in Bar Kokhba's army was critical, and in spite of their commander's admonitions, the local leaders at En-Gedi failed to obey his orders: "From Simeon ben Kosiba to the men of En-Gedi, to Masabala and to Jonathan son of Be'ayan, peace. You sit, eat, and drink from the property of the House of Israel, and care nothing for your brothers."

Another letter points to the importance of En-Gedi as a spice-growing center. Bar Kokhba orders the property of an En-Gedite to be confiscated, but strictly forbids any damage to the spice plantations. One of the Greek documents reveals the exact pronunciation of the name of the leader of the revolt: Χωσιβα — Kosiba.

The finds from the Cave of the Letters enrich our knowledge of the material culture of this period. For the first time in Israel, objects have been found made of perishable materials — objects the manufacture and use of which are often mentioned and described in the Mishnah in many *halakhot*. The most important finds, however, are the scores of documents — the largest group of complete documents yet uncovered in the Judean desert.

Y. YADIN

BIBLIOGRAPHY

Y. Yadin, *IEJ* 11 (1961), 36–52; 12 (1962), 227–57 • H. J. Polotsky, *ibid.*, 258–62; *idem, EI* 8 (1967), 46–51 (Hebrew) • Y. Yadin, *The Finds from the Bar Kokhba Period in the Cave of Letters*, Jerusalem, 1963; *idem, Bar Kokhba*, New York, 1971 • G. Howard and J. C. Shelton, *IEJ* 23 (1973), 101–02.

THE NAḤAL MISHMAR CAVES

The area assigned to Expedition C headed by P. Bar-Adon included Naḥal Mishmar, Naḥal 'Asahal, Naḥal Ḥoled, and the southern bank of Naḥal Ḥever. In 1962, the expedition continued its activities in the same sector with the addition of Naḥal Zohar and Naḥal Ḥemar. After an extensive survey of the area, efforts were concentrated in the excavation of the caves in Naḥal Mishmar.

Naḥal Mishmar, descending from the Judean Desert to the Dead Sea Valley, drops abruptly in a steep cliff from about 270 meters above sea level at the cliff top to 30 meters below sea level at its foot.

The following caves were excavated:

Cave of the Treasure, Cave 1. This cave is situated about 50 meters below the cliff top, with a sheer drop of 250 meters. Two springs rise from the side of the cliff about 250 meters below the cave. Their waters flow into a small pool and into several ponds in the valley. The cave is a natural one, having a wide entrance and two chambers with deep crevices along the sides, smaller recesses in the walls, and two tunnels below the floor. The cave measures 12 by 14 meters and is from 1 to 3.5 meters in height. The crevices are from 5 to 6 meters long, .5 to 2 meters wide, and from .4 to 2.5 meters high. Traces of a narrow trail, which was wide enough for at least one man, can be distinguished along the cliff on the north, though erosion and landslides make passage impossible today. Descent to the cave can be achieved only by the use of ropes and ladders.

Caves 2 and 3 were for the most part burial caves, and are connected to cave 1 by an inner corridor. Cave 2, situated about 15 meters north of cave 1 at a slightly higher level, is a rather small cave with two chambers. Cave 3 is located about 20 meters west of cave 1. Its entrance, on the south, is very low and narrow, and its one chamber measures 5 by 6.8 meters.

Two structures were discovered on surface level. Structure A (2 by 2 meters), built on the edge of the cliff above caves 1 and 2, served as an observation point as it possessed an excellent view overlooking all the high ground in the region, as well as the entire valley. Near the building and on a slightly lower level were found Roman sherds, indicating the presence of a Roman campsite. Structure B is located about 150 meters northwest of the observation post. It consists of an oval-shaped stone enclosure, 37 meters long and 27 meters wide at its center, with two entrances, both 4.5 meters wide, one on the east and the other on the west. A rectangular building (4 by 5 meters) with rounded corners on its east side stood in the southern part of the enclosure. The walls (.6 meter thick), built in dry construction without mortar, are preserved to a height of four or five courses, about .8–1 meter high. Chalcolithic sherds were found on the floor of the structure. The enclosure was examined for the first time by Y. Aharoni in 1955, and in 1960–62 trial soundings were carried out by the Naḥal Mishmar Expedition. Judging by the wide openings of the enclosure, it seems

hardly likely that it was a sheepfold, and it probably served the occupants of the neighboring caves for ritual purposes. Enclosures similar in form and size have been discovered by M. Stekelis at 'Ala Ṣafat (see Megalithic Monuments) and at Tuleilat Ghassul, all located in dolmen fields. After discovering human burials in some of these enclosures, Stekelis suggested that they were connected with funerary rites, and he dated them to 3200–2850 B.C.

CHALCOLITHIC PERIOD. As in most of the caves in the Judean Desert, traces of occupation from the Chalcolithic period were discovered also in most of the caves excavated or examined in Naḥal Mishmar. The most important and interesting finds came from the Cave of the Treasure. The occupation level here was some 2 meters thick and contained many layers of ash around fireplaces, as well as household utensils and ornaments of pottery, bone, shell, ivory, copper, stone, and flint. Organic material was uncovered in an excellent state of preservation due to the extreme aridity of the Judean Desert. There were also remains of cloth, a loom, food, articles of leather, wood, and straw as well as the principal find — a cache of metal vessels.

Pottery. Most of the pottery vessels were discovered in caves 1, 2, and 3. Few of the vessels were found intact. The many sherds included parts of the sides, rims, and bases, some with mat impressions, various handles of hole-mouth jars, store jars and pots, large and small bowls (some with traces of soot on their rims were probably used as lamps), a pottery spoon, and churns. The pottery is generally of good quality, particularly the small bowls, which are made of levigated clay. Most of the vessels were covered with a slip or wash of bands of various colors, including light and dark brown, and all shades of red, white, and chrome. The decoration included thumb-indented, incised, and herringbone designs. There were plain and thumb-indented ledge handles, lug and bar handles, and small and large loop handles, some double, thumb-indented, incised or stamped, plain and thickened at their ends. All these features are also characteristic of the Ghassul and Beersheba cultures and other Chalcolithic sites in the Judean Desert. A few unusual vessels, whose forms and decorations are altogether new and as yet have no parallels in other sites, were also found.

Both pages, counterclockwise: Naḥal Mishmar, cave of the Treasure; The treasure, as found in the cave; Crown, from the Cave of the Treasure.

Stone Vessels and Ornaments. Concave and rectangular stone vessels used for pounding and grinding were found, as well as stone and flint rounded hammers of various sizes, most of them with one side smoothed or denticulated, and all showing signs of blows. Spindle whorls of stone and various flint tools were also found: blades, a chisel, the tang of an arrowhead, and bone awls. There were also ornaments: a flat ivory disk (7.5 centimeters in diameter) perforated in the center and decorated with two circles of holes on both sides. A similar object was found at Beersheba. Necklaces of shells, bones, and semiprecious stones were also found.

Textiles. Many fragments of well-preserved cloth were discovered in the cave, some in the burials. The majority were of flax, and a small part was of wool. The remains of a garment in two colors found on a body in cave 2 were sent for Carbon-14 testing (see below). Remnants of cloth were also found with the treasure. A scrap of material had been left in the hole of a mace-head, threads in the hole of a shaft and in the perforations of a horn and of an ivory object, and a piece of cloth was stuck to a sherd of a hole-mouth jar.

Straw and Wicker Objects. Many straw objects, some completely preserved, were discovered in this level. A straw sieve, complete with its meshed bottom, lay near the fireplace. It resembles a large bowl, the upper diameter measuring 38 centimeters, and the lower one 20 centimeters. The interstices in the bottom measure 2–3 by 2–3 square millimeters. The remains of the many cereals found nearby indicate that it was used for sifting cereals. There were also straw platters, remains of mats and baskets plaited in various ways, as well as plaited ropes of various thicknesses, and the large well-preserved mat (120 by 80 centimeters) in which the vessels of the cache had been packed.

Leather Objects. A pair of sandals were found, one only in fragments, the other almost whole, 26 centimeters long, with parts of the sole and the thongs. From these remains, the method of sandal making in the Chalcolithic period was seen to bear no resemblance to that of the Bar Kokhba period, of which many sandals were found in the Judean Desert Caves. A well preserved piece of a leather coat sewn with tendons was also found.

Food, Cereals, Vegetables, and Fruit. Near the fireplaces and in other areas in this level were remains of food, including uncarbonized spikelets and grains of wheat and barley. This was the first discovery in Israel of the ancient remains of uncarbonized cereals. Also found were lentils, onions, garlic, olives, dates, and acorns.

D.V. Zaitschek, who studied the plant remains, found the wheat to be of emmer, the cultivated two-grained glume wheat. This species of wheat, discovered here for the first time in an excavation, is the "missing link" between the two-grained wheat (the ancestor of cultivated wheats discovered by A. Aaronsohn) and the durum wheat. This find has great importance for the study of the origin and development of cultivated wheat. The other remains of grain include einkorn wheat, the most primitive of the cultivated wheat species, also found here for the first time in Israel, and cultivated two-row barley.

Animals. Many animal bones were uncovered in this level. They were identified by G. Haas as sheep, deer, mountain goats, and various kinds of birds.

A Weaving Loom. Carved wooden sticks, bone awls, and double-bladed bone spatulas, with one round or pointed end and the other perforated, were found. Similar objects have appeared at other Chalcolithic sites, but here for the first time a thread had remained in the hole of one of the spatulas. Carved wooden plaques, some flat, concave or double-bladed, were discovered, with a gloss from use. These apparently served the same purpose as the spatulas, i.e., as weaving shuttles. They were found in the same area as the two wooden spatulas, one longer than the other, and terminating in carved knobs. The comparison of these objects with scenes on early paintings shows them to comprise a horizontal loom with all its accessories.

Pottery and stone whorls, some rounded, and some elongated, were also found. Similar whorls have been found at Tuleilat Ghassul, Beersheba, and other sites. The elongated whorls are called loom weights. These whorls and parts of carved wooden spatulas, which do not belong to the horizontal loom, suggest that there was also a weighted loom in the cave.

Burials. Twenty-one skeletons were found in caves 1, 2, and 3. Seven were of children, six of women, and eight of men. The skeletons were

Opposite page: Standard decorated with ibex heads.

examined by G. Haas and H. Nathan. The skeletal type is that of the Cappadocia, a secondary Mediterranean type, whose center was in the Caucasian Mountains and Armenia. This type was discovered at Beersheba and, according to recent examinations by G. Haas, also at Tuleilat Ghassul.

Most of the skeletons were laid in a straight position, although some had their legs flexed. Chalcolithic pottery was found beside the skeletons.

The Cache. A hoard of 429 vessels wrapped in a straw mat was discovered in a natural niche in the north wall of the passage leading to chamber B in cave 1. Apart from six hematite vessels, six of ivory and one of stone, all the objects were made of copper. The cache is astonishing in the beauty of its objects and the excellence of their workmanship, and in the unexpectedness of encountering such objects in a cave in the desert. Nothing of this kind has ever been found in Israel or other countries. Only a few of the objects could be compared to earlier finds, whereas the majority are new and strange types.

The cache included about twenty copper chisels and axes of various sizes (from 15 to 35 centimeters long) with straight, thick or thin sides (from 3 millimeters to 3 centimeters) and straight, rounded, and splayed blades, either sharp or blunt. Also included were about 240 copper mace–heads of various sizes (from 3 to 6 centimeters in diameter and weighing from 110 to 710 grams). They vary in shape, being rounded, flattened, oval, disk-shaped, denticulated, and were decorated with incised or relief designs.

Six hematite mace-heads were also of varying sizes and shapes. About eighty copper wands, or standards, from 10 to 40 centimeters long were also found, most of them hollow, although a few were solid. Some were plain and some decorated with incised bands and herringbone patterns, knobs, branches, flattened or round projections or figures of birds and animals, such as ibexes, deer, buffalo, wild goats, eagles, and also with a human face.

Ten copper crowns, generally similar in form, but of varying ornamentation and sizes (from 9 to 17.5 centimeters in height, from 15.6 to 19.1 centimeters in diameter and from 928 to 1971 grams in weight). The decorations included architectural designs, birds animals, human faces, a star, herringbone patterns, horns, spirals, and zigzag lines.

Five sickle-like implements, made from hippopotamus tusks, measured from 30 to 40 centimeters in length. All are perforated with from 47 to 73 holes, and the central perforation had a projecting collar-shaped neck. An elongated, slightly concave box made of ivory was also found.

Also included in the cache are small baskets, a pot, and various flagpoles and scepters, a perforated triangle, horned-shaped vessels, hammers, pointed implements, etc.

One unfinished copper mace-head illustrates the method of producing and casting the objects. Although all the others are well polished, this single mace-head has a very rough surface. In its center is a perforated projection, showing that it was produced in a full mold, apparently by the lost-wax process (cire perdue), the casting being carried out through the hole. Objects damaged during the casting were repaired by welding.

DATE OF THE TREASURE. The fact that the objects of the cache were packed and concealed together in one mat indicates that they are a homogeneous group belonging to a single period. Its owners dug down to a depth of two meters in order to reach the niche that served as the hiding place. It is also certain that, aside from the two layers from the Chalcolithic and Bar Kokhba periods, there is no trace of occupation or even of visits to the cave.

The cache was first dated by the objects, such as mace-heads, chisels, and axes, known from Chalcolithic sites. Two mace-heads and fragments of a copper chisel were also found in Chalcolithic levels in Naḥal Ṣeelim. The upper part of a hollow copper standard and also a small fragment of an object made from a hippopotamus tusk (5 by 6 centimeters) were found in excavations at Beersheba. No parallel had been known for this object until the discovery of the cache. The hoard included other typical Chalcolithic features: the human face on the figurine, which resembles faces appearing on Chalcolithic ossuaries; the horned gate on one of the crowns is similar to a horned facade also found on an ossuary; the star on the crown is similar to that on the fresco at Tuleilat Ghassul and the birds also have Chalcolithic parallels.

Carbon-14 tests carried out on the mat and on bits of wood stuck in the wands confirmed the archaeological evidence, even though the tests yielded

Opposite page: Crowns from the Cave of the Treasure; Top, decorated with a gate and birds.

dates ranging broadly between the thirty-fifth and twenty-eighth centuries B.C.

SUMMARY

The great number of the Chalcolithic finds from the caves in Naḥal Mishmar illustrating the dress, footwear, food, crafts, household utensils, and ornaments of the occupants, indicate a prosperous way of life and a high cultural level, a completely unexpected phenomenon in the caves of the desert.

The valuable objects of the cache were without doubt publicly owned, and it appears that they were used by the occupants of this cave as well as by those of the other caves excavated in the Judean Desert. The thickness and large number of occupation levels in the cave indicate that the occupation was of long duration. The large enclosure on the plateau above the Naḥal Mishmar caves seems to have served as a local cult site while the large temenos at En-Gedi (q.v.) apparently served as the regional center. However, it is difficult to determine what constituted the basis of the economy of the settlers and why they chose to inhabit these desert caves, whose approach was so difficult and hazardous. Judging from the form of the burials and the funerary offerings, they seem to have believed in a life after death. The end of the occupation of the Judean Desert caves was caused by some unknown event, which put an end to all the Chalcolithic settlements in Israel, and as a result of this sudden occurrence the treasure was hidden in the cave.

The objects of the treasure were apparently the ritual equipment from a temple, either at En-Gedi, or another central site in the area. The excavator is of the opinion that most of the objects are fertility symbols, whose origins should be sought in the culture of Mesopotamia and Iran. The anthropological and metallurgical studies are also in agreement that the producers of these objects were influenced by the cultures of these lands.

The treasure opens up new horizons in the culture of this period in Israel, its art and crafts, religion and ritual, and the cultural and material connections with other countries.

IRON AGES I–II. Sherds and other remains from the Iron Age I were found in cave 4. This was the first discovery of finds from this period in this part of the country. Only Iron Age II pottery has previously been uncovered in the caves of the Judean Desert. Objects made of iron, as well as pottery from the Chalcolithic period, were also found in cave 4, which apparently served shepherds as a temporary halt and was not used as a permanent dwelling.

BAR KOKHBA PERIOD. A rich collection of material from the Bar Kokhba period was found in the two stamped-earth floors in the upper level of the Cave of the Treasure and also in cave 2. These finds included a great number of sherds of storage jars, jugs, juglets, cooking pots, lamps, fragments of a jug and a bottle of glass, stone "measuring cups," a stone mortar and pestles.

Among the rocks that had fallen from the ceiling and covered the Chalcolithic level were well-made mortars and grindstones. Also found were remains of cloth and sandals, various straw objects, an iron hook, and remains of cereals and fruit.

Three fragments of papyri were preserved, as well as five ostraca written in Hebrew and Greek, pieces of blank parchment, probably of a scroll, and isolated illegible letters on sherds of storage jars.

The following written documents were found: 1. a small papyrus fragment on which the letters ג, י, ת, ג, ו were well preserved. 2. a badly damaged papyrus, with many lines of writing, but only two could be deciphered by B. Lifshitz. They contain names followed by the appellative ἀδελφός ("brother"), as in the documents from Naḥal Ṣeelim and Naḥal Ḥever; Lifshitz suggests that this is a title or rank used in the army of Bar Kokhba. On the back of the papyrus were the remains of eight lines containing names and the symbol for wheat, and to the right, numbers including 15 and 32; 3. a damaged papyrus, apparently the remains of a promissory note; the lines are blurred, but at the end of one line can be read the word נפשה (על) and in another line the "son of Dramenes. Witness."

On the Greek ostracon are written the letters IAK. The four Hebrew ostraca apparently all bear the word זוזין. One may be marked with the contents of the jar, either wine or oil, and another seems to be a receipt of payment for a quantity of oil.

P. BAR-ADON

BIBLIOGRAPHY

P. Bar-Adon, *IEJ* 11 (1961), 25–35; 12 (1962), 215–26 • B. Lifshitz, *ibid.*, 59–62 • H. Nathan, *ibid.*, 65–69 • D. V. Zaitschek, *ibid.*, 70–72 • P. Bar-Adon, *The Cave of the Treasure*, Jerusalem, 1971 (Hebrew).

JUDEAN DESERT CAVES — Wadi Murabba'at

IDENTIFICATION. Wadi Murabba'at is a deep ravine (up to 200 meters) descending from the Judean Desert to the Dead Sea. Its northern slopes are sheer while the southern are steeply sloped. Dotting the cliffs are caves, four of which contained important remains from the Chalcolithic period onward, and especially documents dating to the Bar Kokhba revolt. The caves are approximately 18 kilometers (11 miles) south of Khirbet Qumran and 25 kilometers (15.5 miles) southeast of Jerusalem (map reference 185110).

The caves had been located in clandestine diggings by Bedouins of the Ta'amra tribe, who were searching for written material. When news of the discovery of Hebrew, Aramaic, and Greek documents in the area reached the directors of the Qumran excavation, L. Harding and R. de Vaux, they began to search for their place of origin, and the Bedouins finally agreed to lead them to the caves. The two archaeologists, together with D. Barthélemy, conducted excavations in the four caves from January 21 to March 1, 1952.

THE CAVES

Cave 1. The opening of the cave is rectangular in shape (4 meters wide and 10 meters high). Just outside it was a cistern and a storage pool from the Roman period. From the entrance the floor inclined upward steeply toward the inside of the cave. The cave itself had the form of a passageway (50 meters long and 4–7 meters wide). Due to the frantic searches of the Bedouins, it was impossible to conduct a stratigraphic investigation, but an examination of the cave nevertheless revealed fragments of wood, leather, basketry, and cloth, small metal objects, including rings, tools, weapons, and several coins. Written material was very scarce. Most of the finds were made close to the cave entrance, and the deeper the investigation proceeded in the interior of the cave, the fewer were the finds uncovered. They were attributed to the Chalcolithic, Iron Age II, Roman, and Arab periods.

Cave 2. The entrance to the cave is very close to that of cave 1. It opens onto a chamber measuring 4 by 6 meters, from which two narrow underground passages (15 meters in length) descend to the slope and lead to a horizontal passageway, approximately 40 meters long. The inhabitants of the cave made equal use of both the chamber and the underground passages. Heavy stone collapses from the ceiling made the excavation difficult. (During the excavation, it was determined that the falls occurred later than the Chalcolithic period, for remains datable to the latter were found beneath them.) In the upper chamber several scroll fragments were discovered beneath stones or in pits that had served as nests for various animals. The upper level of the chamber yielded several pieces of cloth from the Arab period and some pottery from the Iron Age II. The majority of the finds, however, belong to the Roman period and include pottery, wooden and metal objects, cloth and leather fragments, and remains of baskets. This upper level had been disturbed, and beneath it lay a 30-centimeters-thick ash layer, which, according to the excavators, was caused by the burning of dung. A still lower layer, this time undisturbed, contained Chalcolithic pottery, flint tools, and an abundance of animal bones.

The Bedouins had also searched the underground passageways, and it seems that most of the scroll fragments acquired from them originated there. Though most of the area had been disturbed, it was possible to conduct systematic excavations in several places. An examination of the waste dumps left from the diggings of the Bedouins revealed two pieces of a large ostracon, inscribed leather fragments, and half of an alabaster vessel dated to the Middle Bronze Age (see below), the first half of which had already been purchased from the Bedouins. The excavation revealed several layers, including, from the bottom upward, a level containing a mixture of earth and collapsed rocks, a 10-centimeter-thick ash level, a layer of red earth (34 centimeters thick) containing Chalcolithic sherds, a level of stone and gravel (36 centimeters) with a few Chalcolithic flints, a black ash level (55 centimeters) with remains of various periods including some Chalcolithic sherds, a Middle Bronze Age II scarab and a few Iron Age II sherds, and a black-earth level that contained only Roman remains. In this upper level, the excavators found a quantity of pottery, leather, and textile fragments, wooden artifacts, and papyrus fragments.

Not far from the excavated area was found the well-known papyrus containing the letter of the elders of Beth Mashiko to Joshua son of Galgula. Above this upper level, the Bedouins had heaped up the earth dug out of their nearby excavation.

Cave 3. This cave is situated approximately 40 meters west of cave 2 and is separated from it by a rock projection. It was impossible to reconstruct the plan of the cave as both its opening and ceiling had collapsed, and part had fallen into the ravine. The excavators distinguished a thin level of settlement with remains of both the Chalcolithic and Roman periods. No written material was revealed. In one of the corners was a slight depression, which was found to contain Iron Age II pottery, two iron knives, and part of a bone plaque decorated with a mesh pattern. In the western end was a pit, some 25 meters deep, which widened out at the bottom to form a space 2 by 4 meters. There was no evidence of human habitation in the pit.

Cave 4. Two hundred meters east of caves 1–3 and at a slightly higher level is cave 4. A low corridor led from the opening to a series of long rooms in a row. Its overall length was approximately 60 meters. The Bedouins who had dug there first had not found anything. The expedition concentrated on the middle room, and though there was no clear stratigraphy, at the bottom of the settlement level there were Chalcolithic sherds with Roman sherds above them.

THE FINDS. The main finds from the Chalcolithic period, as stated above, were discovered in caves 1 and 2. The pottery was handmade of coarse clay with only a small amount of tempering material added. A few complete vessels were found, some of them burnished. The common types are cornets, chalices, goblets, deep bowls with straight sides, hole-mouth jars, several jugs with lug handles, and a few thumb-indented ledge handles. Several of the bases bore mat impressions. Three types of decoration were in use:

1. Red or brown wash covering the outside of the vessel with a thin band left plain along the inner edge of the rim. Some vessels were decorated with horizontal lines near the base. 2. Incised decoration, usually in a herringbone pattern. 3. Relief decoration, formed by a rope or thumb-indented clay strip. The large quantity of flint tools that was found were mostly scrapers. An outstanding example is a fan scraper (110 by 135 millimeters). Blades, knives, axes, and several arrowheads were also found. Among the stoneware there were two basalt whetstones and a small limestone bowl with four rectangular projections around its rim instead of handles.

The bone artifacts included awls, needles, and a few spindles. A wooden ax handle was also uncovered, whose flint blade (not found) was originally attached with a leather strip.

The excavators distinguished two phases of the Chalcolithic period at Wadi Murabba'at. The first is dated to the Middle Chalcolithic, approximately the mid-fourth millennium B.C., and the second, to which the burnished ware belonged, was dated to the Late Chalcolithic. It was not established whether the Chalcolithic settlement at Wadi Murabba'at was continuous or seasonal.

The finds from the Middle Bronze Age II are relatively scarce. The Hyksos scarab found in cave 2 is of special interest. It is engraved with a beetle and two ankh signs. On the basis of Egyptian parallels, the scarab was dated by the excavators to the Fifteenth Dynasty. Pieces of an alabaster juglet and two bronze needles were also found. The remains of two wooden combs have exact parallels in Middle Bronze Age II tombs at Jericho and Thirteenth Dynasty tombs in Egypt. Several sherds from the same period were also discovered in cave 2. The excavators related these finds to a temporary settlement that existed for a brief period during an early stage of the Middle Bronze Age II. It was possibly settled by fugitives who sought shelter in the caves.

The Iron Age finds include a small amount of pottery with such types as decanters, a lamp with seven wicks, cooking pots and store jars. The excavators dated all the pottery to the eighth–seventh centuries B.C., during which period, they believed, the site also served as a temporary refuge rather than a permanent settlement.

The bulk of the finds are to be dated to the Roman period. They include a large amount of pottery of all types, which were dated by similar finds in Jerusalem and Khirbet Qumran to the second and beginning of the third century A.D. Many remnants of weapons, including a blade of a pilum — the javelin used by the Roman legionnaires — several triple-headed arrowheads and a flat arrow, an iron arrowhead of the equilateral triangle type, larger than was usual, which the excavators believed had been fired from a catapult, and several javelin heads including one with a socket. Of special interest was a wooden stamp belonging to the Roman army with a Latin inscription of two lines: "C/enturia Annaii/ Gargiliu[s]", i.e., Gargilius of the Anaiian century. The first name is Latin while the second is an African name that was especially common during the first–second centuries A.D. The remaining artifacts consist of iron nails, various tools, a big iron key, many wooden and stone spindles decorated with various incised geometric patterns, remnants of sandals (including a child's sandal), and bone dice. An unusual discovery was a set of implements that the excavators believed were used by a doctor.

The textile fragments, for the most part wool with some linen and cotton, also belonged to this period. Some of the cloth was dyed and decorated with various patterns.

Apart from two coins, all the rest were purchased from the Bedouins, but the excavators were convinced of their authenticity. The coins included a Hasmonaean coin of Matthias Antigonus (40–37 B.C.), a coin belonging to Agrippa I (A.D. 42/43), two procuratorial coins from the time of Nero (A.D. 58/59), one coin from the First Revolt (A.D. 69/70), a city coin of Ashkelon from the time of Trajan (A.D. 113/114), a city coin of Tiberias from the days of Hadrian (A.D. 119/120), nine coins from the Bar Kokhba revolt, and two coins with the emblem of the Tenth Legion.

On the basis of the evidence found in the caves, and especially the written documents, some of which were dated (see below), the excavators concluded that the caves were settled during the Roman period from the first century B.C. on. At this time, there was only a temporary settlement there, as during the First Revolt. A larger and more developed settlement existed during the Bar Kokhba revolt, when the area served as a refuge for the fleeing rebels and their families (indicated by the discovery of the child's sandal). The site

Opposite page: Fragment of a Hebrew letter; from the 8th century B.C.; This page: Letter of the administrators of Beth Mashiko to Yeshua' ben Galgula; Bottom: Letter of Simeon ben Kosiba to Yeshua' ben Galgula.

was in due time overrun by Roman army units, whose weapons, etc., have survived. A small unit continued to be stationed in the area until the end of the second century A.D. — one of the documents is attributed to the days of Commodus (A.D. 180–192).

Caves 1 and 2 were also in use during the Arab period. From this period have remained two eighth–ninth centuries A.D. lamps, a coin (in cave 1) that was minted in Ramla in the eighth century A.D., and several inscriptions, one of which mentions the year A.D. 938/39. Other fragments of Arab pottery were dated to the fourteenth–fifteenth centuries A.D. The elders of the Bedouin tribe relate that at the beginning of the twentieth century guano was extracted from the caves and sold in the Bethlehem markets as fuel.

Among the documents is a papyrus fragment of the eighth century B.C. and various biblical fragments, including a Torah scroll, of which portions of Genesis, Exodus, and Numbers have been preserved. Not a great deal of this scroll has survived, for it was torn already in antiquity. The caves also yielded several fragments of Deuteronomy, a piece of the right-hand edge of the text of Isaiah, and a scroll of the Twelve Minor Prophets with parts of twenty-three columns containing considerable portions of Amos, Obadiah, Jonah, and Micah. This last scroll was found sometime after the end of the excavations in a crevice used for burial, not far from the Murabba'at Caves. Of special interest are the documents from the time of Bar Kokhba, one letter was even sent in his name. Some Greek, Latin, and Arabic papyri, as well as Greek and Latin ostraca, were also found.

It should be kept in mind that the publication of the Wadi Murabba'at material preceded that of the first season of excavations in Naḥals David, Ḥever, and Mishmar, making any comparison of the material impossible. It was subsequently established that the finds from Wadi Murabba'at complement the other evidence from the various canyons in the Judean Desert and form a single assemblage.   E. STERN

BIBLIOGRAPHY

R. de Vaux, *RB* 60 (1953), 245–67 • R. de Vaux, E. H. Crowfoot, E. Crowfoot, in: P. Benoit, J. T. Milik, R. de Vaux, *Discoveries in the Judean Desert* 2, Oxford, 1961 • S. Yeivin, *'Atiqot* 1 (1955), 95–108 (English Series).

JUDEIDEH, TELL

IDENTIFICATION. Tell Judeideh is an ancient site in the Shephelah, about 2 kilometers (1 mile) north of Beth-Govrin (map reference 141115), situated 398 meters above sea level. Most scholars agree with J. Jeremias that the site is to be identified with Moresheth-Gath — the birthplace of the prophet Micah (Micah 1:1; Jeremiah 26:18), and one of the cities captured by Sennacherib in his campaign against Judah in 701 B.C. (Micah 1:14). Moresheth-Gath is mentioned in the Book of Micah as being in the vicinity of Lachish and Mareshah. This identification is also based on Eusebius (Onomasticon, 134:10), Hieronymus, and the Medeba Map where it is shown north of Beth-Govrin.

The city is perhaps mentioned among those which Rehoboam fortified, but the name in the list was corrupted by haplography. Therefore instead of "and Gath, and Mareshah" (II Chronicles 11:8), one should read "Moresheth-Gath and Mareshah."

EXCAVATIONS

Tell Judeideh was excavated in 1899–1900 by the British Palestine Exploration Fund under the direction of F. J. Bliss, assisted by R. A. S. Macalister. This excavation was one of four carried out at mounds of the Shephelah — the other were Azekah (Tell Zakariya), Mareshah (Tell Sandaḥannah), and Tell eṣ-Ṣafi. It was one of the first stratigraphic excavations conducted in Palestine. The report of the excavation, published in 1902, greatly advanced archaeological research, but it is still a pioneering work and deficient in some respects.

The ancient settlement was spread over the natural hill, an elongated rectangular area about 580 meters long. The excavations were concentrated in the southern part of the hill, at the site of the ancient citadel. In this area of 2.5 hectares surrounded by a wall (about 250 meters long, 100 meters wide), the depth of the occupational debris is 3–6 meters, whereas in the northern part of the hill its maximum depth is only 1.5 meters.

The excavators traced the line of the wall and made six soundings down to virgin soil. The total area of the soundings was about 86 square meters.

RESULTS OF THE EXCAVATIONS

Three main periods were distinguished in the

history of the site: 1. Pre-Israelite (i.e., Canaanite); 2. Jewish (Israelite II); 3. Hellenistic-Roman.

Very few remains of the Bronze Age were uncovered. From the scanty material published in the report, it is difficult to assign exact dates. The excavators were of the opinion that the site was abandoned at the end of the Bronze Age and remained unoccupied until the end of the Judean Kingdom.

From the Iron Age II, thirty-seven handles stamped with *lamelekh* seals were discovered. The handles include almost all of the known types: the two- and four-winged types and the four cities (Ziph, Hebron, Socoh, *Mmsht*). Building remains were also found, but they are not described in the report.

The main finds belong to the Roman period. On the southern part of the hill, there was a military

Left: General plan; Right: Plan and section of the headquarters—Herodian period.

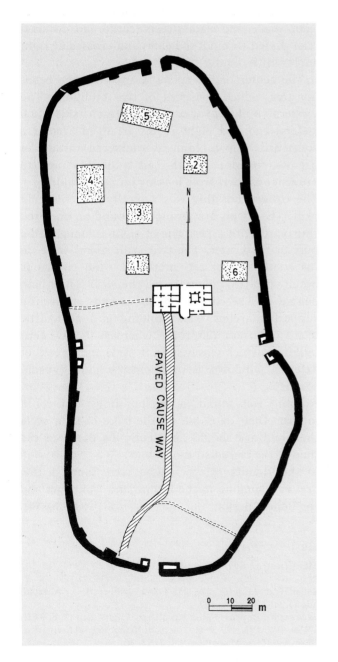

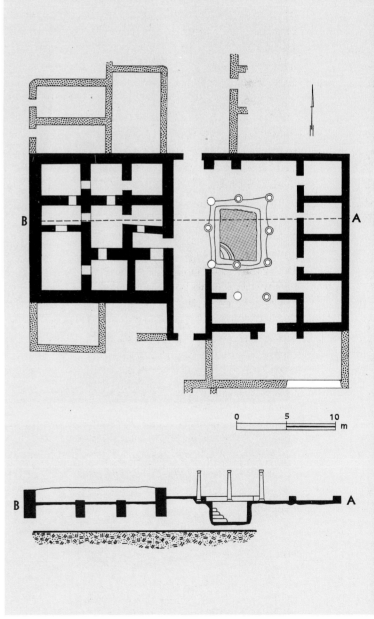

Top: Lamelekh *seal impressions on handles of storage jars — Four-winged scarab and inscription* lamelekh Hbrn*; Bottom: Two-winged scarab and inscription* lamelekh Socoh.

enclosure in the Early Roman period, surrounded by a wall with four gates, and the headquarters in the center. The wall, 3.35 meters thick, was built of slightly dressed stones, laid dry in horizontal courses. It was strengthened by projections inside the wall, which jutted 1–1.5 meters into the city. Sixteen projections were exposed, but it is reasonable to assume there were more. The four gates point north, south, east, and west, and are flanked by square internal towers. The gates were well preserved, some of them to a height of 2.1 meters, with pillars, sockets, and thresholds. The gates were double winged. As was usual in military camp plans, the main streets (cardo and decumanus) passed through the gates and crossed at right angles in the center of the camp.

In the center of the enclosed area was the headquarters, which consisted of two buildings. The western building was square (each side 13.6 meters) and had eight rooms arranged around a courtyard. The building was entered through a narrow corridor, which had a double turn to prevent outsiders from looking into the building.

The eastern building was typically Hellenistic in plan. The rooms are arranged around an enclosed courtyard with a peristyle of eight columns and a pool in the center. The two main rooms were on the south side of the courtyard — the *prostas* (a porch with two columns) and the *oikos* (guest hall) behind it. The columns of the *prostas* apparently supported arches. This building is a Hellenistic men's quarters (andron), whereas the western building, which was eastern in style and devoid of external windows, is the women's house (gynaeconitis).

Nothing was found in the buildings that could indicate their date, but on the basis of their style the buildings should apparently be dated to the time of the Herodian dynasty.

In the vicinity of the mound were found a few graves belonging to the Bronze and Iron Ages and the Roman period.   M. BROSHI

BIBLIOGRAPHY

Identification of the Site: J. Jeremias, *PJB* 29 (1933), 42–53; Abel, *GP* 2, 392 • M. Avi-Yonah, *EI* 2 (1953), 151 • Z. Kallai, Enc. Miqr. 4, 421–23, 741–42 (Hebrew) • Aharoni, *LB*, 54, 90, 292, 314, 339.
Excavation Reports: Bliss-Macalister, *Excavations*, 7, 8, 44 ff, 89–90, 107, 195, 199 • H. Thiersch, *Archaeologischer Anzeiger* 1908, 384 ff. • Watzinger, *DP* 2, 28–30.

KADESH-BARNEA

IDENTIFICATION. Kadesh-Barnea was the most important station of the Israelites during their wanderings in the desert and their religious and judicial center at that time (Deuteronomy 1:2 ff). It can be located with certainty from its description in the Bible (Numbers 34:4; Joshua 15:3). The suggestion of C. L. Woolley and T. E. Lawrence to identify it with Tell el-Qudeirat in northern Sinai has generally been accepted. This mound is situated near the junction of two ancient routes: "the way to Shur" leading to Egypt and a branch of the Via Maris running from the Mediterranean shore (from el-'Arish or Rafiaḥ) to the Gulf of Elath.

The area of the mound is approximately three dunams. It stands near 'Ein el-Qudeirat ("Water of Meribah" and En-Mishpat in the Bible), which is the richest spring in Sinai, watering the largest oasis in northern Sinai. The name "Kadesh-Barnea" may have originally referred not only to the mound but to the entire oasis as well. This oasis was also protected by several other fortresses. The mound dominates the road crossing the oasis.

EXPLORATION

In 1914, Woolley and Lawrence surveyed northern Sinai on behalf of the Palestine Exploration Fund. In the course of their work, they examined Tell el-Qudeirat and the remnants of a fortress on the site, prepared a plan of the remains, and described the site in detail for the first time.

Late in 1956, an expedition of the Department of Antiquities, under the direction of M. Dothan, undertook an exploratory excavation on the mound. The expedition sought to clarify the plan of the fortress, its method of construction, and the periods of occupation of the site. The line of the walls was uncovered, the interior of one of the towers was examined, and a deep sounding was made down to virgin soil. Several walls and floors in the casemate wall were excavated, and a section of the glacis was exposed.

After the completion of Dothan's excavation, the plan of the fortress as drawn up by Woolley and Lawrence could be corrected. The changes added related mainly to the eastern section of the citadel, the openings connecting the inner part of the fortress, and the casemate wall as well as the nature of the glacis. The chronology of the site was established mainly on the basis of the finds. Although much important material on the history of the site was added, a reliable stratigraphy is still lacking because of the limited area excavated.

RESULTS OF THE EXCAVATIONS. Three main periods were distinguished on the mound.

Period I. No remains of buildings were found from this period, which predates the fortress. Evidence of a conflagration and potsherds, however, were found under the walls. Similar potsherds were found in the glacis, which dates from period II. Most of the pottery is handmade and includes bowls and deep pots, which were perhaps used for cooking, and hole-mouth jars. Several of the vessels have pairs of ledge handles under the rim or on the side. Judging from similar finds from the lowest level at Ezion-Geber and from excavations and surveys in the southern Negev, this pottery is to be dated to the tenth or beginning of the ninth century B.C.

Period II. In this period the fortress at Kadesh-Barnea was built. It is a rectangular structure (21 by 60 meters) with a casemate wall containing rooms of varying lengths. Several rooms had doorways opening onto the inner courtyard. Square towers stood in each corner of the fortress and in the middle of each side, in all, a total of eight towers. No gate was found, and it is possible that the fortress was entered through a single narrow opening.

Erected on ground slightly higher than the bed of the adjoining wadi, the fortress was surrounded by a glacis, except on the side of the wadi, where the steep embankment afforded a natural defense. The glacis, with a gradient of about 40 degrees and consisting mainly of beaten clay covered with large stones, encircled the lower part of the wall up to a height of 2 to 4 meters.

The lower part of the casemate wall, the greater part of which is sunk in the glacis, was built of rubble, except for the towers which were made of dressed stones. The second story of the fortress was brick as evidenced by the rubble of bricks (measuring approximately 20 by 12 by 15 centimeters), which had collapsed on the floor of the rooms in the lower story.

Most of the finds, especially those discovered on the floors of the casemate rooms, belong to the last phase of the fortress. In the earlier phases the rooms of the fortress were apparently cleared of debris periodically, so that no material accumulated for long periods of time.

The ceramic finds date mainly to eighth–seventh centuries B.C., but some potsherds seem to indicate a date in the ninth century B.C. for the construction of the fortress. Typical vessels from the eighth–seventh centuries include bowls with disk bases, deep cooking pots with two handles, and, in particular, sack-shaped storage jars without necks. The fortress, which is of a type common in the Israelite period, may have been erected in the reign of Jehoshaphat and defended the southern approaches of Judah up to the end of the First Temple period. It may also have served as an administrative center.

Period III. Some evidence of occupation, especially in the eastern end of the courtyard, was found from the period following the destruction of the fortress. In this period, only a few structures built inside the courtyard of the fortress were used, while the walls remained in ruins. The last period of occupation of the site can be dated on the basis of the finds to the fifth–fourth centuries B.C. These finds include "Persian" bowls with ring bases, an Attic lecythus and a jar with high basket handles. On this vessel is painted the Hebrew letter *shin,* in the form usual in the Persian period, and also the symbol ∧, which may designate the numeral five and thus indicate the capacity of the jar. The *shin* may be an abbreviation of the word *shemen* ("oil"). Since the liquid measure of the period was the *hin,* the jar seems to have contained 5 *hin* of oil. Occupation of the site came to an end in the Persian period, perhaps toward its close. The settlements of the Roman and Byzantine periods shifted to a nearby height.

SUMMARY.

There are indications that the first permanent settlement at Kadesh-Barnea was established in the tenth century B.C. (period I). A casemate fortress, of the type characteristic in the kingdom of Judah, was apparently erected in the ninth century, perhaps during the reign of Jehoshaphat (period II). No building phases can be distinguished in the fortress, but according to the latest finds, it was destroyed at the end of the Judean monarchy. After its destruction the last occupation (period III) on the mound was limited mostly to the courtyard of that structure, where finds from the fifth–fourth centuries B.C. were uncovered.

M. DOTHAN

BIBLIOGRAPHY

C. L. Woolley–T. E. Lawrence, *APEF* 3 (1914–15), 62–71 • N. Glueck, *AASOR* 15 (1935), 118 ff. • R. de Vaux–R. Savignac, *RB* 47 (1938), 88 ff. • B. Rothenberg–Y. Aharoni, *Tagliyyot Sinai,* Tel Aviv, 1958, 104 ff (Hebrew) • Aharoni, *LB,* index • M. Dothan, *IEJ* 15 (1965), 134–51; R. Cohen, *IEJ* 26 (1976), 201–202.

*Opposite page: The mound, looking south; This page,
top to bottom: Israelite fortress, schematic cross-
section (reconstruction); Plan of the Israelite fortress;
Israelite fortress, southern outer wall of the casemates.*

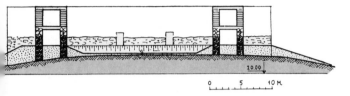

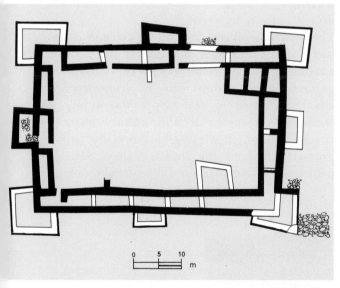

KEBARA CAVE

IDENTIFICATION. The Kebara Cave is situated in dolomitic rocks on the western slope of Mount Carmel, about 50 meters above sea level, 2 kilometers (1 mile) south of the police station of Zikhron Ya'akov and 400 meters from the Haifa–Ḥederah highway.

The cave, which is not deep, consists of a hall about 17 meters long and 14 meters wide. The walls contain many projections, recesses, and holes made by nesting birds and bats. In the ceiling of the cave, there is an open chimney about 20 meters high. The entrance to the cave is high and arched and faces west.

EXPLORATION

The cave was discovered by M. Stekelis in 1929. The entrance was blocked at that time by a stone fence, and the cave itself served as a resting place for sheep, its floor being covered with sheep and bat droppings. Large stones fallen from the ceiling were scattered over the floor. The terrace in front of the entrance to the cave was also covered with stones and earth. An investigation of the terrace yielded microlithic tools.

In 1931, Dorothy Garrod and T. D. McCown made a trial sounding at the entrance to the cave (without having any knowledge of Stekelis' trial excavation) and discovered Natufian remains. In the spring of 1931, F. Turville-Petre and Dorothy Baines excavated in the cave, on behalf of the British School of Archaeology in Jerusalem and the American School of Prehistoric Research. They distinguished the following levels, from top to bottom:

A. Mixed level containing pottery from the Bronze Age to recent times. Thickness .3–.75 meter.

B.   Natufian (Mesolithic) .5–2 meters.

C.   Kebaran, .25 meter.

D_1. Middle Aurignacian.

D_2. Middle Aurignacian.

E.   Middle Aurignacian.

F.   not excavated.

Level B. Near the entrance to the cave, a collective burial was discovered at a depth of about 1 meter with the crumbling bones of men, women, and children laid in no specific order and intermixed with stones. No funerary offerings were discovered.

699

The lithic industry of this level comprised about a thousand sickle blades with abrupt or Helwan retouch, the gloss from use discernible on the edges. Also found were lunates with abrupt or Helwan retouch. Among the microliths are triangles, trapezes, bladelets with parallel re-touched sides, thirty-six burins, among them angle burins, bec-de-flûte, and prismatic forms as well as borers. In addition to the assemblage there were also end scrapers, round scrapers, and carinated scrapers, large and coarsely trimmed implements, such as cutting implements, picks, and scrapers. Bone implements included one hundred awls, four harpoons with one row of barbs, fish hooks, gorgets, a broken comb, four hundred pendants, beads made of carnivore and ox teeth, gazelle toe bones, and bird bones.

Of special interest is a sickle haft (.38 meter long) with the end carved in the form of a goat's head. A similar haft (.23 meter long) and two other bone objects bearing a carved bull head and a deer head were probably sickle hafts too.

Turville-Petre ascribes this complex to the early phase of the Natufian culture.

Level C. The lithic complex of this level is predominantly microlithic. Among the implements are elongated triangular bladelets, with retouch on two sides only, spiky points, and curved bladelets. Regular-sized implements were also found: end scrapers, carinated and semi-carinated scrapers and several burins. The presence of what seemed to be charred human bones suggested cremation of the dead. Dorothy Garrod named this culture Kebara because of its distinctive lithic characteristics.

Levels D, E. In these levels Turville-Petre discovered remains belonging to the Middle Aurignacian, but due to his illness and subsequent death they were not included in his first report (after his death Dorothy Garrod prepared the second report for publication). In levels D_1 and D_2, the most common implements are various kinds of scrapers (75.2 percent in D_2 and 73.4 percent in D_1), whereas in level E their relative proportion decreases to 56.4 percent.

The lithic assemblage in level C (Kebaran culture) was found throughout the area of the cave in a stratum only .25 meter thick. On stratigraphic grounds this culture can be considered an advanced phase of the Upper Paleolithic. Assemblages belonging to this culture were discovered throughout Israel, especially in the Coastal Plain and the Jordan Valley. Since the nature of this complex, as well as its chronological

Left: The Kebara Cave; Opposite page, left: Bone artifacts, fishhooks, harpoons, etc.; Right: Sickle handle carved in the form of a young gazelle.

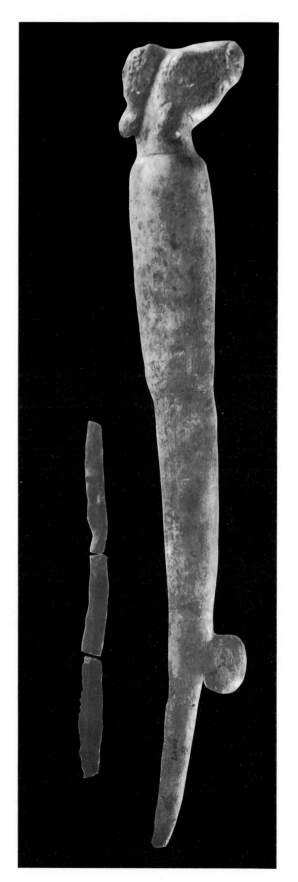

setting and age, were unclear, it was decided to resume excavations in the Kebara Cave, in the hope of clarifying this culture.

In 1951, excavations in the Kebara Cave were renewed on behalf of the Hebrew University and the Department of Antiquities and continued until 1957, and were again resumed in 1964 on behalf of the Hebrew University and the Haifa Municipality.

Excavations on the terrace yielded no material of the Kebara culture. Turville-Petre, in his time, had not reached bedrock inside the cave, and excavations were therefore concentrated in that area. It became clear that the prehistoric strata were not horizontal but sloped in two directions, north–south and east–west, forming a kind of deep basin in the center of the cave.

The excavations inside the cave revealed about thirty occupational levels, twenty of which belonged to the Upper Paleolithic, ten to the upper phase of the Middle Paleolithic and two levels to the lower phase of the Middle Paleolithic. The excavators penetrated to a depth of 10.5 meters below surface level, without, however, reaching bedrock.

In the level belonging to the upper phase of the Middle Paleolithic, the charred fragments of a human skull and several teeth were discovered in 1957. In the lower phase of the Middle Paleolithic, the skeleton of an infant (about two years old) was uncovered in 1965. It was found near a fireplace, in a shallow grave topped by three stones.

The total thickness of the Middle Paleolithic layers reaches 4 meters. Several "living floors" were discovered inside the cave, containing remains of numerous animals. The kitchen middens were concentrated mainly near the walls of the cave. Stone-built fireplaces were also discovered.

Carbon-14 tests yielded the following ages: 34690 ± 500 (GRO 2551); 42000 ± 1000 (GRO 2561).

M. STEKELIS

BIBLIOGRAPHY

F. Turville-Petre, *Journal of the Royal Anthropological Institute*, 1932, 271–76 • D. M. A. Bate, *ibid.*, 277–79 • M. Stekelis, *IEJ* 2 (1952), 141; 3 (1953), 262; *idem, IV Congress Cronica*, see Jisr Banat Ya'aqub-Inter. de *Cièncìàs Prehist. y Protohist.* Madrid, 1954, 385–89 • D. A. E. Garrod, *Proceedings of the Prehistoric Society* (1954), 155–92 • M. Stekelis, *RB* 62 (1955), 84; *idem, IEJ* 14 (1964), 227 • E. C. Saxon, *Journal of Archaeological Science* 1 (1974), 27–45 • T. Shick and M. Stekelis, *EI* 13 (Hebrew, in press).

KEDESH, TEL

IDENTIFICATION. Tel Kedesh (Tell Abu Qudeis) is situated almost midway between Taanach and Megiddo in the Jezreel Valley. It is a nearly circular mound, covering an area of about 10 dunams, and rising about 6–7 meters above its surroundings. On its northwestern edge is a group of small springs used by shepherds from nearby villages to water their flocks. The presence of these springs can explain the permanent settlement on this spot in antiquity. The soil around the site is heavy and swampy, and was rendered fit for cultivation only in recent years when a broad channel was dug near the mound.

In 1968, excavations were conducted on the mound by E. Stern on behalf of Tel Aviv University. The purpose of the excavations was to examine the stratigraphy of the site and to establish its identification and possible historical connection with the Kedesh mentioned in the biblical story of Deborah's war.

This page: Incense altar of limestone—Israelite period; Opposite page: Tel Kedesh. Section through the mound.

The area selected for excavation was the western slope of the mound where eight strata of occupation were exposed.

Stratum I. In this top stratum were uncovered sections of walls apparently dating from different phases of the Arab period (seventh–eighth centuries A.D.).

Stratum II. Dates to the Late Roman period (third–fourth centuries A.D.). Remains of a very large, stone-flagged building, with a cement-lined storage pool in one of its rooms, were found on the summit of the mound. Parts of additional structures were discovered near the foot of the mound, indicating that occupation extended over this entire area.

Stratum III. A gap of about a thousand years separates stratum II from stratum III, which embraces the Persian and the beginning of the Hellenistic period (i.e., it spans the end of the sixth to the beginning of the third century B.C.). Building remains from this stratum were found on the summit and the slope. The finds included local as well as imported Attic and Cypriot wares.

Strata IV–VII. The next four strata all belong to the Israelite period. These strata were well preserved for the most part, with walls and floors lined with stones, clay, or ground chalk. The most important building was a large structure in stratum IV, which was only partly exposed in the excavated area. It contained one long chamber with an entrance that led to a stone-flagged courtyard. Inside the chamber were a number of jar bases stuck in the floor, and adjacent to them was a limestone incense altar with four horns. These finds led the excavator to conclude that the building served as a cult place. The building remains in the four

Israelite strata showed that occupation of the mound during these phases was confined to its summit only.

Careful examination of the ceramic remains showed that the earliest stratum (VII) belonged to the first half of the twelfth century B.C. The other three strata fit within a relatively short time span (the tenth to the first half of the eighth century B.C.). This examination also revealed that the Israelite occupations were destroyed at least twice in wars, these destructions sealing off both the earliest (stratum VII) and the latest (stratum IV) occupations.

Stratum VIII. This was the lowest level excavated. It yielded sherds of local and imported Mycenaean ware, which dated the stratum to the fourteenth–thirteenth centuries B.C.

The discovery at Tel Kedesh of a level from the twelfth century B.C., assumed by many scholars to be the period of Deborah's war, and especially the discovery of a cult place with an altar (which testifies to a tradition of holiness associated with this site), lends support to the mound's identification with the Kedesh mentioned in Judges 4:11, i.e., the dwelling place of Heber the Kenite. This locality is clearly linked with the battle on the Kishon near "Taanach by the waters of Megiddo" (Judges 5:19). The whole description fits the site of Tel Kedesh surprisingly well.　　　E. STERN

BIBLIOGRAPHY

J. Garstang, *Joshua, Judges,* London, 1931, 301 • W. F. Albright, *BASOR* 62 (1936), 26–31; 68 (1937), 25 • R. Giveon, *Journal of Jewish Studies* 8 (1957), 157–59 • B. Mazar, *JNES* 24 (1965), 297–303 • Y. Aharoni, in: *Near Eastern Archaeology in the Twentieth Century,* New York, 1970, 254–70 • E. Stern–I. Beit-Arieh, *Excavations and Studies,* Essays in Honor of S. Yeivin, Tel Aviv, 1973, 93–122 (Hebrew).

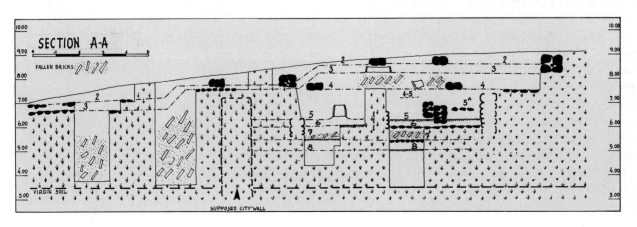

KEFAR BIR'AM

THE SITE AND ITS EXPLORATION. An abandoned village northwest of Gush Ḥalav, where the ruins of two ancient synagogues were found. The place is not mentioned in ancient sources apart from the itineraries of medieval Jewish pilgrims. Rabbi Samuel son of Simeon (1210) mentions the ruins of these synagogues, one of which (called the *bet midrash*) was outside the city and the other within the city. Rabbi Moses Basula (1522) and others speak of the beauty of the existing remains, especially of the doorways and columns still standing. All ascribed the construction of the synagogues to Rabbi Simeon bar Yoḥai. In the second half of the nineteenth century, many explorers visited the site. E. Robinson, E. Renan, V. Guérin, and members of the British Survey of Western Palestine described the ruins as well as the doorway of the small synagogue outside the village. In the year 1905, the synagogue in the village was excavated by H. Kohl and C. Watzinger on behalf of the Deutsche Orient-Gesellschaft. No remains of the second synagogue were visible at that time. In recent years the site was again cleared on behalf of the Israel Department of Landscaping and Preservation of Historical Sites, and additional architectural fragments were discovered. Parts of the building have been restored.

Of the large synagogue inside the village (15.2 by 20 meters) the beautiful facade with its doors and windows has been preserved practically undamaged up to the upper cornice of the lower story. The facade faces south in the direction of Jerusalem. Unlike other synagogues, a porch (5.35 meters wide) was built along the length of the facade. On the east side one column of this porch has been preserved in situ complete with part of the architrave connecting it to the building as well as a pedestal of a corner column. The porch was surmounted by a pediment with an arch in its center, as can be deduced from a fragmentary architrave, which is partly straight and partly arched. Eight columns supported the porch, six in front and one on either side between the corner columns and the building. The columns have

Synagogue of Kefar Bir'am.

Attic bases and the capitals are molded with ovolo, cavetto, and abacus.

The facade is built of ashlar stones and is provided with three entrances—a large doorway in the middle and two smaller entrances on the sides. The middle entrance (2.65 meters high and 1.42 meters wide) has molded jambs and a lintel with a *tabula ansata*. A low relief on the lintel depicts two Winged Victories ("Nike") bearing a wreath. The figures had been deliberately mutilated. The convex frieze above the lintel is decorated with a vine branch issuing from an amphora. Above the frieze is a cornice. On either side of the lintel was a console in the form of a double spiral. One console has been preserved in situ, but its direction does not fit the cornice. A molded arch, which served as a window, rises above the cornice.

The two side entrances, although much simpler, are similar to the central doorway. The convex frieze above the western lintel is decorated with a rope pattern and the one above the eastern lintel with a pattern of laurel leaves or scales. Above each lintel is a rectangular window surmounted by a relief of a pediment decorated on its sides with vine tendrils.

On the sill of the eastern window is carved a Hebrew inscription which reads "Built by El'azar son of Yudan"—presumably the name of the artisan who erected the synagogue.

The facade of the lower story terminates in a cornice rising 5.3 meters above the floor; part of the cornice has been preserved in the eastern corner. The facade undoubtedly was two stories high and terminated in a Syrian pediment, but no traces of such a pediment have been found.

The interior of the synagogue is divided by two longitudinal and one transversal row of columns into a nave (6.2 meters wide) and narrow aisles which surround the nave on three sides. The floor is paved with flagstones. One column and several pedestals were found in situ, and others were scattered throughout the area. The pedestals stand on stylobates. No capitals were uncovered, but it can be assumed that they were similar to those in the porch. The aisles were about 5.3 meters high, which was also the height of the cornice in the facade of the building. No remains of the upper story were found.

Among the finds of special interest are the head of a lion and a fragment of a frieze decorated with a meander pattern and various figures.

Of the small synagogue outside the village no remains have survived. Two doorways were still seen in the sixteenth century, but only the main entrance was still standing in the nineteenth century. This synagogue was also provided with three entrances. There are photographs of the main gate and of fragments of columns found in the area. According to a plan prepared by C. Wilson (unpublished), there were only two rows of columns in the synagogue.

The doorway was built of two molded monolithic jambs and a decorated lintel carved with a relief of a pair of Winged Victories bearing a wreath, similar to the relief above the central lintel of the first synagogue. The images were already completely blurred by the nineteenth century. Beneath the relief, on the lower band of the lintel, was the Hebrew inscription: "May there be peace in this place and in all the places of Israel. Jose the Levite, the son of Levi, made this lintel. May blessing come upon his deeds. Shalom." A fragment of this inscription is preserved in the Louvre. The artisan Jose, son of Levi, also made the lintel of the synagogue at 'Almah, as is attested by the inscription found there.

SUMMARY

Kefar Bir'am must have been a flourishing Jewish settlement in the third century A.D., since it could afford to build two elaborate synagogues. Remains of two synagogues in one town have hitherto been found only in neighboring Gush Ḥalav. Because of the excellent state of preservation of the facade and porch, the synagogue at Kefar Bir'am occupies an important place among Jewish architectural remains, being a fine example of the characteristically rich, monumental style of Galilean synagogues. The inscription on the lintel constitutes an important addition to the scanty epigraphic material found in the early synagogues.   N. AVIGAD

BIBLIOGRAPHY

Conder–Kitchener, *SWP* 1, 230–34 • Kohl–Watzinger, *Synagogen,* 89–100 • Sukenik, *Ancient Synagogues,* 24–26 • S. Yeivin, *BJPES* 3 (1936), 117–21 (Hebrew) • Goodenough, *Jewish Symbols,* 201–3 • R. Amiran, *EI* 3 (1954), 178–81 (Hebrew); *idem, IEJ* 6 (1956), 239–45.

Below: The facade of the large synagogue; Opposite page, counterclockwise, top left: Head of a lion, from the synagogue; Plan of the large synagogue; Lintel of the small synagogue; Fragment of a relief of the zodiac.

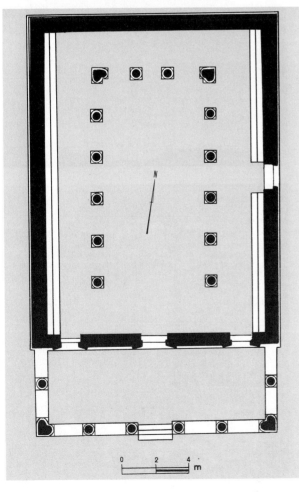

KEFAR GIL'ADI

In the area around Kibbutz Kefar Gil'adi, a survey conducted by J. Kaplan in 1957 revealed the existence of three new sites. Two ancient sites were already known in the area — the large mound north of the kibbutz, where the former village of Abil el-Qamḥ once stood (identified with the biblical Abel Beth-Maachah), and Khirbet Niḥa which lies northwest of the kibbutz. The three new sites (from north to south) include 1. a site north of the Rawaḥina spring with Neolithic and Chalcolithic remains, 2. an area of tombs and mausoleums south of the kibbutz, called Givat ha-Shoket, 3. a small flat mound south to Givat ha-Shoket with a spring nearby. This small mound was occupied mainly in the Israelite period and could well be Janoah, one of the towns conquered by Tiglath-Pileser III in the land of Naphtali (II Kings 15:29). This identification is based on the fact that Janoah appears in the biblical list between Iyon and Abel Beth-Maachah, and Kedesh and Hazor, and also on its similarity with the name Niḥa. Khirbet Niḥa itself was occupied from the first century B.C., when the area of Givat ha-Shoket served as its burial ground. Two of the sites excavated by J. Kaplan are described below.

SITE NEAR THE RAWAḤINA SPRING

Excavations were conducted at the site in September, 1957, and November, 1962, on behalf of the Israel Exploration Society. An area of 200 square meters was exposed, and four strata were distinguished: strata I–III, Chalcolithic and stratum IV, Neolithic. The top stratum (I) contained the lower parts of round silos built of stone slabs. The pottery found at the bottom of the silos resembles Ghassulian ware. In the two strata II–III were uncovered foundations of a building of rubble with pottery similar to the Chalcolithic ware of Jericho VIII and the Wadi Rabah culture. Stratum IV, beneath strata I–III, contained two occupation phases, the lower phase IV-b, resting on virgin soil, and the upper phase IV-a, with a wall 1.15 meters thick, built of large rubble stones. The flint implements were similar in both phases and included axes, adzes, hoes, arrow- and spearheads, blades, and denticulated sickle blades. Most of the pottery in these two phases belonged to the dark-faced

burnished ware known from Cilicia and Syria, and especially from the Amuq Plain. Also in phase IV-b were found, for the first time in Israel, sherds of cord-marked ware known from R. J. Braidwood's excavations at Tabat el-Ḥamam in north Syria. Noteworthy among the finds was a clay fertility figurine excavated in phase IV-a. Radiocarbon tests of charcoal from phase IV-b gave the date: 8905 ± 320 B.P. The pottery from this phase represents some of the earliest found in the ancient Near East, and compares roughly in date with the earliest pottery excavated at Chatal Hüyük, Anatolia.

In summary, it can be stated that the Neolithic remains at Kefar Gil'adi are closer in character to

those found in Neolithic sites of Lebanon-Syria than to those excavated thus far in Israel.

THE MAUSOLEUM NEAR GIVAT HA-SHOKET

The mausoleum was first explored in September, 1957, on behalf of the Israel Exploration Society. Excavations were carried out in November, 1961, on behalf of the Department of Antiquities.

The excavations exposed the lower part of a mausoleum (9 by 9 meters), with walls, 1.8 meters thick, built of two rows of ashlars with a fill of small stones. Three superimposed layers of burials were found on the floor. To the first layer belongs an empty sarcophagus incised on one of its short sides with the Hebrew inscription "Hezekiah." The mausoleum was evidently constructed to preserve this sarcophagus. The second layer included a complex of seven rectangular graves that filled a cavity in the rock below the floor of the mausoleum. The walls of the first grave were plastered and decorated with panels of floral motifs, leaves, and birds in three colors. Although most of the graves contained coffins made of thin lead sheets, the second grave had a heavy lead coffin ornamented with reliefs depicting Hercules in a gabled frame, a roaring lion also in a gabled frame, Corinthian columns, and panels of grape clusters, vine tendrils and birds. Inside the coffin was found a rare gold diadem inlaid with semi-precious stones and also a gold chain bracelet with greenish stones. Several glass vessels of the third century A.D. were found in some of the other graves. The third layer, underlying the seven tombs, yielded a marble sarcophagus that was partly concealed in the rock. Its lid is decorated with rosettes on the short sides. One of the long sides of the sarcophagus bears a Greek inscription painted in red: ΗΡΑΚΛΕΙΔΟΥ ΠΠ. Inside this sarcophagus was a sheet-lead coffin, containing a human skeleton. This lead coffin was actually the inner lining of a wooden coffin, which had almost totally disintegrated. Apparently, when the pit was dug for Heraklides' marble coffin, Hezekiah's sarcophagus was shifted aside and later restored to its original place. The same also happened with the digging of the tombs — then, too, the sarcophagus was moved aside when necessary and afterwards returned to its original position.

CONCLUSION

It was established that the mausoleum was used for burials in two separate periods. In the first period (strata I and III) Hezekiah and Heraklides were interred. Heraklides was most likely the son of Hezekiah and built the mausoleum to commemorate his father and probably also with the intention of being buried there after his own death. The first period dates not later than the Severan dynasty (A.D. 193–235). The second period begins in the time of Diocletian (A.D. 284–305) with the digging of the first graves in stratum II close to the years 290–295. The last of the seven graves in this stratum was probably dug in A.D. 310, and if so, the second period thus extended from approximately A.D. 290 to 310.

J. KAPLAN

BIBLIOGRAPHY

Y. Aharoni, *Enc. Miqr.* 3, 704 (Hebrew) • Abel, *GP* 2, 354 • R. and L. Braidwood, *Syria* 21 (1940), 183–226 • J. Kaplan, *IEJ* 8 (1958), 274; idem, *RB* 64 (1958), 411–12; 70 (1963), 587 • F. Hole, *Syria* 36 (1959), 149–83 • J. Kaplan, *EI* 8 (1967), 104–13 (Hebrew).

Opposite page, top: Fragment of the lead sarcophagus from the mausoleum; Bottom: Silos, from the Chalcolithic period; This page: Ornaments on lid of lead sarcophagus from the mausoleum.

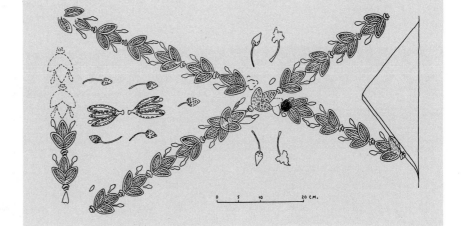

KEFAR NEBURAYA

The site lies about 3 kilometers (2 miles) north of Safed and is generally identified with Kefar Neburaya of the Talmudic period. In writings of Jewish travelers of the Middle Ages, the site appears as Nevarta. The Arabs used the dual form Nabratein for the two ruined sites on the two banks of Wadi 'Amukah. On the southern bank are the remains of an ancient synagogue, mentioned by E. Renan, C. Wilson, V. Guérin, and H. H. Kitchener. In 1905, H. Kohl and C. Watzinger excavated the site.

The Synagogue is one of the smallest in the Galilee (about 16 by 11.5 meters). Little has survived of the building. Of its walls only one course of ashlar stones or the foundations have been preserved. The facade of the building, which had a single entrance, faces south in the direction of Jerusalem.

The hall of the synagogue is divided by two rows of four columns each into a nave (4.25 meters wide) and two aisles (2.2 meters each). Benches probably stood along the walls. The floor was paved with stone slabs. The columns stood on square pedestals, one of them bearing an unusual relief of a hare. Near the northern wall was found a lintel decorated with a relief of a vase from which tendrils issue in all directions. This find points to the presence of an additional entrance in the northern wall.

In the southern wall the threshold of the main entrance was unearthed. Near it lay a stone door-post, 2.5 meters high, which indicates the height of the doorway. In front of the entrance a lintel (2.8 meters long) was found. It has a molded profile, which terminates in a frieze decorated with a pattern of laurel leaves. In the center of the lintel is a laurel wreath enclosing a representation of the seven-branched candlestick (menorah). Run-

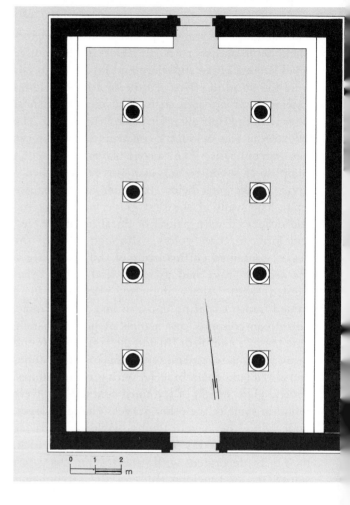

Above: Plan of the synagogue; Below: Inscribed lintel.

ning along both sides of the wreath is a Hebrew inscription in low relief which reads: "[According] to the number 494 years after the destruction [of the Temple], the house was built during the office of Ḥanina son of Lezer and Luliana son of Yudan."

The date, as mentioned in the inscription, corresponds to the year A.D. 564, but on the basis of the style of the lintel and of the building itself, the synagogue is to be ascribed to the third century A.D. Thus this is not an original building inscription contemporary with the lintel, but it is probably a later addition commemorating the restoration of the early synagogue.

N. AVIGAD

BIBLIOGRAPHY

S. Klein, *Sefer ha-Yishuv* 1, Jerusalem, 1939, 94 (Hebrew) • Conder–Kitchener, *SWP* 1, 243–44 • Kohl–Watzinger, *Synagogen*, 101–06 • Goodenough, *Jewish Symbols* 1, 203–04 • N. Avigad, *Rabinowitz Bulletin* 3 (1960), 49–56, Pl. 13.

KEISAN, TELL

Tell Keisan (in Hebrew Tel Qison) is one of the largest ancient sites in the country (nearly as great as Megiddo). It is situated 8 kilometers (5 miles) due southeast of Accho in the heart of the long coastal plain of Zebulon (map reference 164253). Its summit is roughly circular, occupying fifty dunams (200 by 250 meters) and is divided into two parts by a slight, narrow depression running across the mound from north to south. The mound dominates the fertile plain below by its height of 25 to 30 meters, and this easily fortified height, with accessible groundwater at the northern end of the mound, explains the continued occupation over the course of many millennia. The mound rises upon a central core of limestone. Bedrock has been exposed at two places through erosion of the trench cut by A. Rowe some forty years ago (see below).

The history of the site is still virtually unknown. Occupation is attested from prehistoric times. Many flint tools, the earliest dating from the Neolithic period, have been found in the nearby fields. The surrounding plain must have been less marshy and more extensively cultivated in antiquity than has been believed. The number of ancient sites discovered within a 10-kilometer radius of the mound attests to an uncommon density of population. At the mound itself, apart from a city of the Hyksos period (Middle Bronze Age II-B–C), two periods in particular appear to have been important: Late Bronze Age–Early Iron Age, and the Hellenistic period. Thereafter the site continually declined in importance and in population, except for two brief reoccupations in the sixth and the twelfth–thirteenth centuries A.D.

Most scholars locate the biblical city of Achshaph at Tell Keisan. This city is mentioned in three passages in the Bible, all in the Book of Joshua. Joshua 19:25 mentions Achshaph among the possessions of the tribe of Asher, but without giving its exact location. Joshua 11:1 and 12:20 are lists of cities of the Israelite conquest. The second of these lists, according to literary criticism, has been reworked by a later (Deuteronomic)

Tell Keisan; Two views of a conical stamp of Psamtik II (6th century B.C.*)*

711

This page, left: General view of the mound, looking south; Below: Byzantine church—east side; Opposite page: Plan of the excavations.

redactor under the influence of a roster of cities fortified by Solomon.

Achshaph is mentioned eight times in Egyptian texts, from 1800 to 1200 B.C. At the beginning of the second millennium B.C., a king writes to Pharaoh that the kings of Accho and Achshaph have hastened to aid him with fifty chariots. Another text (Papyrus Anastasi I, thirteenth century B.C.) contains the following question: "Come, set [me] on the way southward to the region of Accho. Where does the Achshaph road come? At what town?" (trans. from Wilson, *ANET*, p. 477). From this we can conclude that Achshaph and Accho were close to one another, with the former situated somewhat to the south. But nothing yet discovered by archaeologists confirms the identification of Achshaph and Tell Keisan. Some scholars have identified this mound with q-s-n in the lists of Thutmose III, with Allammelech or with Mishal.

In 1935, the Nielson Expedition to the Near East excavated a stratigraphic trench across the southeast slope of the mound. The results were published soon after by A. Rowe. Further work (carried out with the collaboration of V. M. Seton-Williams) opened a series of cross trenches running from east to west along the length of the mound and stratigraphically connected to Rowe's trench. These revealed the existence of an important Hellenistic city of the third to second centuries B.C. These

KHELEIFEH, TELL EL-

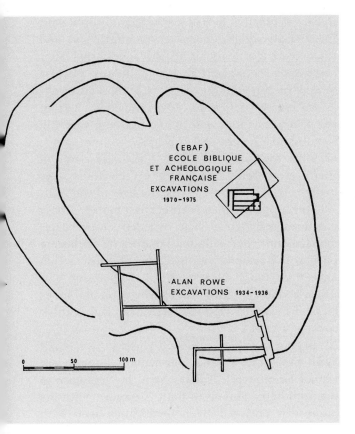

(EBAF)
ECOLE BIBLIQUE
ET ACHEOLOGIQUE
FRANÇAISE
EXCAVATIONS
1970-1975

ALAN ROWE
EXCAVATIONS 1934-1936

0   50   100 m

results remain unpublished.

In 1970, the École Biblique et Archéologique Française of Jerusalem initiated a program of excavation under the direction of R. de Vaux, who was especially interested in the little-known transition period between the Bronze Age and the Iron Age. After de Vaux's sudden death in 1971, the excavations were continued by his assistant J. Prignaud and a team of graduates of the École Biblique et Archéologique. Two adjacent areas (A and B) opened on the eastern part of the mound revealed a Byzantine installation (which earlier indications had suggested might be a Persian building), and several levels of occupation on the slope from the Iron Age II and the Persian period.

P. BENOIT

BIBLIOGRAPHY

A. Rowe et al., *QDAP* 5 (1936), 207–09 • J. Prignaud, *RB* 79 (1972), 227–38 • J. Briend, *ibid.*, 239–46 • A. Lemaire, *ibid.*, 247–54 • M. Join-Lambert, *ibid.*, 255–62 • A. Spycket, *ibid.*, 263–74; *idem, RB* 80 (1973), 384–95 • W. Fulco, *RB* 82 (1975) (in press). A volume of studies on Tell Keisan will be published shortly in the series "Cahiers de la Revue Biblique" (Paris) • J. Prignaud, *IEJ* 22 (1972), 177–78; 249; 23 (1973), 259.

IDENTIFICATION. Tell el-Kheleifeh is a low mound with Iron Age and Persian remains, located some 500 meters from the present north shoreline of the Gulf of Aqabah, about midway between its eastern and western ends. It was first discovered by F. Frank in 1933. After excavation by N. Glueck, on behalf of the Smithsonian Institution, Washington, D.C. and the American Schools of Oriental Research, its identity with Ezion-Geber was generally accepted. It was at Ezion-Geber that Solomon established his fleet of Tarshish ships ("in Ezion-Geber, which is beside Eloth, on the shore of the Red Sea, in the land of Edom" I Kings 9:26). Glueck searched in vain for the remains of Ezion-Geber and/or Elath near or at the site of modern Aqabah at the northeast end of the Gulf of Aqabah. This area, with its strong springs of sweet water, fertile soil, fine anchorage, and command of the crossroads to and from Arabia, make it seem a natural choice for the location of ancient Ezion-Geber and Elath. It is possible that Iron Age I–II remains may be buried under the debris of Aqabah, or they may have been washed almost completely away by the devastating freshets that periodically inundated the site when diversion dams did not exist or were not kept in repair.

It seems quite possible also that an Iron Age I–II fortress existed, in general conformity with the practice of the period, on one of the hills overlooking the fertile plain and springs of Aqabah. The fact remains, however, that Tell el-Kheleifeh is the only site thus far found on the north shore of the Gulf of Aqabah, whose pottery and other datable remains correspond with the history of Ezion-Geber and of Elath. If in the final result Tell el-Kheleifeh is not to be identified with Ezion-Geber/Elath, it must then be considered an industrial and maritime satellite of the two places, a strongly fortified caravanserai and a granary city.

EXCAVATIONS

Excavations were begun at the northwest corner of Tell el-Kheleifeh where the most important building of the site was immediately exposed. It was 13.2 meters square, with the outside walls 1.2 meters thick and the partition walls about 1 meter

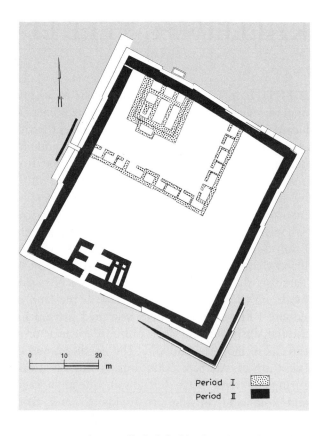

Above: Tell el-Kheleifeh, plan of periods I and II;
Below: Room 76, with typical bricks.

Period I

Period II

thick. Originally, it had consisted of six rooms, three small square rooms at the north end and three rectangular rooms to the south, the latter being each 7.4. meters in length. It was the best built structure on the site, with its mud bricks measuring 40 by 20 by 10 centimeters. Part of the southern outer wall of the building was still standing to a height of 2.7 meters.

Each of the walls had two horizontal rows of apertures piercing the width of the walls. The lower row was a meter above the base of the walls and the upper row 70 centimeters higher. These apertures apparently held wooden cross beams inserted into the walls for bonding or anchoring purposes. Examples of this type of construction have been found at Sendschirli, Boghazköy, and Samaria (and cf. I Kings 6:36). The outer and inner faces of its walls were plastered over with a thick coating of mud.

A sloping rampart of mud bricks was built against the outer sides of this main building, but it cannot be known if it dates from the first stage of the building. This well-built structure with its glacis was enclosed by a fortification wall with salients and recesses on its outer face and casemate rooms against its inner face. Each side of the

enclosure wall was 45 meters in length and was divided into three salients and two recesses, each 9 meters in length. It was built of bricks somewhat larger (about 43.5 by 23.5 by 13 centimeters) than those of the "storehouse granary" and its glaçis, and it is possible that a certain interval of time elapsed between the construction of the two, but probably only a short one, for it is difficult to envisage the military post with its storage rooms standing by itself, even with its glaçis. The building, as well as the casemate wall with its salients and recesses, has been attributed to the time of Solomon.

In the middle offset of the south side of the wall was a 2.5-meter-wide gateway, with the outer entrance originally at the east end and the inner entrance at the west end. The gateway was in line with a massive later gate. Both gateways pointed toward the sea. The enclosure wall proper, including the salients, measures from 1.05 meters to 1.1 meters in width and with the addition of casemates, from 3.95 meters to 4.1 meters. Similar casemate walls from Solomon's time have been found at Hazor, Megiddo, and Gezer (qq. v.).

The buildings of period I may have been destroyed in the invasion of Pharaoh Shishak in the last quarter of the tenth century B.C.

At the beginning of period II, a new series of massive fortification walls of mud brick was erected. The glaçis-strengthened central structure was no longer in the center of the site but at its northwest corner. The new outer mud-brick fortification consisted of a large inner wall and a smaller outer wall, each strengthened by a glaçis, with a dry moat between them. The inner wall, with its comparatively slight salients and recesses and further strengthened by a strong glaçis with corresponding offsets and insets tied into it above its foundation levels, was a particularly massive affair. It was originally some 8 meters high, about 2 meters wide at the top and 4 meters wide at the base. About 3 meters beyond the base of its glaçis was the thinner outer wall, which seems to have mirrored the construction features of the inner one. The dry moat between the two walls had a stamped-clay and mud-brick floor. At the corners of the inside wall were towers overlooking its supporting glaçis. The scheme of double-walled outer defenses with a dry moat between the walls can be paralleled at the Moabite site of Khirbet el-

Medeiyineh overlooking the Wadi Themed, and at other sites.

On the south side, near the southeast corner of the double wall fortification was a massive, four-chambered gate, with three pairs of doorways and two opposite sets of guardrooms between them. It is very similar to the massive gateway of Megiddo (IV-A), which Y. Yadin has shown was built long after the time of Solomon, perhaps by Ahab. Period

Top to bottom: Faience figurine of a cat. Twenty-Second Egyptian Dynasty, 9th–8th centuries B.C. (enlarged five times); Incense burner and seven-wicked lamp, 7th–6th centuries B.C.; Bowl with potter's mark, 7th–6th centuries B.C.

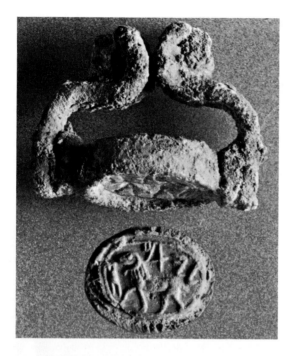

II may represent a reconstruction by Jehoshaphat of Judah, who reigned about 870–846 B.C. He was the king who made the abortive attempt to revive the sea trade between Ezion-Geber and Arabia and Africa (I Kings 22:48; II Chronicles 20:36, 37). As a result of economic decline, coupled with the growing political weakness of Judah, the importance of Ezion-Geber seems to have weakened, and after the time of Jehoshaphat, it is no longer mentioned in the Bible.

Ezion-Geber may have been destroyed again during the successful rebellion of the Edomites against Jehoshaphat's son Jehoram (Joram) (II Kings 8:20–22; II Chronicles 21:8–10), shortly after the middle of the ninth century B.C.

Nearly seventy years had passed between the destruction and abandonment of Ezion-Geber and the rebuilding of a new city (period III) on its sand-covered ruins. In this new city, a seal signet ring with the inscription "Belonging to Jotham" was found. The reference is probably to Jotham, King of Judah, the successor of Uzziah. Underneath the inscription is a horned ram and in front of it an object that N. Avigad has identified as a bellows or a metal bar. In the city of period III, which was apparently built by Uzziah, the guardrooms of the gateway were blocked up and other changes were made in various constructions of the city.

During the war of Ahaz and Rezin, King of Aram, and Pekah, King of Israel (about 733 B.C.), the city was again destroyed, and the Edomites rebuilt it anew (period IV). This city, in which several sub-periods are distinguished, lasted from about the end of the eighth century to the end of the sixth century B.C. The freedom regained by Edom from Ahaz was never again threatened by Judah, which was not strong enough thereafter to dispute Edom's control over the 'Arabah and Elath. Edom itself, however, despite periods of efflorescence, apparently became progressively less able to take full advantage of its independence.

A series of jar handles, belonging to the first phase of period IV, which probably extended well down into the seventh century B.C., were stamped with an Edomite inscription reading, "Belonging to Qausanal, the Servant of the King," i.e., an official of the King of Edom. The first part of the theophorous name of Qausanal or Qosanal, namely Quas or Qos, is that of a well-known Edomite and subsequently Nabataean deity. Also belonging to

period IV were the fragments of a large jar, which was probably used for transporting incense and spices from Arabia. On two of its pieces were incised the first ancient South Arabic letters in Minaean script discovered in a controlled excavation in greater Palestine. Other objects found in the course of the excavations show connections with Egypt.

The Babylonian conquest brought an end to Edomite rule over the city of period IV. It was destroyed before the end of the sixth century B.C. Over its ruins was built a new industrial city of period V, which lasted from the late sixth or early fifth century B.C. down to the end of the fifth or the beginning of the fourth century B.C. Trade on an extensive scale was still carried on with Arabia as evidenced by Aramaic ostraca, including wine receipts. Fragments of black-glazed Greek pottery indicate that goods were exchanged with Greece in the fifth–fourth century B.C. Tell el-Kheleifeh was abandoned thereafter and the subsequent Nabataean settlement was located farther to the east of Aila, close to present-day Aqabah.

N. GLUECK

BIBLIOGRAPHY

F. Frank, *ZDPV* 57 (1934), 208–78 • N. Glueck, *BASOR* 71 (1938), 3–18; 72 (1938), 2–13; 75 (1939), 8–22; 79 (1940), 1–18; 80 (1940), 3–10; 82 (1941), 3–11; *idem, AASOR* 15 (1935), 26–37; 42–45; 47–48; 138–39; 18–19 (1939), 3–7 • G. Ryckmans, *RB* 48 (1939), 247–49 • N. Avigad, *BASOR* 163 (1961), 18–22 • B. Rothenberg, *PEQ* 1962, 5–71 • N. Glueck, *BA* 28 (1965), 70–87 • J. Naveh, *BASOR* 183 (1966), 27–30 • N. Glueck, *ibid.*, 188 (1967), 8–38; *idem, EI* 9 (1969), 51–59 (English); 10 (1971), 120–25 (Hebrew) • B. Mazar, *ibid.*, 12 (1975), 46–48 • Z. Meshel, *ibid.*, 49–56 (both Hebrew).

Opposite page, top: Ring and seal: lytm*—perhaps belonging to the Judean king Jotham, about 758–743* B.C.; *Bottom: Room 38; two ovens and a storage jar; This page: Aramaic ostracon listing shipments of wine, 5th–4th centuries* B.C.

KINNERET

A tomb discovered when a shelter was dug near the houses in Kibbutz Kinneret, was excavated in July, 1940, by B. Mazar, with the participation of I. Dunayevsky and P. Bar-Adon. The site lies at a distance of 1.25 kilometers from Beth-Yeraḥ (Khirbet Kerak) and may have been one of Beth Yeraḥ's burial sites in the Early Bronze Age.

The tomb was hewn out of soft rock not far below ground level. It consisted of a square-shaped court (2.3 by 3 meters) with rounded corners and an elliptical burial chamber (approximately 3.38 by 2 meters), to which a step led down from the courtyard. Since the floor of the tomb was only 1.2 meters beneath the rock, the chamber could be entered only by crawling. To prevent the collapse of the chamber's rock roof, a pillar was left in the wall.

The bones and funerary offerings were originally laid on the floor of the chamber. Once the space on the floor was completely occupied, the bones and offerings were covered with a layer of sand, which then served as the base for further burials. Three superimposed burial layers of this type were unearthed. After the entire chamber had been filled up, burial was begun in the courtyard.

All three levels belong to a single brief period. The bones were either completely or partially burned, while others were only charred. It seems that the bodies were first consigned to flames and the bones later interred in the cave tomb together with funerary objects.

Inside the burial chamber fifty intact pottery vessels were found as well as a considerable quantity of potsherds. Only four vessels were found in the courtyard. The pottery is a homogeneous group dating to the late Early Bronze Age II, and many of the vessels have parallels in strata of that period at Beth Yeraḥ. Only a few sherds, found in debris on the west side, appear to be of earlier date. The pottery included jugs, jars, and juglets, cups, goblets, bowls, and platters. Two juglets in particular should be noted. They are made of a greenish clay and decorated with rows of triangles filled with dark-brown dots on a cream-colored slip. Below the triangles is a zigzag line between two horizontal lines similar to designs on the Syrian pottery well known from the First Dynasty royal tombs at Abydos. The First Dynasty has also acquainted us with the large, narrow-necked jug with one loop handle projecting from the rim to the shoulder and two tiny vertical handles on the elliptically shaped body. The clay is brown, and the burnish is vertical. Other vessels also have parallels both with pottery from Early Bronze Age II strata in Palestine and in Egyptian First Dynasty tombs. It should be noted that no sherds of Khirbet Kerak ware were found in the tombs, indicating that it predates Early Bronze Age III.

More than three hundred beads and other articles of jewelry were found in the cave tomb. Among these was part of a necklace with two gold beads and two cylindrical ruby beads. The beads found are mostly spherical, cylindrical, elliptical, conical, and biconical and are fashioned of gold, copper, faience, ruby, crystal, jasper, quartz, pottery, and mother-of-pearl. Fragments of ornamented bone plaques and a limestone pestle were also uncovered. Another noteworthy find is a round plaque of beaten gold decorated with bands and bosses arranged symmetrically around a central perforation. The ornamented portion displays four arms of dots emerging crosslike from the center with embossed sections occupying the spaces between the arms. Both in technique and design, the plaque resembled the pendants from the tombs of the second half of the third millennium at Alaca Hüyük in Anatolia.

B. MAZAR

BIBLIOGRAPHY

B. Maisler (Mazar), *BJPES* 10 (1942), 1–9 (Hebrew); *idem*, *QDAP* 12 (1946), 106 • R. Amiran, *IEJ* 2 (1952), 100 f. • W. F. Albright, *BASOR* 93 (1944), 26 • H. J. Kantor, in: *Relative Chronologies* (R. W. Ehrich, ed.), Chicago, 1956, 8 f. • B. Mazar, Ruth Amiran, and N. Haas, *EI* 11 (1973), 176–93 (Hebrew).

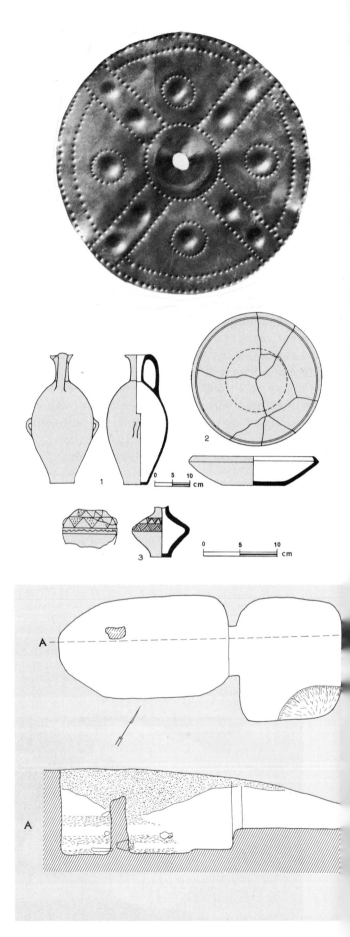

This page, top to bottom: Plaque of beaten gold, from the tomb; Selection of pottery from the tomb; The tomb — Plan and section.

KINNERET, TEL

IDENTIFICATION. Tel Kinneret (Tell el-'Oreimeh) is a high, small mound located near the northwestern outlet of the Sea of Galilee (Lake Kinneret), above the rich springs of 'En-Hashiv'a (Heptapegon). The site was of importance because it dominated the fertile valley, particularly its southern section, as well as the important branch of the Via Maris which descended from the Horns of Hattin and passed at the foot of the mound before climbing toward Hazor.

The suggestion of G. Dalman and W. F. Albright to identify the site with biblical Chinnereth has been accepted by scholars, since it was the most important fortified town on the western shore of the Sea of Galilee in the Late Bronze and Iron Ages.

The name first appears in Thutmose III's roster of conquered towns, dated to about 1468 B.C. (number 34), and in an Egyptian papyrus from approximately the same period (Papyrus Leningrad 1116–A), which lists rations of grain and beer supplied to the emissaries of various towns of Canaan. In the Bible, the city is included among the Canaanite towns which struggled with the Israelites in the north of the country (Joshua 11:2), in the list of fortifications of the tribe of Naphtali (*ibid.* 19:35) and, finally, in the description of Naphtali's invasion by Ben-Hadad I, ruler of Aram-Damascus (I Kings 15:20).

EXCAVATIONS

Limited trial digs were undertaken on the site by P. Karge in 1911, A. E. Mader and A. M. Schneider in 1931–32, and R. Bea in 1939, on behalf of the Görresgesellschaft, the German Institute for Oriental Research.

Since only brief reports of the excavations have been published, it is possible to make only the most general observations here. The trial trenches and cross sections in the various parts of the mound yielded remains of settlement from the Late Bronze Age, Iron Age I–II, and Roman period. Most of the pottery found belongs to the Late Bronze Age, and the massive stone wall, sections of which were uncovered in various places along the mound's slopes, has also been attributed to that period. The city apparently declined in importance in the Iron Age II–C, and it was probably destroyed by Tiglath-Pileser III in the year 733/32 B.C. (cf. II Kings 15:29).

Among the major finds, the excavators mention the fragment of a pottery cult object, which they assigned to the reign of Ramses II. They found on the surface of the mound an Egyptian scarab bearing the name of Queen Tiy, the wife of Amenhotep III. Mention should also be made of another surface find (in 1928), a fragment of an Egyptian stele dating either to the reign of Thutmose III or of Amenhotep II, recording a victory over foreigners from the land of Mitanni　Y. AHARONI

BIBLIOGRAPHY

Identification: G. Dalman, *Orte und Wege Jesu*, Gütersloh, (1924), 140 • W. F. Albright, *AASOR* 2–3 (1921–22), 36 f.; 6 (1924–25), 24 f.
Excavations and Finds: P. Karge, *Rephaim*, Paderborn, (1917), 172 f. • W. F. Albright–A. Rowe, *JEA* 14 (1928), 281 ff. • A. E. Mader, *Biblica* 13 (1932), 297 • R. Koeppel, *ibid.*, 298–308 • A. Bea, *ibid.*, 20 (1939), 306–08.

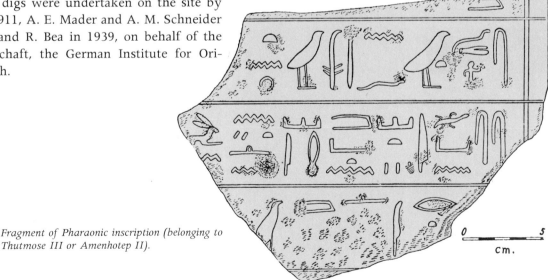

Fragment of Pharaonic inscription (belonging to Thutmose III or Amenhotep II).

KUDADI, TELL

Tell Kudadi (Tell esh-Shûni), a small mound rising about 8 meters above sea level, is situated on the northern bank of the Yarkon estuary. Trial excavations were conducted at the site in 1936 by P. L. O. Guy on behalf of the Department of Antiquities of the Mandatory Government. More extensive excavations were carried out in the winter of 1937–38 by the Hebrew University under the direction of E. L. Sukenik and S. Yeivin, with the participation of N. Avigad. Most of the mound had been washed away by the sea and the Yarkon, and some of it was also destroyed, before the excavations, during the construction of a lighthouse and a breakwater.

EXCAVATIONS

The remains of two buildings were discovered, which had probably served as fortresses at various stages of the Israelite Kingdom. The fortresses were built to protect the entrance to the Yarkon River against invaders from the sea. The first fortress was probably constructed in the ninth century B.C. It was erected on a sandstone substructure 3 meters high, with walls 7 meters wide. The eastern wall has survived for a length of 33 meters, and of the southern wall 14 meters has survived. All other parts of the substructure were completely destroyed. It was probably rectangular or square with a central courtyard. Above its massive walls was a row of rooms built around the courtyard, six of which are still extant. The walls of these rooms were built of stone and have survived to a height of .6 meter. They were found filled with clean sand. The upper parts of the walls, which were completely destroyed, were probably of brick. The courtyard of the building was entered from the east.

On the ruins of this building was built a second fortress. A segment of about 30 meters of the east wall erected against the front of the first building is still extant. This second wall, about 2.5 meters thick, was built with offsets and recesses. A road paved with rubble stones led to a gate in the wall. Two burned layers and two floors of this structure lay above the rooms of the first fortress. They contained pottery from the end of the ninth and the eighth century B.C. This building was probably destroyed by the army of Tiglath-Pileser III (732 B.C.) when the Israelite settlement at nearby Tell Qasile was also razed. Pottery from the seventh century attests to the continuation of settlement at this site.

A wall 17 meters long and .75 meter thick and built of rough stones was cleared about 20 meters north of the fortress. The wall, strengthened with ashlar piers at intervals, was attributed to the Persian period. Scattered over the whole site were building remains and pottery from the Persian to the Byzantine periods. A mosaic paved pool from the Byzantine period was found above the wall of the second fortress. N. AVIGAD

Tell Kudadi: general plan of the excavations.

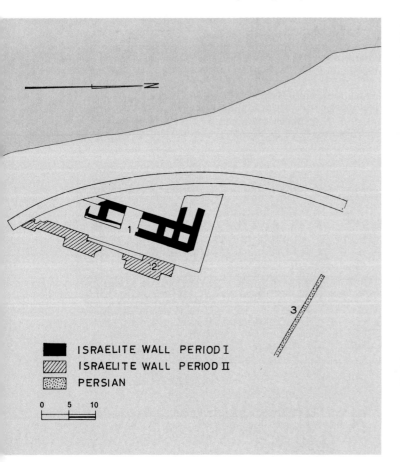

ISRAELITE WALL PERIOD I
ISRAELITE WALL PERIOD II
PERSIAN

0   5   10

BIBLIOGRAPHY

E. L. Sukenik, *QDAP* 8 (1938), 167–68.

Kurnub. Fresco room. Top: general view of the southern wall.
Bottom: Eros and Psyche shown on the western wall — beginning of the third century A.D.

KURNUB

IDENTIFICATION. Kurnub lies 40 kilometers (25 miles) southeast of Beersheba at the junction of the Jerusalem-Hebron-Elath and Gaza-Beersheba-Elath roads. There was probably also a road in antiquity connecting Kurnub with Eboda. The Arabic name of the site, "Kurnub," does not preserve any trace of the original name. R. Hartmann's suggestion to identify Kurnub with Mampsis is generally accepted today.

HISTORY

Mampsis is first mentioned in the mid-second century A.D. by Ptolemy (Geography 15 : 7) where Μάφ (other readings: Μάφις, Μάφα) and ἐοῦσα are listed together with the cities of Idumaea.

The city is later mentioned in Roman and Byzantine sources. Eusebius (Onomasticon 8:8) relates that Tamar is one day's journey from Μάμφις, on the road from Hebron to Aila. He adds that in his time there was a garrison stationed there. Hieronymus calls the site Mampsis. It seems that Mampsis also appears in the tax edict of Beersheba (beginning of the sixth century A.D.). Hierocles (A.D. 530) lists Mampsis together with the other cities of the province of Palestine Tertia. On the Medeba Map an arched gateway supporting a pediment and flanked by two towers appears under the name Μάμφις.

A further reference to Μάμφις appears in one of the Nessana Papyri (PC 39, probably from the mid–sixth century A.D.). This papyrus contains two rosters of cities together with the taxes imposed on them. In the first list, Mampsis appears (line 4) between Sobila and Carmel, and its tax is the fourth largest in the list. This however is no indication of the size of the settlement, since cities like Elusa and Beersheba, though larger than Mampsis, paid fewer taxes. In the second list, Mampsis (line 17) follows Beersheba and precedes Moleatha. Here, too, the cities are not listed according to geographical criteria only.

Some scholars have identified Kurnub with the letters *mmšt* occuring on *lamelekh* seals. There is, however, no archaeological proof for such an identification since no Israelite pottery has been found at Kurnub or its surroundings. It is furthermore not at all certain that *mmšt* is indeed the name of a town. The modern Hebrew name of Mamshit was adopted not on the strength of this identification, but in an attempt to restore the original Semitic form of the name Mampsis.

History of Exploration. In a marginal note on the map of U. J. Seetzen's voyage (1807), the name "Kurnub" appears together with the Arab names of the other Negev towns. Seetzen saw there the remains of a fortress at the foot of a low hill, as well as traces of vineyards and orchards. E. Robinson, who viewed the site from a distance in 1838, described it as a city built of cut stone. He subsequently distinguished the remains of what appeared to be churches or other public buildings. E. H. Palmer visited the site in 1871, but left only a short description of the ruins. The first detailed description of the site was provided by A. Musil (1901), who also drew a plan of the ruins. He noted that the city was surrounded by a wall flanked by towers and had churches in both the western and eastern parts of the city. On Musil's plan the eastern church is shown in a separate walled area shaped like a triangle. This description is of particular importance since this eastern area was subsequently damaged by later building. Musil also noted the large tower in the western part of the town and the well in the valley to its south. C. L. Woolley and T. E. Lawrence drew up another plan of the remains in 1914 but without furnishing much detail. They recorded, however, the sites of the dams and the watchtowers around the city. The city wall was described by them as a rather weak defense against the Bedouins. They also noted the gates of the city as well as the remains of a large building near the big tower in the western part of the city. A large structure north of the eastern church is called by them a serai. In their opinion the public buildings occupied about one quarter of the total area of the city. J. H. Illife visited Kurnub in 1934 and found there Nabataean pottery and terra sigillata ware.

The most recent and most detailed survey was carried out by C. E. Kirk and P. L. O. Guy in 1937, on behalf of the Palestine Exploration Fund, following the construction of a police station on the site. Dissatisfied with the plan of Woolley and Lawrence, they drew up a new, more detailed one. North of the town, near the northern gate, they found the remains of two very large buildings, which had been covered by dunes. They also discovered a cemetery about one kilometer north of the town, with Nabataean pottery, terra sigillata ware, and black-glazed sherds on the surface. In the city proper, the surveyors noted the two large buildings built of ashlar stones (appearing on their plan as A and B) and attributed them to the Roman rather than to the Byzantine period. They further established that the two churches had probably been squeezed into an already existing town plan which had been completed a considerable time before their construction. In the eastern quarter of the city, the surveyors noted a large building, about 40 meters long, with a row of rooms on either side of a central corridor.

In 1956, S. Applebaum, on behalf of the Hebrew University, carried out trial soundings near the inner side of the western wall of the city. He discovered nine levels in four occupation strata, as follows: II, fifth to seventh centuries A.D.; V, fourth to fifth centuries A.D.; VIII, fourth century A.D.; IX, third century A.D. or earlier. Applebaum dated the beginning of settlement in the excavated

Kurnub (Mampsis), general plan: 1. Building I, Palace. 2. Building II, tower. 3. Western church. 4. Building XV. 5. Building V, bathhouse. 6. Building VII, pool. 7. Building XII. 8. Eastern church. 9. Main gate. 10. Water gate. 11. Building VIII, caravanserai.

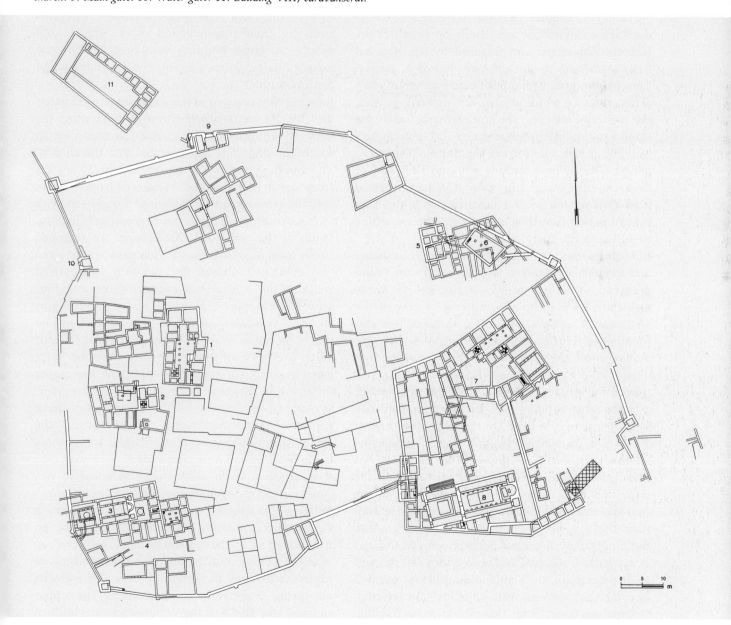

area (2.5 by 2.5 meters) to the third century A.D. At the end of this century, building activity was resumed, and at the end of the fourth century or at the beginning of the fifth, a large part of the settlement was destroyed. At this time, the Western Church (see below), erected only a short time earlier, was also damaged. In the sixth or seventh century, there was a short period of intensive building activity, and during this time the city's street plan—visible today—was drawn up. The excavator ascribed the building of the city wall to this period.

EXCAVATIONS

From September 15, 1965, to October, 1967, and again in the summer of 1971, large-scale excavations were carried out at Kurnub, on behalf of the Hebrew University, and financed by the National Parks Authority, under the direction of A. Negev. The excavations were conducted in five main areas: the city fortifications, the western quarter, the eastern quarter, the caravanserai, and the Nabataean and Roman cemeteries. The pottery and building remains date from the Middle Nabataean period (end of first century B.C. and first half of first century A.D.), the Late Nabataean period (first half of the second century A.D.), the Late Roman period (fourth century A.D.), the Byzantine period, and the Early Arab period.

Middle Nabataean Period. Nabataean potsherds and fragments of Eastern sigillata ware were found scattered over the surface of the site (Western sigillata ware is completely absent). A coin of the Nabataean King Aretas IV (9 B.C.–A.D. 40) was also found. The remains of several structures from this period could be identified. The large building (fortress?) discovered in the northeast, the highest part of the city, is probably also from this period, as is the large building near the northern wall. The latter consists of a large courtyard, with a row of rooms on its northwest side and long narrow storerooms on the southeast. The building was demolished when the large pool was built on the same spot and later the city wall. Part of the building lies outside the area enclosed by the wall from the Late Roman period. Remains of another building from the same period were discovered beneath the courtyard of the Western Church and to the north of it. This building also extended beyond the western wall adjoining the church. Occupation layers from this period were also dis-

covered under the towers of the northern gate, together with painted Nabataean pottery and numerous coins, and under the eastern wing of the palace. There fragments of "Herodian" lamps and Eastern sigillata ware were discovered together with Nabataean lamps. Other finds from this period were uncovered in the cemetery (see below).

Late Nabataean Period. During this period, the town plan was completed in its essential components. The layout of the streets was determined largely by the location of the mansions of the rich. The main street cut through the town from north to south, separating the public buildings from the residential area. Three buildings in the quarter west of the main street were identified as Nabataean by their masonry and other architectural details. A large building (building XII) in the eastern quarter forms a separate self-contained and fortified unit.

Building XI is situated in the southwestern corner of the city. Its western half was destroyed when the Western Church was built, and the rooms of its southern wing were incorporated into the church. The building measured approximately 27 meters from north to south and 35 meters from west to east. In a courtyard in its center is a cistern with arches, roofing and keystone preserved in situ. South of the courtyard three rooms are arranged in the form of a basilica—a wide nave set between two elongated aisles. The western and eastern walls of the central hall contain doors and four arched "windows." Mangers built into the sills of the "windows" indicate that the elongated rooms served as stables. Other rooms are situated north and east of the courtyard. Another door gives access to a staircase leading to the upper floor, built around a strong rectangular pier. Several stone courses of the upper story have survived. In the Byzantine period, the plan of the building underwent several changes, some doors being blocked and new ones added.

A short street leads north from this house to two other buildings belonging to the same period.

Building II is a square tower (10 by 10 meters) with a courtyard containing a roofed water reservoir on its western side. The outside walls of the tower are of ashlar stones, and the lower courses are built of rather hard stone, the length of some of the blocks measuring 3 meters and even more. The upper courses, like those of the upper story, are built of smaller and softer stones. The entrance to the building was through a door on the west, which led to three rooms (4 by 4 meters each) with high narrow windows and stuccoed walls. The western-most room gives access to a stairway built around a heavy square pier showing typical Nabataean tooling. The stairway leads to the upper story, of which two courses are preserved in situ as are also the threshold and the doorposts of the building. The whole building still stands to a height of about 5 meters. This tower seems to have been the administrative center of the city, serving also as an observation post. A paved courtyard containing a water reservoir extends to the west of the building. The lower part of the reservoir is cut into the rock, the upper part being built of hewn stones. To the west of the courtyard are long narrow storerooms.

Building I, adjoining building II, is a structure of considerable size (length from north to south 35 meters, width 20 meters). It consists of two separate units on a somewhat asymmetrical plan, which were built within a short time of each other and joined together. Because of its unique plan and splendor, the excavators assumed this to be the palace of the governor or the military commander. The entrance was in the south through a narrow corridor with steps occupying the entire width of the corridor leading down to an inner courtyard (19 by 6 meters). West of the corridor is a guard-room. Along the western and northern walls of the courtyard stood a colonnade of square pillars supporting arches. On it were probably placed round columns so that the colonnade reached the balcony of the upper story. A door in the southeastern part of the courtyard leads to a hall whose western part is elevated. Two engaged pillars and two columns, preserved in situ, separate the two areas. The column bases do not belong to any of the classical orders and are apparently Nabataean. The floor of the hall was probably made of wooden planks. Another doorway in the courtyard, near the first one, leads to a room on a lower level. In the southern wall of this room between the arches of the roof were built cupboards, probably for storing documents.

West of the courtyard are additional rooms built on bedrock. They may have served as storerooms. A door in the southwestern corner of the courtyard

Western part of the city.

gives access to a stairway, almost completely preserved, leading to the rooms and balcony on the upper floor. Only a few courses of this story are still extant. Signs of building and floors from an earlier period were found in the rooms east of the courtyard. On the floors and between them were found Nabatean painted sherds, lamps, and coins together with "Herodian" lamps. A Nabataean house was apparently situated there in the first half of the first century A.D. An arched passage (7.5 by 4 meters) leads to the other, more sumptuous part of the building, consisting of six rooms paved with stone slabs. The bases and capitals of the doorposts have non-classical moldings. One typical Nabataean capital was discovered in situ. The voussoirs show typical diagonal Nabataean tooling. This part of the house, the north, west, and east sides, was probably the residential wing. The outer walls of the house are constructed of carefully smoothed ashlar stones. Inside, the doors and adjacent walls as well as the arches are built of ashlar stones. The rest of the walls are built of chipped stones. Traces of white plaster appear on these walls.

Building XII, another building from the same period, is situated in the eastern part of the town. It forms a building complex of several units about 40 by 40 meters, all erected during the same period. The facade of the building, oriented northwest, is 40 meters long and has a single entrance

Building II. Late Nabataean period.

that leads to a large room with arches. Doorways in the western wall of this hall give access to the western wing of the building.

A doorway in the southern wall of the hall opens onto a large courtyard irregular in form, from which stairways lead to the upper stories of the western and eastern wings. The latter unit included a large stable, built like that of building XI, and two storerooms, in one of which were found fragments of papyri from the Byzantine period.

The excavation was concentrated mainly in the northwestern wing of the building. A doorway in the northeastern corner of the large courtyard opens onto an inner court (15 by 6 meters) surrounded on three sides by a porch with square pillars. On the western side and in the center of the southern wall of the courtyard are staircase towers leading to the upper stories of the units surrounding the inner court. The courtyard itself is paved with stone slabs.

The typical Nabataean capitals and other architectural elements definitely attest to the Nabataean origin of building XII.

The Pool. A large pool (about 18 by 10 by 3 meters) is situated on the northeastern side of the city wall at a slight distance from building XII. Its outer walls are built of large hewn stones, and the inner ones of hewn, but not smoothed, stones. Four engaged pillars in the northern and southern walls and four pillars in the center of the pool indicate that the structure was roofed, probably with a wooden roof since the distances between the pillars are too great to be spanned by stone slabs. A short water conduit leads from the city wall to a square water tank attached to the eastern wall of the pool. The water was brought to the pool by pack animals from a small spring in the Mamshit Valley. The pool was apparently built in the Late Nabataean period and continued in use in later periods as is indicated by the water conduit, which was built together with the later city wall.

Late Roman Period. Because of their excellent construction, the buildings of the Late Nabataean period served the population also in the Late Roman period. Evidence for the occupation of the city in this period is supplied by pottery and numerous coins found in and around the city. It appears that at this time the first city wall was built. As can be seen in many sections of the wall, a thin wall rather like a fence was first constructed (70–80 centimeters wide), and a later and broader wall was added to it. The early wall had two faces, the outer one being plastered, whereas the later wall had an outer face only. The wall encompassed an area of about 40 dunams. In the Late Roman period the city seems to have had only one gate, on the northern side. The road ascending from the gate does not correspond to the main street of the Nabataean period.

The clearest evidence of the Late Roman period was discovered in building XII. In the debris of the staircase in the southern part of the inner court, a bronze jar was discovered containing a hoard of 10,500 silver coins of the Middle and Late Roman periods. To the first period belong four denarii of Rabel and of Gamilat (A.D. 75–106) and about 2,000 denarii and numerous tetra-drachms of Trajan and Hadrian (98–137). From the second period there are coins of Septimius Severus (193–211), Geta (198–212), Caracalla (188–217) and Elagabalus (218–222). Most of the coins were struck in Syria and sent to Jerusalem for the use of the Roman army. This very valuable hoard testifies that at the beginning of the third century

Building XII. Late Nabataean stable (at right). Troughs in the stable (at left).

there was considerable (military? economic?) activity at Mampsis. Another find from the same period came from a small room (3 by 3 meters) at the entrance to the staircase where the hoard was found. In this room two bands of frescoes were found covering the upper half of the room and the ceiling vaults. They depict men and women walking with various objects in their hands. One scene apparently shows Leda and the Swan. The lower

This page: Painted Nabataean dishes from mourner's meal in the cemetery of the Middle Nabataean period; Opposite page: Earrings from the cemetery of the Late Nabataean period.

band contains various standard decorations, among them a small panel depicting two winged beings sitting on a couch, who are identified by a Greek inscription as Eros and Psyche. On the stones of the arches naked men and clothed women hold palm fronds in their hands. Their feet stand on the wall and their heads reach the center of the arches, where the head of a young man is depicted in a medallion. These wall paintings were influenced by the third century A.D. paintings of Roman Africa.

The cemetery northeast of the city is probably also to be attributed to the Late Roman period (see below).

Byzantine Period. During this period the Late Nabataean buildings underwent only minor changes. The lintels bearing Christian symbols and the abundant Byzantine pottery found on the floors of the buildings attest that they continued in use in this period too. There are various signs, such as the location of the churches, that the plan of the town had been fixed hundreds of years earlier but the settlers in the Byzantine period adapted their buildings to the existing plan, and avoided as far as possible any damage to buildings found on the site (although almost half of building XI from the Nabataean period was demolished during the construction of the Western Church).

FORTIFICATIONS. At the beginning of the Byzantine period, the Late Roman city wall was strengthened by doubling its width. The original course of the wall was retained for the most part. At the corners and several other spots, the wall was reinforced by towers and salients. In the construction of the wall, its line was adapted to considerations of the city's topography as well as the presence of several earlier buildings. The wall, which reaches a total length of about 900 meters, is built of chipped stones laid in straight courses with a fill of pebbles set in clay mortar where the stones did not fit together exactly. The inner face of the wall is filled with pebbles and earth. Here and there, some segments of the wall are built with reused hewn stones. Trial soundings carried out in several sections showed that under the foundations of the double wall there was an earlier wall, probably also from the Late Roman period.

The wall has two gates, a main gate in the north and a smaller one in the west, both situated nearer to the western quarter of the town. The northern gate is protected by two towers of unequal size.

Soundings showed that the towers had been erected, at least in part, in the Late Roman period and that in the Byzantine period their walls were strengthened. Nabataean and Early Roman potsherds were discovered under the later pavements, but no building remains. The gate chamber, which was paved with stone slabs, was roofed with three arches in the Byzantine period. The iron armor covering the doors of the gate was found in the rubble. Under the armor were signs of a violent conflagration, probably from the time when the Arabs stormed the city. The western gate is no more than an opening in the wall protected by two strong pillars. To the same period is to be ascribed the blocking of two posterns in the wall.

The Eastern Church — Church of Saints and Martyrs — is built on the highest point of the city, in the southern part of an enclosure which was probably the original nucleus of the city. The church complex includes the church proper, a chapel, a baptistery, annexes (a monastery?), and a small bathhouse. The entire complex measured 55 by 25 meters. A broad flight of stairs leads to three entrances in the northern wall of the atrium (15 by 18 meters), the four sides of which were surrounded by a colonnade. In the center of the atrium was a cistern (6 by 5 by 4 meters). The roof of the cistern was supported by four arches, and the water was supplied by four gutters in the corners of the atrium. Traces of the gutters and the drains that carried the water under the floor of the atrium were found. From the atrium (there was no narthex) three entrances open onto the nave and two aisles. The interior measurements of the church proper are 27.5 by 15 meters, the width of the nave being equal to that of the two aisles together. The ceiling of the nave was supported by two rows of columns and by two engaged pillars in each row. A raised bema was reached by two steps. The church included a central inner apse, as well as a prothesis and a diaconicon without apses. The altar stands on the axis of the apse, to its west. A bench composed of three steps extends around the apse. In the excavations in the prothesis and the diaconicon in the summer of 1971, remains of a cult of saints and martyrs were dis-

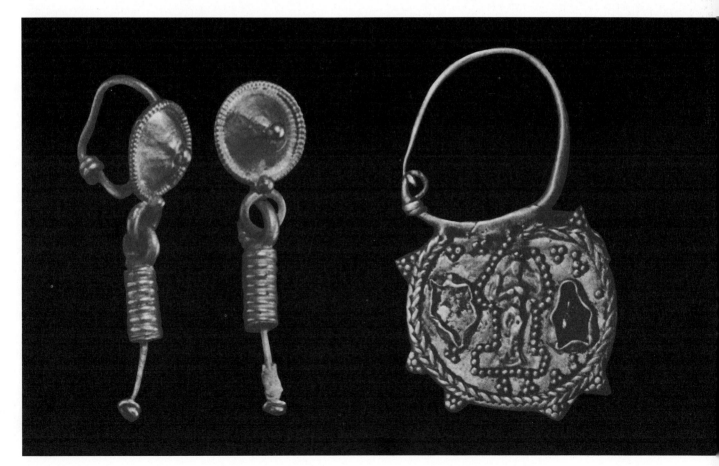

covered. Reliquaries were built into the floors of these two rooms. Above them stood small altars. In one of the reliquaries in the diaconicon, a fragment of a leg bone was found. The paving stone above the reliquary had a hole through which libations could be made. Remains of an ambo standing on a marble base were found northwest of the bema. The aisles were paved with marble slabs and the nave with mosaics of simple geometric patterns. Opposite the main entrance and in front of the bema, two large crosses are represented in the mosaic. Along the southern wall of the southern aisle are two stone benches. Three doorways in the western wall of the atrium give access to the five annex rooms. One of them was a bath with two sitting bathtubs. A staircase in the southeastern corner of the atrium leads to a gallery on top of the colonnade. A door in the center of the southern wall of the church opens into the chapel, in the eastern part of which is a

raised bema without an apse. South of the chapel is the baptistery, with a cruciform font set into the floor. These southern annexes were constructed later than the church proper and the western annexes. Because the rooms in the south are built against the city wall, they show an irregular pattern. The line of the wall was moved when the annexes were erected. Alterations can be distinguished in the church, as for example, changes in the stairway leading to the atrium and the blocking of entrances in the aisles.

The northwestern corner of the church is built against a tower, similar in form and plan to building II, but somewhat smaller (8 by 8 meters). It consists of four rooms and is entered from the east. The entrance room is on the southeast, and also contains stairs, the lower ones built of stone, and the upper ones probably of wood, as may be deduced from a beam found in the rubble. The doors of the rooms are arched. The walls of the

Both pages, counterclockwise: Facade of the bathhouse—Late Roman and Byzantine periods; The Eastern church; Plan of the Eastern church.

tower are made on the outside of well-dressed ashlars, but most of the stones were removed to be used in the construction of the Turkish police station.

The Western Church — the Church of Nilus — is situated in the southwestern corner of the city, near the wall. West of the church is an atrium surrounded by colonnades and having a small cistern in its center. The inner measurements of the church are 17.5 by 10 meters, but aside from the fact that it is smaller then the Eastern Church, the two are nearly identical in plan. The Western Church also has annexes on the southern side, but no baptismal font. From the surviving architectural remains (the church was destroyed by a violent conflagration, and parts of wooden beams and roof tiles were found in the debris together with stone and marble fragments), it seems however to have been more elaborate than the Eastern Church. The aisles were paved with stone slabs, the nave and the intercolumnar spaces with colored mosaics. The western field of the nave is covered with octagonal medallions filled with birds and baskets of fruits, all on a background of geometric patterns, spirals, double axes, and the like. The central field is a geometric carpet containing a dedicatory inscription (mentioning a certain Nilus who built this holy place). In front of the bema two peacocks are represented standing at the sides of an amphora from which a vine emerges. On a narrow band between the peacocks and the steps of the bema, there are another three dedicatory inscriptions, again naming Nilus and two wardens of the church. Mosaics of intersecting circles and various other geometric patterns also appear in the bema, except for the area of the altar, the axis of the apse and to its east. The intercolumnar spaces are paved with geometric panels, continuous bands of flowers, and a band with representations of assorted fruits, a checkered pattern, a swastika, and other geometric designs.

The Dating of the Churches. The inscriptions in the Western Church contain no dated or other evidence by which the date of its construction can be determined. The only indication for dating the Eastern Church is the presence of the two crosses in the mosaic pavement. Since it was prohibited to depict the cross on the floors of churches after A.D. 427, the excavator concluded that the building was erected prior to this date, especially as, according

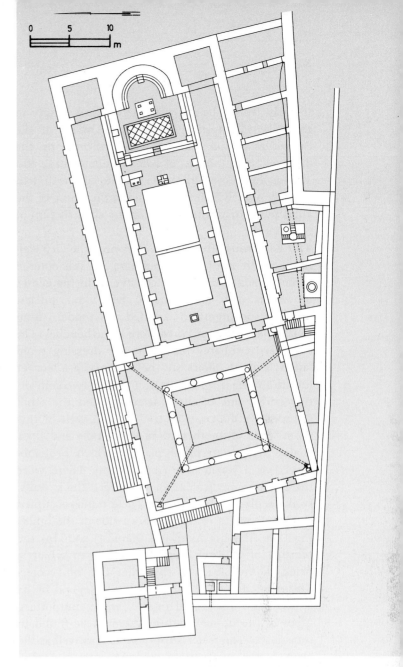

to early Byzantine sources, there was a colony in this city (Mampsis?) in the early phase of the Byzantine period. This is also confirmed by the discovery of a number of coins of Constantine and Theodosius. Coins from the middle of the fourth century A.D., which were found in the filling of the altar, point to an early date for the construction of the church.

The Bathhouse (building V) lies near the city wall in the north, not far from building XII. It is entered from the south through a courtyard, in the center of which was an enclosure with four pillars, probably belonging to a roofed colonnade. Along two walls of the courtyard were stone benches. The courtyard probably served as the dressing room (apodyterium). Stairs in the northeastern corner lead to a room (frigidarium) containing two cold sitting baths, one of them octagonal and the other rounded. A doorway in the western wall of this room leads to another room with walls and floor coated with waterproof plaster, which probably served as a warm bath (tepidarium). There were three hot rooms (caldaria), with very thick walls, sunk deeply into the ground. These rooms occupied the entire width of the northern side of the building. The first hot room (on the east) contains the remains of a water-heating stove, from which a brick channel leads to the other two hot rooms. The columns of the hypocaust and several of its arches were discovered in situ, while the pottery pipes of the upper heating system were found in the rubble. The water-supply system as well as the waste-water evacuation system were also discovered. The bathhouse can be dated only approximately. Although all the pottery found there belongs to the Byzantine period, this is not conclusive, since such pottery was also uncovered in typical Nabataean buildings. Thus the bathhouse, which was in use in the Byzantine period, could have been built in the Late Nabataean or Late Roman period.

Building XII contains abundant evidence for its continued use during the Byzantine period. Lintels of doors leading from the inner courtyard to various rooms show crosses, palm fronds, and other Christian symbols (including a kind of sundial often encountered in Kurnub). In the entrance to the room containing the wall paintings and on its floor were found numerous fragments of Greek papyri, which may also belong to the Byzantine period. Traces of typical Byzantine building have been discovered in a street leading from the western city wall to building I (the palace) and in the street between the wall and the enclosure of building II (the tower). The Byzantine constructors narrowed the street and squeezed their simply built houses into the enclosures of the Late Nabataean buildings. This is clear evidence that the number of inhabitants in the city increased in this period, a phenomenon known from other towns of the Negev.

The Caravanserai. This large structure lies a short distance outside the city wall near its northwestern corner. It consists of a huge court, a large hall to the west, and rows of rooms along its northern and eastern sides. The eastern part of the caravanserai was built on the remains of a Nabataean structure. The dating of the caravanserai to the Byzantine period still requires clarification.

Early Arab Period. No building remains or repairs from this period can be identified with certainty, but the numerous graffiti on the stones of the apse of the Eastern Church attest to the presence of the Arab conquerors. These graffiti contain verses from the Koran and dedications. It may be assumed that the Arabs converted a part of the church into a mosque. Since no pottery aside from Byzantine ware was found, it seems that the conquerors abandoned the site a short time after its conquest.

The Cemeteries. Three cemeteries have been located in the city: the Byzantine necropolis at a distance of about 500 meters west of the town, the Nabataean necropolis, about 800–1000 meters north of the city, and a third cemetery, discovered about 200 meters northeast of the city, probably to be attributed to the Late Nabataean period or to the time of the annexation of the Nabataean kingdom to the Provincia Arabia.

Extensive excavations were carried out in the northern cemetery. As early as 1937, G. E. Kirk and P. L. O. Guy discovered there black-glazed pottery and typical Nabataean ware and identified the area as a cemetery. In a survey carried out at the beginning of the recent excavations, only Nabataean, Early and Middle Roman pottery, as well as a few Byzantine sherds were found. In all, twenty-five burials and funerary structures were excavated. The tombs usually consisted of two parts: the grave proper, sometimes built as a

This page, right: Dedicatory inscription in the Western church; Below: The Western church.

stonecase covered with stone slabs in which the wooden coffin was placed, or a pit about two meters deep in which the coffin was deposited. Above the tomb a monument was erected, and sometimes a stele was placed in front of the monument. Only the base of most of the monuments has remained, the stones above the surface having all been carried off. Two monuments in fairly good condition can furnish information on their construction. Three types of monuments are distinguished: a solid square structure (with a base 2 by 2 meters), a solid rectangular monument (1.2 by 2 meters), and a hollow square monument (about 4.8. by 4.8 meters). It seems that the solid monuments were in the shape of a stepped pyramid while the hollow ones were built like mausoleums rising above the tomb.

The burials could be dated by objects found in some of the tombs. Silver denarii of Trajan were found in two tombs, and in one tomb were clay seals for sealing documents, made from impressions of city coins of Petra from the time of Hadrian. One tomb of an ossuary type contained a large amount of human bones as well as a coin from the year 4 of Rabel II (A.D. 74), two Early Roman lamps, and a painted Nabataean bowl. It is not clear when the bones in this tomb were collected. Quantities of gold jewelry were found in the tombs, including figures of a goddess and of dolphins, which held a place of honor in Nabataean art. On the ancient top soil of the cemetery were found the remains of funerary meals near the tombs. These consisted of hundreds of vessels, mainly bowls and cooking pots. A few of the vessels are of the painted pottery type. Outstanding is a small bowl decorated with

Above: Seal impression, from tomb 107; Below: Ossuary or communal burial; tomb 108.

painted dolphins. The coins, pottery, and other finds date the cemetery to the first half of the first and first half of second centuries A.D. In the summer of 1971, several additional tombs were excavated in the west part of the cemetery. These are dated by pottery lamps and vessels to the late second–third centuries A.D. The tombs differ in manner of burial. In the early burials the body was deposited on the ground, but in the later it was laid in a stone-built cist.

The Northeastern Cemetery was discovered in 1967. Two monuments of the solid rectangular type are similar in tooling and manner of construction to those in the northern cemetery. The symbol of Dushara was carved on one of the stones. Two Roman inscriptions were found, one of a cavalryman of the Cohors I Augusta Thracum, the other of a centurion of the Legio III Cyrenaica. Military units were stationed in the Provincia Arabia from its very inception and included a garrison at Mampsis, which guarded the road ascending from the 'Arabah. Four other tombs in this cemetery do not have tombstones built above them, but only large boulders. The tombs here are arranged side by side in very strict order, unlike the northern cemetery where they were built haphazardly. All the burials in this cemetery were of the cremation type, the monuments being built on the site of the pyre.

The Western Cemetery. A few trial soundings only were carried out in this cemetery, dating from the Byzantine period. It is the largest of the three cemeteries at the site. The remains of a large building in the cemetery probably belonged to a chapel.

CONCLUSIONS

The city of Kurnub (Mampsis?) is unique among the Negev towns. The quality of its construction is outstanding, and its public buildings occupy an extensive area of the town, much larger than in the other cities. It appears that Kurnub was not founded with the initial penetrations of the Nabataeans into the Negev but only at a later date. The new station was perhaps established to replace the Nabataean center at Eboda, which was destroyed toward the middle of the first century A.D. At the same time the caravan road Petra–Naḥal Neqarot–Eboda–Elusa–Gaza was apparently abandoned, and importance passed to the new road leading from Petra to Kurnub along the 'Arabah, through the so-called Ascent of the Aqrabim. Kurnub's prosperity after the incorporation of the Nabataean kingdom into the Provincia Arabia parallels the previous prosperity of Eboda, which was due probably to the construction of the Via Nova Traiana in Transjordan. If this site is indeed Mampsis, its prosperity in the Late Roman period is equally comprehensible, since at that time a military unit was garrisoned there to guard the road from Jerusalem to Aila. Occupation of the site continued during the Byzantine period, probably due to the necessity of maintaining contact with Transjordan. Unlike the other towns in the Negev, agriculture did not play an important role in the city's economic life, since little agricultural land was available in its surroundings. As the latest coins found on the site are not later than the middle of the sixth century A.D., it seems that Kurnub was destroyed by an earlier Arab incursion, preceding that of 634, in which the other towns of the Negev were conquered.   A. NEGEV

BIBLIOGRAPHY

Robinson, *Biblical Researches*, 616, 622 • F. Krause–H. L. Fleischer, *Kommentar zu Seetzen's Reisen*, Berlin, 1859, 403 • Musil, *Arabia Petraea* 2, 25–28 • C. L. Woolley–T. E. Lawrence, *PEFA* 3 (1914–15), 121–28 • W. F. Albright, *JPOS* 4 (1924), 153, n. 1; 5 (1925), 44–45, n. 70 • J. H. Iliffe, *QDAP* 3 (1934), 133 • G. E. Kirk, *PEQ* 1938, 216–21, 236–39; 1941, 64 • S. Applebaum, *BIES* 23 (1959), 30–52 (Hebrew) • A. Negev, *Christian News from Israel* 18 (1966), 17–23; *idem, IEJ* 17 (1967), 46–55; 121–24; *idem, Raggi, Zeitschrift für Kunstgeschichte und Archäologie* 7 (1967), 67–86; *idem, Bible et Terre Sainte* 90 (1967), 6–17; *idem, RB* 75 (1968), 407–13; *idem, PEQ* 1969, 5–14; *idem, IEJ* 19 (1969), 89–106; *idem, Israel Numismatic Journal*, 1970, 27–31, *idem*, in *Sefer Braslavi*, Jerusalem 1970, 403–20, (Hebrew); *idem, Archaeology* 24 (1971), 166–71; *idem, Jahrbuch für Numismatik und Geldgeschichte* 21 (1971), 9–12; *idem, IEJ* 21 (1971), 110–29; *idem, Antike Welt* 3 (1972), 13–28; *idem, RB* 80 (1973), 364–83; *idem, RB* 81 (1974), 397–420; *idem, Journal of Jewish Studies* 25 (1974), 337–42; *idem, IEJ* 24 (1974), 153–59 • A. Kloner, *EI* 12 (1975), 167–70 (Hebrew).

LACHISH

IDENTIFICATION AND HISTORY. A prominent city in the Shephelah, which was occupied, with several interruptions, from the Chalcolithic period to the Persian period. Its remains were uncovered at Tel Lachish (in Arabic, Tell ed-Duweir), situated near the border of the Shephelah, about 30 kilometers (18.5 miles) southeast of Ashkelon (map reference 135108). In 1878, C. R. Conder proposed Tell el-Ḥesi as the site of Lachish, and this identification remained unchallenged until W. F. Albright questioned it in 1929, proposing Tell ed-Duweir as its site. He based his identification on Eusebius (120:20), who states that Lachish was a village in the seventh mile from Eleutheropolis (Beth-Govrin) to the Negev (Daroma), and on the size of the mound, which is four times as large as Tell el-Ḥesi. Since the excavations, the identification of Tell ed-Duweir with Lachish has been generally accepted.

The Canaanite royal city of Lachish is first mentioned in the el-Amarna letters of the fourteenth century B.C. (Numbers 328, 329, 332), and in a contemporary letter discovered at Tell el-Ḥesi. In the Bible, it figures in the account of the Israelite conquest among the five cities of the coalition that fought Joshua at Gibeon and were defeated by him (Joshua 10:5). After the King of Lachish was put to death, the city was conquered (*ibid.* 10:26, 32–33) and included in the territory of Judah (*ibid.* 15:39). Lachish again appears in the Bible only some three centuries later when it is listed among the cities fortified by Rehoboam (II Chronicles 11:9). Amaziah, King of Judah, fled to Lachish from a conspiracy against him in Jerusalem "but they sent to Lachish after him, and slew him there" (II Kings 14:19; II Chronicles 25:27). During Sennacherib's expedition to Palestine in 701 B.C., Lachish played an important role in the defense of the country. The siege of the city and its conquest are described in detail in parallel passages in the Bible (II Kings 18; II Chronicles 32; Isaiah 36) and in Assyrian sources (documents and reliefs in the king's palace in Nineveh). According to an Assyrian document, Sennacherib, after returning to Assyria, left a garrison in Lachish. A century later Nebuchadnezzar, King of Babylon, conducted a campaign to Palestine in which Lachish and Azekah were the last cities to be conquered (Jeremiah 34:7). With the fall of Jerusalem in 586 B.C., the city of Lachish was also destroyed and abandoned until the time of the return from the Babylonian Exile when "Lachish and the field thereof" were resettled (Nehemiah 11:30).

EXPLORATION

From 1932 to 1938 the Wellcome-Colt Archaeological Research Expedition (from 1933 called the Wellcome–Marston Expedition) spent an average of six months of the year at the site under J. Starkey's direction. This came to a tragic end with Starkey's murder in January, 1938. He was succeeded for the remaining three months of the

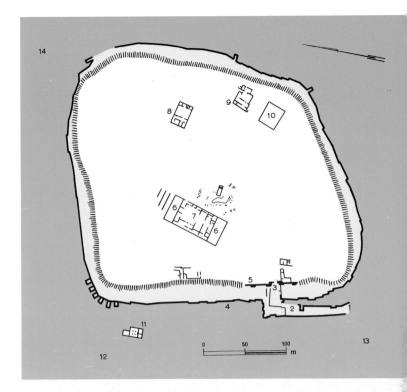

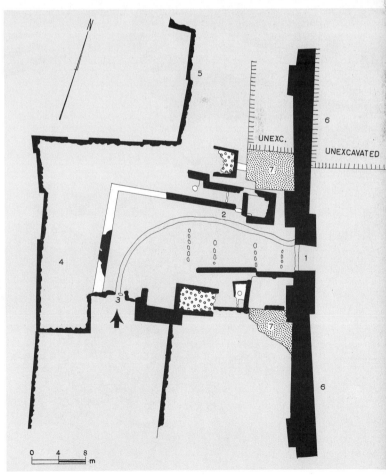

Both pages, counterclockwise: Aerial view, from the west; Gate complex: 1. Inner gate. 2. Drainage channel. 3. Outer gate. 4. Bastion. 5. Outer wall. 6. Inner wall; 7. Bricks of earlier gate.
Plan of the site: 1. Approach road to the gate. 2. Outer gate. 3. Inner gate. 4. Outer wall. 5. Inner wall. 6. Israelite palace. 7. Persian palace. 8. Solar shrine. 9. Hellenistic structure. 10. The great shaft. 11. Fosse Temple. 12. Cemetery 100–200. 13. Cemetery 500. 14. Cemetery 4000; Bronze dagger with Proto-Canaanite inscription—MBA II-B.

season by L. Harding. Olga Tufnell and other members of the expedition, with contributions from other experts, prepared the publication of the excavation which was completed in 1958.

EARLY SETTLEMENTS

An extensive plain northwest of the mound produced many flint implements, the earliest of which are ascribed to the Aurignacian. On a central spur stood the collapsed stones of a ruined dolmen. From its position it appeared to be the focal point of a troglodytic settlement. By the Late Chalcolithic period and probably before, a community was settled in numerous caves, artificially enlarged and transformed into comfortable dwellings, provided with door sills, sunken hearths, and lined storage pits.

A significant find was a small piece of diorite, of a quality mined only in Nubia during the First to the early part of the Third Egyptian Dynasties. Engraved lines visible on the edge of the fragment may have been part of a *serekh*, a suggestion of contact with Egypt at the beginning of the dynastic period (and cf. nearby Tell el-'Areini and Tel Arad). In this period, which is equivalent to the Early Bronze Age II in Palestine, the troglodytic settlement broke up, and the inhabitants abandoned their dwellings, which were subsequently used as communal graves by the new town in the Early Bronze Age III and later.

The first 1.8 meters above bedrock in the northeast section of the mound retain some contact with Early Bronze Age I–II, but above that point there was a leveling off of the surface and at around 2.5 meters, a potter had left lumps of clay and an unfinished hole-mouth jar still in position on the floor. From 1.5 to 1.8 meters fragments of Khirbet Kerak ware were found, and so far Duweir is the farthest site to the southwest which has produced this type usually ascribed to Early Bronze Age III.

It is noteworthy that Khirbet Kerak ware is altogether missing from the burials in the abandoned cave dwellings in the northwest settlement, even though Early Bronze Age III ware is present in the caves, as for example cave 1519, which contained a large quantity of red-burnished pottery.

There is no layer of ash or burning to mark the end of the Early Bronze Age at Duweir, in contrast to other cities in this period, such as Jericho, where the Early Bronze Age levels terminated in destruction by fire. However, a lack of sherds between 3.3 and 3.6 meters in the northeast section suggests an interruption in the occupation.

Middle Bronze Age I. In this period, newcomers arrived who were not immediately concerned with rebuilding the towns they had destroyed, and few buildings can be attributed to them. Knowledge of this phase is derived from their varied burial customs and from the offerings placed in the tombs.

One hundred and twenty tombs were cut into and under the exposed scarp on the edge of the northwest settlement. Few of the chambers were intact, and many were too small to take more than one tightly flexed body. Nearly all traces of human remains had disappeared. The chronological position of cemetery 2000 in relation to others representing this culture elsewhere falls in the main later than that of cemeteries 1500 and 200 at Tell el-'Ajjul (q.v.), though there is some overlap, and a relationship also exists with strata H–I at Tell Beit Mirsim. Other phases, or as Kathleen Kenyon prefers, other ethnic groups are represented at

Opposite page: Fosse Temple—phase III; This page, below: Restored plan of the Fosse Temple—phase III; Bottom: Fosse Temple—phases I–III (left to right).

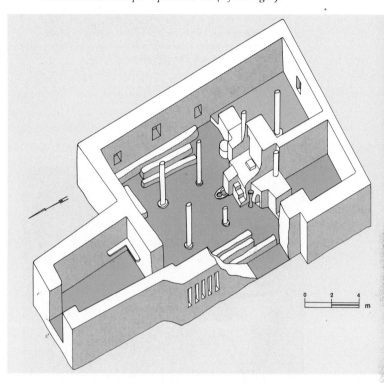

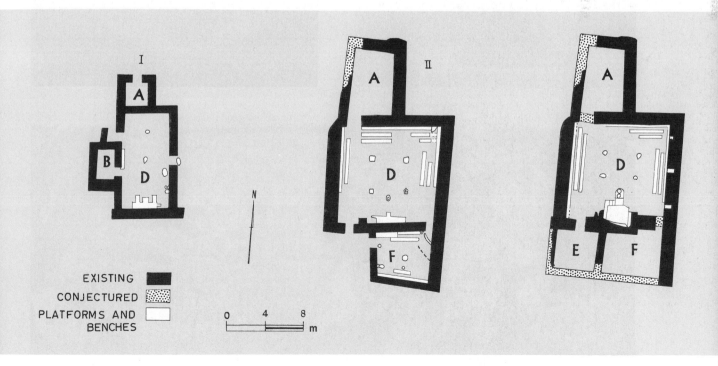

EXISTING ▆
CONJECTURED ⬚
PLATFORMS AND BENCHES ☐

0   4   8
m

This page, clockwise: Jug and lid—glazed blue and black pottery from Fosse Temple, phase III; Reliefs on ivory pyxis, from the Fosse Temple, phase III; Mycenaean kylix from the Fosse Temple, phase I; opposite page: Cosmetic flask made of an ivory tusk, from the Fosse Temple, phase III.

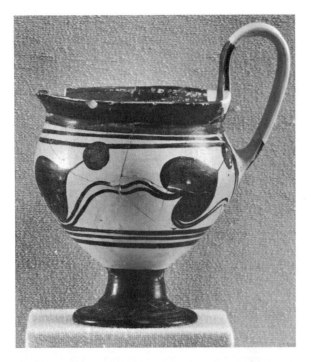

Jericho by different tomb shapes and burial customs.

Middle Bronze Age II. Tombs. The early stages of this period are absent here, nor are there substantial deposits of the red-burnished bowls, represented at Tell Beit Mirsim by strata G–F, and in the Courtyard Cemetery at Tell el-'Ajjul by group 3. The earliest Middle Bronze Age graves which have come to light at Duweir are roughly equivalent to groups 4 and 5 at Tell el-'Ajjul. Grave 173 underlies the packing of the Middle Bronze Age escarpment near the northwest corner, and grave 145 cut in the same ledge of bedrock was almost certainly covered in the same way before the fill slid down into the fosse. In the opinion of the writer, part of the contents of the tombs in cemeteries 100–200 low on the slopes near the site of the Fosse Temple (see below) precede the tombs at Jericho, and cease before the beginning of the tombs at Jericho.

Early Canaanite Inscription. Several tombs in the deserted northwest settlement also belong to this phase of the Middle Bronze Age, dating perhaps to the eighteenth rather than the seventeenth century B.C. Among them is tomb 1502, which contained a dagger inscribed with four signs, including the "human head" sign. This is one of the three Canaanite inscriptions from the Middle Bronze Age II–B found in Palestine and one of the earliest known attempts at alphabetic writing.

Defense Systems. The construction of massive earthworks is an exclusively Middle Bronze Age characteristic in Palestine. They are usually oriented to the cardinal points of the compass. Traces of such fortifications have also been found at Duweir, and their presence may account for the relative lack of erosion on the slopes.

In 1932–33, when the section at the northeast corner was excavated, alternate horizontal layers of brown and gray debris were exposed between 3.6 and 6.6 meters, although it was only later that the significance of this fill and of the white plaster surface which capped it was recognized. In the following season, patches of a sloping lime-plastered surface were exposed at the northwest corner of the mound, which had been cut by the foundations of the Iron Age wall and buttresses. The shallow fosse was traced for 140 meters on the west side of the mound.

The correct horizon for deposits contemporary

with the period of use of the Middle Bronze Age defenses was not reached by the Wellcome Expedition, and evidence is confined to sherds found immediately above the plastered surface, which appear to be Middle Bronze Age in character, and to the latest contents within the embankment fill.

In the upper layers were Middle Bronze Age sherds covered with white lime wash and decorated with colored bands and wavy lines. Similar sherds were found in strata G–F at Tell Beit Mirsim and elsewhere. When the limits of this White Wash Ware are fixed in the Middle Bronze Age pottery sequence, that decision will help to establish the structural date of the Middle Bronze Age earthwork. Meanwhile, the period between 1750 and 1700 B.C. still appears most probable, though it may prove necessary to raise the date of the Middle Bronze Age graves under the embankment fill. By the time debris from within the city had reached the summit of the bank and had overflowed its plastered surface, the earthwork can no longer have been an effective defense.

Late Bronze Age. Fosse Temple and Tombs. Near the northwest corner of the mound, a small building planned on a north-south axis was erected on debris in the obsolete fosse. Now known as the Fosse Temple, the sanctuary of the first phase formed a rectangle 10 meters long by 5 meters with subsidiary rooms on the west and north. A mud bench with three projections, which appears to be the focus of the building, backed against the south wall. Much of the apparatus of the cult was preserved on and near this shrine or altar. On the demolition of structure I, only the position of the shrine remained unchanged in the new temple (II) and among other improvements the width of the sanctuary was doubled. The north room was lengthened, and a new chamber was built out to the south. The shrine maintained its benchlike character but was built of undressed stone. No major innovations were made in the sanctuary or existing anteroom of structure III, although an additional room was built out to the south to balance it. The shrine, however, developed in two phases within the occupation of structure III and became a platform, approached by three steps with an altar in front.

The extreme maximum range for structure I may be 1600–1450 B.C. Its use ceased perhaps with the

establishment of Egyptian suzerainty by Thutmose III, in about 1468 B.C. This event was followed by a prosperous age for Lachish during the remainder of his reign and those of his successors, Amenhotep II and Amenhotep III (1413–1377 B.C.). These kings are represented in the tombs by many scarabs bearing their names. There may have been an interval in the life of the city to coincide with the end of structure II and the desertion of city level VII, as seen in the northeast section at 9 meters. From the contents of the Fosse Temple and the tombs, a date in the reign of Ramses II, which ended around 1234 B.C., would be indicated for the destruction of the Late Bronze Age city (level VI). W. F. Albright dates its destruction to the fourth year of Pharaoh Merneptah on the basis of an Egyptian hieratic inscription which has the date ''in the fourth year,'' though it may be extended by a scarab of Ramses III, exactly matched at Megiddo in stratum VII–A, into the first half of the twelfth century.

Inscriptions. It has been seen that Lachish was in contact with Egypt throughout the period of its empire, and further proof exists in the bowls from level VI inscribed in Egyptian hieratic, which are datable on paleographic grounds to the Nineteenth–Twentieth Dynasties. An attempt to produce a coffin inscription in monumental hieroglyphs was less successful. Almost contemporary with these are five short Canaanite inscriptions from the Late Bronze Age. Their reading is difficult. Two Canaanite votive inscriptions from the thirteenth century B.C. demonstrate the diffusion of the script in this period. One is read *bšlšt*, and the second is generally read *mtn....'lt*.

Iron Age. Levels V–IV. The absence of any biblical references to Lachish from the days of Joshua to those of Solomon's son Rehoboam accords with the apparent lack of much building activity on the mound between the twelfth and tenth centuries B.C., although further excavation could perhaps prove otherwise. However, the use of the northwest corner of the Bronze Age palace, embedded in the charred ash of its destruction, by the builders of palace A as the foundation for the corner of their Iron Age building, suggests that in this quarter at least there was no intervening occupation. A trial cut beyond and below the

Opposite page, top: Ivories, from the Fosse Temple. Bottom: Scarab seal. Between the wings of the beetle appear the name Smkh *and the Egyptian* ankh *sign (life), Below the beetle:* laḥimelekh; *This page, below: Bird figurine, stratum III; Right: Figurine on a hollow column base, stratum III.*

southeast corner of palace B (see below) revealed brick walls, part of the so-called Late Bronze Age government storerooms, which were themselves cut into by later rubbish pits, but there was no trace of burning between them and the foundations of palace B to correspond with the devastation at the northwest corner.

The stone podium, 32 meters square, of palace A was only the sub-structure of a missing building. It encased the ruins of the Bronze Age palace and is perhaps comparable in construction to David's Millo (Hebrew "filling") in Jerusalem. It is assumed at present that palace A (level V) was the center of Rehoboam's walled city, and if it could be proved, the 6-meter brick wall that was partially cleared on the western edge of the mound could be attributed to Asa. This wall was exposed in section north of the gateway and is known to continue for a short distance beyond. As part of the level IV defense system, it may have remained in use until the destruction of level III.

The extension of the citadel to the south for an additional 46 meters (palace B) could have been initiated by Jehoshaphat during his recorded building activities in Judah. At some time thereafter, a strip was added along the east wall of palace B, forming the foundation of an enlarged building or of a separate porch (palace C), which underwent several phases of construction and repair. There was a flight of steps leading up to it,

and under these stones two earlier stairways were partially preserved. On the rise of the oldest stairway, among other graffiti, the first five letters of the early Hebrew alphabet had been scratched.

Nothing remained of the building or buildings that once stood on the podiums (palaces A–C) except some patches of lime floor, but quantities of stamped jar handles found on the southern end suggests that a building had stood nearby in the eighth or seventh century B.C.

Houses. Levels III–II. The only large city area exposed during 1932–38 lay south of the citadel and was designated as level III. This was only a small part of the 75 dunams enclosed within the walls, and the ruins lay buried under debris, which varied in depth from a few centimeters to a meter-and-a-half, according to the slope of the ground. Two groups of houses were excavated, the first stood high on the south slope of the citadel, descending in terraces to a point where erosion had destroyed even the floors, leaving no trace of any buildings that may have intervened between them and the street of shops, which lined the roadway leading into the city from the gate. Here also, erosion had swept the higher ground almost clear of buildings and brought an accumulation of debris down toward the gate, thus preserving the houses near it to a substantial height. Masses of broken jars, some with stamped handles, were found in these rooms, which were poorly built of stone and brick with mud or cobbled floors, all deeply covered with charred ash.

Biblical and Assyrian sources both show that Lachish fell to Sennacherib about 700 B.C., and that event should be reflected in the wholesale marks of destruction preserved in the buildings of level III. Even though no earlier level has yet been excavated in full, it is clear from the examination of the two opposite corners underlying the Iron Age palace, and of the West Section, that there was no great burned level between that of levels VI and III. The brick wall, which was apparently built during the reign of Asa, continued in use until the time of Hezekiah, and the gate towers, which may have stood for more than a century, were then buried under their own collapsed superstructure, over which other roadways passed, beaten hard

This page: Trepanned skull, IA II; Opposite page: Plan of the Residency.

by the passage of many feet. In the reconstruction after 700 B.C., a stone gateway replaced the underlying brick gate towers, and the space each side of the road was left clear. Not long afterward, further disaster befell the city. Burning covered the threshold of the level II gate, and a charred heap just inside seems to represent the remains of a wooden door. In a further stage of defensive preparation, the width of the doorway was reduced. Remains between the inner and outer gate built over the once free-standing bastion were equally evocative of catastrophe, and it was to the burning of the final phase that the ostraca from the guardroom were assigned (see below).

This interpretation of the evidence has not gone unchallenged, and most archaeologists prefer to attribute the destruction of level III to the Babylonian attack in 597 B.C. But in the writer's opinion, which is shared by L. H. Vincent, Y. Aharoni, and Ruth Amiran, level III was destroyed by the Assyrians, for there is no other evidence on the site to substantiate the existence of the well-documented Assyrian campaign. The second phase of level II (containing the Lachish ostraca) must be lowered in date to a time between the Assyrian and the Babylonian expeditions. In this event, the pottery from level III becomes especially significant because the other great cities fell to the Assyrians two or three decades earlier, and only at Lachish is there an excavated destruction level dating from the end of the eighth century.

In the southeastern corner of the city was found what the excavators called the Great Shaft (22 by 25 by 25 meters). This was apparently an abortive attempt in the time of Hezekiah to construct a water reservoir within the walls. This gigantic task, involving the removal of 14,285 cubic meters of rock, remained unfinished, however, and the shaft filled up from the seventh century onward.

Tombs. The broken domestic pottery from the city is supplemented by funerary deposits, including hundreds of complete vessels, some burnished by hand on a deep red slip and others burnished by wheel, a technique which became common around 800 B.C. In some isolated cases the inhumations were relatively undisturbed, but often bones and offerings were piled in a mass with skulls lined up against the walls. Three skulls had been trephined, and one individual at least had survived the operation.

Lachish Ostraca. Twenty-one ostraca were found at Lachish. This is the most important epigraphic collection from the time of the First Temple period. Eighteen of the ostraca were uncovered in 1935 in the guardroom between the inner and outer city gate, where they lay buried in a mass of burned pottery fragments, many of which may have originally been inscribed. They were written in

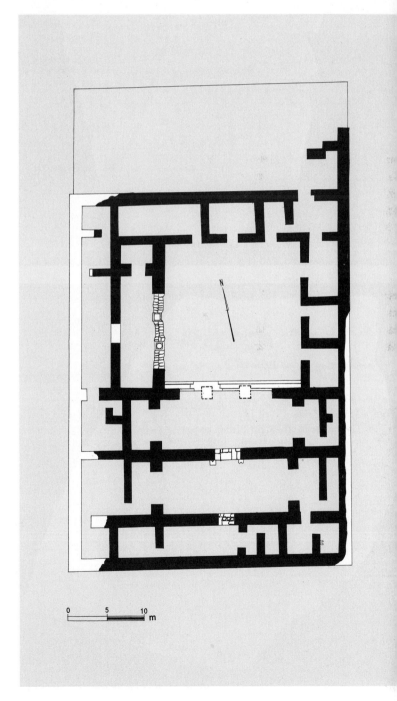

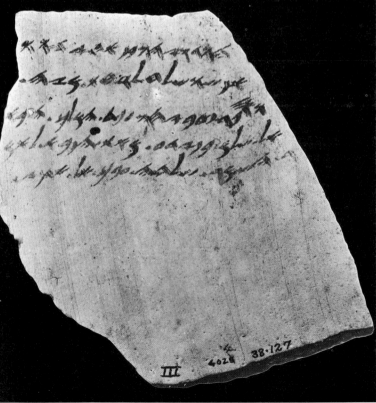

ancient Hebrew script, in biblical style, presumably during the reign of Zedekiah, about 590 B.C., and were mostly addressed to "my lord Yaush," an army commander. They were sent by a subordinate, stationed at some point where in normal times he could watch the signals of Lachish and Azekah. More ostraca were discovered in 1938 in rooms built against the east wall of palace B–C, attributed to level II. One of them was found embedded in burned debris. It opens with a date: "In the ninth (year)..." It will be recalled that the Babylonians laid siege to Jerusalem in the ninth year of King Zedekiah.

Persian Buildings. Level I. The capture of Jerusalem encouraged the Edomites to overrun southern Palestine, and eventually Lachish became an administrative capital in Idumaea. A house on the west side of the mound with an Aramaic ostracon high in its fill may belong to the late sixth or early fifth century B.C.

In this period a new city wall and gateway replaced those of level II, and some poorly built rooms round a courtyard nearby may have served as a guardhouse. But most impressive must have been the uppermost building, situated on the platform of the razed citadel, which had been cleared of ruins to provide a level surface for the so-called Residency. It was built on the open-court plan, approximately 50 by 37 meters, with steps and porticoes leading to halls and private quarters. According to the scant evidence of the pottery it was in use from the mid-fifth to the mid-fourth century B.C.

Northeast of the Residency stood the so-called Solar Shrine measuring 27 by 17 meters and built of the same quality stone and plaster. A bronze lamp with fifth-century parallels and a limestone altar are its most striking contents, but the range of its use is uncertain. The final phase of the shrine may date early in the second century B.C. Another building, 25 by 16 meters, lying north of the Great Shaft, is provided with squared pillars like houses of level III–II, though it is built over that destruction. The date of its final phase, tentatively ascribed to the fourth–third centuries B.C., may require revision in the light of future excavation elsewhere.   OLGA TUFNELL

Left, top: Lachish ostracon No. 6; Bottom: Lachish ostracon No. 3, reverse.

THE EXCAVATION OF THE SOLAR SHRINE

In the summers of 1966 and 1968, two brief seasons of excavations were carried out in the area of the building known as the Solar Shrine by Y. Aharoni on behalf of the Hebrew University, Tel Aviv University, and the Israel Exploration Society, in collaboration with the University of North Carolina. The excavations were undertaken in order to clarify the date and early history of the temple in the light of its striking similarity to the temple at Arad.

The excavations fixed the date of the Solar Shrine in the Hellenistic period on the basis of Late Persian material found beneath its foundations and Hellenistic sherds in the foundation trenches of its walls.

Structures from levels dating to the end of the

Right, top: Horned stone incense altar, from the Tenth–century B.C. *shrine; Bottom: Tenth–century* B.C. *shrine, west of the Hellenistic temple.*

Below: Incense burners and pottery from the Tenth–century B.C. *shrine; Opposite page, top: Juglet with clay* bullae *showing Hebrew seal impressions; Bottom: Stone* maṣṣebah *and burnt Asherah(?), beneath Hellenistic temple.*

Late Bronze Age and the Iron Age (strata VI–II) were discovered beneath the temple and in its vicinity. A street, bordered by buildings and industrial installations, ascended toward the west. A small storeroom of stratum II contained a rich assemblage of early sixth-century pottery, a Hebrew ostracon with a list of names each preceded by the letter lamedh, six inscribed shekel weights, as well as a unique find: a juglet containing seventeen clay bullae. These were stamped with Hebrew seal impressions and bore traces of papyri and strings on the reverse sides. This collection of bullae was used to seal papyri, and after the documents had been opened the bullae were kept in the juglet.

Remnants of a high place from the Israelite period (strata V–III) were uncovered beneath the interior of the Hellenistic temple. These included a raised area, a large upright stone (massebah), the buried remains of the trunk of an olive tree (Asherah?), and several pits *(favissae)* with broken stone stelae and votive objects. West of it was a small rectangular room (about 3 by 4 meters) with plastered benches along its walls and a raised platform in its western corner. On the benches and in a heap of ruins near the platform was a large collection of cult vessels, including a stone incense altar with horns, four pottery incense burners, chalices, bowls, lamps, and other pottery vessels. This small cult room, attributed to stratum V, was destroyed in the latter part of the tenth century B.C.

These finds strengthen the assumption that the later temple was based on the tradition of an earlier cult in the area, and that it may have been a Jewish temple, similar to the Yahawistic temple at Arad. The Hellenistic period is the latest occupation level at Lachish, and there is no historical record that its occupants were other than Jews (cf. Nehemiah 11:30).

Further evidence for the long tradition of a cult at Lachish is furnished by the following:

1. Sennacherib's reliefs of the capture of Lachish showing two decorated incense burners at the head of the procession of spoil bearers.

2. More than 150 small stone incense altars from the Persian period found in several caves at the foot of the mound. One bore an Aramaic inscription, which should probably be read:— לבנתא (ש)י(או)ש בן מחליה מלכ(ש) i.e., "Frankincense [altar] Ya['u]sh son of Maḥalyah from Lachi[sh]."

The name testifies that its donor was a Jew.

3. A building from the Late Persian to Early Hellenistic periods was excavated by J. L. Starkey southeast of the Solar Shrine. Aside from the fact that one of its walls is constructed of a row of square pillars, its plan, size, and orientation are almost identical with the plan of the Solar Shrine. In its main room was found a stone incense altar in the form of a shrine. It is quite probable that this structure is yet another temple, which preceded the Solar Shrine in the area, equally indicating the existence of a long tradition of a Jewish cult. Y. AHARONI

THE 1973–75 EXCAVATIONS

Excavations at Tel Lachish were resumed in 1973 by the Institute of Archaeology of Tel Aviv University and the Israel Exploration Society, under the direction of D. Ussishkin. The first three seasons of excavations took place in 1973–75, as part of a long-term systematic study of the site and its history. Excavations were started in three areas: the Iron Age palace-fort (area P), a section at the edge of the mound (areas E and S), and the Iron Age city-gate complex (area G). The choice of these areas took into account the difficulties of digging a large mound on a relatively small scale, the need to continue the excavation areas and follow the results of the previous excavations, and the special importance of this Judean city.

Area P. The northern end of the Iron Age palace-fort was completely excavated by J. L. Starkey, who noted remains of an underlying Canaanite monumental building. Excavations in 1974 revealed not one structure as previously believed, but two superimposed large Canaanite buildings.

The earlier building was possibly a palace. Several rooms were exposed with massive walls over 2 meters thick, constructed of bricks on stone foundations and plastered over. In one large room, the brick wall was based on a row of large ashlar stones. Three architectural stages were distinguished in the structure, which may have had two stories. Two rooms contained a large amount of pottery, mainly storage jars, which indicate that the rooms may have served as storerooms. The structure was destroyed by fire, probably in the early part of the Late Bronze Age, and some of its walls, being covered with burned debris, were preserved to a height of more than 2 meters.

The later building seems to have been a palace, or more probably a temple. It was destroyed by fire

Area of the Judean city gate showing the exposed left half of the level III inner gate house, with the inner gate and city wall of level II above it.

at the end of the Late Bronze Age, and its stone-work and contents were robbed, possibly by squatters, who settled in the area after the destruction of the building. The main architectural feature of the building is a large hall or courtyard, which was only partly excavated. Against its eastern wall was constructed a monumental stone staircase, which apparently led to a raised, plastered platform extending above the line of the eastern wall of the building and possible beyond it. The axis of the staircase has an exact east–west orientation. The staircase probably contained seven steps, but only the lower four steps were preserved. A broad stone slab stood in front of the lower step. It bore an incised circle, about 54 centimeters in diameter, in its center, probably to indicate the position of a stand. A stone parapet flanked the lower steps, joining two octagonal columns that flanked the fourth step (the stone base of the left-hand column was found in situ while the place of the right-hand column is still concealed).

A large plastered installation, probably for holding liquids, was built against the eastern wall of the building to the right of the staircase. A row of columns was erected along the same wall, to the left of the staircase. The round column bases were found in situ. They were attached to the wall of the building by a narrow plastered "wall," thus forming a kind of pilaster. At least the central column base, and probably the other two bases as well, carried tapering octagonal columns of stone. Broken sections of columns matching these bases in size were recovered in the building and its vicinity by Starkey and in the present excavations. The walls of the building were decorated with painted plaster, small fragments of which were scattered all over the area. The plaster fragments

Section at the western edge of the mound. The ladder is leaning against the earlier brick city wall of level III, on which lie the city walls of levels II–I.

are of different colors, and some show remains of painted decoration.

A small room opening onto the above hall (or courtyard) was excavated near the latter's northeast corner. The contents of the room indicate that it may have served as a storeroom. The rich though fragmentary finds include several pottery stands, many bowls, sherds of a Mycenaean chariot vase, a painted stone lid, fragments of alabaster bowls, gold foils, pieces of iron, fragments of faience vessels decorated in Egyptian style, beads, and fragments of ivory boxes (?).

Below: Three royal Judean storage jars from the storerooms behind the level III city gate; Bottom, left: Monumental stone stairway in the LBA edifice; Right: Stone column bases in the LBA monumental building.

Further investigations were carried out at the Iron Age palace-fort. Starkey's conclusions that the preserved building is only the substructure and that it contained three stages (Podea A–C) were confirmed. The present surface of the building, i.e., its floor level, was cleared, and several trial cuts were made into the foundations. A fragment of an hieratic inscription dated to the thirteenth-twelfth centuries B.C. was discovered in the foundation fill. It contains the sign for "(regnal) year 10" but being broken it could be any number from ten to nineteen. The king's name is missing.

Areas E and S. This section is located at the western side of the mound, opposite the southwest corner of the Iron Age palace-fort. Here the Iron Age city walls and habitation levels were un-

earthed. Sections of three superimposed city walls were uncovered at the edge of the mound. The upper one dates to the Persian–Hellenistic period (Starkey's level I), the second one is the latest Judean city wall (level II), and the lower one is the early Judean city wall. The last was built of bricks on stone foundations. Starkey had unearthed a small section of the wall, which was 6 meters thick. The section of the wall recently unearthed has a rectangular tower more than 6 meters thick, while the wall itself was only about 4 meters thick. It seems, therefore, that Starkey, too, had unearthed a section of a tower.

Area G. The excavation of the inner city gate of level III was started in 1938 and resumed in 1974 in the northern (left) half of the gatehouse. The gate consists of six chambers, three on each side, and seems to be larger than similar gates at other sites. The innermost pier on the left side was destroyed when the drain of the level II gate was constructed. The innermost left gate chamber contained an installation whose function is not clear. The gatehouse was destroyed in an extensive fire.

The central left gate chamber and a storeroom adjacent to and behind the gatehouse produced a number of typical royal Judean storage jars, which were all crushed by the collapse of the gatehouse in the conflagration. Similar royal storage jars were found in contemporary burned houses in area S. The storage jars that were reconstructed include several with four plain handles, three jars stamped *lamelekh Hebron* with a four-winged scarab in the naturalistic as well as the schematic styles, and two jars with a royal stamp of the two-winged type. These two jars also have private stamps impressed on the handles not bearing the royal stamps. Together with one or two specimens recovered by Starkey, the jars of this type found at Lachish form a unique assemblage of complete, stamped royal storage jars.

D. Ussishkin

BIBLIOGRAPHY

H. Torczyner et al., *Lachish 1*, London, 1938 • Olga Tufnell et al., *Lachish 2 (The Fosse Temple)*, 1940 • Olga Tufnell et al., *Lachish 3 (The Iron Age)*, 1953 • Olga Tufnell et al., *Lachish 4 (The Bronze Age)*, 1958 • Y. Aharoni, *IEJ* 18 (1968), 157–69; *idem, Qadmoniot* 4 (1969), 131–34 (Hebrew); *idem, Leshonenu* 35 (1971), 3–6 (Hebrew); *idem, Investigations at Lachish: The Sanctuary and the Residency (Lachish V)*, Tel Aviv–Tokyo, 1975 • D. Ussishkin, *IEJ* 24 (1974), 272–73; 25 (1975), 166–168; *idem, BASOR* 223 (1976), 1–13.

LOD

IDENTIFICATION. Lod is first mentioned in the list of Canaanite towns conquered by Thutmose III in the fifteenth century B.C. It appears later only in the genealogical list of the tribe of Benjamin in connection with the wanderings of the Elpaal family and their settlement in the northern Shephelah (I Chronicles 8:12). B. Mazar accordingly considers — and correctly so, it would seem — that the town lay in ruins during most of the Late Bronze and Iron Ages and was resettled only in the time of Josiah. Lod is also mentioned among the people returning from Babylonian Exile (Ezra 2:33; Nehemiah 7:37, 11:35). The town is frequently mentioned in the Hellenistic and Roman periods. Under the Emperor Septimius Severus, it was granted the status of a city and received the name of Diospolis. After the Arab conquest its earlier name was restored.

The ancient mound is situated near the southern bank of the Aijalon Brook (Wadi el-Kabir). It is completely covered by modern buildings, except on the northern side where there are few houses and where the edge of the mound was cut away thus forming a section 2.5 meters deep.

EXCAVATIONS

In December, 1951–January, 1952, J. Kaplan conducted trial excavations at the site on behalf of the Department of Antiquities. Three small areas were examined: 1. the northern edge of the mound; 2. the two sides of a small ravine; 3. a level area north of the above-mentioned cut. In area A, a trench (10 by 2.5 meters) was dug running from the base of the mound toward the upper part. Here below surface level, part of a circular structure built of rubble was exposed. Beneath this structure a mud-brick wall was founded on the sterile whitish sandy soil. These two lower strata were found to be identical with the lowest strata of the mound visible in the cut. Altogether, four phases of occupation could be distinguished in the section in the mound, all dating to the Early Bronze Age I.

In area B on the two banks of the small ravine, a dump of gray earth was discovered with pottery of different periods, mainly of the Chalcolithic cultures of Israel: Wadi Rabah, stratum VIII of Jericho, and Ghassulian ware. The pottery of the first two types included sherds of jars with bow rims, splay-ended loop handles, and black-burnished ware. Among the Ghassulian sherds were lug handles with triangular section, cornets, and churns.

In area C were found shallow cavities, the remains of pits dug into the whitish sand, which contained Neolithic pottery. Most of the pottery was characteristic of Jericho IX ware, including simple and coarse ware made with a large quantity of straw, plain burnished ware, and decorated pottery with a red-painted chevron pattern, as well as typical Jericho IX handles, such as rough loop handles, cylindrical knob handles, and triangular-shaped ledge handles. Although from an un-stratified excavation, the Jericho IX material found at Lod affords a unique opportunity of examining this rare assemblage at a site far from the Jordan rift, its place of discovery.   J. KAPLAN

BIBLIOGRAPHY

Abel, *GP* 2, 370 • Z. Kallai, *Enc. Miqr.* 4, 430–31 (Hebrew, see literature there) • J. Kaplan, *'Alon* 5–6 (1954), 39 (Hebrew); *idem, The Chalcolithic and Neolithic Settlements in Tel Aviv and its Environs,* Tel Aviv, 1958, 24–27 (in stencil); *idem, EI* 5 (1957), 9–24 (both Hebrew); *idem, BASOR* 156 (1959), 15 ff.; *idem, JNES* 28 (1969), 197–99.

View of the excavations.

AL-MAFJAR, KHIRBET

IDENTIFICATION. Al-Mafjar is the current name of a group of ruins lying on the north bank of Wadi 'n-Nuway'imah in the Jordan Valley, about 2 kilometers north of Jericho (map reference 194144). No ancient name is known, and the site although proved to belong to the Umayyad period, remains unidentified in ancient literature.

EARLY HISTORY

A deposit of Iron Age pottery on the northern outskirts of the site has given rise to the conjecture that hereabouts was the biblical site of Gilgal. Of Byzantine Gilgal there is no vestige, unless its monastery somewhere in this vicinity was the source of certain re-used columns carved with crosses, which supported arches in the courtyard of the palace.

THE SITE

A boundary wall (Arabic: *ḥayr*) with semicircular buttresses alternating on its two faces, enclosed a demesne, or perhaps a game park, extending for a mile or more along the north bank of Wadi 'n-Nuway'imah. Within it, toward the west, stood three principal buildings, a bath, a mosque, and a palace, aligned from north to south along the west side of a common forecourt. The forecourt had a gate on the south side and rooms or stables on its perimeter. Farther to the north stood a fourth building, perhaps a khan or workmen's quarters. At the center of the forecourt an octagonal stone-built pavilion sheltered a square pool and fountain. An aqueduct brought water by an open channel from 'Ein ad-Duyuk and 'Ein 'n-Nuway'imah rising at the foot of Jabal Quruntul, 4 kilometers to the west-northwest. In its course, the aqueduct twice crossed the valley by bridges (one of them still standing), filled a reservoir, and turned three or more water mills.

Unused roof tiles, half-carved architectural details, and fresh builders' waste showed that the palace and mosque were left unfinished. But furnace ashes and lime-encrusted pipes proved that the bath, first to be built, was both completed and put to use. All three buildings had been overthrown by an earthquake (probably in A.D. 746).

All the buildings were of ashlar, cut from a soft limestone conglomerate quarried locally. In each of the buildings, vaulting was employed in both cut stone and brick, as well as timber roofing with earthenware tiles. Floors were of mosaic, bituminous limestone flags, or lime cement.

Palace. The palace was a square building of two stories, with round towers at the corners, a rectangular gate tower at the middle of the east side, another square tower on the south, and half-round towers at the middle of the west and north sides. It was planned round a central courtyard enclosed by four arcaded galleries, which gave access and shelter to the ground-floor rooms.

The arrangement of these rooms, singly or in pairs, some of great size, others small, suggested that they were not intended for domestic use but rather for the accommodation of guests or servants, or for storage and stabling. On the south side a small room was furnished as an oratory with a mihrab. Flights of stairs on arches at two opposite corners of the courtyard gave access to a second floor, where evidence suggests that the living rooms were placed, together with the privies, of which a downward drainpipe at the northeast corner provides the sole evidence. Some of the second-floor rooms on the east side must have been decorated with wall paintings, for many fragments

Plan of the site: 1. Forecourt. 2. Ornamental pool. 3. Enclosed courtyard, surrounded by living rooms. 4. Small mosque. 5. Large mosque. 6. Large reception hall. 7. Bathhouse, caldarium. 8. The diwan *(reception hall).*

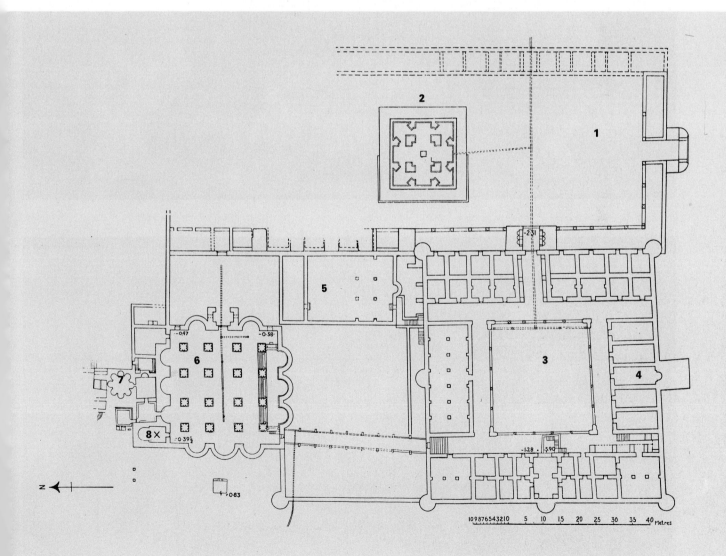

Lachish. Decorated pottery from the Fosse Temple — LBA.

of floral and figured designs painted on plastered masonry were recovered from the ruins. A spirally fluted column and a series of niche fragments set in a concave wall from somewhere above the gateway suggest the possibility that a reception room may have occupied that important position on the second floor.

In the west gallery of the courtyard, a descending stairway led down to a mosaic-paved area preceding an underground vaulted room equipped with a water spout, wall benches, mosaic floor, and a stepped barrier, behind which a brick-lined and waterproofed space at the back could be used for bathing.

The entrance to the palace was through a vaulted passage with benches on either side, giving access to the east walk of the courtyard and preceded by a vaulted porch set in the base of a projecting tower. The porch, too, was furnished with benches on either side and embellished with carved ornamental niches built into the walls above. A double-leafed door between the porch and passage was framed by splay-faced jambs and lintel, all decorated with carved panels. The lintel was composed of a hexagonal keystone set between two long cantilevers. The gate tower was flanked by arcaded galleries in two stories facing the forecourt and sheltering at ground level a row of single rooms with external doors. The position of these rooms, opening only outside the palace, reinforces the impression that the ground floor was primarily for the use of guests or servants.

Mosque. The Mosque, recognized by a mihrab with flanking colonnettes in its south wall, was a rectangular enclosure (23.6 meters by 17.1 meters) lying close to the north side of the palace. The southern end, up to two fifths of the total area, was sheltered by a roof carried on two rows of three arches, set parallel to the south wall and resting on columns and engaged half-columns with acanthus capitals. There are signs that neither the whole of this structure nor the roof had been completed.

Pool and Pavilion. The forecourt pool was a shallow basin, 16.2 meters square, supplied by a fountain on a square pedestal in the middle. The pavilion above it was a regular octagon, built on eight-angle piers set within the edges of the basin and four exceedingly massive L-shaped piers in the center. All of these were linked in two concentric rings by arches, of which the central four carried a square superstructure rising above the roof of the surrounding octagon. The central square was lighted by three arched windows in each side, and surmounted by a brick dome. The roof of the octagon was enclosed by an ornamental stone parapet, and its outer corners were decorated with sculptured figures in relief. The form of the superstructure could be inferred with some certainty from scanty but sufficient fragments recovered from the low mound of debris.

Bath. A small enclosed courtyard served as a common approach to both the mosque and the bath. The latter consisted of a domed porch on the east, a hall or frigidarium, a domed reception room, a series of relatively small bathing rooms, a stoke room, and a latrine. Its remains were preserved in sufficient quantity for a convincing reconstruction of its upper walls and vaulting.

The dominating feature of the bath was the frigidarium, some 30 meters square, its roof rising to a central dome surrounded by concentric ranges of vaults of successively narrower spans. The four outer walls enclosing this structure were strengthened by three semicircular half-domed exedrae on each side except the east, where a projecting rectangular porch replaced the central exedra. The vaulting system was of brick and rested on sixteen massive stone piers in four rows, carrying arches in each direction, and so spaced as to define two broad axial naves intersecting at the center between narrower aisles on each side. The vaults of the nine central bays in this system were raised above the outermost aisle or ambulatory, as it may be called, by clerestory walls pierced by round-headed windows.

The three middle bays of the southern aisle, together with the three exedrae facing them, were enclosed by a stepped barrier forming a plunge pool some 20 meters long and 1.5 meters deep. This must have been filled from a spout entering at a higher level than the surviving masonry. Pilasters built against the walls and piers enclosing the pool may have carried a curtain. The remaining exedrae and the walls between them were fitted with wooden benches and square built-in niches as if for the convenience of bathers undressing. The central exedra on the west, axially facing the entrance of the bath, was in a more pretentious style than the rest, with horseshoe-shaped niches at two levels between carved colonnettes, and a semi-dome built in radial as opposed to horizontal courses. From the keystone of this structure, cut in the form of a cross, depended a stone chain and pendant, the whole more than five feet long and cut from one stone.

The main entrance was through a projecting rectangular porch, which presented a high open archway to the east and was covered by a hemispherical dome resting on a cylindrical drum lightened by fourteen niches containing plaster statues. Four pendentives carried the drum wall. Both the facade and the interior of the porch were encrusted above a certain level with carved stucco.

Jug with impression and molded decorations.

Besides the frigidarium, the bath proper comprised four smaller rooms appended to its north side and entered by a door in one of the exedrae. Two of these rooms, fitted with marble floors and wall benches, were unheated. The inner one had two small receptacles about the size of a hip bath built into one of its walls and piped to receive two separate liquids. The two remaining rooms stood on hypocausts heated by two furnaces, from which smoke flues and hot-air pipes rose in the thickness of the walls. The first room to be entered was square and had a round niche, which must have contained a *labrum*, in the far wall directly above the furnace. The second room, which could only be entered from the first, was circular in plan and ringed about with eight horseshoe niches between slender columns. In the niche directly opposite the door an aperture admitted steam from a boiler placed directly outside it and above the second furnace. The two adjoining niches were also fitted to hold *labra*. Here, clearly, beneath a dome of some sort, from which traces of glass mosaics have survived, was the place of maximum heat and moisture.

At the northwest corner of the frigidarium stood the reception room, entered by a door at the north end of the west ambulatory. Here, by a branch of the same stairs that descended to the mosque was the owner's private way from his apartments to the bath. The reception room was a small chamber, something less than 5 meters square, extending into an apsidal dais raised 50 centimeters above the main floor level and covered by a barrel vault and semi-dome. The main chamber had wall benches on either side of the same height as the dais. It was lighted by eight windows set high up in a drum wall resting on pendentives and carrying a brick dome. The floors of both the room and the dais, and also the surfaces of the benches, were finished with mosaic, and the whole interior of the room, from the benches to the crown of the vaults and dome, was encrusted with carved plaster. The windows were fitted with carved plaster grilles.

Date. The date of Khirbet al-Mafjar can be inferred within close limits. The bath was completed within the caliphate of al-Hisham (A.D. 724–743), and the palace was still under construction during the one-year reign of al-Walid ibn al-Yazid. There are grounds for believing that the owner and builder was not Hisham himself, however, but his extravagant and loose-living nephew and successor, whose assassination in A.D. 744 may well have been the cause of its abandonment. The general context of Hisham's reign is established by two small fragments of marble slabs inscribed in ink with short Arabic texts addressed to "the Servant of God, Hisham, Commander of the Faithful," which were found with a number of other inscribed fragments among builders' waste beside the southwest corner of the palace.

Workmanship. The texts and certain masons' graffiti indicate that the artisans engaged on the construction were both Greek- and Arabic speaking, and included Christians, Jews, and Muslims. One fragment had a Hebrew alphabet transliterated into Arabic. The builder's craft was strongly influenced by Sassanian architecture. Thus the entrances to both palace and bath were through high arches inspired by the Iwan facades of Persia and Iraq. Composite piers in both buildings,

and certain ornamental details of small scale, betray a dependence on the clustered columns of Sassanian brick architecture. For the first time in Palestine, carved stucco was employed extensively as a surface ornament and as a material for balustrades and windows. Facades were crowned with crenellations of a form familiar only in Sassanian art and its derivatives. In both stucco and painted ornaments, Sassanian motifs — geometrical, floral, animal, human, and mythological (e.g. the *senmury* and winged horse) — were of frequent occurrence.

Vaulting and Arches. Wherever they could be measured, stone arches proved to be struck from two centers separated by distances varying from one fifth to one twelfth of the span. Brick and stone were equally employed for vaulting, and in close conjunction. The problem presented by the interpenetration of vaults of differing span and height, whether in stone or brick, were tackled without evasion. A good example is seen in a groined cross

Stucco screen (reconstructed).

759

vault used to span the porch of the palace, a short-armed cross in plan, having on the main east–west axis a cut-stone tunnel vault 4.66 meters wide, intersected in the middle by another of slightly smaller span. The archivolt of the main vault, facing the forecourt, was carved with a series of twenty-one radiating niches between colonnettes. At the intrados of the arch, the profile of this ornament, consisting of alternate hollows and ribs, was transmitted horizontally under the vault, giving it a lobed aspect as seen from the front. The surface of the transverse vault was lobed with the

*This page, right: Figure of a warrior;
Below: Carved panel, from the palace;
Opposite page: Female statue, from the palace.*

same profile, and at the intersections the groin stones were cut with stereotomic exactitude, transmitting the ornament to right and left through a right angle. Within the gate, a passage forming the inward prolongation of the porch was again cross vaulted, but in brick. This had too far disintegrated to be measured, but it had left impressions on a stucco incrustation, which enabled its form to be reconstructed as a long tunnel penetrated from each side by two narrower vaulted bays. For covering square compartments, the builders were also accustomed to using domes, which appear always to have been in brick. Transition from the square to the circular plan was effected, in all cases that could be observed, by means of spherical pendentives of cut stone. In each case the brick dome was raised on a stone masonry drum wall lightened by niches or windows or both.

Stone Sculpture. The builders upheld local tradition by admitting only acanthus ornament for capitals, albeit in a far from orthodox style. Elsewhere, in the carving of string-course moldings, window frames, door jambs, lintels, and niche heads they employed the guilloche and other conventional classical ornaments as well as a wide range of floral motifs based freely on the acanthus, palmette, vine, rosette, and other plant forms, including composite fantasies whose derivation from Sassanian ornament is clearly seen. Of the figural reliefs from the octagonal pavilion, only the scantiest fragments survived. They appear to have represented full-length figures, originally colored, larger than life. The best example of coloring on stone scuplture was an acanthus capital, probably destined for the facade of the palace, which was painted red and blue and also gilded.

Plaster Sculpture. Plaster sculpture was extensively used for decorating wall surfaces, arches, and ceilings, for columns, capitals, cornices, and niches, for windows and balustrades, and for ornamental statuary, both human and animal. In the palace and bath, built as they were over a period of years, several groups of sculptors were employed. The finest mural decoration was displayed in geometric and floral panels and moldings of great delicacy and interest on the walls and vaults of the bath reception room. In the same room, the technical accomplishment of the sculptors was exhibited in the treatment of the four

pendentives, each of which carried a floral wreath of minute acanthus leaves, deeply undercut, encircling a winged horse of Sassanian type carved in very high relief. Above these, the dome was crowned with a giant rosette of larger acanthus leaves, also boldly undercut, set radially to frame six human busts about an open flower at the center.

On the facade and interior of the bath porch, and on the walls of the entrance passage to the palace, geometric panels with conventional floral fillings closely resemble certain Sassanian revetments. But on the vaulted ceiling of the palace entrance a vast design of scrolling vines, peopled by animal, bird, and human figures in high relief, is inspired, presumably, by some painting or mosaic of Mediterranean origin. Window grilles and balustrade panels, the latter bearing a different design on each

762

face, display an almost unlimited variety of geometric compositions, concentric or orientated, and many graceful floral fillings and border scrolls, of which the most interesting are those which draw inspiration from the exotic flowers depicted by Sassanian artists in textiles, metal-work, and architectural sculpture. To the same source may be traced a number of details on the walls and vaulting of the bath reception room.

In a class by themselves stand two groups of carved plaster statues or high reliefs, which were recovered from the entrance passage to the palace and from the facade and interior of the bath porch. Of these, some are human figures, nearly life size, male and female, who stood erect in stiffly frontal poses framed in niches. Others are animals — wild sheep, ibex, and gazelle — kneeling in rows on cornices below the statue niches. The human figures include one arrayed as a Roman soldier, with mailed shirt, round shield, and spear (now missing). Others are gymnasts or swimmers, naked except for a loincloth. Others again are female figures, of a single type — apparently dancers — but with varied details. All were elaborately coiffured with braids and ringlets, earrings and rosettes. Below the headdress, opulent forms stood naked to the hips, holding in each hand a posy or a basket of flowers. From the hips a pleated and flowered skirt was suspended by a thick twisted cord, leaving exposed small feet adorned with anklets.

Opposite page: Mosaic pavement in the diwan *(reception hall) near the bathhouse; This page: Mosaic pavement in the large reception hall, from the west.*

That all the figures were colored is revealed by traces of red, black, white, and yellow paint visible on the headdresses, features, costumes, and posies.

One statue stood alone, a bearded princely figure wearing ankle-length trousers, full-bottomed surcoat edged with beads, and a jeweled belt. His hand rested on the hilt of a sword, probably suspended by a baldric. This figure, fully colored with golden brown hair touched with crimson, black eyelids, crimson and flowered garments, stood in a central niche above the entrance to the baths, and represented undoubtedly a caliph (probably al-Walid). At his feet two lions squatted in heraldic pose, their tails raised, and glared outward.

Mosaics. The frigidarium of the bath and both parts of the reception room were paved with colored stone mosaics, the whole vast expanse of which was preserved almost intact. The floor of the frigidarium was divided into rectangular and circular panels or carpets, reflecting in all probability the articulation of the vaulting. Throughout this area, the designs were with one small exception abstract in character — interlacings, diaper, and basketry patterns. The effect is that of a great spread of rugs. On the chord of the apse at the center of the west side of the hall, a panel 45 centimeters square contains a composition representing a bulbous form of vaguely human and female aspect, from the base of which sprouts a leafy stem. On the right is a yellow-handled knife, pointing sharply upward. The intention of the panel is a symbolic allusion to sexual reproduction.

CONCLUSION

Al-Mafjar, then, with its bath preceding the palace in time, was not an official residence but the spring or winter resort of the caliph designate. The preponderance of non-domestic rooms in the palace, the ample benches at its entrance, the outward-looking arcades, and three-doored mosque, all denote a numerous retinue and hospitality lavishly dispensed. The brilliant reception room, secluded domestic apartments, and private approaches to mosque and bath show that princely state and protocol were maintained, at least for some purposes. Horsemanship, poetry, song, and wine were the passionate pastimes of al-Walid, and all were honored in the appointments and ornament of al-Mafjar. The balmy climate of the *ghor*, abundant fresh water, enclosed estate, and sumptuous architecture provided a congenial setting for the life of aesthetic hedonism, which the assassination of the caliph in A.D. 744 extinguished.

R. W. HAMILTON

BIBLIOGRAPHY

Early Visits: *SWP* 3, 211 • F. J. Bliss, *PEFQSt*, 1894, 177.
Preliminary Reports: D. C. Baramki, *QDAP* 5 (1936), 132; 6 (1937), 157; 8 (1938), 51; 10 (1942), 153.
Greek Inscriptions: M. Schwabe, *QDAP* 12 (1946), 20.
Pottery: D. C. Baramki, *QDAP* 10 (1942), 65.
Sculpture: R. W. Hamilton, *QDAP* 11 (1945), 47; 12 (1946), 1; 13 (1947), 1; 14 (1950), 100.
Comprehensive Report: R. W. Hamilton and O. Grabar, *Khirbat al-Mafjar*, Oxford, 1959 • R. W. Hamilton, *Levant* 1 (1969), 61–67 • K. A. C. Creswell, *Early Muslim Architecture* 1, part 2, Oxford, 1969, 545–77 • Eva Baer, *IEJ* 24, (1974), 237–40.

Both pages, counterclockwise: Sculptured decoration in the dome of the reception hall; Inscription mentioning the Caliph Hisham (A.D. 724–743). Ink on marble; Ostracon with Arabic and Hebrew letters; Restoration of the bathhouse.

EL-MAḤRUQ KHIRBET .

El-Maḥruq is a rocky hill overlooking the Beth-Shean–Damiya–Jericho road, and the Succoth Valley on the eastern side of the Jordan.

Three main areas at the site were excavated in 1974 under the direction of Z. Yeivin, archaeological staff officer in Judea and Samaria.

EXCAVATIONS

Early Bronze Age. The earliest settlement excavated dates to the Early Bronze Age II and is spread over more than 250 dunams. Three phases of the Early Bronze Age II could be distinguished in this area (area C). The earliest phase (stratum 3) was founded on bedrock, and leveled with a stone and earth fill. In the south, a long supporting wall was built to form a terrace on which houses were erected.

Several rooms were uncovered in this well-preserved stratum. One room, which served as a dwelling (5 by 6 meters), contained the stone base of a pillar in its center. Low benches ran along the walls, both walls and benches being smoothly plastered. A second, adjoining room, with a fine brick floor, served as a granary. A rich collection of Early Bronze Age II pottery came from this stratum.

The next phase (stratum 2), not quite so well preserved, belongs to a denser settlement, which re-used walls of the earlier stratum. The pottery is basically the same as that of the previous stratum.

Little was preserved of the latest phase (stratum 1). The foundations show a re-use of the stratum 2 walls, including the stone terrace wall (2 meters high), traces of brick walls above this as well as above the previous stratum 2 walls. Part of the brick city wall of this settlement was found at the southern edge of the site.

As regards the architecture and pottery, there is no essential difference among the three strata, except for the presence of a few Khirbet Kerak (Early Bronze Age III) sherds in stratum 1.

Iron Age. The other period uncovered at el-Maḥruq dates to the Iron Age. This period is represented by two isolated towers, one at the northern edge of the site (area A) and the other in the center (area B).

The tower in area B is a round structure 19.5 meters in diameter from the tenth–ninth centuries B.C. Its foundations lie on a brick building of the Early Bronze Age II settlement. The tower consists of three concentric circular walls of stone. The inner circle (8 meters in diameter) seems to be a solid structure built on a pavement of small stones, which were apparently laid to level the area. This core was surrounded by a second stone wall (about 10 meters in diameter), built above a fill of about 1 meter above the rock. A well-built brick fill connected the core and the wall. The outer circular wall (19.5 meters in diameter) was the strongest, overlying the rock surface and cutting through the Early Bronze Age II remains and a foundation trench. It was preserved in sections to a height of 3 meters.

The area between the outer and middle circular wall was divided into eight rooms. The dividing radial walls, built partly of brick and partly of stone, were undoubtedly constructed at the same time as the second wall. A 1-meter gap between the outer edge of the radial walls and the outer wall was filled in by a ramp-type structure, which was on a lower level than the outer wall, and contained two entrances leading to the rooms. In some of the rooms two stages of plaster pavements were found with tenth–ninth century B.C. pottery

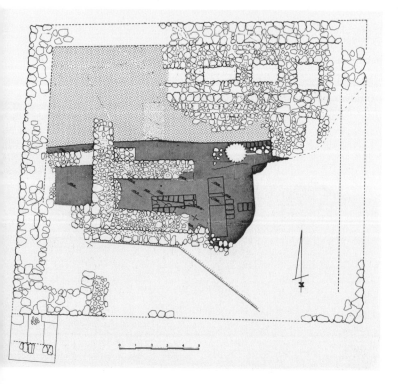

Opposite page: Plan of the square fort; This page: Plan of the round fort.

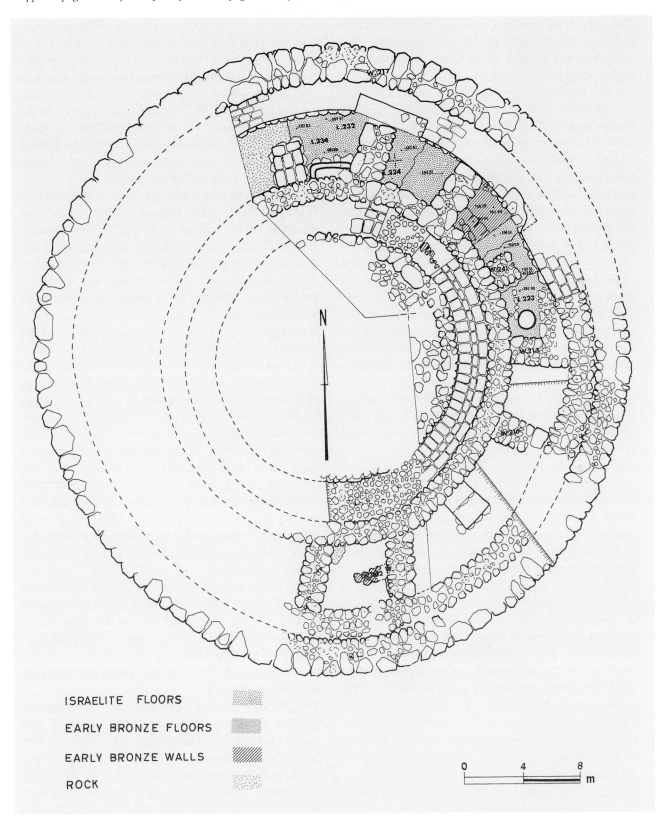

N

ISRAELITE FLOORS

EARLY BRONZE FLOORS

EARLY BRONZE WALLS

ROCK

0   4   8

m

in situ. The level of these pavements is in the main equal to that of the base of the middle circular wall.

The ramp-type structure was constructed of stone and brick on the inner side of the outer wall. This ramp apparently also served for ascending to a higher level in the tower.

On the northern edge of the site (area A) was a second tower built over the remains of the Early Bronze Age II. Three Early Bronze Age II phases of settlement were noted in this area. The earliest phase included the corner of a building erected on bedrock. The second phase consisted of a well-built city wall of square bricks on a stone foundation. The corner of the wall, located in the northeast sector of the site, measured about 3 meters in width and is preserved to a height of 5 meters. On the outside, the wall is abutted in its lower part by a glacis built of clay and brick rubble, and in the upper part of gravel, taken from the hewn fosse separating the site from the continuation of the spur. The third and latest Early Bronze Age II phase succeeded the destruction of the second phase. In this last phase, some of the ruins of the previous wall were covered with stones and chalk, which served as a base for a new brick fortification, which generally followed the line of the earlier wall. Part of two rooms of this later fortification were preserved.

Above the remains of the Early Bronze Age II wall was a square tower from the Israelite period, in which two phases of construction are evident. The tower in the first phase is divided into two long parallel rooms and a third adjoining room. Its walls are narrow and are made mostly of a brick superstructure on stone foundations. In the second phase, the structure was enlarged to form a square monumental tower (24 by 20 meters) built of walls 4 meters thick. One of these walls was a party wall for a row of rooms, which it surrounded. The ceramic finds in this tower are very similar to those in the round tower (area B), although they are somewhat later, dating perhaps to the early ninth century B.C.

Except for these two isolated towers no other trace of an Iron Age settlement was encountered at el-Maḥruq. Z. YEIVIN

BIBLIOGRAPHY

Z. Yeivin, *IEJ* 24 (1974), 259–60; *idem*, *Qadmoniot* 7 (1974), 102–04 (Hebrew).

MAKMISH

The site is situated on a small hill in the area of sand dunes near Herzliyah, about 400 meters northeast of Tel Mikhal, which lies on the seashore and about 150 meters north of Wadi el-Gharbi (map reference 13141744). The ancient name of the site is not known. Tel Mikhal itself has not been excavated, but potsherds gathered on the mound showed that it was occupied from the Middle Bronze Age to the Hellenistic period.

EXCAVATIONS at Makmish were carried out in October, 1958, and August, 1960, under the direction of N. Avigad on behalf of the Museum Haaretz in Tel Aviv with the cooperation of the Institute of Archaeology of the Hebrew University. In the northwestern corner of the hill, the excavators found remains of buildings in which three phases could be distinguished.

Iron Age. In the lowest level were discovered the remains of a square structure (10 by 10 meters), which lacked partition walls and showed no signs of supports for a roof. This was most probably an open enclosure surrounded by brick walls on foundations of rough stone. Of the southern wall, six courses of bricks (.4 meter wide) were still standing. The floor of the enclosure consisted of a thick layer of beaten red earth. On its surface and embedded in it were numerous potsherds, bone fragments, and ashes. In the center of this enclosure was a simple stone platform containing large deposits of ashes in the four corners. Several flat stone slabs found lying on the ground probably served as "tables".

The remains suggest that this enclosure was a place for gatherings, where fires were lighted and meals cooked. It may have been one of the High Places mentioned in the Bible, where sacrificial meals were held (I Samuel 9:12–13, 23–25). The date of the structure can be fixed by the pottery to roughly the tenth century B.C.

The Persian Period. On the sand covering the remains of the enclosure, a larger building was erected (about 15 meters long). This building was probably a sanctuary. Although its plan could not be definitely established, it appears to have had two rooms, which were built in separate stages. A larger room was built first, and a smaller chamber was later added north of it.

The best-preserved part of the sanctuary is the eastern wall, where one stone course, and in some places two courses, are preserved above floor level. The entrance was found in this wall. Its doorposts consist of pillars built of ashlar. The rest of the wall is built of undressed stones. On the eastern side is a courtyard in which were found two round plastered basins, one (1.1 meters in diameter) sunk into the floor, and the other (1.5 meters in diameter) built above floor level. An open plastered drain (preserved for a length of 5.2 meters) runs from east to west and was apparently connected with the sunken basin. It can be assumed that the basins were used for cultic purposes.

Within the area of the building, and outside it on the northern slope of the mound, numerous figurines were found, most of them of clay and a few of stone. The clay figurines, the majority of which are hollow mold-made terra-cottas, represent seated men wearing high pointed headgear and fondling the end of a long beard, or pregnant women, women with children in their arms or supporting their breasts with their hands, etc. Among the stone figurines is a distinctive type made in the classic Cypriot style of the fifth century B.C. Figurines in Egyptian, Persian, and Greek style were also discovered.

The other finds included several small decorated limestone incense altars, beads of semi-precious stones, colored glass pendants in the form of human heads, faience objects, bronze bracelets,

View of the eastern wall of the sanctuary and the court.

etc. It can be assumed that all these objects were offerings brought to the place of worship, which was probably dedicated to a fertility cult. The figurines and the other finds as well as historical considerations indicate that this cult was practiced by the Phoenician inhabitants of the settlement on the nearby mound in the Persian period.

Hellenistic Period. After the earlier sanctuary had fallen into ruin, the site was used as an open-air cult place, i.e., a High Place. The ruins of the building were leveled to form an open area, and in the courtyard a small rectangular altar was erected. From the Hellenistic pottery and several Ptolemaic coins found in the area, it can be concluded that the site was used until the second century B.C.

The Cemetery. In the sand dunes between the sanctuary and the seashore is a large cemetery, which was used by the settlement of Tel Mikhal. During construction work on the site, several tombs were examined under the supervision of A. Kempinski. The tombs are rectangular pits covered with stone slabs, with the walls faced with stone slabs or coated with red earth. Among the burial offerings were a Greek lecythus, local pottery of the Persian period, alabaster vessels, a bronze mirror, a Hebrew seal, a Tyrian coin from the fourth century B.C., etc. The tombs are contemporary with the Phoenician sanctuary.

N. AVIGAD

BIBLIOGRAPHY

N. Avigad, *IEJ* 10 (1960), 90–96; 11 (1961), 97–100.

Clay figurines: pregnant women and a bearded man with pointed hat.

MALḤATA, TEL

IDENTIFICATION. Tel Malḥata (Tell el-Milḥ) is situated at the confluence of the Malḥata (Wadi Milḥ) and the Beersheba rivers. The mound, which lies next to rich wells, is about 15 dunams in area, and its summit rises 14 meters above the plain. It consists of two parts, an eastern and a western, the eastern being twice as large and 2–3 meters higher than the western part. The remains of a Roman fort are visible on the surface along the perimeter of the east side of the mound.

The site is generally identified with the Roman fort Moleatha, but there is no consensus as to its identification in earlier times. F. M. Abel suggested Moladah, a Simeonite town (Joshua 15:26, 19:2; I Chronicles 4:28), while J. Garstang and B. Mazar located there Hormah–Zephath (Numbers 14:45, 21:3; Deuteronomy 1:44; etc.) and Y. Aharoni

proposed Canaanite Arad, the "Arad of the House of Yeroham" of Shishak's list. M. Kochavi proposed to identify the site with Baalath–Beer (Joshua 19:8, shortened form Bealoth, *ibid.* 15:24) mentioned together with Ramoth-Negev as the two eastern-most Simeonite cities. This identification is based on the proximity of Ḥorvat Uzza (Ramat Negev, as is evident from the Arad ostracon No. 24) to Tel Malḥata, and on the important wells and the abundance of pre-Israelite remains alluded to in the Hebrew place name.

EXCAVATIONS

Two seasons of excavations were conducted at Tel Malḥata by M. Kochavi, the first during July–August, 1967, under the auspices of the Arad Expedition and the second during July–August, 1971, as part of the Tel Beersheba Expedition.

Since the cemetery on the mound is still in use, only two trenches, 10 by 40 meters, were allowed for excavation. One trench was dug on the northern slope (trench W) of the higher (eastern) side of the

Tel Malḥata. View from the north.

mound and the other on the southern slope (trench Z) of the lower (western) side of the mound. Virgin soil was reached only outside the city wall.

Four periods of occupation were distinguished: 1. Chalcolithic period–Early Bronze Age; 2. Middle Bronze Age II; 3. Iron Age; 4. Roman–Early Arab periods.

Period 1. Remains of this period did not appear in a stratigraphic context. The abundance of sherds and flints from this period found in the deepest layers reached so far and their concentration on the river bank opposite the mound points to the existence of an extensive settlement at that time.

Period 2. Three strata of this period were uncovered at the base of the trench dug in the eastern side of the mound (trench W.). The town of this period was apparently confined to this side and extended over an area of about 10 dunams. The date of its establishment could not be ascertained since the excavation did not penetrate beneath the three uppermost strata of this period. An earthern rampart was exposed, built of six alternating layers of clayish soil and riverbed gravel, each layer supported by a stone battered wall founded on virgin soil. The outer face of the rampart was plastered and formed a glacis with a 30-degree incline. Against a 1-meter-wide outer wall, a group of rooms was built on top of the rampart. Three strata were distinguished, the last of which had been destroyed by fire. White-slip V Cypriot ware found in the uppermost stratum, dated the end of period 2 to the sixteenth century B.C.

Period 3. Remains of this period were uncovered

in both trenches. The earliest stratum exposed dates to the middle of the tenth century B.C. A brick city wall, 4–4.5 meters thick, appeared in both trenches. The wall, built directly on Middle Bronze Age II debris in trench W, was founded on a 5-meter-high rampart at the lower part of the mound (trench Z). The rampart was made of riverbed gravel and was stabilized on its outer lower slope by a cobblestone covering, forming a stepped glacis. Near the city wall in trench Z two major phases of this stratum were noted consisting of superimposed, well-built, thick, lime-plastered floors and plastered brick walls. Both phases are connected with the wall and probably belong to a public building. The tenth-century city was destroyed by the end of the century and was followed by a short-lived unwalled settlement, best seen in trench W, where a habitation level containing several fireplaces was found directly above the stump of the tenth-century city wall. The last Iron Age phase at Malḥata began with a new city wall, 3–3.5 meters wide, built on the remains of the earlier wall. The wall is best preserved in trench W. It was constructed of brick, plastered inside and outside, and was supported on the steep slope by a huge earthern rampart. Part of a tower of this wall was also found projecting 8 meters and with more than thirty brick courses preserved to a height of 10 meters. Inside the wall there were three rows of small rooms, 2.5–3 meters wide. Five buildings with such rooms were discovered. Only the last one was destroyed by a conflagration. In trench Z a typical Israelite

"Edomite" pottery.

Lachish. Fragment of wall painting from the temple —LBA.

storehouse, 15 meters long and 7 meters wide, was uncovered. It consisted of three long rooms divided by two rows of pillars. The middle, narrower room had a beaten earth floor, and the other two rooms had stone pavements. The storehouse was in use throughout the period. Its floors were raised, and the original pillars built of round drums were later replaced by square monoliths. This phase dates to the ninth–seventh centuries B.C. Most of the finds, however, date from the last destruction level, probably from the last years of the Judean Kingdom. These include the latest types of Judean pottery as known from Arad VI, En-Gedi, and Ramat-Raḥel. About 30 percent of the pottery has Jordanian affinities, and a comparison with the pottery of Umm el-Bayarah, Tawilan, and Tell Kheleifeh shows it to be Edomite ware. An Aramaic ostracon with a list of private names, such as Azanel and Danel also hints at the same ethnic origin. This last rich phase also contained shekel and *Neṣeph* weights, a mirror, a bone handle, a decorated limestone incense altar, a complete store jar with a rosette stamp on one of its handles, and an archaic East Greek oenochoe, probably of Rhodian origin.

Period 4. Two rooms of the Roman fort were

excavated in trench W. They were paved and contained stone-lined "sleeping bunks," fireplaces, etc. The finds date the final use of the fort to the Umayyads (eighth century A.D.).

CONCLUSIONS

Tel Malḥata, an important center on the eastern fringe of the Beersheba plain, was founded in the Chalcolithic period but became a fortified town only during the Middle Bronze Age. It is the southeasternmost Hyksos fortification known and was surely part of the southern line of forts that guarded the southern border of Palestine at that time. There is a gap in occupation through most of the Late Bronze Age, but a new fortified city was built by the mid-tenth century B.C. The destruction of the early Israelite city should be attributed to Shishak's raid. The rebuilt walls continued in use until the Babylonian conquest. The Edomite pottery is probably the first archaeological evidence of Edomite expansion through southern Judea, as known from the prophecies of Jeremiah and Obadiah. M. KOCHAVI

BIBLIOGRAPHY

Abel, *GP*, 2, 391–92 • B. Mazar, *JNES* 24 (1965), 297–300 • Aharoni, *LB*, 184–85 • M. Kochavi, *IEJ* 17 (1967), 272–73; *idem, Qadmoniot* 3 (1970), 22–24 (Hebrew).

Both pages, counterclockwise from bottom: Iron age stone rampart — View from the south; superimposed pillar building — View from the west; Selection of pottery from the end of the Judean Kingdom.

MAMRE

IDENTIFICATION. Ramat el-Khalil is an ancient cult site situated on the highest point of Jabel er-Ramah (Jebel el-Betraq), 3 kilometers (2 miles) north of Hebron, 1,024 meters above sea level. Most scholars consider it the site of "Abraham's terebinth," which is first mentioned by Josephus (*Antiquities* I, 186; *War* IV, 533, and cf. Mishnah, *Ma'asar Sheni* 5:2), who states that it stood some six stades (about 1.2 kilometers) from Hebron. According to Jerome (*Commenteria in Jeremiam* 31; Zechariah 9:2), Hadrian brought prisoners there from Judea to be sold as slaves after the Bar Kokhba uprising (cf. *Chronicon Paschale* ad ann. 119). Julius Africanus (frag. 19) and Eusebius (*Demonstratio Evangelica* 9) mention the pagan altar at Terebinithus. According to Eusebius (*Historia Ecclesiastica* X, 18) and Socrates (*Vita Constantini* III, 53), the Emperor Constantine ordered the altar to be destroyed when he built his church there. The Bordeaux Pilgrim (A.D. 333) and Eusebius describe the place as an important market and the religious center of the south of the country. The market is also mentioned in the Palestinian Talmud as Botnah ('*Abodah Zarah* I, 39d; cf. Judith 1:9; Midrash *Canticles Rabbah* 4 fin; *Sifrei Deuteronomy* 306 calls the place Beth Ilanim). According to the Bordeaux Pilgrim, it was the site of Abraham's terebinth and the well dug by him, and also the site of the church built by the Emperor Constantine. The Medeba Map (about A.D. 560/65) testifies that the church still existed in the sixth century. The traveler Arculf (about A.D. 670) mentions it as still standing in the seventh century. In the tenth century, the structure was a quarry for building material. In the thirteenth century the Arab village of Ramah was built there.

Relying on ancient traditions, several scholars, including A.E. Mader and K. Galling, considered it the site of Mamre — the part of Hebron where Abraham resided (Genesis 13:18, 23:19, etc.). The view of others, however, who locate Mamre either within the town of Hebron (W. F. Albright) or on the hill of Namra north of it (F. M. Abel, B. Mazar), seems more acceptable.

EXPLORATION

In 1837, G. H. von Schubert found remains of occupation at this site, including a masonry enclosure known as Beit el-Khalil or Ḥaram el-Khalil (*el-Khalil*, "[God's] friend," is the Arabic name for Abraham). In 1926, 1927, and 1928, Mader, on behalf of the German Görresgesellschaft, excavated the Constantinian church in the east part of enclosure and clarified the site's history.

EXCAVATION RESULTS

The enclosure covers an area of 3.5 dunams (49.35 by 65 meters = approximately 7/8 acre), and is surrounded by a strong wall. Investigation of the temenos disclosed the following phases: A paved way, 446 meters long, was found leading up to the center of the west wall of the Haram. West of the wall at this point were uncovered the foundations of two towers of the Ḥaram, containing pottery of the Iron Age II (ninth–seventh centuries B.C.). These were probably entrance towers to the temenos. Sections of stone paving belonging to two periods earlier than the wall were found within the south wall of the temenos. Numerous building stones, apparently of the period of the monarchy, were found re-used in the fill below the Byzantine basilica and in the Arab cistern in the west of the temenos. The direction of the paving stones indicated that the extreme eastern part of the court extended farther south in the period of the monarchy. This deviation was corrected in the time of Herod. M. Gisler dated the first pavement to the Judean monarchy (the time of Rehoboam — cf. II Chronicles 11:7, 10) and the second to the Hasmonaean period (possibly the reign of John Hyrcanus, who captured Hebron in about 128 B.C.). According to Josephus (*War* IV, 533), Abraham's terebinth had existed from the time Hebron was founded. And indeed the temenos yielded pottery of the early phase of the Middle Bronze Age II, although no other remains attributable to that period were found.

The wall of the enclosure consists of two faces of dressed blocks with a rubble fill. The blocks are laid as headers and stretchers set on their narrow edges. Larger blocks were used in the upper courses. The blocks are smooth dressed and un-drafted, with central bosses of no great size. The wall contains re-used masonry of the Early Roman period. All these features are characteristic of the buildings erected by Hadrian in Jerusalem and at Odruh in Transjordan.

The foundation of a sill and the lintel of an older

structure were found in the west wall. The enclosure wall also contained a window through which spectators outside could see what was happening within the temenos. The south wall stood on an older foundation. Along the north wall was uncovered a fairly long sector of a pre-Hadrianic wall. It was composed of huge dressed blocks with drafted bosses, with the remains of piers abutting on the front — typical features of Herodian work. Such dressed blocks have been found in Herod's temple at Jerusalem, in the Phasael tower, and in the Ḥaram at Hebron, and similar piers are found in the last structure. Four periods were distinguished in the east wall: Herodian, Hadrianic, Byzantine, and Arab. It was therefore clear that the enclosure in its present form was built under Hadrian, its construction doubtless being connected with the emperor's journey from Jerusalem to Gaza (A.D. 130). The Hadrianic wall was laid over remains of the Herodian peribolos, which had two ceremonial entrances, one in the west and one in the north wall. In Hadrian's time there was probably an entrance in the north side only. There were indications that the Herodian temenos was never finished, and what had been built was destroyed during the Roman capture of Hebron in A.D. 68.

On the rebuilding of the temenos under Hadrian, a shrine was erected abutting the eastern limit of the enclosure. Only three walls of the shrine survived, and these were incorporated into the Constantinian church. They are distinguishable from the walls of the church by their being bonded into the east peribolos wall of the Hadrianic temenos. A fragment of the altar mentioned by the sources has been preserved west of the narthex of the Byzantine church. In the east area of the Ḥaram were found Corinthian capitals of second-century style, a stele of Hermes, the head of a statue of Dionysus, a miniature altar, and other finds, all evidence of the existence of a cult building, perhaps of the god Hermes. Hundreds of coins of the second and third centuries were also found. Among the sacred enclosures similar to the Hadrianic shrine are those of Zeus Madbachos in Jebel es-Sheikh Baraqat in northern Syria, of Zeus at Ḥosn Suleiman (Betocaice) southeast of Homs, and of the temple at Mushennef (Neila) in Hauran. All these were completed in the second century A.D.

Constantine's church is the oldest known of its type. It is mentioned in sources from the fourth century onward. The basilica was built in the form of a broad house, 20.1 by 16.45 meters, in the eastern third of the temenos, thus filling the entire sacred area, since the west part of the temenos was the atrium of the church. The church

Western wall of the enclosure.

included an apse, nave, and aisles, a narthex on the west and sacristies (prothesis and diaconicon) at the ends of the aisles on the north and south. Although this arrangement is rare, it has parallels in fourth and fifth century churches in northern Syria. Abraham's terebinth stood in the atrium. Two phases were discernible in the apse, pilasters and a new floor being added in the second. Mader inclined to date the second phase to the patriarch Modestus, who repaired the building after the Persian invasion in A.D. 614. The apse, however, may have been part of the Hadrianic temple, and the second phase would then have belonged to the Constantinian church. Mader does not reject this interpretation. Rooms apparently serving to house pilgrims visiting Abraham's terebinth were built north and south of the church in the Byzantine period.

The position of Abraham's terebinth is marked by a gap in the paving northeast of the well in the atrium. The well yielded numerous coins of Constantine. In and around the well were remains from the pre-Herodian to the Arab period. Notable among these were fragmentary Greek inscriptions, especially of the Severan period and the fourth and fifth centuries (prayers, one be a certain Paragorios, perhaps a Jew whose name was Menahem). Also found were 1,331 coins ranging from the Hasmonaean to the Crusader period. It should be noted that no coins were found of the emperors from Vespasian to Hadrian.

S. APPELBAUM

BIBLIOGRAPHY

For a list of ancient sources and archaeological studies, see the excavation report of A. E. Mader, *Mambre, Die Ergebnisse der Ausgrabungen im heiligen Bezirk, Ramat el-Halil in Süd-Palästina*, Freiburg in Breisgau, 1957; see also R. de Vaux, Mambre, *DB Suppl.* 5 (1957), 753–58.

Left: Plan of the church. 1. Nave. 2. Aisles. 3. Prothesis. 4. Diaconicon. 5. Narthex. 6. Foundations of "Abraham's altar". 7. "Abraham's well"; right: Enclosure wall fron the Herodian period.

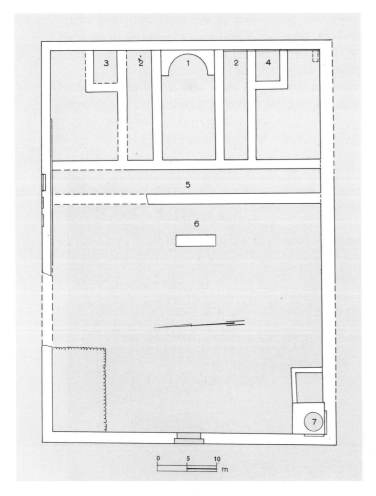

MA'ON

IDENTIFICATION. The city of Ma'on in the region of Besor, about 20 kilometers (12.5 miles) southwest of Gaza and .5 kilometer southwest of Kibbutz Nirim, is today known as Khirbet el-Ma'in. It was apparently the center of the Saltus Constantiniaces from the fourth century A.D. onward. The place was known as Menois, and it formed the western boundary of the Limes Palaestinae. A unit of Illyrian horsemen was stationed there.

THE SYNAGOGUE

A synagogue, which was discovered during road construction, was cleared in the spring of 1957 and 1958 by S. Levy on behalf of the Department of Antiquities. Of the western part of the synagogue, almost nothing has survived, and only scant remains were found of the rest of the building. A section of the northeast wall, built of ashlars and orientated toward Jerusalem, is still standing. This wall contained a semicircular apse with a small pit in its floor, which probably served as the synagogue's treasury chest. In front of the apse was a small bema (.6 by .75 meter) built of ashlars. In the excavator's opinion, it was here that the Ark of the Law stood. It is more likely, however, that the Ark was fixed in the apse and that the bema served some other purpose. On the basis of the meager remains, especially those of the floor, it can be assumed that the building was a basilica (about 17 by 15 meters), divided by two rows of columns into a nave and two aisles. The aisles and the southern part of the nave were paved with limestone slabs, but the rest of the nave was paved with a decorated mosaic. This may indicate that there was possibly an additional story (women's gallery) above the aisles and the southern part of the nave. The remains of a plastered pool (a *miqve*?) and a cistern were found east of the synagogue, but it was not ascertained whether they belonged to the synagogue.

The Mosaic Floor was published by M. Avi-Yonah. The western part of the pavement, about one third of its total area (10.2 by 5.4 meters), was destroyed during road construction. The mosaic was laid in a blaze of color, a rich palette of eighteen shades of red, brown, green, yellow, black, white, and orange. On either side of the small bema near the apse, the floor has two small rectangles decorated with geometric patterns. In front of the apse is an inscription set in a *tabula ansata* (see below). The main field of the mosaic consists of a single panel (8.9 by 4.95 meters) surrounded by a border of stylized flowers pointing alternately inward and outward. The border itself is flanked by two bands of stepped triangles. The panel is divided into fifty-five round medallions, arranged in eleven horizontal rows with five medallions to a row, or in five vertical rows of eleven medallions. The medallions are formed by a vine trellis with clusters of grapes, leaves and tendrils issuing from an amphora in the central medallion of the bottom row. Jewish symbols are concentrated in the upper row of medallions, near the apse. The top two medallions in the axial row contain a seven-branched menorah on a tripod, with the feet shaped like lions' paws. On a horizontal bar at the top of the menorah are seven burning oil lamps, which are depicted as made of glass. Flanking the menorah in the top row of medallions is a pair of lions with their heads turned toward it. On either side of the menorah's stem are two ethrogs, with a ram's horn (shofar) on the right and a lulab and another ethrog(?) attached to it on the left. Two palm trees with a pair of doves at their feet appear in two medallions on either side of the menorah's shaft. The eight remaining medallions in the axial row (between the menorah and the amphora) are filled with baskets, bowls, a goblet, an amphora, and a bird in a cage. Animals and birds appear in the other medallions of the mosaic and are identical on both sides of the axial row.

The Jewish symbols are typical of the synagogue mosaics of the Byzantine period. Lions in pairs are familiar from the mosaics in the synagogues of Beth Alpha and Hammat-Gader. The style of the mosaic pavement is similar to that of the mosaic pavement of the synagogue of Gaza, completed in A.D. 508/09 and that of a church dated to the year A.D. 561/62 that was uncovered in the Besor region in 1917 and is now preserved in Australia (see Churches). From a comparison of these mosaics, Avi-Yonah concluded that the Ma'on mosaic and the church pavement had apparently both been produced by artisans from the same workshop and that the synagogue mosaic had evidently been laid

during the first three decades of the sixth century A.D. The remains of an earlier mosaic floor were found 5 centimeters below the Ma'on pavement. Earlier floors have also been uncovered below mosaic pavements of the synagogues at Beth Alpha, Eshtemoa, En-Gedi, and elsewhere. From the available evidence, it is impossible to ascertain whether the earlier floor also belongs to the synagogue.

The inscription in front of the apse, which was deciphered and published by S. Yeivin, is an Aramaic dedication of four lines, of which the three upper lines on the right side have been damaged. It reads as follows: "Remembe[red] for good be the whole congregation [who ha]ve contributed this mosaic [and furtherm]ore Daisin and Thoma and Judah who have donated [the] sum [of] two denarii." The execution of the letters is of a very poor standard. The artisans may have been unfamiliar with the script.

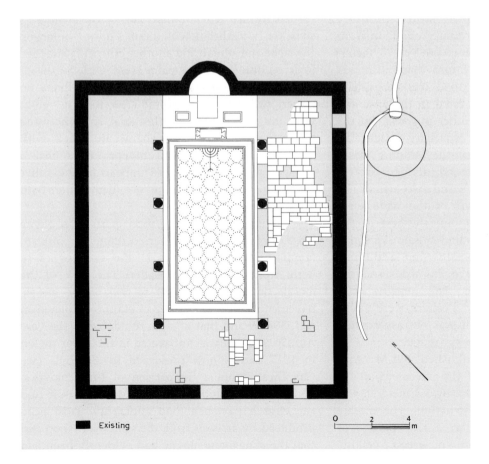

Existing

0   2   4
             m

Both pages, counterclock-wise, from top: Section of the mosaic pavement; Plan of the synagogue; Section of the mosaic pavement; Drawing of the mosaic pavement.

Among the small finds are coins dating from the fourth to the sixth centuries A.D. and also carved bone ornaments, including a small plaque with an amphora which may have served as an inlay of the Ark of the Law.

This synagogue is an outstanding example of the late type of synagogue, especially those of the sixth to the seventh centuries A.D. Like them it is provided with an Ark of the Law in an apse oriented toward Jerusalem, and is the first synagogue of this type discovered in the Negev.

D. BARAG

BIBLIOGRAPHY

For the Site: M. Avi-Yonah, *The Holy Land,* Grand Rapids, 1966, 120, 162 • Abel, *GP* 2, 180.
For the Synagogue: S. Levy et al., *Rabinowitz Bulletin* 3 (1960), 6–40 • S. Levy, L. Y. Rahmani & M. Avi-Yonah, *EI* 6 (1961), 77–93 (Hebrew) • A. Grabar, *Cahiers Archéologiques* 12 (1962), 117, 124; 16 (1966), 10 ff. • Goodenough, *Jewish Symbols,* 9, 17; 12, 48 • M. Avi-Yonah, *EI* 12 (1975), 191–93 (Hebrew).

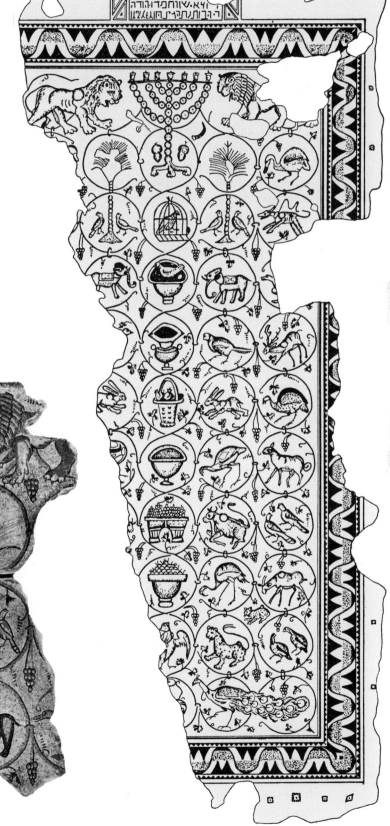

MARESHAH (Marisa)

IDENTIFICATION. It is generally agreed by scholars that Mareshah (Marisa) is to be identified with Tell Sandakhanna, located about 2 kilometers (1 mile) south of Beth-Govrin and 30 kilometers (18.5 miles) east-southeast of Ashkelon (map reference 140110). This identification is based on references in the Bible and in Josephus where Marisa is mentioned in the vicinity of towns in the eastern Shephelah. It is also corroborated by Eusebius, who located it 2 miles from Beth-Govrin (Onomasticon 130:10). In the light of this literary evidence, E. Robinson established the location of Marisa as a large mound south of Beth-Govrin, i.e., Tell Sandakhanna. Although V. Guérin and the British Survey sought to identify Marisa with Khirbet Marash, 1 kilometer south of the above-mentioned site, W. F. Petrie found there only Roman remains, leading him to conclude that Marisa should be identified with Tell Sandakhanna itself. F. J. Bliss was of the same opinion even before his excavation of the latter mound. The identification was definitely verified by the excavations, especially by the inscription discovered in a tomb near the mound mentioning the Sidonian community "residing in Marisa" (see below).

HISTORY OF THE SITE

Mareshah appears among the cities of Judah (Joshua 15:44) and in the "genealogies" of the settlements (I Chronicles 2:42) as belonging to the Calebites. In the Bible, no mention is made of its being a Canaanite city prior to the Israelite conquest. During the reign of Rehoboam, Mareshah was one of the fortified cities defending the southwestern approaches of Judah. Zerah the Ethiopian, who invaded the country in the time of Asa, reached Mareshah (about 900 B.C.), but was repulsed in the major battle fought in the Valley of Zephathah (north of Mareshah according to the Septuagint [II Chronicles 14:8–9]). After the destruction of the First Temple, Marisa, together with all of southern Judah, became Edomite territory. In the Hellenistic period, it replaced Lachish as the main city in western Idumaea (see, for example, the Zenon papyri, 259 B.C.). During the Hasmonaean wars, Marisa served as a base for

attacks on Judea, and therefore suffered acts of retaliation by the Maccabees (I Maccabees 5:66 should be read Μαρισαν [Marisa], not Σαμαρειαν [Samaria] and also II Maccabees 12:35). In the Hellenistic period, and perhaps even in the Persian period, a Sidonian community settled in Marisa. Hyrcanus I captured Marisa together with all of Idumaea (Josephus, *Antiquities* XIII, 257; *War* I, 63), and the city remained in Hasmonaean hands (*Antiquities* XIII, 396) until Pompey's conquest of Judea (*Antiquities* XIV, 75; *War* I, 156). The city was rebuilt by his successor, the Consul Gabinius (*Antiquities* XIV, 88; *War* I, 166) and was probably handed over to Herod together with all of western Idumaea in 40 B.C. In the same year, the Parthians utterly destroyed the "strong city," which was never rebuilt (*Antiquities* XIV, 364; *War* I, 269). Thereafter Beth-Govrin replaced Marisa as the capital of the district.

EXCAVATIONS

Tell Sandakhanna was partially excavated in June–August, 1900, by F. J. Bliss and R. A. S. Macalister, under the auspices of the British Palestine Exploration Fund. This was part of a series of excavations carried out in the Shephelah in the years 1898–1900. The mound is about 152 meters in diameter. At its summit (357 meters above sea level) was found a stratified accumulation 3.6–6.1 meters thick. The excavators identified three strata: two Hellenistic and one Israelite ("Jewish"). They first excavated a network of squares (each 3 square meters) until they discovered walls directly beneath the surface. After three days of digging, they began uncovering walls and rooms, clearing three walls of each room and piling up the debris against the fourth wall. They uncovered the whole upper stratum and established the plan of the entire city in the last phase of its occupation. In one area (block II, see below), an exploratory pit was sunk (15 by 9 by 5.5 meters). In 1902, Bliss published his report of the excavation, and five years later H. Thiersch published a detailed analysis of his report, which is still of value today.

The city in its last phase was almost square in plan (158 meters from east to west. 152 meters from north to south) and covered an area of about 24 dunams. It was surrounded by a wall with square and rectangular towers. Aside from the corner towers (of which the northwestern one is outstanding), three towers were discovered in the western wall, three in the southern wall, and one in the eastern wall. In the northern wall a corner and an angle were found, but no tower. Near the angle, inside the wall, was discovered a large structure, perhaps the remains of a gate. The wall was constructed on a foundation of rough stone, and is built in part of limestone cut like bricks, and laid in headers and stretchers (15 by 52 by 28 centimeters). On the east, the wall is built of large blocks of stone laid in mortar. No gates were found. The gate that Bliss thought he found near the southeastern corner is actually a tower, the remains of which are preserved up to the threshold of the door. It can be assumed, however, that the gates were located at the ends of the main streets. The Hippodamian system (based on a grid) is easily recognized in the original plan of the city: two parallel main streets running east–west (A and Θ in the report); and three north–south streets (E + B, Z + Γ, H + Δ) intersecting the main streets at right angles. The width of the streets varies from 2 to 6 meters. In most of the streets, there were remains of paving. The main street contained the remains of a drainage system. The municipal drainage network branched off to the private houses, but the excavators did not examine it in detail, confining themselves to uncovering the upper stratum without destroying buildings. The grid of streets bounded twelve blocks of buildings. One of these blocks of buildings (I, between E, Θ and A streets) located near the eastern wall, was evidently the religious, administrative, and military center. Another (block II between A, H, Z, and streets) was the commercial center.

Block I was square in form (each side 45 meters long). In its center, there was an enclosed court, surrounded by rooms and halls of various sizes. To the west an additional row of six rooms of equal size opening onto street E was added to the inner row of rooms. The former were apparently offices or guardrooms. A small building (9 by 3 meters) in the center of the court was divided into three compartments. Some scholars assume that this was a temple erected in the time of Gabinius in honor of an Idumaean trinity of gods, as yet not identified. It seems that one of the tutelary deities of the city was Apollo (perhaps the Idumaean god Qos). The court surrounding the temple may have been an outer court. In all events, this was clearly a very important building for its court to occupy so large an area in so crowded a city.

Block II is also a square structure (each side 42 meters long) consisting of two courts. One, extending along street A, was paved with stones. The other (24.5 by 15.2 meters), to the south of the first court, was surrounded by a porch, of which the foundations were cleared. West of the first court was a large house with a small enclosed court in the center. The rest of the block consisted of smaller rooms. Apparently the northern court was a marketplace and the southern one a caravanserai. Since, as was mentioned above, there was a Sidonian colony at Marisa and nearby Ashkelon was a Tyrian city (according to Pseudo-Scylax), it seems reasonable for Marisa to have kept up contacts with maritime countries.

Two types of buildings were distinguished in the city: a large building consisting of rooms surrounding an enclosed court and a small building with rooms not arranged in a clear plan. In several buildings were discovered remains of hearths, basins, shelves, and steps leading either to the roof or to the cellar. One house in the south of the city contained a granary. In the middle of one of the northern blocks was a storeroom(?) with thick walls and a barrel-vaulted ceiling. From the few architectural fragments and from the plans of the buildings, it is evident that the architecture of the city was a blend of Hellenistic and eastern elements, corresponding well with the history of the city. The remains also included Ionic and Corinthian capitals of large and small columns, capitals of pillars, and panels decorated with rosette and meander motifs.

The excavations revealed that the original Hippodamian plan was distorted in the final phase of the city. Streets were blocked by rooms, or were diverted from straight courses into crooked paths. Toward the end of the city's existence, the inhabitants were apparently no longer prepared to accept the urban plan imposed on them from above, and each individual adapted it to his own needs and to his eastern way of life, without heeding the public welfare. The excavators are of the opinion that during the final siege of the city the wall was breached on the southwest where no building remains were discovered. In the debris in this spot were found the tablets bearing the execration inscriptions (see below).

In an earlier phase, the city was surrounded by a different wall which, judging from its remains, enclosed a slightly larger area. The excavators assumed that the two walls were linked and that the outer one served to support the rough-stone foundation upon which the first wall was erected. They concluded that the two walls were built at the same time. This explanation, however, does not seem plausible. It seems more likely that the lower wall belongs to the early phase of the Hellenistic city, of which several rooms were discovered in the trial trench sunk in the center of the city. Under these rooms, at a depth of 3.05 meters was found a "Jewish" stratum from the Israelite period. The finds from this stratum include seventeen *lamelekh* seals—eleven of the double-winged type and six of the four-winged type—from various cities: Hebron, three; *Mmšt*, three; Socoh, six; Zif, two; and three seals bearing illegible names.

The Finds. A large quantity of Hellenistic pottery was found in the excavations. It comprises the richest pottery repertoire of this period discovered in Palestine. Among the finds were 328 Rhodian handles as well as complete Rhodian jars. The seal impressions on the Rhodian handles date from the beginning of the third to the end of the second century B.C. The imported ware also included early types of *terra sigillata* or Samian ware, a ribbed bowl, and sherds of Megaran bowls.

Three inscriptions were discovered from the Hellenistic period. They were deciphered by C. Clermont–Ganneau. One, an inscription on a cylindrical base, is a dedication to Arsinoe II, queen of Egypt, the wife of Ptolemy IV Philopator (221–203 B.C.). The second inscription, carved on a limestone fragment, mentions only one of the royal names of the Ptolemaic dynasty — Berenice. The third inscription, carved on the base of the huge statue of an eagle and dedicated to Apollo by "...s the son of Kraton," is also from the Hellenistic period. These inscriptions in honor of the Ptolemaic dynasty may perhaps be connected with the victory march of Ptolemy IV in Palestine after his success near Rafah in 217 B.C.

Of special interest are sixteen small (5–8 centimeters high) lead figurines. Most of them are figures of humans (male and female), with slightly rounded heads, on which the eyes, nose, and mouth are indicated. The figures are bent in different positions and their hands or feet (or sometimes both) are bound with iron, copper, or lead wire, or tied to instruments of torture(?). The figurines were found in the row of rooms surrounding the court in block I, which the excavators named the Seleucid barracks. The figurines apparently served magical purposes. A person wishing to curse his enemy with rheumatism or another kind of infliction, made a small figurine in his image, bound or tied it, and set it near the temple of the god. The practice of magic of this sort must have been common in Hellenistic Marisa, as is evidenced by the discovery of fifty-one limestone tablets and fragments, some in cursive Greek, in the southwestern corner of the city, apparently in the fill. Four of the tablets contained Hebrew inscriptions in a square script, not yet deciphered. Two other inscriptions were written in an unknown script (demotic Coptic?). The Greek inscriptions were deciphered by R. Wünsch. On small fragments in Greek appear phrases and isolated names. One tablet apparently contains a list of the days of the week for the whole year (the tablet is divided into seven columns). Each day is designated by the letters ΓΔ (day of good fortune), or in reverse order ΔΓ (day of ill

This page: The mound and caves in the vicinity; opposite page: Upper level of the city — Hellenistic period.

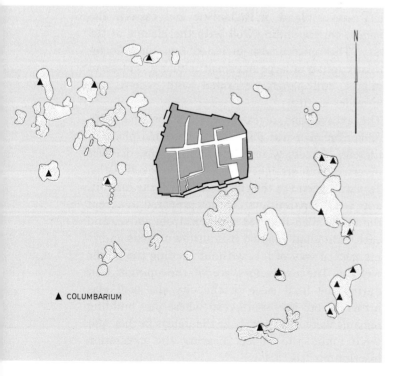

▲ COLUMBARIUM

fortune). On one fragment the letters are written from right to left (Δᴿ), apparently under the influence of Semitic writing. The long passages (one is of twenty-three lines, and two are of seventeen lines) are prayers and appeals to unspecified gods who are called "fatherly or motherly spirits" and "the virgin of Hades" (Ταρτάρου Κόρη). Among the supplicants appear Semitic names (Adam Zabatos), Roman names (Rusticus, Crispa), (Egyptian names (Thoargos, Aegyptos, Memnon) and many Greek names. Thus, one Panklus complains that Philonides and Xenodikos brought harm and illness upon him, causing him to lose his position in the house of Demetrios. Panklus entreats the god to make them dumb and sterile in retribution. In another inscription, the above-mentioned Adam Zabatos calls upon the god for help—he has been in prison for three years, and in the meantime his enemy Theon has had his property confiscated. In prison he suffers cruelty, he is chained and beaten continuously.

Chronology of the Strata. The Israelite stratum can be dated to the final years of the Judean Kingdom. Although on the basis of the finds the founding of the second, middle, stratum is difficult to date with certainty, nevertheless, judging from the Ptolemaic inscriptions—even when disregarding such external documents as the Zenon papyri—Marisa emerges as a very prominent center in the Early Hellenistic period. Albright and others have suggested that the city was destroyed by the Hasmonaeans, but this hypothesis is difficult to accept in the light of the numerous Hasmonaean coins discovered in the excavations. (A total of sixty-one coins were discovered: thirteen Ptolemaic, nineteen Seleucid, twenty-five from the time of John Hyrcanus (I or II), one Herodian, and two Greek coins of unclear provenance). We can accept this hypothesis only if we assume that the numerous coins bearing Hyrcanus' name are evidence of a Hasmonaean occupation force stationed in the city, and the absence of coins of

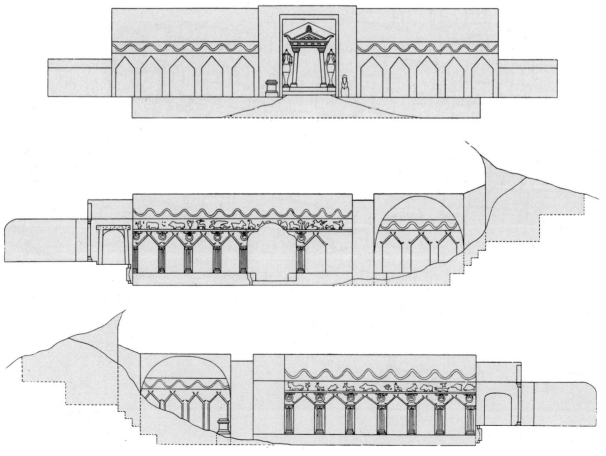

Alexander Jannaeus proves that the city was deserted in his time. The tomb inscriptions however clearly indicate that the Sidonian colony existed at the site at least until 103 B.C., i.e., some years after the Hasmonaean conquest, and up to the ascension of Jannaeus himself. Furthermore, it does not seem plausible that the upper city built by Gabinius in about 56 B.C. was destroyed in 40 B.C., since it is difficult to conceive that within only sixteen years such drastic changes could have been affected in the original Hippodamian plan. It seems more likely — also in the light of the discoveries at Samaria — that the settlement did not cease with the Hasmonaean conquest, but rather during the rule of this dynasty, the "orientalization" of the original layout of the Hellenistic city took place. If this is so, then the middle stratum should be attributed to the beginning of the Hellenistic period, and the city of the upper stratum is to be assigned to the Seleucid period (after the attacks of Judah Maccabeus?), when Idumaean–

Both pages, counterclockwise: Tomb 1. Sections; scene from Tomb 1; Tomb 1, looking east; Elephant and rhinoceros, from Tomb 1.

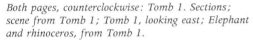

Sidonian Marisa was rebuilt. With the Hasmonaean conquest, the city took on a typically oriental character. Gabinius changed nothing except the government and the composition of the population, nor did he built anything, except perhaps the temple itself.

Tombs and Caves on the Outskirts of the Mound. During the excavations, sixty-three caves hewn in the rock of the slopes of the hill were investigated. These caves served as living quarters or as industrial installations (for wine- and oil-presses). In several caves were found columbaria, and among these, A-Suk, the largest remains of this type thus far found in the country. Many of the caves are bell-shaped. They are approached by steps, which in several cases have banisters, a feature unique to Marisa. Several of the caves were still in use in the Byzantine period, as is evident from the inscriptions and crosses painted on the walls. As early as the 1900 excavations, several shaft tombs were discovered — trough-shaped graves covered with stone slabs. In one of the shaft tombs was a figurine of Aphrodite, which was erroneously attributed to the Hellenistic period. The finds include bone and glass fragments, metal pins, cosmetic utensils, etc. On the basis of the finds, the tomb was dated to the third–fourth centuries A.D. The walls of one tomb are decorated with painted angels, peacocks, doves, clusters of grapes, and wreaths. This cave is dated to the Byzantine period.

In a survey conducted by the Israel Department of Antiquities, forty-five additional burial caves were partially excavated and examined, most of them of the loculus type.

The most important tombs in the vicinity of Marisa were discovered by grave robbers in 1902, after the completion of the excavations. On their discovery, religious fanatics from Beth-Govrin broke into the tombs and effaced some of the figures in the wall paintings. As soon as the incident became known, Petrie and Thiersch, who were in Jerusalem at that time, rushed to the site and with the assistance of the Dominican Fathers from the French School of Archaeology in Jerusalem, succeeded in copying (within three days) the paintings and inscriptions of two of the painted tombs (A and B) and of two other tombs (C and D), where the remains of drawings could no longer be distiguished clearly. The contents of these tombs found their way to the antique dealers of Jerusalem, and only a few were published. In 1925, the Dominicans excavated several more tombs (termed tombs E, F, and G in the series).

TOMB A is the largest (22 by 17.5 meters) and most richly decorated tomb. It consists of an entrance hall, an ornamented entrance, and a hallway from which the three burial chambers are entered. On the right side of the entrance to the middle burial chamber was the pedestal of a statue. To the left of the entrance stood an altar. There were fourteen loculi in the middle hall — seven on each side — with gable-shaped facades. Beneath them, two long benches run along the length of the wall. In the rear wall is a recess, flanked by pilasters, which served as a passage to another three burial rooms. In the north burial chamber, there are five loculi in the long walls and four in the short wall opposite the entrance. The south chamber has five loculi in the long walls and three in the short wall.

The main interest of the tomb is in its wall paintings and inscriptions. The recess in the middle burial chamber leading to the rear burial room is decorated with a triangular pediment similar to that of a Greek temple. The pediment is ornamented with a stylized leaf design, and below it runs a Doric frieze. The two pilasters flanking the entrance are painted red and have a rosette under the capital. On either side of the pilasters are tall black-painted amphorae, the one on the right surrounded by a white band, and that on the left by a red band. The amphorae are covered with lids painted in the same colors. Long wreaths stream

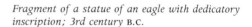

Fragment of a statue of an eagle with dedicatory inscription; 3rd century B.C.

from the lids. The amphorae resemble the urns used by the Greeks to hold the ashes of the dead. At the base of the recess are carved the legs of beds (cline). In front of the recess on either side of the pediment are two eagles with outspread wings standing on a wreath running the entire width of the wall. Under each eagle there is a yellow (gold) table standing on three lions' feet. On each table stands a white (silver) incense burner set on a base in the form of three griffons. The wreath on which the eagles are perched runs along the top of the tomb. Beneath the wreath, a continuous frieze of hunting scenes and animals extends from the southwestern corner to the opposite northwestern corner. The first figure in the hunting scene is a youth blowing a long trumpet. To his left is a rider whose horse has a beautifully decorated saddle, and below him, a running hunting dog. The rider is hurling a spear at a leopard already wounded and bleeding from a wound in its breast, where an arrow is stuck. Another hunting dog attacks the beast from the rear. Above the rider is written, "The rider's white horse," and above the hunted beast, the word "leopard" (ΠΑΡΔΑΛΟC). A (palm?) tree, painted black, separates the leopard from a lion with a mane, stalking to the left. Although the drawing is clearly of a lion, for some reason it is called "panther" in the inscription above it. The figure of the next animal was destroyed when one of the loculi was enlarged. To the left of the break is depicted a huge bull collapsed on bent forelegs, with blood running from its mouth. To the left of the bull a large snake is writhing. Behind the bull are a giraffe (called a "camel tiger" in the inscription) facing left and a boar, facing right. To the left, there is a griffin with a lion's body and eagle's head and wings. Facing in the same direction is a running deer with long horns curling at the ends, and a striped body, called ΟΡΥΞ. Again a tree similar to the previous one separates the deer from the red rhinoceros or hippopotamus ambling to the left, and above him is written "rhinoceros." To his left walks a war elephant, painted black, and equipped with a saddle for the mahout, and a canopy. The figure to the left of the elephant was destroyed, but above it is the inscription ΑΙΘΙΟΠΙΑ, Ethiopia, apparently the symbol of Africa. This terminates the frieze on the right side. Continuing on the opposite side are two fish, one with the trunk and nose of

an elephant, and the other with the head of a rhinoceros. Left of them is a red alligator, with an ibis (ΙΒΙΣ) perched on its back. Behind them are a hippopotamus (without inscription), a wild ass struggling with a snake, two unidentified animals (one similar to a field rat, and the other to a tapir with a horn on its snout), a porcupine, and a rat. At the end of the frieze stands a lion with a human face and beard. Beneath the frieze are drawings of laurel wreaths, tied with red ribbons, and below them, at the tops of the pilasters between the loculi are painted Ionic capitals. In the corridor above the altar is a drawing of a red cock, and near the entrance to the middle hall is an image of Cerberus. Thirty inscriptions and five graffiti, all in Greek, were found in the tomb. Above the entrance to the burial chamber to the right of the above-mentioned recess is the epitaph of Apollophanes, the son of Sesmios, who lived for seventy-four years and was the head of the Sidonian colony in Marisa for thirty-three years. Many members of his family are buried in this tomb. The names of the fathers are generally Semitic, while the names of the sons are Greek. The Idumaean names (Babas and names compounded with "Qos") attest to the assimilation of the Sidonian family to the population among whom they dwelled. The Greek names are evidence of gradual Hellenization. The dates found are according to the Seleucid era (from 196 to 119 B.C.), and the Hasmonaean or city's era(?) (from years 1 to 5). One inscription of three lines is either a poetic dialogue between a pair of lovers or a letter addressed to a lover. The interpretation of this dialogue has aroused much debate as to whether it is actually a poem or merely a letter. In another carved inscription, the priest Miron and a woman named Kalypso are mentioned. It is to this Kalypso that the "poem" is attributed.

TOMB B situated south of tomb A, is similar in plan, but smaller. From the hallway, one enters the central hall which has five loculi on each side. Behind it is another hall, from which seven burials branch off. In the hall north of the passageway, there are eight loculi or burial rooms. They had not yet managed to cut loculi in the sides of the southern hall. Above the loculi are painted garlands, and among them, round wreaths. Large amphorae, similar to those in tomb A, are painted on either side of the entrance to the central hall. On the pilasters between the central hall and the one behind it are depicted tall candelabra, with burning candles. Beside each candelabrum are two small figures. Near the door of the last burial room (XVII) is painted a man crowned with a wreath and wearing a striped tunic, who walks blowing a double flute. Behind him walks a woman wearing a multi-colored dress and playing a harp. On the other side is a libation sacrifice and, behind it, a tripod and cantharus. In tomb B twelve inscriptions were found dating from 188 to 135 B.C.

TOMBS C–F are small but built on similar plans.

The burial caves at Marisa are similar to caves

Below: Wall of the columbarium; bottom: Hellenistic jars near one of the columbaria.

found at Alexandria from the time of the Ptolemaic dynasty and also to the Phoenician burial caves of the Hellenistic period. However, the problem of the origin of this cave type requires further investigation. The paintings are characterized by a mixture of Semitic religious elements (the Syrian eagle) and Greek sepulchral elements (decorated jars, the flute and harp players, Cerberus, the cock). The animal frieze is undoubtedly influenced by the Ptolemaic menagerie drawings, which are known to have existed in Alexandria in the Hellenistic period. Under Aristotle's influence, there was much popular interest in the natural sciences at that time. From descriptions of the menagerie of Ptolemy II (according to Agatharkos) we know that it included lions, leopards, and other felines, rodents, buffaloes from India and Africa, a wild ass from Moab, large snakes, a giraffe, a rhinoceros, and various birds — these are in fact some of the very animals represented at Marisa. The griffin was a Persian legacy. The animal with the human face was a version of the Assyrian Lamassu (a fabulous creature with a lion's body, eagle's wings, and human face, statues of which guarded the palace entrances). The fishes with elephant face and rhinoceros face are taken from the legends based on the belief of Greek scholars that an exact correspondence existed between land and marine animals. Another example of this belief is provided by the Roman mosaic at Ostia. The Hellenistic "travel stories" are replete with descriptions of animals of this kind, which were found, they claimed, in remote corners of the earth. The animal frieze at Marisa is a unique document of its kind in the Hellenistic world. Only Roman mosaics show influences from the same Hellenistic-Egyptian sources from which the artist at Marisa drew his inspiration.

M. AVI-YONAH

LATER EXCAVATIONS

A columbarium cave 70 meters west of the wall of Marisa was excavated in 1972 under the direction of A. Kloner on behalf of the Department of Antiquities and Museums. The cave lies alongside an olive-press registered by R. A. S. Macalister as cave 21. The two caves belong to the lower town that extended around the Hellenistic mound.

The cave excavated in 1972 is square in shape, each side 9 meters long and 4 meters high. Approximately 200 niches were hewn out of the walls of the cave. They measured from 20 to 25 centimeters in height and depth.

The construction of the cave was accomplished in three phases. In the first stage, the cave was dug out through two openings in the ceiling. Doorways were then cut into two of the cave's walls, and steps were carved out of the rock to give access to these openings. In its final stage the cave was widened, and as a result the niches in one wall were destroyed. A passageway was hewn connecting the cave with the olive-press.

Some of the niches contained pottery, including bowls. In one niche four lamps were discovered. A large quantity of pottery, some of it in perfect or nearly perfect condition, as well as numerous sherds were found in debris piled up along the walls and in the center of the chamber. The pottery included local and imported types. Most of the vessels — the jars and cooking pots — were too large for the niches and were thus placed against the walls. The pottery found in the niches and in the fill of the room all dates to the Hellenistic period, from the third century B.C. to the middle of the first century B.C. The bones of goats, pigs, and sheep were also found.

Examination of the material in the bowls and in the niches as well as of soil samples established that the niches and the cave in general were used neither for cremations nor for the raising of doves.

A. KLONER

BIBLIOGRAPHY

Identification: Robinson, *Biblical Researches* 2, 67 • W. M. F. Petrie, *PEFQSt* 1890, 224 • F. J. Bliss, *ibid.*, 1900, 336 • Bliss–Macalister, *Excavations*, 67 ff.
Excavations: Bliss–Macalister, *Excavations*, 52–61, 67–68, 107, 124–34, 154–87 • Clermont–Ganneau, *RAO* 4, 152–58 • H. Thiersch, *Archäologischer Anzeiger* 1908, 392–413 • Watzinger, *DP* 2, 12 f. • W. F. Albright, *BASOR* 43 (1931), 12.
Tombs A–D: F. S. Bodenheimer, *The Fauna of Biblical Lands* 2, Jerusalem, 1937, 1–9 (Hebrew) • Bliss–Macalister, *Excavations*, 200, 209, 238–54 • J. P. Peters–H. Thiersch, *Painted Tombs in the Necropolis of Marissa*, London, 1905 • W. F. Albright, *BASOR* 85 (1942), 18–27 • Watzinger, *DP* 2, 17–20 • Goodenough, *Jewish Symbols* 1, 65–74.
Tombs E–G: W. J. Moulton, *AJA* 19 (1915), 63–70 • F. M. Abel, *RB* 34 (1925), 267–75.
1961–1963 Survey: E. Oren, *Archaeology* 18 (1965), 218–24.
Inscription in Tomb A: R. Ganszniec, *Bull. corr. hellén.* 48 (1924), 516–21 • H. Lamer, *ZDPV* 54 (1931), 59–67 • *Supp. epigr. gr.* 8 (1937), No. 244.
On the Origin of the Caves: Y. Ben-Arieh, *BIES* 23 (1959), 176–93; 24 (1960), 266–82 (Hebrew); *idem, IEJ* 12 (1962), 47–61.
Columbarium Cave: E. Oren, *PEQ* 101 (1968), 56–61 • A. Kloner, *Qadmoniot* 6 (1973), 113–15 (Hebrew).

MARWA

IDENTIFICATION AND EXCAVATIONS. A tomb of the Roman period, situated near the Arab village of Marwa (or Maru), 7 kilometers (4.5 miles) northeast of Irbid in Gilead. The tomb was excavated in 1935 by C. C. McCown and A. Bergman (Biran) on behalf of the Department of Antiquities of Transjordan. Other tombs, still unexplored, were found northeast of this tomb (among them some with wall paintings).

The facade of the tomb faces south. Five loculi of the *Kokhim* type had been cut into the north wall and six into the east wall of the burial chamber. An arcosolium was hewn out near the entrance, and beside it appears a painted Greek inscription. The arcosolium and its front wall are covered with plaster bearing paintings. The tomb had been rifled in the Byzantine period, and since little was found in it, it could not be clearly dated.

The importance of the tomb lies in its wall paintings. The colors employed by the artist included black, blue, red, dark and light brown, and gilded yellow. The figures of a man and a woman appear in the arcosolium, seated on folding stools and flanked by a Cerberus (the three-headed watchdog at the entrance to Hades) on the left, and a basket of fruit on the right. Above the man and woman, whose faces had been deliberately obliterated, the artist had drawn a garland of flowers. On the wall below the arcosolium are depicted three female masks, festooned in floral wreaths. The hair style and the cut of the man's beard may be assigned to the Severan period. The costume (chiton, himation) is Greek rather than Roman, while the loose hair style betrays Eastern influence. The artist had obviously intended to impart a divine character to the two principal figures by adorning their heads with a *kalathos* (a basket-shaped crown of wild-flying locks) and by placing a staff in the hand of the male figure and a torch (the symbol of Persephone) in the hand of the female figure. On the inscription, most of which is indistinct, the word πλούτων, the name of the god of the underworld, can still be read. This inclined the excavator to assume that the figures were meant to represent a deceased couple in the form of Pluto and Persephone who, as indicated in the inscription, dwelt in Hades. It is not clear to what school the drawings are to be ascribed, but the Greek influence is obvious. The excavator was of the opinion that this school was peculiar to Transjordan and that the tomb was to be assigned to the end of the second, or to the third century A.D.   S. APPELBAUM

BIBLIOGRAPHY

C. C. McCown, *QDAP* 9 (1939), 1–30.

Wall painting in the arcosolium.

MASADA

IDENTIFICATION. Masada is situated on the top of an isolated rock cliff, on the border between the Judean Desert and the Dead Sea Valley, about 25 kilometers (15.5 miles) south of En-Gedi. On the east the rock falls in a sheer drop of about 400 meters to the Dead Sea. Its western side is about 100 meters above the surroundings, and its northern side is 45 meters above the Mediterranean Sea. The cliff top is rhomboid shaped, measuring about 600 meters from north to south and 300 meters from east to west in the center. Its highest parts are in the north and west. Masada's natural approaches are difficult and comprise the White Rock on the west (the Leuce of Josephus), approaches on the southern and northern sides of the cliff and the Snake Path on the east.

The name "Masada" appears only in Greek transcription (Μασαδα). The name may be an Aramaic form of hameṣad, "the fortress."

HISTORY OF THE SITE

The only source that describes Masada is the writings of Josephus Flavius (*Jewish Antiquities* and *The Jewish War* — see bibliography). According to *War* VII, 285, the high priest Jonathan, built the first fortress at the site (Μηδάβων) and called it Masada. Some scholars consider this Jonathan to have been Alexander Jannaeus, but in another passage (*War* IV, 399), the foundation of Masada is attributed to "ancient kings." In 40 B.C., Herod fled from Matthias Antigonus and escaped to Rome. His family and his brother Joseph took refuge in Masada with eight hundred men to defend them (*Antiquities* XIV, 361–62, *War* I, 264, 267). During the siege by Antigonus, they escaped dying of thirst when a sudden rainfall filled the crevices and ponds on the summit. Herod, on his return from Rome, succeeded in rescuing them (*Antiquities* XIV, 390–91, 396, 400; *War* I, 286–87, 292, 294). According to *War* VII, 280 ff., "Herod furnished this fortress as a refuge for himself, suspecting a twofold danger: peril on the one hand from the Jewish people, lest they should depose him and restore their former dynasty to power; the greater and more serious from Cleopatra, queen of Egypt." Thus he probably began building the fortress between 73 and 31 B.C.

Although there is no information on Masada immediately after Herod's death, it seems probable that a Roman garrison was stationed there. At any rate, such was the case in A.D. 66, when the site was captured "by strategem" by Menahem, the son of Judah the Galilean (*War* II, 408, 433). After Menahem was murdered in Jerusalem, Eleazar son of Jair, son of Judah (i.e., Menahem's nephew), fled to Masada and was its "tyrant" until A.D. 73. During this time, Masada served as a refuge for the persecuted. Simeon the son of Giora also stayed there for a time. In A.D. 72, the Roman governor Flavius Silva marched against Masada with the Tenth Legion, its auxiliary troops, and thousands of Jewish prisoners of war. After Masada's conquest, Silva left a garrison at the site. Masada is also briefly mentioned by Pliny in *Natural History* V, XVII, 73.

HISTORY OF EXPLORATION

Masada was correctly identified for the first time with the rock es-Sebba in May, 1838, by the Americans, E. Robinson and E. Smith. They did not visit Masada themselves but viewed its northern cliff through a telescope from En-Gedi. Smith suggested identifying the site with Masada. Robinson believed that the building visible on the northern cliff was Herod's palace.

In 1842, the American missionary S. W. Wolcott and the English painter Tipping visited Masada and left amazingly accurate descriptions and drawings.

In April, 1848, an expedition sent by the American naval officer J. W. Lynch visited the site, anchoring off the Dead Sea coast. They were the first to identify the "holes" in the northwestern cliff as water reservoirs and noted the "square structure" (i.e., the lower terrace of the northern palace).

The Frenchman F. de Saulcy visited Masada in January, 1851. He dug in the Byzantine chapel, finding remains of its mosaic floor. He also drew the first plan of Masada and the Roman camps.

The Frenchman E. G. Rey visited Masada in January, 1858, and correctly attributed the mosaic remains from the upper terrace to Herod's palace.

A turning point in the exploration of Masada came with the British Survey of Western Palestine. For the first time, in 1867, C. Warren climbed Masada from the east, tracing out the Snake Path. After surveying the site in March, 1875, C. R. Conder published more accurate plans of the buildings and the Roman camps. It was Conder who first suggested identifying (erroneously) the western building with Herod's palace.

The first detailed study of the Roman camps was carried out by the German scholar, A. V. Domaszewski. In 1909, together with R. E. Brunnow, he published their studies in *Die Provincia Arabia*. Domaszewski mainly studied camps B and C. The German G. D. Sandel visited Masada in 1905. He noted the water reservoirs in the northern cliff and observed that they were fed by canals that collected rainwater from the wadis. In 1929, the Englishman C. Hawkes advanced the study of the Roman camps, which he examined with the aid of aerial photographs.

However, the principal turning point in the investigation of the site was made by the German, A. Schulten, who spent a whole month at Masada in 1932. His plans of the building and of the Roman camps laid the foundation for all later studies. Schulten, however, made some fundamental mistakes in his conclusions. He attempted, for example, to locate the Snake Path in the north, and concluded that the buildings on the three terraces in the north were fortifications connected with this path. He also agreed with Conder's mistaken proposal that Herod's palace, described by Josephus, should be identified with the western building.

The recent studies of Masada, which culminated in the excavation of the site, were carried out by enthusiastic Israeli scholars and amateurs, foremost among them S. Guttman. He traced the exact line of the Snake Path, and, together with A. Alon, examined Herod's water system (1953). Guttman also discovered and restored the gate of the Snake

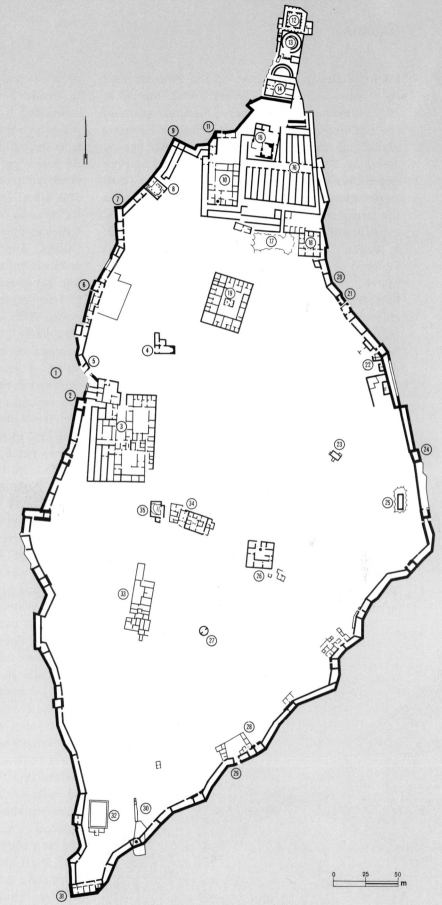

Opposite page: Aerial view, looking southeast. Silva's camp seen in right foreground; This page: General plan.
1. Top of ramp. 2. Tower 1276.
3. Western palace. 4. Byzantine church. 5. Western gate. 6. Tower 1028. 7. Casemate 1039. 8. Synagogue.
9. Tower 1049. 10. Building VII.
11. Water gate. 12. Northern palace, lower terrace. 13. Northern palace, Middle terrace. 14. Northern palace, upper terrace. 15. Large bathhouse.
16. Storerooms. 17. Quarry. 18. Building VIII. 19. Building IX. 20. Casemate 1102. 21. Snake path gate.
22. Zealot's living quarters. 23. Byzantine cave dwelling. 24. Tower 1133. 25. Open cistern. 26. Building XII. 27. Columbarium. 28. Miqve.
29. Southern gate. 30. Cistern.
31. Southern bastion. 32. Large pool.
33. Building XIII. 34. Building XI.
35. Miqve.

Path. He also partly excavated and reconstructed the Roman camp. A. M. Livneh and Z. Meshel in 1953 published the first nearly accurate plans of the buildings of the northern terraces, correctly identifying them with Herod's palace described by Josephus. As a result of these discoveries, survey expeditions were organized on behalf of the Israel Exploration Society, the Hebrew University, and the Department of Antiquities and Museums. One expedition directed by M. Avi-Yonah, N. Avigad, J. Aviram, Y. Aharoni, S. Guttman, and I. Dunayevsky, surveyed the site for ten days during March, 1956. These investigations confirmed the identification of the structures on the northern cliff with Herod's palace, and added to the information on the storehouses and "the western building." A new detailed map of Masada was also prepared.

THE MASADA EXCAVATIONS 1963–1965

Excavations were conducted at Masada under the direction of Y. Yadin from October, 1963, to April, 1964, and again from December, 1964 to March, 1965. The permanent staff members included D. Bahat, Malka Batyevsky, A. Ben-Tor, I. Dunayevsky, G. Foerster, S. Guttman, E. Menczel, and D. Ussishkin. In these excavations almost all of the built-up area of Masada was uncovered, and a trial sounding was made in camp F. The following account is based on the results of these excavations.

HERODIAN PERIOD

The Water System. Since Masada lacked any permanent source of water, one of Herod's first

Storeroom (locus 139), after reconstruction.

tasks was undoubtedly the construction of a system to ensure a supply of water. This system, also mentioned by Josephus, consisted of three components: a drainage system to carry the rainwater from the valleys in the west; a group of cisterns in the lower part of the northwestern slope; and another group of cisterns on the summit of the rock.

THE DRAINAGE SYSTEM carried rainwater from the Masada Valley in the south and the Ben-Jair Valley in the north. Dams were constructed in both valleys, and the water flowed through open channels built on a moderate slope into the cisterns. The aqueduct in the Masada Valley is very wide (1.4 meters) and supplied water to the upper row of pools. This well-plastered aqueduct is almost completely buried beneath the Roman camp, but sections of it are still visible near the Masada Valley. A vault, which carried the aqueduct above the ravine, was also preserved near the rock face. The second aqueduct conveyed the waters of the Ben-Jair Valley into the lower row of cisterns.

THE CISTERNS were cut into the slope of the rock in two parallel rows, with eight in the upper row and four in the lower. They were mostly square in shape. Each cistern had two openings: a lower one, at the level of the aqueduct, for the inflow of water and a slightly higher opening connected with steps for drawing out water. Each cistern could hold about 4,000 cubic meters, and their total capacity was about 40,000 cubic meters.

A winding path led from the upper row of cisterns to the Water Gate near the Northern Palace (see below). A number of large reservoirs was also cut into the summit of Masada, on the north, south, and east sides. Water was brought to these reservoirs along the winding path and the Snake Path by men or beasts of burden. In order to shorten the way, channels were constructed from the Water Gate and from the Snake Path to the main reservoirs on the summit. Water from the lower pools was poured into these channels, and it flowed into the reservoirs by force of gravity. In addition to these reservoirs, smaller cisterns were found in the various buildings (especially in the palaces), which supplied water independently of the reservoirs.

The Wall and Gates. Masada is enclosed on all sides by a casemate wall (except for the northern tip, see below, the palaces), whose circumference measures 1,400 meters, or 1,300 meters in a straight line, which corresponds exactly with the 7 stadia of Josephus' description. The wall is built of dolomite stones quarried from the cliff itself and only slightly cut. The stones were laid in two faces and the spaces between them filled with smaller stones. Both sides of the wall were covered with white plaster. The outer wall is 1.4 meters thick, and the inner wall 1 meter thick. The width of the casemates is about 4 meters (8 cubits in Josephus). The average width of the wall is thus some 6.5 meters. The length of the casemate rooms varies according to the terrain, the turns in the wall, etc. The longest casemates are on the average 35 meters long, the medium-sized 15 meters, and the shortest about 6 meters. Altogether there are seventy rooms, thirty towers, and four gates. The rock on which the wall was constructed was not leveled in most places, and the floors of the rooms were consequently uneven and full of pits and steps, some quite high. Since all the roofs were horizontal and 4 to 5 meters high, and the rock surface sloped in different directions, the top of the wall was not even but stepped.

The Towers were built at unequal distances from each other, according to the terrain and for tactical considerations. The shortest distance between them is 35 meters and the longest 90 meters. The towers are in fact small casemates, about 6 meters wide. Their inner walls were widened on the side facing the fortress, to form a kind of platform by which the tower could be ascended. Some of the towers also had stairs leading to the top. Each tower had at least one entrance, usually near the northern partition wall.

The Gates. The four gates from the time of Herod were all built on the same general plan: a square room with two entrances, one in the outer wall and one in the inner wall, and benches built along the walls.

THE SNAKE PATH GATE is situated in the northeastern sector. Its walls are coated on the inside with plaster and decorated with a panel design. The floor is paved with square, dressed stone slabs. A small casemate opening into the gate on the south side was probably a guardroom.

THE WESTERN GATE. Remains of this gate were found in the middle of the western wall. It too had benches along the walls. A path led to the gate from the west, and remains were found of the ramp on which the path was built.

THE SOUTHERN GATE (Cistern Gate). This gate was situated in the southeastern section of the wall, 150 meters northeast of the southern edge of the cliff. It led to a group of cisterns in the southeastern cliff and was a kind of inner gate and consequently not built with the same extravagance as the other gates, nor was it provided with benches.

THE NORTHERN GATE (Water Gate) was uncovered in the northwest corner of the wall. It was similar in plan to the Snake Path Gate. Its location near the large reservoirs north of the large bath-

The palace, built on three terraces on the edge of the northern cliff.

Bathhouse; view of the hypocaust and caldarium. Entrance to the tepidarium seen on the left.

house indicates that it was used mainly for bringing water from the upper row of cisterns along a special path whose remains are still visible (see above). This gate was apparently also the gate for the northern part of Masada. It was constructed in the second phase of Herodian building — after an earlier gate built north of it went out of use — inside a casemate north of the large square in front of the administrative building (building VII).

THE CANCELLED GATE. The remains of a paved gate were found north of the Water Gate near the western corner of the wall of the Northern Palace. This gate went out of use when a wall was built joining the casemate wall and the palace wall in the second phase of building (see below). It was the original entrance gate to Masada, and through it water was brought up. Its entrance was north of building VII, and it served as the gate between the northern complex and the rest of Masada. In the later building phase, it was replaced by a gate constructed to its south.

INNER GATES. Three other gates were found near building VII and the Water Gate. They belonged to the internal organization of Masada, centered on the large square north of building VII.

The gate east of the Water Gate was intended to block the entrance to the Northern Palace, the large bathhouse, and the storehouses. The gate adjoining the northwest corner of building VII served in the Herodian period as the entrance to the special storerooms attached to building VII. A third gate situated west of the early gate was the main passage between the northern complex and the rest of Masada. These three inner gates belong to the second phase of Herodian building.

Storehouses. The storehouses for food and weapons are of two types: public storehouses and storehouses attached to special buildings (palaces and administrative buildings).

PUBLIC STOREHOUSES. This complex of storehouses stands in the northern complex, south of the Northern Palace (buildings V and VI). It is subdivided into two blocks: the northern block (V) consisting of long storerooms (20 by 3.8 meters) and a right-angled corridor, which is a kind of double storeroom. Each room has a single entrance in the south, except for the eastern storeroom, which also has an opening on the east leading to a casemate storeroom. The floors and ceilings of the storerooms are plastered with clay.

This block of storehouses was erected after the building of the large bathhouse had started, and its western wall almost touched the wall of the bathhouse (see below). The southern block (VI) is larger and consists of eleven elongated storerooms (27 by 4 meters) with entrances in the northern end.

Oil, wine, flour, etc., were each stored in a separate room in special jars. The fifth storeroom from the west was completely plastered with hydraulic mortar, and in its floor three plastered pits were set at equal distance, apparently to facilitate the pouring of liquids from one jar to another. In the northern end of the second storeroom from the west were two rows of small depressions, apparently to hold the jars upright. The two blocks of storehouses were separated by a corridor running from east to west and forming the northern branch of the corridor surrounding the main block of storehouses on the west, south, and east.

STOREHOUSES ATTACHED TO BUILDINGS. Three storehouses were constructed west and south of building VII (see below): a long storeroom on the west side of the building and two smaller storerooms south of it. Special commodities were apparently stored here, since they were entered through a separate gate — the above-mentioned inner gate adjoining the northwestern corner of building VII. Two more storehouses running from east to west were situated south of the southern block of storehouses. These groups of storehouses were apparently constructed in the second phase of building, to increase the capacity of the existing storehouses, and especially for costly articles or objects of special importance (weapons?).

The Palaces consists of four groups: 1. the palace-villa (Northern Palace); 2. the ceremonial and administrative palace (Western Palace); 3. three small palaces near the Western Palace, which probably housed the royal family; 4. elaborate buildings resembling the small palaces, adjoining the Western Palace and the blocks of storehouses, which were possibly residences for high officials and administrative centers.

The Northern Palace-Villa was built in three tiers on the northern edge of the cliff. This is the palace of which Josephus gives a detailed description. The upper tier contained only living quarters, the other two tiers being taken up by luxurious structures intended for entertainment and relaxation.

THE UPPER TERRACE consists of two main parts: 1. a semicircular balcony bounded by two concentric walls, on which probably stood two rows of columns; 2. living quarters south of the balcony, consisting of two rooms on the east and west sides of an open court. Their walls were decorated with paintings in geometric and floral designs and the floor was paved with black-and-white mosaic with hexagons, overlapping circles, and rectangles.

The inner sides of the court were covered by a roof supported by columns parallel to the walls. The columns on the upper terrace were of the Ionic order, and many were discovered nearby. The entrance to this terrace — the main entrance to the palace — is situated on the east side. Entry was through an open square in front of the southern wall of the terrace, up an impressive staircase leading east–west to an open area in the east end of the square. This open area was built above two storerooms roofed by a barrel-shaped vault. From here one passed through a doorway (with a bench next to it) into a narrow trapezoid-shaped entrance hall, bounded by the east wall of the living quarters and the casemate wall. Another doorway opened onto a small square entrance and led west to a corridor separating the balcony from the living quarters. Two stages of building were distinguished in the entrance complex. In the first stage, the entrance was approached by a rock-cut staircase. In the second stage a sloping wall replaced the staircases and the entrance was as described above. In this stage, the small bathhouse on the eastern cliff of the upper terrace went out of use. Both stages belong to the Herodian period.

THE MIDDLE TERRACE approximately 20 meters beneath the upper one, contains a circular building and a complex of buildings south of it.

THE CIRCULAR BUILDING. Of this structure the foundations of two concentric circular walls have survived. The outer wall has a diameter of 15.3 meters and the inner wall 10 meters. The top of these walls is covered with rectangular sandstone slabs. A building had stood on these foundations, but nothing of it has been preserved. In the empty space between the two walls lay collapsed stones, including carved stones such as capitals and column drums. The circular structure was a kind of tholos with two rows of columns supporting the roof. The foundations of the walls were based on the uneven surface of the bedrock, and the rock descended toward the north. The walls are consequently higher in the northern part of the terrace. The empty space between the concentric walls was intended to decrease the pressure on the outer wall, built at the edge of the cliff.

THE SOUTHERN COMPLEX, to the south of the circular building, consists of three parts: a staircase in the west, a large hall in the east, and a roofed space in the center.

THE STAIRCASE. The lower part of the staircase was made of stone around a built pillar, and the upper part was made of wood. The staircase, which connected the middle and upper terraces, was hidden from view from the outside.

THE EASTERN HALL was decorated with wall paintings imitating marble paneling.

THE MIDDLE SPACE between the staircase and the eastern hall was open on the north side. Its roof was supported by several square pilasters built against the southern rock and the walls of two other rooms.

This complex served for entertainment and relaxation. Its ornamental style is characteristic of Late Hellenistic buildings.

THE LOWER TERRACE is about 15 meters beneath the middle terrace and 35 meters below the upper one. Its buildings were erected on a raised square area (17.6 by 17.6 meters), built at the edge of the cliff by means of supporting walls. In the center of the area was a square area surrounded by porticoes. The inner wall consists of columns, with windows cut between them. These columns are in fact two half-columns, the inner ones standing on high pedestals and the outer ones standing on the floor. The outer sides of the porticoes were also colonnaded, apart from the southern wall, the rock face, which was plastered and half-columns were attached to it. All the columns are made of sandstone, plastered and fluted drums. The capitals were in Corinthian style and coated with gold paint. The lower parts of the porticoes were decorated with wall paintings in panels and rhombuses. An empty space was left between the foundations of the western portico to lessen the pressure on the outer wall. The floor of the portico was of wood. The walls of the central area were also decorated with frescoes on the lower part. It can thus be assumed that at least the sides were

roofed to protect the wall paintings, but it is doubtful whether the whole central area was roofed over. The entrance to the central area was through the southern portico.

A SMALL BATHHOUSE situated east of the square structure was reached by descending a built staircase. The bathhouse contained a cold room (frigidarium) with steps plastered with hydraulic mortar, a corridor-like warm room (tepidarium), and a hot room (caldarium) built above the heating chamber (hypocaust). The floor of the caldarium rested on small round columns made of mud bricks. The floor of the bathhouse was partly paved with white mosaic.

A STAIRCASE at the western edge of the cliff led down from the middle tier to the lower one. Like the middle terrace, the buildings of this level were also intended for pleasure.

The Western Palace (IX–X) is the largest residential building at Masada. Its total area is almost 4,000 square meters. The building is situated near the wall in the middle of the western side, a little south of the Western Gate. The excavations showed that this was the main administrative and

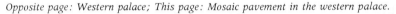

Opposite page: Western palace; This page: Mosaic pavement in the western palace.

Below: Limestone "measuring" cups.
Bottom: Shekel coins, in situ.

ceremonial palace. The palace consists of four blocks of buildings: the royal apartments (in the southeast); the service wing and workshops (in the northeast); the storerooms (in the southwest); and the administrative wing and residence of the palace officials (in the northwest).

The main entrance to the palace was in the north. The gate in the middle of the north side led to a long and wide corridor, which in turn gave access through additional gates similar in plan to the other gates at Masada, to the service and administrative wings and also to the royal apartments.

THE ROYAL APARTMENTS. This wing was built around a large central court. In the middle of the southern part of the court was a roofed hall, with 2 Ionic columns in its north side open to the court. The walls of the hall were decorated with white plaster in panels. Three entrances in the hall led into the throne room in the southeast corner of the wing. In the plastered floor in the southeast corner of the room were four depressions, which probably held the legs of a throne or a canopy. On the west side of the court were the bedrooms and dining rooms. Another hall, which also led to the throne room, occupied almost the entire length of the eastern side of the block. This hall could also be entered through a rear entrance on the east. Two columns stood on its north side, which was the south end of a small court. On the floor of the hall was a magnificent richly colored mosaic whose design consisted of a central medallion with intersecting circles and a border containing geometric and plant designs (grape and fig leaves and pomegranates). A corridor and official rooms separated the hall and the throne room. The service rooms of the palace were situated north of the court. In the northeast corner of the wing was the bathhouse of the residency. It consisted of a caldarium with bathtubs (heated through a rear room), an immersion pool with cold water, and other installations. All the floors of the bathhouse were paved with mosaics, and even the corridor contained a multi-colored mosaic in geometric design.

Parts of this wing had several stories (particularly the service wing), reached by three staircases: one near the eastern entrance, another inside the mosaic hall, and a third in a separate room north of the large courtyard.

THE SERVICE WING AND WORKSHOPS were also built around a large court. On its north side were several dwelling units composed of an open court and two rooms, similar to building IX (see below). The other sides of the wing were occupied by workshops and other service rooms.

THE STOREROOM WING consists of one very long storeroom (about 70 meters long) on the extreme west and three smaller storerooms between it and the palace proper. Special doorways in the palace led into the storerooms, but there were also outer entrances (mainly on the south), through which the storerooms were stocked. Another row of storerooms abutted the southern wall of the royal apartments. All these storerooms, as well as a few units near the eastern entrance and and the administrative wing in the northwest, belong to the second building stage of the palace (see below).

THE ADMINISTRATIVE WING AND RESIDENCE OF THE PALACE OFFICIALS is situated in the northwestern corner of the Western Palace. It is composed of three blocks of building. The northernmost building was particularly elaborate, resembling the small palaces (see below) and the building on the southeast side of the public storehouses.

The Small Palaces. Three small palaces (buildings XI, XII, XIII) stood in close proximity southeast of the Western Palace. They were built on the plan of the royal apartments in the Western Palace (especially buildings XI and XII), with a central court and a hall with two columns in its southern part. The hall leads to a large room in the southeast corner. This room could also be reached from the east, through a corridor and a special waiting room.

The small palaces (and another building near the public storehouses and two buildings northwest of the Western Palace) were constructed on a roughly similar plan. They were most probably used by palace officials.

Building VII is situated west of the southern block of public storehouses. It consists of a central court surrounded on all sides by a row of rooms, with an additional row on the south side. The main entrance was from the north, from the square south of the Water Gate. Storerooms were attached to the building on the east and south. These probably held special goods (weapons, choice wine, etc.), as is indicated by the fact that they were reached by a separate entrance.

Building IX, situated south of building VII on a small hill, differs in plan from the other buildings at Masada. It consists of a row of dwelling units around a central court. Each unit contains an open court and two small rooms. In all, there were nine dwelling units, three on each side of the building with the exception of the eastern side, which contained the main entrance and two large halls. Square halls with their roofs supported by four columns in their center were found in the southwest and northwest corners. This building probably served as the barracks for officers of the guard.

The Bathhouse. In addition to the bathhouses in the palaces, Herod built a large and magnificent bathhouse in the northern complex of Masada, south of the upper terrace of the Northern Palace and west of the northern strorehouses. The bathhouse consists of four rooms and a large open court entered from the northeast corner of the building. The court had a kind of square exedra on the north side and a small pool with plastered steps beside it. The open court had roofed-over porticoes on the west, north, and east sides. Their capitals were of Nabataean style. The entire floor of the court was paved with mosaics similar to those in the upper terrace of the Northern Palace. The mosaics in the three porticoes are surrounded by a black rectangular border. In the center of the court the mosaic is laid in three nearly square carpets. It was decorated with black and white triangles in the middle carpet and beehive-shaped hexagons in the flanking carpets. All the designs are in black. In the center of each of the three carpets was a square medallion with a richly colored design, which has not been preserved. The lower part of the walls of the porticoes were decorated with painting of panels and rhombuses. THE ENTRANCE ROOM (apodyterium) is situated in the northwest side of the bathhouse. Its walls were decorated with paintings of panels, and the ceiling with geometric and plant designs, as is evidenced by the plaster fragments found on the floor. The floor was originally paved with a black-and-white mosaic which was replaced in its second phase by a pavement with alternating black-and-white triangular tiles.
THE WARM ROOM (TEPIDARIUM) was entered through a doorway in the south wall of the apodyterium. Its walls, too, were decorated with

paintings of panels, and its floor also was originally paved with mosaics and in the second phase with black-and-white square and triangular tiles. The black triangles were laid with their bases tangent to the white squares, and the white triangles were laid against the black squares.
THE COLD ROOM (FRIGIDARIUM) occupied the northwest corner of the bathhouse and was entered through the warm room. It is in fact a stepped pool, which was plastered with hydraulic mortar. In the early phase, the pool could be filled through two small openings.
THE HOT ROOM (CALDARIUM), HEATING CHAMBER (HYPOCAUST) AND FURNACE (PRAEFURNIUM). The caldarium was the largest room in the bathhouse, extending over nearly half the area of its east side. Its walls are especially thick and contain two recesses: an apse in the north wall and a rectangular niche in the south wall. The apse had originally contained a round flat basin *(labrum)*, made of quartz, fragments of which were found. The water for this basin came from outside the building through a lead pipe. In the opposite rectangular niche, there was a bathtub *(balneum)*. The floor of the caldarium was laid on small columns of the hypocaust (the heating chamber). Some two hundred columns about 65 centimeters high were found, most made of round clay bricks, and some of stone. All the walls of the hypocaust and caldarium were faced with vertical rows of rectangular clay pipes made in segments. These segments were perforated on their narrow sides so that the hot air also flowed sideways. As in the other rooms, the floor of the caldarium was also originally paved with mosaics, and in a later stage laid with black-and-white slabs, arranged in a pattern resembling that of the warm room, but with larger slabs (30 by 30 centimeters). To the east of this room was the furnace *(praefurnium)*.
THE SWIMMING POOL, cut out of rock, was found southeast of the Western Palace, near the small palace XI. It has wide plastered steps and was entered from the east through a long wide corridor. In the wall of the corridor and in the south and west walls of the upper part of the pool were niches where clothes could be left.
The Columbarium. In the southern part of the summit was a circular building (7.5 meters in diameter), which had no doorways and was divided into two parts by a wall with an opening.

The building was in Herodian style, and its outer face was well plastered. Small niches (about 16 centimeters wide, high, and deep) are set in horizontal rows in the inner face and on both faces of the dividing wall. Each row had about eighty niches, six rows out of a possible ten being preserved. In the excavator's opinion, this building received the urns containing the ashes of cremations of the gentile garrison force.

Pottery and Other Finds. The numerous sherds found in the fill of the Herodian floors and their comparison with vessels from the buildings themselves made it possible to identify the Herodian pottery, including terra sigillata ware, Augustan lamps, elongated and pointed amphorae, and others. Many amphorae for storing wine were dated the year of the consul C. Sentius Saturninus, i. e., 19 B.C. and were inscribed with their destination — to Herod, king of Judea.

SUMMARY OF THE HERODIAN PERIOD

The results of the excavations have established that the original buildings on Masada were erected by Herod. No structure from an earlier period has yet been definitely identified. Herod's buildings were found to have been constructed over a long period of time, and this is attested by the change in

Miqve in southern wall.

plans, mainly in two stages of planning, during the construction itself and later.

During the first building stage the upper and lower water systems were cut in the rock, and the original Water Gate was constructed. The main palaces, the large bathhouse, and a large part of the storehouses also belong to this stage. In the second stage of construction, most of the wall was erected, and the main block of storehouses and the storerooms near the palaces were enlarged, and the other public buildings were constructed. After the completion of the wall, several changes were introduced in the layout of the gates, especially in the northern complex, which was completely isolated to keep it out of bounds for those entering Masada through the new Water Gate or the Western and Eastern Gates.

BETWEEN HEROD AND THE REVOLT

A Roman garrison was stationed at Masada between the period of Herod and the Revolt (A.D. 66–73). The clearest evidence from this period are the numerous coins of the Herodian dynasty and the Procurators, and several pottery vessels with Latin inscriptions. It seems likely that some of the changes and additions made in the public buildings were carried out during this period.

THE PERIOD OF THE REVOLT (A.D. 66–73)

A great number of finds from the period of the Revolt were uncovered in the excavations. They will be described here in context with the Herodian buildings used during the Revolt and the dwellings built by the Zealots, the public buildings erected

Plan of the synagogue in its two phases.

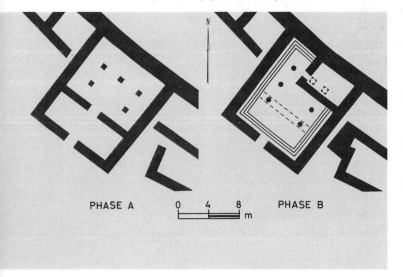

PHASE A   0   4   8   PHASE B
m

by the Zealots and their contents, and the evidence for the fall of Masada in A.D. 73.

The Herodian Buildings During the Revolt. The Herodian buildings—the many sumptuous palaces and the small number of living quarters—were not very suitable dwellings for the Zealots and their families. Most of the buildings (except for the storehouses) were adapted as dwellings, command posts, etc. The ornamental architectural parts, such as the capitals and column drums, were employed in the Zealots' dwellings as building material, fill, and also as benches, tables, and other furniture. The Zealots were especially in need of planks and other wood that had been used in building or adorning the Herodian structures. Many of the floors were dismantled to be used as building material in the Zealots' quarters.

THE NORTHERN PALACE. Because of its location and layout, the northern villa-palace could not be adapted as normal living quarters or as a public building. Its importance during the Revolt was in its strategic defensive position and for control of the sources of water. Capitals and drums from the three tiers of the palace were found reused in various parts of the Zealots' quarters. Many of the architectural parts, the wooden floors and ceilings, were removed. The Zealots used only the living quarters of the upper terrace of the palace, and this without the decorative architectural details. This part was probably used for the administration of the northern complex. A large heap of burned arrowheads uncovered in the middle terrace may indicate that it served as a defense post. Many finds from the last stage of the Revolt were discovered on the lower terrace. It was covered by a thick burned layer, which contained several coins of the Revolt, as well as a large quantity of olive and date pits, and other food remains. Beneath the collapsed debris covering the small bathhouse on the east were found the remains of three skeletons, a man, woman, and child. Near them lay an ostracon inscribed in Aramaic, fragments of a *tallith* (prayer shawl), hundreds of silvered scales of armor of copper, and scores of arrows. The woman's scalp complete with braids and sandals lay beside her. These appear to be the remains of one of the commanders of the Revolt and his family.

THE WESTERN PALACE. The absence here of cooking ovens, wall partitions, and other domestic installations indicate that this building was not used for normal dwelling purposes. It seems to have been used as general administrative offices. In the large mosaic hall were found hundreds of burned arrows and scores of coins dating to the Revolt. There were also a few ostraca, some apparently inscribed with the names of priests. A thick conflagration layer covered most of the palace, especially the throne room.

THE SMALL PALACES (buildings VIII, XI, XII, XIII), were adapted as dwellings for a large number of families. Remains of ovens were found in most of the rooms, their soot covering part of the wall paintings. Partition walls were constructed by the Zealots, dividing large rooms or courts into several smaller living units. Many rooms showed signs of fire and in the layer of ashes were found household goods together with shekels and other coins dating to the Revolt. Signs of burning were generally found in one of the main rooms, where the furniture and family property were apparently gathered together and deliberately set on fire.

BUILDING XI was suitable for dwelling even during the Revolt. Families inhabited all the living units as well as the large central court. Several wealthy families were among these, as indicated by remains of luxury vessels (of alabaster and gold), found in the rooms. Two hoards of shekel and half-shekel coins were discovered in rooms in the northwest. One hoard, hidden beneath the floor in a cloth bag, included nine shekels (of the Years One, Two, and Three of the Revolt) and twenty-eight half-shekels (of the Years One, Two, and Three). The second hoard, discovered nearby in an unusual bronze jug (a sort of chest) contained six shekels and six half-shekels (of the Years One, Two, and Three). Several special washing installations, which were connected with the large swimming pool, were added to the building.

BUILDING VII was also inhabited by a large number of families. Several rooms showed many traces of fire, in which were fragments of glass vessels, food remains (large piles of dates), and weapons. Many changes were made in the building during this stage, mainly to provide ritual baths and other bathing pools.

THE STOREHOUSES continued in their original use. A few rooms, completely destroyed by fire, contained hundreds of smashed store jars for food, all of one type in a separate room. Several other rooms, on the other hand, were totally empty and showed no signs of fire. It can thus be assumed that most of the storerooms containing food were burned, and only a few were left undamaged, to prove perhaps, as related by Josephus, that the reason the defenders died was not lack of food.

Many of the vessels in the storehouses belonged to the Herodian period, as is shown by the Latin and Greek inscriptions on them. The new owners, however, are indicated by the Hebrew and Aramaic inscription (mostly names), written on the jars in ink and charcoal. Scores of bronze coins from the Revolt were found scattered in a layer of ash on the floor of one of the storerooms. A group of special jars for wine and oil bore the Hebrew letter ת, perhaps indicating that these vessels were intended for priestly dues and tithes. Hundreds of ostraca found near the storehouses and inscribed with single letters (see below) were most likely used for some system of food rationing. In the large storehouses of the Western Palace (especially in the long one) was a thick layer of ashes containing hundreds of smashed store jars. In these storerooms special goods, such as fig cakes, were kept as is attested by Hebrew inscriptions on the vessels: "pressed figs," "crushed pressed figs," and "dried figs."

THE BATHHOUSES. All the bathhouses and bathing pools continued to be used during the Revolt, but alterations were carried out in some of the buildings, especially in the large bathhouse. Immersion and bathing pools were added as well

Aerial view of the synagogue and adjoining casemate wall.

as *miqves* (see below). Small bathhouses in the form of stepped bathing pools were installed in some of the buildings.

THE WALL. All the rooms of the casemate wall and the towers were used as living quarters by the Zealots and their families. While the small rooms were inhabited by a single family, the large rooms were partitioned to form several living units. In many cases, rooms or courts were added to the casemates. Many of the domestic utensils of the Zealots were found in the rooms of the wall: clothes, leather articles, baskets, vessels of glass, stone, and bronze, etc. In contrast to the public buildings, most of which had been razed by fire, few of the dwellings in the wall and its surroundings were burned, and their contents were found strewn on the floor, on ovens, and other cooking installations, and in niche-cupboards in the walls. Piles of charcoal with remains of various articles were found in the corners of some of the unburned rooms, indicating that the families had collected their personal belongings and set fire to them. Hundreds of coins of the Revolt were discovered in the rooms of the wall, and among them a hoard of seventeen silver shekels found in locus 1039 (three of them shekels of the Year Five) and a number of fragments of biblical and sectarian scrolls (see below). The towers served mainly as public rooms or workshops, such as tanneries and bakeries. In one of the towers some 350 bronze coins of the Revolt lay scattered next to a cooking stove.

THE TRANSIT CAMP. In order to solve the problem of housing, the Zealots also built several groups of huts. These were wretched dwellings of mud and small stones. They were mainly concentrated around the Herodian structures (buildings XI, XII, XIII, IX), adjacent to the wall, and in open areas in the southern part of the summit. Some of these huts (called "transit camps" by the excavators) were probably built during the last stages of the Revolt, when there was an influx of fugitive families. Most of the coins from the Year Four of the Revolt came from these huts.

Religious Buildings. Apart from the transit camps, the only other structures built by the Zealots were for religious purposes: *miqves*, a *beth midrash*? (school), and a synagogue.

THE MIQVES (ritual baths). Two *miqves* were found, one on each end of the summit, built accord-

ing to halakhic law: namely, part of their water was supplied by rainwater flowing directly into it and not pumped. The southern *miqve* was built inside and adjoining a casemate (room 1197 near tower 1196). It consists of three pools coated with gray water-proof plaster. The larger pool has three steps. It stored the rainwater collected from the roof and surroundings through a conduit. Between the conduit and the pool was a sump, in which the sediment settled. The second pool, for immersion, is smaller and has two steps. The two pools are connected by a hole, two fingers wide. A third, smaller pool served for the actual washing before immersion. Outside the casemate were several other rooms connected with the *miqve* such as dressing rooms, etc. One room contained rows of small niches in the walls where the bathers left their clothes. In front of the *miqve* was an entrance hall with benches whose roof was supported by columns made from drums and capitals taken from Herodian structures.

The northern *miqve* was built in the east side of the central court of building VII. Three pools with a drainage system were situated in the northeast corner, with the dressing room, etc. — mostly destroyed — in the southeast corner.

THE BETH MIDRASH? (SCHOOL). Palace XIII housed a large number of families during the Revolt. Many huts were built onto it, to form a kind of self-contained block. In the north part of this block was an elongated hall with a bench extending around three of the walls. A bench or narrow table stood lengthwise in the center of the room. This hall (built in a north–south direction) was clearly of a public character, and may very likely have been a *beth midrash*.

THE SYNAGOGUE is situated in the northwest section of the casemate wall, west of building VII. During the period of the Revolt, it was rectangular in plan (internal measurements 12.5 by 10.5 meters) and built in a northwest direction, i.e., facing Jerusalem. The entrance was in the middle of the southeast side. A room (3.6 by 5.5 meters) in the northwest corner was covered with a thick layer of ashes, containing fragments of glass and bronze vessels. Four tiers of mud-plastered benches extended along all the walls of the building, except for the wall of the room in the northwest corner, which had only one bench. The benches were made out of building remains, including broken capitals taken from the lower terrace of the Northern Palace. The building has two rows of columns, with three columns in the south row and two columns in the north row. Scores of lamps of Herodian type were uncovered in a corner of the building. An ostracon inscribed *ma'aser kohen* ("Priest's tithe") was found in another corner. Beneath the floor in one corner were discovered fragments of two scrolls, hidden in pits dug into the upper floor, and then refilled with dirt and pebbles. The scroll in the northern pit contained parts of Deuteronomy and the scroll in the southern pit contained parts of Ezekiel. The building in this form was erected in the period of the Revolt, and it can be stated with certainty that it was a synagogue. The bench facing Jerusalem was probably reserved for the elders, who sat with their faces toward the congregation. This is the earliest known synagogue and the only one preserved from the Second Temple period.

Test pits and cross sections made beneath the floor of the synagogue revealed an earlier stage of construction (from the time of Herod). It was built on a different plan. There was no corner room, and an entrance room extended along the facade on the eastern side. Columns ran along the west, north, and south walls, five in all. It is possible that this early building also served as a synagogue, for not only is it oriented toward Jerusalem, but the arrangement of the columns has a certain resemblance to that in early synagogues in the Galilee. The Zealots enlarged the building and built benches along the walls and the northwest room, in which the Scriptures were kept. To carry out these alterations in the building, they removed the wall between the entrance room and the hall, and also the two columns in the northwest corner. These were placed on the foundations of the old dividing wall between the hall and the entrance room.

North of the synagogue was a plastered water pool built during the period of the Revolt, perhaps for the use of the synagogue. Two casemates, north of the synagogue, were covered with thick conflagration layers containing the remains of wooden furniture, shekels, and fragments of scrolls. Scrolls were also found in another casemate (1039) situated several meters from the synagogue.

ZEALOT REMAINS

In addition to the three skeletons found in the lower terrace of the Northern Palace, a large heap of skeletons was found in a small cave a few meters below the wall in the southern cliff. It contained twenty-five skeletons, fourteen of men, six of women, four of children, and one of an

Cosmetic utensils found in zealots' dwellings; kohl spoons, lid of a mirror, comb and perfume flasks.

embryo. Remains of clothing were among the skeletons. Although it is difficult to establish whether these skeletons are of the defenders of Masada during the Revolt, it seems a reasonable assumption. Most of the skulls are of the type found in the Nahal Hever caves, and so can be assumed to be Jewish.

THE FINDS

Coins. Many bronze coins of the Revolt were found on the floors of the dwellings and the public buildings, some in large hoards (of 350, 200, and 100 coins) either scattered in a very small area or thrown in a heap in disorder. The most common coins are the usual bronze *prutah*. However, several scores of rare coins dating to the Year Four of the Revolt were also found. These coins were found mainly in dwelling huts and in the southern part of the summit. It can be assumed that they were brought to Masada by groups who joined the defenders of Masada during the last year before the fall of Jerusalem or soon after. The coin finds include thirty-seven shekels and thirty-five half-shekels in the three large hoards, and other finds of groups of two or three, or single coins. The following chart shows the distribution of the coins of the Revolt according to the year of their minting:

Above: Ostracon–"tag", inscribed on top row Yehoḥanan; Below: Ostraca; Bottom: Fragment of the Psalms Scroll (verses 85:1 ff.)

Total		ONE	TWO	THREE	FOUR	FIVE	UNIDENTIFIED
				Year			
Shekels	37	3	20	3	2	3	6
Half-Shekels	35	7	15	11			2

Among the coins of the Revolt were some tens of coins from the period of the Procurators.

The Ostraca. More than seven hundred ostraca of various kinds were discovered (including inscriptions on jars). Most of them are written in Hebrew or in Aramaic, with some also in Greek or Latin. The Hebrew and Aramaic inscriptions are also important for paleographic research, for their date can be set exactly between A.D. 66 and 73. The ostraca also add to our knowledge of the social organization of Masada and the national and religious character of the defenders.

1. TAGS WITH LETTERS. About half of the ostraca found are a kind of tag with single or a combination of several letters. Most of them were discovered near the storehouses, and they seem to have been connected with the food-rationing system of the Zealots during the siege.

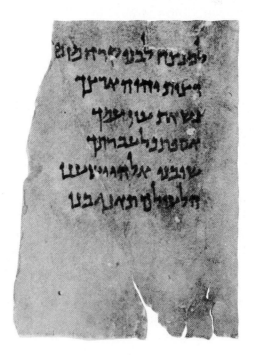

2. TAGS WITH NAME FORMULAS. This group consists of some tens of tags inscribed with one of the following three inscriptions:

1. Yehoḥanan, an *alpha*, and a *yod* in Paleo-Hebrew script; 2. Yehudah, a *beta* written right to left, and the letter *samekh* in Paleo-Hebrew script; 3. Simeon with a *gimel* in regular script, and a *daleth* in Paleo-Hebrew script. Most of these were found near the storehouses, either scattered or in groups of the same type. Twelve tags with the Simeon formula, for example, were found in a group near the southern storeroom of building VII. Perhaps these were special vouchers bearing the names of units or commanders, or the names of those in charge of the priests' dues and tithes, etc.

3. TAGS WITH SINGLE NAMES were found in various places, usually alone. Only one name is inscribed on these ostraca, of a male or a female, as for example, "daughter of Demaly," "daughter of Karta," "son of Karzela," "son of Hata," "Atat Jacob," etc. A special group discovered in one of the rooms of the Western Palace may be inscribed with the names of priests, Yo'ezer, Yosh'ayah, Hezekiah, Dostas. These tags may have designated ownership by priests or Levites of objects or food, or they may have served as "lots."

4. LISTS OF NAMES. Four large ostraca were found in various places on the surface of Masada inscribed from top to bottom with names and a number beside each name, as for example, "son of Yeshua 21." These seem to have been administrative or military lists.

5. "LOTS". In locus 113, beside the inner gates commanding the entrance to the storehouses, the Water Gate, etc., were discovered a strange group of eleven small ostraca (and a twelfth ostracon which was left incomplete due to a defect in the sherd). They are all written in the same handwriting, and each one was inscribed with a single name. The names appear to be nicknames: Benanatam, Haemeky, Benafty, Zida, Malta, Grida, Joab. The sherd inscribed Ben-Jair is of special interest, apparently being that of Eleazar ben-Jair. These ostraca may be the "lots" mentioned by Josephus: "they made the same rule for casting lots for themselves, that he whose lot it was to first kill the other nine, and after all, should kill himself." It appears, therefore, that Masada's last defenders were Jair's commanders who had been left to the last and who then cast lots among themselves.

6. INSCRIPTIONS DESIGNATING PRIESTLY TITHES. This group includes the ostracon inscribed *Ma'aser Kohen* ("Priest's tithe"), which apparently means the "tithe of the tithe," and the jars inscribed with a large **ת** in ink or charcoal. Also included in this group are the ostraca inscribed: *Leqodsha* לקודשא and לטהרת הקדש כשר (ין).

7. NAMES OF OWNERS were found inscribed on many store jars, for example, *Khana rba 'qbya* "the high priest, Aqavia;" "Simeon son of Yehosef;" "Yehosef son of Eleazar;" "Jacob son of Ezra." "Nahum son of Eleazar;" and many others.

8. THE CONTENTS. A special group of store jars, most of them from the storehouse of the Western Palace, bore inscriptions such as "crushed pressed figs," "dried figs," and "pressed figs."

9. LETTER. This ostracon was discovered on the lower terrace of the Northern Palace, beside the three skeletons. The letter is written to "(...)M son of M'azy," on the subject of the payment of the sum of 500 denarii.

The Scrolls. The remains of fourteen apocryphal, biblical, and sectarian scrolls were found. All were torn and in bad condition, and were either thrown on the floor or hidden beneath it. These are the first scrolls discovered outside of caves in a dated archaeological stratum.

Biblical Scrolls. PSALMS. 1. Fragments discovered in casemate 1039, south of the synagogue. The psalms are written in two columns. The scroll contained parts of chapters 81 to 85. The division of the Psalms and the text are identical with the Masoretic Text, except for one variant; 2. a small fragment discovered in casemate 1103, north of the Snake Path Gate. The scroll contains nearly the entire Psalm 150, and is also identical with the Masoretic Text. The blank space to the left of the text shows that it was the last Psalm on the parchment, corresponding to the Masoretic Text and unlike the Septuagint and Psalms Scroll from Qumran.

GENESIS. A small fragment from locus 1039 containing several sections of Genesis 46:7–11. It can be dated by the script to the first century B.C. It contains several slight textual variations.

LEVITICUS. 1. A small fragment found in casemate 1039, containing half of eight lines of Leviticus 4:3–9. The text corresponds throughout to the Masoretic Text; 2. Large fragments of Leviticus found torn and crumpled in a corner of the square between the Northern Palace and the large bath-house. It contains a large part of chapters 8 to 12, and is identical with the Masoretic Text, with spaces between the chapters.

DEUTERONOMY. Fragments of this scroll were found hidden beneath the floor of the synagogue. The top of the last parchment with several verses from chapter 33 was mainly preserved. To the left of the text was a wide blank sheet, which was rolled up and sewn to the scroll to make it easier to unroll it.

EZEKIEL. Fragments of this scroll were hidden beneath the floor of the synagogue. Large portions of chapters 35–38 were preserved including chapter 37 (the vision of the dry bones). It was also identical with the Masoretic Text, apart from a few unimportant variants.

Apocryphal and Sectarian Scrolls. BEN SIRA. Substantial fragments of chapters 39–44 of the lost Hebrew original of the *Wisdom of Ben-Sira* were discovered in casemate 1109, south of the Snake Path Gate. The text is written in two columns (like the above-mentioned Psalms), in a minute script which can be ascribed to the first century A.D. The text is for the most part identical

Heap of skeletons, as found in the cave.

with the medieval Ben Sira manuscript found in the Cairo Geniza.

BOOK OF JUBILEES. A tiny fragment found in a garbage heap in a tannery tower, beside the Western Palace, where it had been thrown by the Roman garrison stationed at the site after Masada's fall. It contains several lines in Hebrew of the ancient text of the book.

SONGS OF THE SABBATH SERVICE. A fragment of a Hebrew scroll discovered in casemate 1039 deals with the songs of the Sabbath Service—each sabbath and its particular song. The fragment found here contains parts of the songs of the fifth and sixth sabbaths. The sixth sabbath fell on the ninth day of the second month. This scroll is identical to the scroll discovered in cave 4 at Qumran. Its contents, style, and the calendar mentioned in it are all characteristic of the writings of the Dead Sea sect. The discovery of this scroll at Masada is of great importance, for it provides evidence for dating the Dead Sea Scrolls and also indicates that members of this sect (apparently Essenes) participated in the Jewish War.

MISCELLANEOUS. Other fragments of apocryphal and sectarian scrolls were discovered, mainly in casemate 1039. These have not yet been deciphered.

THE ROMAN SIEGE AND GARRISON

The tremendous effort of Flavius Silva to conquer Masada is still clearly visible in the surroundings of the fortress: the siege wall (circumvallation), camps, and assault ramp. S. Guttman excavated part of camp A, and trial soundings were made by the 1963–65 expedition in camp F, the large camp northwest of the rock and Silva's command headquarters. The main aim of the expedition was to determine the date of the smaller camp, situated in the southwest corner of camp F. It was established that this small camp was built by the garrison left at the site after the conquest of Masada. All the finds found on the upper of its two floors are attributed to the end of the first and beginning of second century. The latest coin found here is from A.D. 105.

Part of the garrison was also stationed on the summit of Masada. Stratigraphic evidence of the fall of Masada was provided by occupation levels above the conflagration layers, found mainly in buildings IX and VII, in the large bathhouse, and in some of the casemates, particularly in the northwest side.

In other places, signs of destruction were noted, which were apparently carried out by the Roman garrison. Coins from these levels include a group of silver coins discovered in the north side of building VII. The latest coin in this group dates to A.D. 111, attesting to the length of their occupation. In various places on the summit were found some Nabataean bowls, which can be attributed to either the period of the Revolt or to the Roman garrison. Large quantities of this type of pottery were also discovered in all the Roman camps. It seems likely that the garrison and siege troops included Nabataean soldiers, and this pottery was used at least until A.D. 73.

THE BYZANTINE PERIOD

Masada was occupied by monks during the fifth and sixth centuries A.D. Three groups of structures date from this period:

Mosaic pavement in Byzantine church.

1. Public Buildings. Two complexes of public buildings were found: the church and the refectories and kitchens.

THE CHURCH is situated northeast of the Western Palace. It consists of a long hall with an internal apse on its east side. The narthex was on the west side; on the northwest side of the hall was the diaconicon and an elongated hall which served as a residence. The floor of the hall was paved with a richly colored mosaic in a guilloche pattern, but most of it had been destroyed in antiquity, and only some sections in the southeast and northwest corners have survived. The narthex was paved with a white mosaic. The tesserae were prepared at Masada, and remains of this industry were found in a workshop near building XII. The diaconicon was paved with a colorful mosaic in red, black, yellow, and white, which was almost completely preserved. It consisted of sixteen circular medal-

lions in a guilloche border. In the medallions are represented rosettes, pomegranates, figs, citrus, grapes, a basket of eggs with a cross, flowers, plants, and geometric patterns. Judging from the style of the mosaic, the construction of the church can be dated to the fifth century.

A REFECTORY AND PUBLIC KITCHEN were found to the west of the church, inside and adjoining the casemate wall.

2. Living Quarters. Small cells built of stone were found scattered in various places. They were used by the monks as living quarters and retreats. The foundations of these cells usually lay on the stones fallen from the Herodian and Zealot structures.

3. Caves. Signs of habitation by monks were also found in caves in the southern cliff and in the center of Masada. The caves on the summit were cut out of the soft rock, and the monks also built rooms and cells beside them.

Chronological and Archaeological Summary

PERIOD	DATE	FINDS
Chalcolithic	4th mill. B.C.	Cave, pottery, cloth and mats
Iron Age	10–7th cent. B.C.	Scattered sherds
Hasmonaean	first half of 1st century B.C.	Coins of Alexander Jannaeus
Herod	40–4 B.C.	Fortress, palaces, storehouses, bathhouses, water system, pottery and coins.
Herodian dynasty and Procurators	4 B.C.–A.D. 66	Additions and alterations to Herodian buildings, hundreds of coins of Archelaus, Agrippa and the Procurators.
The Jewish Revolt	A.D. 66–73	Dwellings, synagogue, *beth-midrash*(?), ritual baths, scrolls, ostraca, coins and articles of daily life, destruction by burning.
Roman Garrison	A.D. 73–111 (at least)	Additional dwellings, alterations to earlier buildings, destruction of mosaics and paved floors, coins, and everyday utensils.
Byzantine	5th–6th cent. A.D.	Church, refectories, and kitchens, monks' cells, caves, pottery and articles of daily use.

EARLIER SETTLEMENTS

The Chalcolithic Period. The earliest signs of occupation discovered in the excavations date to the Chalcolithic period. These remains were uncovered in a cave in the lower part of the southern cliff. Cup marks were found in the floor with remains of plants, mats, cloth as well as a few Chalcolithic sherds.

The Iron Age. A few scattered sherds from the Iron Age II were found in several places, including the middle terrace of the Northern Palace. No buildings of that period were found, however, and it can thus be assumed that these sherds were left by individuals who for some reason lived at Masada from time to time.

The Pre-Herodian Period. To this period belong some of the upper cisterns. A large number of coins dating to Alexander Jannaeus were also found. This may perhaps indicate that the "Jonathan the priest," mentioned by Josephus, should be identified with Alexander Jannaeus and not Jonathan the Hasmonaean. In this connection should be mentioned a burial near camp F, which contained a Roman silver coin from the second half of the second century B.C. Such coins continued in use until the time of Alexander Jannaeus, and the burial may perhaps date from this period.

Y. YADIN

BIBLIOGRAPHY

Josephus Flavius, *Jewish Antiquities* XIV, XV; idem, *The Jewish War* I, II, IV, VII • Robinson, *Biblical Researches* • S. W. Wolcott, *Bibliotheca Sacra* 1, 1843 (also in: *The History of the Jewish War by Flavius Josephus*, A New Translation, by R. Traill, Manchester, 1851) • J. W. Lynch, *Narrative of the U.S. Expedition to the Jordan and the Dead Sea*, Philadelphia, 1849 • S. W. M. Van de Velde, *Syria and Palestine*, Edinburgh and London, 1854 • F. de Saulcy, *Round the Dead Sea and in the Bible Lands*, London, 1854 • E. G. Rey, *Voyages dans le Haouran et aux bords de la Mer Morte*, Paris, 1860 • R. Tuch, *Masada, die herodianische Felsenfeste nach Fl. Josephus und neuern Beobachten*, Leipzig, 1863 • H. B. Tristram, *The Land of Israel*, London, 1865, Passim; idem, *The Land of Moab*, London, 1873 • C. Warren, *PEQ*, 1860, 146 ff. • Conder–Kitchener, *SWP* 3 (1883), 417–21 • G. D. Sandel, *ZDPV* 30 (1907), 96 f. • Brünnow–Domaszewski, *Die Provincia Arabia* 3, Strassburg, 1909, 220–99 • C. Hawkes, *Antiquity* 3 (1929), 195–260 • A. M. Schneider, *Oriens Christianus* 6 (1931), 251–53 • W. Borée, *JPOS* 13 (1933), 140–46 • A. Schulten, *ZDPV* 56 (1933), 1–185 • A. Alon–S. Guttman, *Mibifnim* 16 (1953), 468–76 (Hebrew) • M. Livneh, *HA-Teva ve ha-Ares*, 10 (1954), 507–14 (Hebrew) • M. Avi-Yonah, N. Avigad, Y. Aharoni, I. Dunayevsky, S. Guttman, *Masada, Survey and Excavations, 1955–56, IEJ* 7 (1957), 1–60 • I. A. Richmond, *JRS* 52 (1962), 142–55 • Y. Yadin, *IEJ* 15 (1965), 1–120; idem, *The Ben-Sira Scroll from Masada*, Jerusalem, 1965; idem, *Masada*, London–N.Y., 1966 • S. Guttman, *With Masada*, Tel Aviv, 1965 (Hebrew).

MASOS, TEL
(Khirbet El-Meshash)

IDENTIFICATION. Tel Masos (Map reference 146069) is situated some 12 kilometers (7 miles) east of Beersheba. Until 1964, it was known only as a small mound of about 5 dunams containing the remnants of a Roman-Byzantine fort and Iron Age II–C remains. In that year, Y. Aharoni, during a survey of the area, discovered a Middle Bronze Age II earthern rampart west of the main well (Bir el-Meshash), and the remains of a huge Iron Age I settlement (about 50 dunams) about 200 meters east of the Roman-Byzantine fort. In the light of these discoveries, and the results of the excavations in the Beersheba Valley (at Arad, Malḥata, and Beersheba), Aharoni proposed to identify Tel Masos with biblical Hormah (Joshua 15:30; I Chronicles 4:30), a city or district already known at the end of the Middle Kingdom as *ḥ'jm* (Egyptian

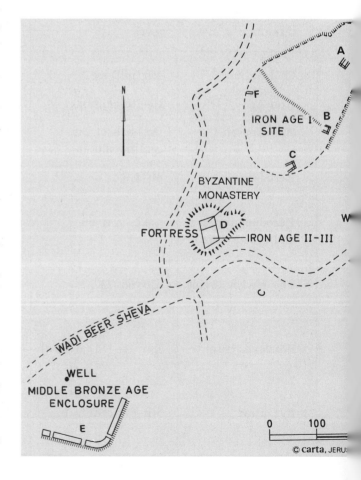

Execration Texts, Number 1) or *ḥ'mj* (Wadi Me-ghara in Sinai). The biblical references conform well with the ceramic evidence at the site. The survey showed that the range of pottery spanned the entire Iron Age I, i.e., from the period of the Israelite settlement when Hormah is first mentioned (about the mid-thirteenth century B.C.) to the early part of David's reign at Ziklag, when he sent the booty of the Amalekites to the city (I Samuel 30:30).

EXCAVATIONS

In 1972 to 1975, three seasons of excavations were carried out at the site by a joint Israeli–German expedition. Remains from the Chalcolithic period, Middle Bronze Age, Iron Age I, II–C, and Byzantine period were uncovered.

Chalcolithic Period. Pits were found in all the areas under debris of the Iron Age I site. The material is almost identical with that of the Beer-sheba Chalcolithic culture.

Middle Bronze Age. At a distance of about 800 meters from the main Iron Age mound close to

Opposite page: General plan of the site; This page, below: Plan of stratum 2; area A; Bottom: Four-room houses; strata 1 and 2.

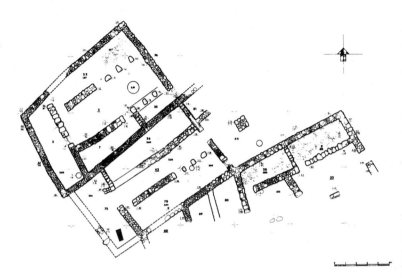

the main well is situated the Middle Bronze Age site, about 10 dunams in area. Earth ramparts originally surrounded the well. Two phases could be distinguished here: 1. an early phase of a fortified building, probably a mud-brick fortress, which was destroyed after a short period of existence; 2. an earthern rampart fort, with buildings attached to the *terre pisée* construction. The two phases were dated by the pottery to the first half of the eighteenth century B.C.

Iron Age I. Five areas (A, B, C, F, H) were examined on the main site. In all the areas, three strata of the Iron Age I were revealed.

STRATUM 3. Found mainly in areas A and C, this stratum represents the first settlement on the site at the end of the thirteenth century B.C. The architecture is very simple, with houses consisting of a broad room opening onto a rectangular courtyard. The pottery dates to the early phase of the Iron Age I.

STRATUM 2. This stratum marks the floruit of the site. Well-constructed houses of the four-room type were excavated in areas A, B, and F, public buildings in areas A and C (a fortress?), and a cult building in area H. Stratum 2 was destroyed by an earthquake, as is indicated by some of the buildings

in area A. Philistine, Phoenician Bichrome, and "Midianite" pottery date this stratum from the mid-twelfth to the middle of the eleventh century B.C.

STRATUM 1 shows a decline of the settlement. Only a few of the buildings destroyed in stratum 2 were rebuilt. A new fortress, smaller than that of stratum 2, was built in area C. The pottery of stratum 1 is of the late eleventh or early tenth century B.C.

Iron Age II–C. West of the huge Iron Age I settlement, a small fortress was erected during the seventh century B.C. and destroyed at the beginning of the following century.

The Byzantine Period. Above the ruins of the Iron Age fortress, a Syrian monastery was built at the end of the sixth century A.D. The monastery included a typical Syrian church with a square apse and a crypt with eight burials in an adjoining chamber. Syriac inscriptions found on stone and plaster indicate that the monastery was destroyed in the eighth century A.D.

CONCLUSIONS

As one of the largest sites in the northern Negev, Tel Masos was of major importance in two periods:

This page: Decorated jugs — Early Iron Age;
Opposite page: Egyptian scarab — stratum 3(?)

1.) In the Middle Bronze Age it controlled, together with nearby Malḥata (Tell el-Milḥ), the east–west road along the Beersheba Valley as well as the south–north road in the direction of Hebron. The two Middle Bronze Age sites, only 6 kilometers apart, can be identified with the late Middle Kingdom district of ḥ'mj (Hormah).

2.) During the Israelite settlement of the Negev, Masos was the largest center in the entire northern Negev area, a fact that clearly indicates its importance at that period. The prosperity of the settlement of stratum 2 at the time of Philistine rule in Palestine suggests that it was incorporated into the Philistine commercial and political system. Masos was abandoned around 1000/980 B.C. and its population moved to nearby Ghara (Tell 'Ira). The identification of Masos with biblical Hormah fully agrees with the archaeological data.

A. KEMPINSKI

BIBLIOGRAPHY

Y. Aharoni, V. Fritz, A. Kempinski, *The Excavation at Tel Masos, First Preliminary Report,* Tel Aviv, 1974, 64–74; idem, *Excavations at Tel Masos, Second Preliminary Report,* Tel Aviv, 1975 • A. Kempinski, *Qadmoniot* 6 (1973), 104–06 (Hebrew) • Y. Aharoni et al., *IEJ* 22 (1972), 243; 24 (1974), 268–69 • V. Fritz, A. Kempinski, *ZDPV* 92 (1976), 83–104.

MEDEBA (Madaba)

HISTORY AND IDENTIFICATION. Medeba is first mentioned in the Bible (Numbers 21:30) in a lament narrating the conquest of Moabite towns at the hands of Sihon, king of the Amorites. The Israelites captured the Kingdom of Sihon, Medeba, and the entire plain surrounding it, and allocated them to the tribe of Reuben (Joshua 13:9, 16). In the days of David, the Israelite commander Joab defeated the Arameans in a bitter battle fought in the vicinity of Medeba (II Samuel 10; I Chronicles 19). The monarchic schism in Israel was exploited by the Moabites, who gained control over Medeba until it was later recaptured by Omri (viz. the Mesha Stele, line 8). It was Mesha himself who subsequently restored the town to its former masters, and it is listed among other Moabite cities in Isaiah's prophecy (15:2). According to I Maccabees 9:36, the Ambri tribe held sway over the area during the Second Temple period. John Hyrcanus captured Medeba at the beginning of his reign (Josephus, *Antiquities* XIII, 255; *War* I, 63) and it remained in Jewish hands until the fratricidal strife between Hyrcanus II and Aristobulus II. Then, according to Josephus (*Antiquities* XIII, 18), Hyrcanus handed the town over to Aretas III, the Nabataean king. A Nabataean inscription found at Medeba and dated to the forty-sixth regnal year of Aretas (A.D. 37/38) testifies that the town at that time was a Nabataean military headquarters under the command of a strategus. With the annexation of the Nabataean kingdom to the Roman empire, Medeba became one of the towns of Provincia Arabia (A.D. 106). It contained a Jewish community in Mishnaic times (*Mikva'ot* 7, 1). Under Roman rule Medeba's northern border was the southern limit of Heshbon and of the Jewish-occupied area of Transjordan (Peraea). Its southern border was the Arnon River (as is attested by the twentieth milestone from the town). Roman Medeba minted its own coins stamped with the image of the town's tutelary goddess and the inscription Μηδάβων τύχη. The population remained Nabataean Arab on the whole. 'Avdalla ben 'Anomi erected a monument in the town in Emperor Antoninus' nineteenth regnal year. The presence of a Christian community in the town is attested by the signature of

Bishop Jaonos at the Council of Chalcedon in A.D. 451. At the end of the sixth and early seventh centuries, the town flourished under the episco-pacies of Sergius (about 578–597), Leontius (about 603–608) and John (617 or 632). Like the other Transjordanian cities, it declined with the Arab conquest. Its identification is based on the Arabic name of the locality Madaba (which has preserved the original Medeba), and on Nabataean and Greek inscriptions discovered there.

Reconstruction of the plan of the church.

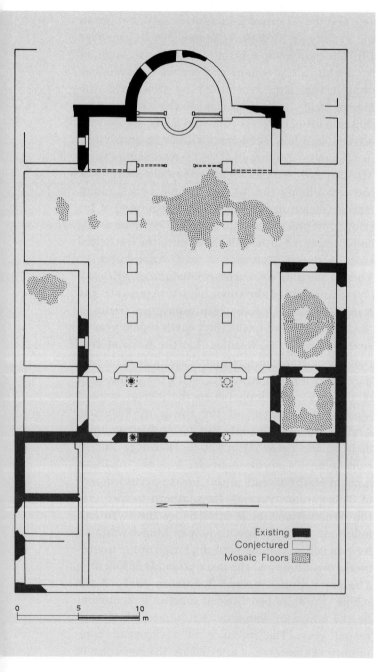

Existing ■
Conjectured □
Mosaic Floors ▨

0   5   10
         m

REMAINS

Medeba is situated on a low hill in the midst of a fertile plain. The ancient city was encompassed by a rectangular-shaped wall whose remains show traces of seven gates. South of the center of the rectangular lies the acropolis, in which ruins of the pre-Roman period were found.

A tomb situated east of the acropolis has produced the only excavated remains of pre-Roman Medeba. In the natural cave, which was used as a burial place by several generations, were discovered more than a hundred pottery vessels, many bronze and iron utensils, beads, scarabs, and other objects. The tomb's rich hoard (published by G. L. Harding and B. S. J. Isserlin) is shown by its objects, includ-ing imported Mycenaean ware, but no Cypriot, to indicate a date about 1200 B.C., i.e., the transition period from the Bronze Age to the Iron Age.

Southwest of the walled area are the remains of a large square reservoir (105 meters long), and west of the walls are the ruins of a church. Outside the northern gate were found the remains of a cistern and two towers (burial or watchtowers) built northwest and southeast of the walls. In the eastern wall of the city was situated the main gate, from which a paved street with colonnades on either side ran for 200 meters in a northwest direction, leading apparently to the town's forum. Near the gate was a square public edifice (20 meters), probably a Roman temple. The remains of another public building and a bathhouse were un-covered in the acropolis, as well as a pool north of the colonnaded street. Several private residences containing fragmentary mosaics from the Byzantine period also came to light. The mosaics showed Greek mythological motifs, especially from the myth of Dionysus, containing the figures of Ariadne, Baccantes, and Satyr.

Ten churches were also found in the ruins of ancient Medeba.

Church 1 stood inside the wall near the north gate and contained the Medeba Map (see below).

Church 2 occupied a position north of and parallel to the colonnaded street and was dedicated to Mary, mother of Jesus. This is a circular struc-ture with an elongated addition built on the east side. It is unclear whether it was dedicated in 574 or 674 in an unknown era in the fifth indiction.

Church 3 stood south of the forum street, 25 meters south of church 2. The structure contains a subterranean chapel (crypt) and is dedicated to Elijah the prophet. Above the crypt is a basilical structure with an inscribed apse and two rows of four columns each. According to an inscription in the mosaic pavement, the crypt was completed in 596, during the episcopate of Sergius, while the main body of the church was possibly completed by his successor, Leontius. The mosaic in the crypt is decorated with two gazelles standing on either side of a "tree of life."

Church 4 stood to the east of church 3. It is a basilical structure (29 by 16 meters) with an inscribed apse, in which a bench for the clergy ran the whole length of the wall, and in its center stood the bishop's throne. The bema is separated by a chancel screen from the hall, which contains two rows of six columns each.

Church 5 was also located east of church 3, but only scant remains of it have survived.

Church 6 was also a basilical structure.

Church 7 was situated southeast of the acropolis. The only trace of the church still extant is a fragment of the chancel screen.

Church 8, situated south of the acropolis, is the largest of Medeba's churches (36 by 21 meters), and hence regarded as its cathedral.

Church 9 (30 meters long) stood outside the town wall, approximately 300 meters west of it. This building also had an inscribed apse. In front of it was an atrium which the same length as the church.

Church 10 was situated in the acropolis.

MEDEBA MAP

Church 1 contains a mosaic floor on which a map of Palestine is represented. It is the earliest map of ancient Palestine. The floor was discovered in 1884 when the foundations of a new Greek Orthodox church were laid. The report of its discovery lay buried in the Patriarchate's archives, while the construction of the new church caused considerable damage to the map. In the year 1896, the Patriarchate's librarian, P. Kleopos Koikylides, visited Medeba, realized the importance of the mosaic, and brought the map to the attention of the scholarly world. Within several years, detailed reports of the discovery were published, and since then interest in the map has not flagged. From the varied and conflicting reports concerning the plan of the church and the place of the map, it is possible to reconstruct a basilical church with a transept (25 by 7.5 meters), in the mosaic floor

of which the map was laid (its total area was approximately 24 by 6 meters). Judging from the map fragment still in situ, it appears to have depicted the entire area regarded as the biblical world — from Byblos (Gebal), Hammath, and Damascus in the north down to No-Ammon (Thebes) in Egypt in the south; from the Mediterranean Sea in the west to Kenath, Bozrah, Rabbath-Ammon, and Petra in the east. Jerusalem is placed in the center of the map. The column near the northern town gate, which served as the egress point to the Roman streets in the town area, seems to have also been the exact center of the map. As was usual in ancient maps, the east is represented in the map's upper section and the west at the bottom. Palestine and its northern neighbors were squeezed into this elongated, narrow framework. However, in order to include Egypt also, the artist depicted the Nile as flowing from east to west. The scale is uneven. The size of cities is exaggerated, and the important areas are larger than the others. Thus the center of the map is executed on an approximate scale of 1:15,000, whereas Jerusalem is shown on a scale of about 1:1,600.

Like all maps, this map also indicated different kinds of settlements: cities, villages, various structures, in addition to illustrations of a topographic nature. Mountains and hills are represented as blocks of color cleft by the black lines of valleys. Mountain ridges and plateaus are both represented in white mosaic. Seas (the Mediterranean and the Dead Sea) are delineated by wavy blue, brown, or black lines. Smaller rivers (the Nile and the Jordan) are the same color as the seas. Brooks, on the other hand, are shown as twin black-bordered blue lines, but the streams flowing in the vicinity of Medeba (the Arnon and the Zered) are exaggerated in size. Aside from the geographic details, the map displays ships on the Dead Sea, fish in the Jordan and the Nile, and a lion pursuing a gazelle in the plains of Moab. The plant world shown includes palm trees in the vicinity of Jericho, Bethagla, Calirhoe, and Zoar, and other scattered plant species. The large cities (Jerusalem, Neapolis [Shechem], Lod-Diospolis, Yavneh, Charachmoba, Ashdod-Yam, Ascalon, Eleutheropolis [Beth-Govrin], Gaza and Pelusium) are presented in bird's-eye view with lavishness of detail, and show the main thoroughfares and public edifices, particularly the churches. The remaining cities, towns, and villages are indicated by conventional symbols of various sizes, depending on the importance of the place in the artist's eyes. Individual edifices are also marked, particularly famous churches built outside the towns, in addition to water installations, ferries, and watchtowers. Legends were appended to localities in black as a rule, but in places where the background is dark, white tesserae were used for the legends. The artist used red tesserae to delineate tribal territories, to inscribe biblical passages, and to mark the names of holy sites such as Jerusalem, Bethlehem, and Mamre. There are four categories of legends in the map: place names only (55); the current name of a locality together with its biblical identification (18); explanation of the site's specific character, i.e., as related to the name of a saint or prophet (11); a summation of important events that took place at the site, as related in the Bible (11). The biblical verses are taken from the Blessing of Jacob (Genesis 49) and the Blessing of Moses (Deuteronomy 33) as well as the verse "A voice was heard in Ramah" (Jeremiah 31:15) and a verse from the Song of Deborah. All the passages follow the Septuagint. The artist attempted to mark all places mentioned in the Gospels and, wherever space permitted, a selection of localities mentioned in the Old Testament. Wherever no biblical names were available (particularly in the Negev area), the artist added new names so as to avoid blank spaces on the map.

An examination of the names reveals that the Medeba Map was based on a Roman route map. Practically all the places mentioned lay along or close to a road. It was made to conform with biblical localities through the use of the Onomasticon of Eusebius, archbishop of Caesarea in the fourth century A.D. and perhaps also by the map originally appended to this volume and no longer extant. Of the ninety-one places mentioned on the Medeba Map, sixty were taken from Eusebius. The Onomasticon, nevertheless, was but one of the sources employed by the cartographer. It appears that Jewish sources were not neglected either. Evidence for this is to be found, primarily, in the transference of Mount Ebal and Mount Gerizim from the vicinity of Shechem to the environs of Jericho (although the names Tur Ebal and Tur Gerizin are listed in their proper places), in the term "Beth Dagon" for "Kefar Dagon," etc. On the Eusebius map, the town outlines were drawn, apparently for the benefit of Christian pilgrims. The latest details appearing in the Medeba Map are Justinian's buildings (the latest being the Jerusalem "Nea" church of A.D. 542), and the map itself can be dated between this year and the year of Justinian's death, i.e., to the middle of the sixth century A.D.

Aside from several fragments (Sarepta near Sidon, a fragment north of Accho, and another adjacent to Safed, containing the name "Agbari"), the entire area between Aenon-Salim, south of Beth-Shean to the confluence of the Nile branches south of Attribis, has been preserved. But this area as well has suffered regrettable damage in places. Other extant portions are those presenting the areas between Jerusalem and the Dead Sea, a strip running eastward from Ascalon to the Dead Sea, the Nile delta, and a section extending from the eastern side of the 'Arabah to the mountains of the Sinai peninsula. Smaller gaps are also to be found in different sections of the map as well as alterations and damage of various sorts. Particularly noticeable are the defaced figures of humans and animals replaced by mosaic patchwork.

The Medeba Map is both historical and geographical in character. Side by side with natural features and contemporary settlements, there are also identifications of biblical sites. The country's natural features have undergone no basic change since the Byzantine era, and consequently little may be garnered from the map as to the land's physical characteristics at the time. Nor has the map any special significance for biblical study, since the majority of the identifications were taken from Eusebius' Onomasticon, and virtually all, save for the most clearly ascertainable (Hebron, Bethlehem, and the like) are not acceptable to present-day scholars. Since the identified localities reflect later traditions, the map is important for the history of biblical study rather than for the research itself. However, the map is primarily valuable for its faithful visual rendering of the country's aspect in the Byzantine age, specifically in its vignettes of the large towns (smaller settlements being rendered as a rule in extremely routine fashion), as well as in the delineation of several buildings (e.g., the churches at Galgala and Beth Zechariah). Even when taking the cartographic limitations of the time into consideration,

Jerusalem is depicted in a precise and faithful representation. Sixteen otherwise unrecorded settlements also appear on the map. The map (composed of two and a half million tesserae, the laying of which must have occupied three artisans an entire year), also bears witness to the interest of the country's inhabitants in the past history of the Holy Land and their own contemporary times.

M. AVI-YONAH

BIBLIOGRAPHY

C. R. Conder, *The Survey of Eastern Palestine,* London, 1889, 178–83 • Clermont–Ganneau, *RAO* 2, 12, 189 • H. Leclerq, *Dict. d'arch.chrétienne et de liturgie* 10, 1931, 807–85 • Saller–Bagatti, *Town of Nebo* 80–82, 147, 226–44 • G. L. Harding, *PEFA* 6 (1953), 27–33 • B. S. J. Isserlin, *ibid.,* 34–47.
The Medeba Map: M. J. Lagrange, *RB* 6 (1897), 165–84 • A. Schulten, *Die Mosaikkarte von Madaba,* Berlin, 1900 • A. Jacoby, *Das geographische Mosaik von Madaba,* Leipzig, 1905 • P. Palmer–H. Guthe, *Die Mosaikkarte von Madaba,* Leipzig, 1906 • R. T. O'Callaghan, *Supplém. Dictionnaire de la Bible* 26, Paris, 1953 • M. Avi-Yonah, *EI* 2 (1952–53), 129–56 (Hebrew); *idem, The Madaba Mosaic Map,* Jerusalem, 1954; V. R. Gold, *BA* 21 (1958), 50–70.
Jerusalem in the Medeba Map: Vincent–Abel, *Jérusalem nouvelle* 4, 922 ff. • F. Thomsen, *ZDPV* 52 (1929), 149–74, 192–220 • J. T. Milik, *Mélanges de l'Université de St. Joseph* 37 (1961), 127 ff.

General plan of the site.

MEGADIM, TEL

IDENTIFICATION. Tel Megadim lies on the coast some 17 kilometers (10.5 miles) south of Haifa and 2 kilometers (1 mile) north of 'Atlit (q.v.) The site was occupied, with long periods of abandonment, from the Early Bronze Age to the Byzantine period. Its principal remains were uncovered in the well-preserved Persian town of stratum II. Three seasons of excavations were conducted on the mound between 1967 and 1969, by M. Broshi on behalf of the Department of Antiquities and Museums, the Israel Exploration Society, and Boston College.

EXCAVATIONS

The Bronze Age. The Early and Middle Bronze Ages are known only through unstratified finds. The Early Bronze Age settlement was considerably larger than the later ones. Abundant material is found from the Early Bronze Age I (gray-burnished ware and hole-mouth jars) and Early Bronze Age II

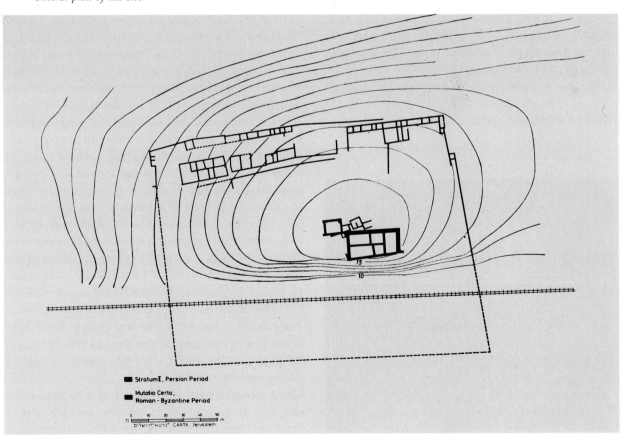

■ Stratum I, Persian Period

■ Mutatio Certa, Roman - Byzantine Period

(platters and a seal impression). After a long period of abandonment the site was re-occupied in the Middle Bronze Age II. The Late Bronze Age city, apparently also preceded by an interruption in occupation, had strong overseas commercial ties, as is indicated by the large amount of Cypriot pottery.

The Persian Period. Three strata of this period were distinguished. Stratum I, the top one, was apparently short-lived and probably settled by squatters who added only a few shoddy walls to the deserted houses of stratum II. As it was close to the surface, this stratum suffered the most from exposure to the elements. Stratum II, the main stratum unearthed, belongs to a well-preserved and well-planned town. It was quadrangular in shape and had a street running parallel to the city wall. Of the town's fortifications, all the western wall was excavated (170 meters long), and part of the northern (100 meters) and southern walls (20 meters). This is mainly a casemate wall, which is best preserved at the northern end of the western wall — in this section eleven casemates were excavated. These were neatly arranged: three large chambers each flanked by two smaller chambers. The width of the casemates is 2.7 meters (6 Attic cubits?). The wall was built of undressed, or slightly dressed, *kurkar* sandstone. The width of each section of the walls is .6–.9 meter. The closest parallel to this wall is the contemporary casemate wall at Tell Mevorakh (q.v.), 21 kilometers (14 miles) to the south, which is of equal width but

Stratum II; room with storage jars in situ — Persian period.

built of ashlar. The wall was not intended to defend the town against a massive military attack but as a protection against pirates — a danger ever imminent for coastal towns in this period — and as storerooms, as is attested by the presence of store jars.

A street, 90 meters long and 2.4–3 meters wide, was unearthed running parallel to the western wall with two insulae west of it and two lanes running at right angles to it. The city gate was located in the south wall at the end of this street. The overlapping of the two lines of the western wall may indicate the existence of a postern — a narrow entrance that could be blocked easily at night or in time of emergency.

This is one of the earliest of the rectangular towns, laid out in the system that became popular from the Hellenistic period onward and later known as the Hippodamian plan.

In the beginning of the fourth century B.C., the town was destroyed and abandoned. The abruptness of its desertion can account for the discovery of a great number of intact vessels, and a rich assemblage of almost the entire corpus of Persian pottery types (in the western part of the country) — from the huge store jars to the smallest juglets. Numerous vessels and sherds of Greek and Cypriot ware testify to an intensive overseas trade. Other finds include small metal objects (bronze fibulae, iron arrowheads), coins, and terra-cotta figurines. Stratum III is represented by well-constructed walls, but no coherent plan could be distinguished here. The excavators could not differentiate between the earlier ceramic ware of stratum III and that of stratum II, and not enough material was found which could suggest the dates of the establishment of stratum III and its destruction. Stratum II flourished in the fifth century B.C. and seems to have come to an end sometime between 399 and 380 B.C., as a result of the invasions of the first two kings of the Twenty-Ninth Egyptian Dynasty, Nepherites (399–393 B.C.) and Achoris (393–380 B.C.), or during the Persian reconquest of the country (380 B.C.). Stratum I might have been destroyed at the time of the Tennes rebellion (351 B.C.), or at the latest, during the campaign of Alexander the Great (332 B.C.).

The Roman–Byzantine Period. In this period the site was not occupied, with the exception of a large building that stood on the peak of the mound.

Medeba. Jerusalem shown on mosaic map.

The building was only partially unearthed (over 300 square meters of floor area), but as is shown by its size and nature of construction — the outer wall is 2.15 meters thick — it was undoubtedly a public edifice. It is very possibly the *mutatio* — a horse-changing station (and possibly also a caravanserai) mentioned by the Bordeaux Pilgrim (about A.D. 330) as Mutatio Certha (or Certa, Cirta). This itinerary relates that the *mutatio* lies 8 miles south of Sicaminos (Shiqmona, q.v.) and that here was the border between Syria-Phoenicia and Palestine. The distance from Shiqmona (12 kilometers) agrees exactly with the 8 Roman miles, and the nature of the building (e.g., large paved courts) also conforms with its identification as a staging post. It is interesting to note that the site still retained its old name: Certa is undoubtedly Qarta, i.e. "town," a Hebrew name for at least two cities mentioned in the Bible and a frequent component of Phoenician place names.   M. BROSHI

BIBLIOGRAPHY

S. Klein, *Ma'asef Zion* 6 (1934), 31, n. 3 (Hebrew) • *Corpus Christianorum*, Series Latina 175, Turnhout, 1965, 12 (Wesseling 585, 1; Geyer 19, 10) • M. Broshi, *IEJ* 17 (1967), 277–78; 18 (1968), 256–57; 19 (1969), 248; *idem, Qadmoniot* 2 (1970), 124–26 (Hebrew) • Stern, *Material Culture*, 19–20, 50, 237 f. et passim.

Above: Clay figurine — Persian period; Below: View of the mound; at left, flagstone pavement of a 3rd–4th century A.D. caravanserai mentioned by the Bordeaux Pilgrim. At right, remains of streets and building foundations of Phoenician town of 6th–4th centuries B.C.

MEGALITHIC MONUMENTS

IDENTIFICATION. Unique monuments, connected with burial rites, have been preserved from prehistoric times. These constructions, built of great undressed stone slabs, are known as megaliths (from the Greek μέγας = big and λίθος = stone). Four types of megalithic monuments are distinguished:

1. dolmen (from the Breton *dol* = table and *men* = stone);
2. cist, stone-case *(ciste)*;
3. menhir, tombstone (from the Breton *men* = stone and *hir* = long);
4. cromlech, stone circle (from the Welsh *crom* = curved and *llech* = stone).

A dolmen generally consists of six large undressed stone blocks. Four of the blocks (each measuring about .9 by .7 by 4 meter and weighing more than one ton) are set edgewise, like the four sidewalls of a box. The fifth block serves as the base of the box, and the sixth one, the largest, serves as the capstone laid over the structure like a table top. The whole structure is covered by a mound (tumulus) of earth or stones, and the base is surrounded by one or more circles of small stones. The function of the surrounding stone circles had been variously interpreted. Most probably they were meant to reinforce the mound of stones and to prevent their scattering. More complex types of dolmens are also found, some formed of a main dolmen with the addition of a corridor with lateral niches or with a long corridor ending in an apse-shaped niche, etc.

Cists (stone-cases) are generally built like the dolmens and are also covered with a tumulus, but their stones are of smaller dimensions. Another type of cist is sunk into a pit in the ground, without a tumulus.

Menhirs are stones set upright like tombstones above ground and reach a height of 1–8 meters, one third of their overall length being embedded in the ground. They are found near megalithic burials.

A cromlech consists of a group of menhirs arranged in a circle.

Megalithic burial fields are as a rule situated near water and woody areas. The water was apparently required for the burial rites, and the woods supplied the logs used for dislodging and levering the rocks and massive stone slabs and for rolling them to the building site. Such megalithic monuments are scattered over extensive areas in Europe, Asia, and Africa.

EXPLORATION

Although the study of megaliths began more than a century ago, their mystery has not yet been unraveled, and strange theories are still proposed as to their function in the pre- and proto-historic cultures. What can nevertheless be stated with certainty is that the dolmens and stone cists served for burials. It is also an unquestionable fact that the menhirs and cromlechs were connected with the cult of the dead. This can be inferred from the fact that they were erected near megalithic cemeteries. At some as yet unknown period, and for some unknown reason, they ceased building these monuments, which from that time have continued to stand towering giantlike above their surroundings and kindling the imagination of all who view them. It is no wonder then that in the course of time they became the subject of numerous folk tales and superstitions.

The first mention of megalithic monuments in Palestine is found in travel books from the beginning of the nineteenth century. In 1817, C. L. Irby and J. Mangles saw a group of twenty-seven dolmens on their voyage from es-Salt to Shechem. These dolmens were later described in detail by the French mission of Albert Duc de Luyenes, which also discovered and published a report of the menhir of Hadjar al-Mansuv in the Hills of Moab. In 1848, Newbold discovered a group of five megalithic structures north of Jerusalem which the local Arabs called the Tombs of the Jews (Qubur beni Israel). Another group of dolmens was seen by F. de Saulcy on the heights of el-'Adeimeh northeast of the Dead Sea. In the report of the British survey conducted by C. R. Conder in 1889, a complete volume is devoted to the description of some seven hundred megalithic structures in Transjordan. The same report also mentions four dolmens in Upper Galilee and two in the Judean Hills. The report of the survey carried out by G. Schumacher in 1886 in Transjordan and Syria mentions numerous megalithic cemeteries, each containing some five hundred to a thousand dolmens. Schumacher estimated that in the region he surveyed there were more than ten thousand dolmens and megalithic tombs. In 1901, L. H. Vincent described dolmens encountered by members of the Dominican order in Jerusalem during trips in the Hills of Moab, in the surroundings of Jerusalem, in the Judean Hills, and in Samaria. Other dolmens were found by P. Karge in Upper Galilee and in the vicinity of the synagogue of Chorozain north of Tiberias during a survey carried out in 1911. A. E. Mader continued this survey, discovering more megalithic monuments in various regions of Western Palestine, especially in Galilee. A. Mallon, G. Dalman, E. Graf von Mülinen, C. Schick, and others described dolmens and similar structures in Transjordan, Western Palestine, and Syria. Other megalithic structures were discovered by W. M. F. Petrie in Sinai and E. H. Palmer in neighboring lands.

Most of the above-mentioned explorers examined the megalithic monuments only on the outside, few of them conducting excavations. Schumacher was the first to excavate (in 1886) three dolmens in the Golan Heights. In them he found calcinated human bones in a state of decomposition and some copper rings. In 1929–30, R. Neuville and A. Mallon excavated a tumulus and several dolmens in a megalithic necropolis on the banks of Wadi 'Adeimeh in Transjordan. The tumulus yielded a burial containing the skeletons of a man, woman, and child. Near the woman were perforated shells and carnelian beads. These skeletons, too, were in a state of decomposition, and their ages could not be determined. In 1929–30 F. Turville–Petre, on behalf of the British School of Archaeology in Jerusalem, conducted excavations in the dolmen field near the synagogue of Chorozain. He cleared twenty-four of the three hundred dolmens discovered there. His finds, which included coins and remains of iron objects, established that the dolmens had been re-used in the Roman period.

Excavations at 'Adeimeh. In 1932, M. Stekelis, on behalf of the Paleontological Institute of Man in Paris, excavated a megalithic necropolis in 'Adeimeh, on the eastern bank of the Jordan, east of Tuleilat el-Ghassul (q.v.), about 5 kilometers (3 miles) north of the Dead Sea and 2 kilometers (1 mile) west of the slopes of the Hills of Moab. The excavations covered the whole area of the cemetery, which comprised nine tumuli and 168 stone cists, sixteen inside the tumuli and the remainder nearby in rows of pits dug into the ground. The bottom and sidewalls of these pits were lined with small slabs of rough stones. Other slabs covered them. The cists, from .5 to 1.52 meters long, contained single burials. The body was buried in a seated position, with the legs flexed and reaching nearly to the chin. Due to the salinity of the soil, the skeletons decayed, as did the remains in the tumuli. Several cists contained whole pottery vessels and flint tools, which could be assigned to the Chalcolithic period. Near most of the tombs were round, oval, or rectangular fireplaces built of small stones, and containing ashes and calcinated bones. Three poorly preserved dolmens built of massive, undressed stones and surrounded by a circle of small stones stood in the vicinity. A cromlech, 30 meters in diameter, projected .35 meter above the ground next to the dolmens. Aside from Ghassulian-type pottery collected on surface level, no other remains were uncovered. The pottery and flint implements in the tumuli and cists are clearly Ghassulian, but it is impossible to establish definitely whether the necropolis indeed belonged to the settlement at Tuleilat el-Ghassul.

Excavations at 'Ala-Ṣafat. In 1942–43, M. Stekelis, on behalf of the Egyptian Archaeological School at Jerusalem, excavated a megalithic necropolis at 'Ala-Ṣafat, about 3 kilometers (2 miles) east of the town of Edom and 20 kilometers (12.5 miles) north of 'Adeimeh. Some of the dolmens had already been recorded in 1817 by Irby and Mangles. Stekelis found 193 monuments on the slopes of the Hills of Moab: 167 dolmens (three of them rock-cut), fourteen cists, and twelve cromlechs. In building the dolmens, the mountain slope was first leveled with a fill of small stones, and only then were the stones of the dolmen sunk into it. Some of the dolmens are built of sandstone quarried in the nearby mountains, while others were hewn out of blocks of rock which were strewn over the slopes. Most of the structures are simple-type dolmens and can be divided into three groups: 1. simple rectangular forms, with or without a gallery, and surrounded by one or two circles of small stones; 2. two-storied structures with two separate entrances cut into the same sidewall; two structures of this type were found, one intact and the other damaged; 3. monolithic dolmens with the crypt in the top part of the rock, and roofed by a large capstone. The entrance (.5 by .53 meter) is cut into one of the walls. Near some of the above structures were the rolling stones which had served to seal the entrance. Tumuli each containing up to four dolmens were also discovered in the necropolis as well as cromlechs of different forms, which were also

Opposite page: Map showing sites of the megalithic monuments; This page, top to bottom: Dolmens at Shamir, and at Ala-Safat.

connected with the cult of the dead.

On the basis of the ceramic evidence, the necropolis was dated to Early Bronze Age. Additional proof for this date is the fact that some of the dolmens have entrances which could only have been cut by metal tools. W. F. Albright assigns the dolmens in Transjordan and in Western Palestine to 6000–4000 B.C. N. Glueck dates them to about 6000 B.C. and even employs the terms "dolmen period" and "dolmen culture." These terms are, however, meaningless since the megalithic monuments were connected with burial rites and the cult of the dead during different periods.

M. STEKELIS

BIBLIOGRAPHY

P. Karge, *Rephaim*, Paderbonn, 1917 • F. Turville–Petre, *PEFQSt*, 1931, 155–66 • M. Stekelis, *Les monuments mégalithiques de Palestine*, Paris 1935 • E. C. Broome, *The Dolmens of Palestine and Transjordania*, Brown University, 1940 (Ph. D. Thesis); *idem*, *JBL* 59 (1940), 479–97 • M. Stekelis, *La Necropólis megalitica de Ala-Safat, Transjordania*, Barcelona, 1961; *idem*, *Mi-Tekufat ha-Even* 3, 1962 (Hebrew) • J. L. Swauger, *ADAJ* 10 (1965), 5–36; *idem*, *BA* 29 (1966), 106–14 • R. W. Dajani, *ADAJ* 12–13 (1967–68), 56–64 • D. Gilead, *PEQ*, 1968, 16–26; D. Webley, *PEQ*, 1969, 42–43; D. Bahat, *IEJ* 22 (1972), 44–46. *idem*, *EI* 11 (1973), 58–63 (Hebrew) • Claire Epstein, *Qadmoniot* 7 (1974), 37–40 (Hebrew); *idem*, IEJ 23 (1973), 109–10; 24 (1974) 254–57; *idem*, *EI* 12 (1975), 1–8 (Hebrew).

Megiddo. General plan of the excavations and areas excavated. 1. Water shaft. 2. Schumacher's trench.

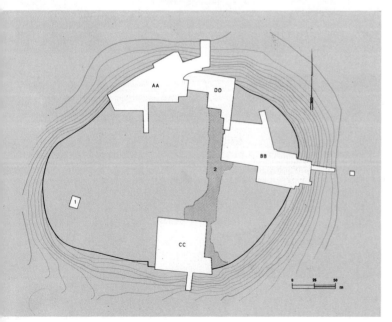

MEGIDDO

IDENTIFICATION. The identification of biblical Megiddo with el-Lajjûn, about 1 kilometer south of Tel Megiddo (Tell el-Mutesellim) was suggested as early as the fourteenth century by Estori ha-Parḥi and in the nineteenth century by E. Robinson. Tel Megiddo is one of the most important city mounds in Palestine. It rises 40–60 meters above the surrounding plain and covers an area of about 15 acres (60 dunams). This areas was enlarged in various periods by a lower city. The position of the mound at the point where the 'Iron ('Aruna) Brook enters the Jezreel Valley gave it strategic control in ancient times over the international Via Maris which crossed from the Sharon into the Plain of Jezreel by way of the 'Iron Valley. This position astride the most important of the country's roads made Megiddo from earliest times until our own era the scene of major battles.

HISTORY

The excavations conducted on the mound have shown that, already in the Early and Middle Bronze Ages, Megiddo was a fortified city of major importance depite the fact that it is not mentioned in historical sources until the fifteenth century B.C. At that time it appears in the inscriptions of Thutmose III. The annals of this pharaoh record that Megiddo led a confederation of rebel Canaanite cities, which, together with Kadesh on the Orontes, attempted to overthrow Egyptian rule in Canaan and Syria. The Egyptian army and the Canaanite chariotry fought the decisive battle of this rebellion at the Qinnah Brook (Wadi Lajjûn) near Megiddo. This is the earliest military engagement whose details have been preserved. After thoroughly routing the Canaanite force in the field, Pharaoh captured a rich booty, including 924 chariots! According to the Gebel Barkal stele, the siege of the city lasted seven months. During this time the Egyptian army harvested the city's fields and took 207,300 *kur* of wheat (apart from what the soldiers kept for themselves).

After his great victory, Thutmose turned Megiddo into the major Egyptian base in the Jezreel Valley Evidence of its importance and military strength is found in three documents. In one of the Taanach letters, the King of Taanach was ordered to send men and tribute to Megiddo. The description of the second campaign of Amenhotep II (about 1430 B.C.) ended "in the vicinity of Megiddo". In one of the el-Amarna letters (*EA* 244), the King of Megiddo requests Pharaoh to return to that city the Egyptian garrison which was stationed there earlier.

Megiddo is mentioned in the city lists of Thutmose III and Seti I, and, in Thutmose's list of Canaanite emissaries (Leningrad Papyrus 1116-A). Among the el-Amarna letters are six sent by King Biridiya (an Indo-Aryan name) of Megiddo to the Egyptian pharaoh. These letters show that Megiddo was one of the mightiest cities in the Jezreel Valley, and that its major rivals were Shechem and Accho. In one of his letters Biridiya mentions that he brought corvée workers from Yapu (Japhia?) to plow the fields of Shunem (a city which, according to another letter, had been previously destroyed). In the Papyrus Anastasi I, dated to the reign of Ramses II, Megiddo is mentioned in a detailed description of the road from the city down to the coastal plain, following the course of the 'Iron Brook.

During the period of the Judges, Megiddo was one of the major Canaanite cities in the Jezreel Valley. It is mentioned in the Song of Deborah: "The kings came and fought, then fought the kings of Canaan in Taanach by the waters of Megiddo" (Judges 5:19; and cf. Joshua 12:21). It is also listed among the Canaanite cities not conquered by the tribe of Manasseh (Joshua 17:11–13; Judges 1:27–28; and cf. I Chronicles 7:29). How or when Megiddo fell into Israelite hands is not known, but it appears during the period of the United Monarchy, together with Hazor and Gezer, among the Israelite cities fortified by Solomon (I Kings 9:15). It is also mentioned as one of the cities in Solomon's fifth administrative district (*ibid*. 4:12).

Thereafter there are few written references to Megiddo, but it is clear that it continued to be one of the major northern cities. Pharaoh Shishak conquered the city during his campaign against Israel in the fifth year of Rehoboam's reign (about 925 B.C.), and it is mentioned in the story of the death of Ahaziah of Judah, during Jehu's revolt (II Kings 9:27). In 733/32 B.C. Tiglath-Pileser III, King of Assyria, conquered the northern part of Israel, and made Megiddo the capital of the Assyrian province of Magiddu. This province included the Jezreel Valley and the Galilee (the

district "of the nations" in Isaiah 9:1). The fact that Josiah's battle against Pharaoh Necho in 609 B.C. was fought at Megiddo (cf. II Kings 23:29; II Chronicles 35:22) indicates that at least for a short time the city was under Judean rule. This was in all likelihood the last period of prosperity in Megiddo's long history, since after Josiah's defeat, nothing more of Megiddo is heard. The strategic role of guarding the 'Iron Pass was assumed by Kefar Othnai, a small village, which after the Bar Kokhba war, became the base of the Sixth Roman Legion. It became known as Legio (in Arabic: el-Lajjūn). Megiddo's military importance and long history as an international battleground was aptly reflected in the Apocalypse of John (Revelation 16:12 ff.) in which "Armageddon" (*Har Megiddon* —"The mount of Megiddo") is designated as the site where at the end of days, all the kings of the world will fight the ultimate battle against the forces of God.

EXCAVATIONS

The excavations conducted at Megiddo were the largest and most extensive ever carried out in Palestine. From 1903 to 1905, the mound was excavated by G. Schumacher on behalf of the German Society for Oriental Research. Schumacher dug a 20–25 meters wide trench running north and south the entire length of the mound. In part of the trench he dug down to the Middle Bronze Age II occupation levels, reaching bedrock in a small section. In his reports, Schumacher described six building levels from the Middle Bronze Age II to the Iron Age. Two large buildings discovered in the trench, the Mittelburg and the Nordburg, were both built during the Middle Bronze Age II and continued in use, with some repairs and additions, until the Late Bronze Age. Beneath these buildings were two unique tombs with false-arch roofs, which some scholars considered the tombs of the Megiddo royal dynasty in the Late Bronze Age. At the south end of the trench, Schumacher uncovered part of a large building dating to the Israelite period (Iron Age), which he called the Palace (Palast) (building 1723 of the Chicago expedition, see below).

Schumacher also made several soundings in different parts of the mound and on the slopes along the city walls. The sections of walls that he excavated belonged mostly to the Israelite city, but some were earlier.

Near the east end of the mound, Schumacher excavated a large Israelite building, which he thought was a sanctuary because of its stone pillars (identified by him as stelae of a sanctuary). He called the building Tempelburg. Similar stone pillars, however, have been found in ordinary houses of the Israelite period. A Proto-Aeolic capital, re-used as a building stone, was discovered in the wall of this building. It was the first such capital found in Palestine.

The small finds of the excavation were published by C. Watzinger in a separate volume. Especially noteworthy are two seals inscribed "(belonging) to Shem'a servant of Jeroboam" and "(belonging) to Asaph," which were found in the ruins of the palace, and a stone incense burner with painted decoration found in the upper (sixth) stratum at the south end of the trench.

In 1925, excavations at Megiddo were renewed by the Oriental Institute of the University of Chicago and continued until 1939, under the successive direction of C. S. Fisher, P. L. O. Guy, and G. Loud. The original goal of the expedition was to excavate the entire mound, removing stratum after stratum, from top to bottom. This ambitious project was carried out successfully for the first four strata only (Persian period to ninth century B.C.). The finds of these four strata and part of the excavation of the fifth stratum were published by R. Lamon and G. M. Shipton in *Megiddo I*.

During the final four years of the expedition, it became evident that the work could not be continued on such a grand scale, and the excavations were thereafter concentrated in two main areas: *area AA* in the north, in the vicinity of the city gate, where the excavators reached stratum XIII (Middle Bronze Age II–A) and *area BB*, in the east, the area of the temples, where bedrock was reached (stratum XX). The expedition reached stratum VI in two additional areas, *area CC* in the south (the area of Schumacher's Palast) and *area DD* in the northeast, situated between areas AA and BB.

The outbreak of World War II put an unexpected end to the excavations. The results have appeared only in a "Catalogue Publication of floor plans and finds" — to quote Loud's definition — and have not as yet been scientifically and systematically published.

Because the east slope of the mound was to be used as a dump for the excavated earth, the expedition first undertook to clear and examine this area before dumping began. Its investigation revealed many burial caves of different periods, which contained rich and varied finds providing valuable additions to the discoveries made on the mound. The finds from the burial caves were published separately by P. L. O. Guy and R. M. Engberg in *Megiddo Tombs*.

The east slope also yielded remains of seven levels of the Early Bronze Age settlements (according to a previous assumption of the excavators the earliest settlement level dated to the Chalcolithic period). These levels, called stages I–VII, were published separately by Engberg.

One of the most significant discoveries was the city's monumental water tunnel. It was fully excavated and made the subject of a separate study, *The Megiddo Water System*, by R. Lamon. The excavators suggested that the tunnel was dug in the twelfth century B.C., but later excavations by Y. Yadin have shown that it was most probably built in the Iron Age (see below). In another separate volume, *Material Remains of the Megiddo Cult*, by H. G. May, were assembled the cult finds of the various levels. The magnificent hoard of ivories (see below) of the Late Bronze Age was published by G. Loud in *The Megiddo Ivories*.

This page: City wall, stratum XVIII. Opposite page, left: High place and temples surrounding it; Right: Sacred area, stratum XV.

THE STRATA OF SETTLEMENT

The excavators numbered Megiddo's strata from I (the latest) to XX (the earliest). In the course of excavations, however, some of these levels were subdivided into A and B.

TABLE OF STRATA AND DATES, ACCORDING TO THE CHICAGO EXPEDITION (ALL DATES ARE B.C.)

STRATUM	PERIOD	STRATUM	PERIOD
XX	before 3300	VIII	1479–1350
XIX	3300–3000	VII-B	1350–1150
XVIII	3000–2500	VII-A	
XVII	2500–?	VI-B	1150–1100
XVI	?–1950	VI-A	
XV	1950–1850	V-B	1050–1000
XIV	1850–1800	V-A	
XIII-B	1800–1750	IV-B	1000–800
XIII-A		IV-A	
XII	1750–1700	III	780–650
XI	1700–1650	II	650–600
X	1650–1550	I	600–350
IX	1550–1479		

THE EARLIEST SETTLEMENT TO THE END OF THE BRONZE AGE

Although scattered potsherds indicated the existence of a Neolithic settlement on part of the mound, no structures were found that could be related to the settlement. A small cave discovered at the bottom of area BB contained only flint tools and bones apparently from the Pre-Pottery stage of the Neolithic period. It is designated in the publication of the Chicago expedition as stratum – XX.

Stratum XX: Only in area BB on the east side of the mound (the area of the Bronze Age temples) did the excavators reach the earliest levels of habitation. The few remains of stratum XX buildings included segments of mud-brick walls of round and square dwellings, pits, and ovens. These structures apparently belong to different stages of the Chalcolithic period, and according to M. Dothan, the round (apsidal) houses are earlier than the square ones.

Stratum XIX: The earliest building of significant size was found in stratum XIX. It consisted of a row of three rooms, enclosed on the west and north by a wall, approximately 3 meters thick. A 30-meter-long segment of this wall was excavated, and no other walls were found leaning on it except the three rooms attached to it on the east. Although its width seems to indicate that it was a city wall, this is unlikely, since it was not built at the edge of the mound, and it may well have just encircled the area to the east of it. The thick wall as well as the walls of the three rooms were built of mud brick on a foundation of a single stone course built with exceptional care. The suggestion of the excavators that the southernmost of the three rooms was a shrine seems very likely, not only because it was the site of later temples, but also because of the room's shape and contents. It was a broad room (4 by 12 meters) with the entrance in the long wall. Set against the west wall, directly opposite the entrance, was a rectangular platform

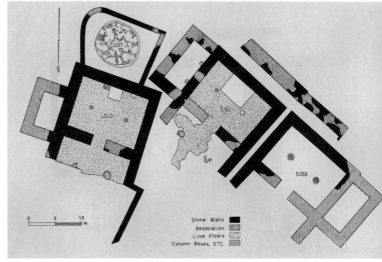

of plastered mud brick — obviously an altar. At a later stage of stratum XIX, another, larger altar was built over the earlier one, completely covering it. The early altar had a step on its south side while the later altar was approached by a step on the east side. In the middle of the room were four flat stones, placed at more or less regular intervals. These may have been the bases of pillars that supported the roof. Near the west wall were three similar stones, one of which was covered by the later altar. Their function is not clear.

East of this building was a spacious courtyard more than 25 meters long, with remains of paving that sloped sharply to the east. The excavators originally suggested that all the structures east of this courtyard were destroyed when the great wall of stratum XVIII was built. However, east of the stratum XVIII wall were found the remains of a row of rooms which may have belonged to stratum XIX (see below). Consequently, it would seem that the large courtyard was enclosed by rooms. The courtyard was paved with stone flags, some of which were laid over with additional slabs, evidently later repairs. On the slabs of the different layers were incised figures of men and beasts (mostly hunting scenes) and decorative patterns. These stone drawings are among the earliest examples of local art found in Palestine. Only a small portion of the ceramic finds of this stratum has been published. The published pottery of strata XIX to XVI shows a mixture of the ceramic finds of these strata. Stratum XIX apparently belongs to a later stage of Early Bronze Age I. The distinct broad-room type of shrine is similar to the Chalcolithic sanctuary at En-Gedi (q.v.) and to the Early Bronze Age II buildings recently excavated at Arad (q.v.).

Strata XVIII–XVI. The settlements of these three strata were dated to the Early Bronze Age II–III. The confusion in the publication of the pottery of these strata indicates that the excavators did not wholly succeed in establishing an accurate and reliable stratigraphy of these lower levels. It is possible, therefore, that many of the walls and other architectural remains were also incorrectly ascribed to their various strata. For this reason, these three strata must remain somewhat unclear, and their plans considered as only the excavators suggested reconstructions.

The major innovation in these strata was the great city wall, which was the largest and strongest wall ever built on the mound. The stone foundations were preserved to a height of more than 4 meters, and it can be assumed that they supported upper courses of sun-dried bricks that have not survived. The wall was built in separate lengthwise sections, between which spaces were left (breaks or joints) of from 5 to 10 centimeters. Its overall width (perhaps at its second stage) was approximately 8 meters, and was made up of two separate sections of some 4 meters each. The excavators were of the opinion that the wall was originally only 4–5 meters wide, and that a row of contiguous rooms was built against its exterior. Sometime during the settlement of stratum XVIII these rooms were destroyed, and an additional 3–4 meter thick wall was built on their ruins. The excavators, however, indicated this addition on the plans of strata XVII and XVI "solely for convenience and clarity of presentation."

On the basis of this row of rooms built outside the wall, Kathleen Kenyon concluded that it was not an additional section of wall that was built over the rooms but a retaining wall, which was intended to level the sloping area. This seems doubtful, however, since retaining walls are not usually so thick. It is more likely, as was stated above, that these rooms were incorrectly ascribed to stratum XVIII and actually belong to stratum XIX. The assumption that these stratum XIX rooms were cut into or covered by the stratum XVIII wall would also explain the irregular shapes of the rooms which are not parallel to the line of the wall (especially room 4057). It would then seem that the original wall was 8 meters thick, and that the "joints" are simply stages in the original building process. A mud-brick wall of equal thickness and dating to about the same period discovered at Beth-Yeraḥ (q.v.) was also constructed in lengthwise sections with thin "joints" between them. The houses

Both pages, counterclockwise: Impression of cylinder seal found in LBA I tomb; Ivory plaque, apparently of Hittite origin — 14th century B.C.; Ivory box decorated with sphinxes on one side, and lions on another, from the ivory hoard found in the palace of stratum VII A, 12th century B.C.; Jug from tomb 912D — LBA II.

abutting the wall on the outside led the excavators to assume that this was a citadel wall rather than a city wall. The west turn of the wall strengthens this assumption, but a citadel wall would not be expected to have houses leaning against it on the outside. It is more difficult to fix the other architectural remains of the Early Bronze Age in a correct stratigraphic order. The plan of this level is fragmentary because no building of stratum XVIII was excavated in its entirety. A wall 3.5 meters thick was uncovered in the area of the stratum XIX shrine. The thickness of the wall suggested that it was part of a public edifice, probably a temple (on the basis of the tradition of temples built on this site throughout the Bronze Age). The other walls excavated do not fit into a coherent plan. According to Kathleen Kenyon, these walls belong to different stages of a continuous settlement, dating from the end of the Early Bronze Age I to the beginning of the Early Bronze Age III.

Left: Decorated clay wall bracket — LBA; Below: Fragment of tablet containing the Gilgamesh Epic.

Strata XVII–XVI. The plans of these two strata are almost identical. The excavators pointed out that stratum XVI is a clear continuation of stratum XVII with minor architectural changes and the addition of some floors. Kathleen Kenyon has shown that the plans of most of the buildings in the two strata are similar. The large eastern building (3177) retained the same floor plan in both strata. The stratum XVII plan represents the wall foundations of the stratum XVI building. The open drainage ditch, which in stratum XVII ran along the surface of courtyard 4002, is the subterranean drainpipe laid beneath the paving of the same courtyard in stratum XVI.

Only in the very center of the area (especially around locus 4037) are discrepancies found between the plan of the buildings of the two strata, and Miss Kenyon suggests that the buildings ascribed to stratum XVI actually belong to stratum XV. The city wall of stratum XVIII continued to exist without alterations (in constrast to the view of Miss Kenyon).

The major architectural innovation in stratum XVII was the large round altar (more than 8 meters in diameter and 1.4 meters high) erected in the middle of the area near the early shrine. Miss Kenyon is probably correct in assuming that the altar of stratum XVII served as the foundation of an identical stratum XVI altar. Built of small rubble stones (cf. Exodus 20:25), the altar is ascended by a flight of steps on the east. It is surrounded by a temenos wall, and the entire area inside the wall was found strewn with a great many potsherds and animal bones — the remains of sacrifices.

The altar was built in the vicinity of the "temple courtyard" of stratum XIX and close to the site of the later temples. It can therefore be assumed that in strata XVII and XVI the altar also stood near a temple which has not been uncovered. West of the round altar were remains of rooms along the two sides of a long narrow lane running east–west. In contrast to the earlier strata, which slope down to the east following the natural contour of the mound, in the later stratum the area was filled in and leveled so that the round altar is raised above its surroundings.

Between the altar and the city (or citadel) wall stood a large building (3177), whose function is not clear. The building consists of large halls and spacious courtyards, most of them paved with pebbles — one of the hallmarks of this stratum. In one of the rooms (Number 5) was a pit and near it a round stone base similar in workmanship to the bases found in the later temples. A paved street, 2–3 meters wide, ran between this building and the wall. The level of the street had been raised several times. Since in some spots the street extended up to and over the edge of the city wall, the excavators concluded that it had covered most of the wall, which consequently was only a retaining wall. This, however, is an unlikely assumption considering the thickness of the wall. It is more probable that the foundations of the wall were slightly wider than the upper course, and the paving stones of the street came up to the wall covering only the part of the foundations that projected below ground level.

Due to the appearance of some Khirbet Kerak ware, strata XVII and XVI should probably be dated to the Early Bronze Age III.

Stratum XV. This stratum is basically different in plan from the earlier strata. Only the round altar continued in use unchanged, although its level may have been raised somewhat. This indicates that the city of stratum XVI suffered total destruction and was rebuilt anew, although a certain continuity is found in the central cult area.

The excavators dated this level to the Middle Bronze Age II-A. Kathleen Kenyon placed it somewhat earlier, in the Middle Bronze Age I. But a study of the small finds and of the ceramic remains indicates that this level too belonged to the Early Bronze Age III.

Three new temples were erected in the vicinity of the round altar: temple 4040 north of the altar, and temples 5192 and 5269 to the west. All three were similar in plan — a broad room, entered through a porch in front of the north side of the hall, which was formed by a 5-meter-long extension of its east and west walls. This type of structure recalls the Aegean megaron except for the broad-room type of hall. The excavators cite examples of similar structures mainly from the Early Bronze Age, and pointed out that the close proximity of the three Megiddo temples is reminiscent of the megaron buildings of Troy II.

The plan of the interior of the three temples was almost identical. Opposite the entrance, in the center of the south wall, stood a square altar.

Below, top to bottom: Ivory wand — stratum VIII;
Ivory handle depicting ruler seated on throne and
receiving victory procession after battle — LBA II;

Plan of temple 2048 in its three phases — strata VIII,
VII–B and VII–A. Opposite page: Plan of the gate
and palace of stratum VII — area AA.

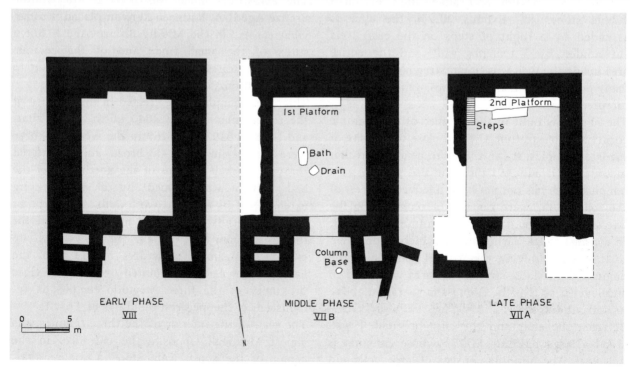

EARLY PHASE
VIII

MIDDLE PHASE
VII B

LATE PHASE
VII A

0   5
m

1st Platform

Bath

Drain

2nd Platform

Steps

Column
Base

N

Steps leading up to the altar from the east were preserved in temple 4040. In the middle of each hall were found two round, well-cut stone bases of columns that had supported the roof. Two other column bases at the north edge of the porch were aligned with the ends of the two wall extensions. The altar, floors, and walls of the porch and main room were all covered with a fine lime plaster. The two western temples were approximately equal in size (5269: 13.75 by 8.9 meters; 5192: 13.6 by 8.9 meters) and were built adjacent to one another. South and east of these temples were the remains of a strong wall, which must have enclosed the temples at least on these sides. Temple 4040 was slightly larger (13.7 by 9.6 meters) and built on a different alignment. The round altar was enclosed with a new temenos wall that extended up to temple 4040.

The pottery of this stratum, as presented in the publication, shows a mixture of Early Bronze Age and Middle Bronze Age I–II ware. Kathleen Kenyon, who examined the pottery and the relationship among the three temples, suggested the following:

1. If the east wall of temple 5192 is extended to the end of the floor preserved in the porch, it will meet the west wall of temple 4040. It must be assumed that the two western temples were built before temple 4040, and that the latter was erected when the western ones already lay in ruins.

2. Most of the pottery ascribed to stratum XV dates to the Middle Bronze Age I and II, but the Middle Bronze Age II pottery was found mainly in tombs. The most common form of burial in the Middle Bronze Age II was in graves dug beneath the floors of houses inside the city, and consequently the excavators found many tombs on the mound itself. Unfortunately, the levels at which these tombs were encountered and excavated were not always accurately recorded and in many cases a tomb find from a later period which had been dug into an earlier one was erroneously ascribed to the earlier stratum. For this reason it is impossible to utilize the rich finds from these tombs in determining the chronology. It can, however, be concluded, that most of the ceramic finds of stratum XV date to the Middle Bronze Age I and that the three temples were built at different stages of this period.

3. In the rebuilt (stratum XIV) north wall of temple 4040 was found a fenestrated bronze axhead (*Megiddo II,* Plate 182:3). This weapon, which is characteristic of the Middle Bronze Age I–beginning of the Middle Bronze Age II-A, dates the late phase of temple 4040 to that period.

4. A section of a wall and a pavement (locus 4009) were found above the round altar and were attributed by the excavators to stratum XIII-B. The wall and floor are obviously later than the altar, and judging from their very close proximity to temple 4040, it seems that they were built after the destruction of that temple. Since all the published pottery from locus 4009 belongs to the Middle Bronze Age I, temple 4040 and the round altar must have lain in ruins before that time.

In an attempt to resolve the stratigraphic problems of this area and to establish the relationship between the three temples and the altar, I. Dunayevsky conducted several soundings in the area. He uncovered several points of contact between the walls of the three buildings. It was found that the wall of a side room attached to temple 4040 (a wall not shown in the publication of the Chicago expedition) ran beneath the eastern wall of temple 5192. This proved that, contrary to Kathleen Kenyon's assumption, temple 4040 was built prior to the two western temples. It also became evident that the temenos wall surrounding

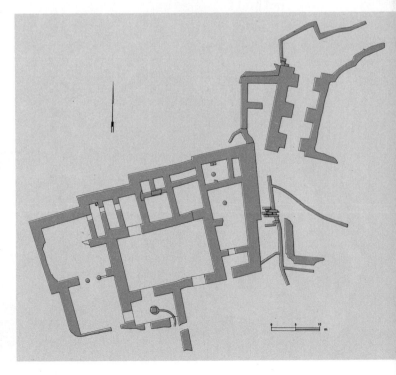

the round altar joined the south wall of temple 4040, proving that the temple and altar must have existed at the same time.

Once the relative stratigraphy of the three temples and the altar had been determined, the chronology of the structures could be reconsidered. It now appears that the temples do not date to the Middle Bronze Age I, but rather to the Early Bronze Age III (note also the similarity of the stone bases found in stratum XVI).

Building 3177 of strata XVII–XVI was apparently not in existence in stratum XV. In its place was erected a new structure, 3160, part of which was excavated in area BB. The most outstanding feature of this new building were two wide stairways ascending from the west. The excavators assumed — probably correctly — that these stairs were used during festivals and rituals, and led to the sacred precinct (the area of the three temples and the round altar). They may have belonged to an east gate whose existence may be surmised from the architectural remains in the various strata.

Between building 3160 and the sacred area was a

5-meter-thick wall that apparently served as a retaining wall of the sacred area. The processional way probably ran along it. The earlier massive wall seem to have continued in use, although the excavators do not include it in the plan of stratum XV.

Stratum XIV. Characteristic of this stratum are small and poorly constructed buildings. In the opinion of the excavators, this level includes at least two separate building levels, but because of the extremely poor state of the remains, it was possible to distinguish between them only where one wall was constructed directly above another. Most of the pottery published from this level dates to the Middle Bronze Age II, but since it comes from tombs, its attribution to this stratum is questionable. The remainder of the pottery is Middle Bronze Age I, with a few pieces typical of the beginning of the Middle Bronze Age II-A (for example, a cooking pot with rope decoration and partially pierced holes [*Megiddo II*, Plate 15:19]). Most of the architectural remains of this stratum therefore probably belong to the end of the Middle Bronze Age I, and a few may belong to the begin-

ning of the Middle Bronze Age II-A. The small buildings of stratum XIV were erected on top of the western temples and in the area of the eastern building (3160). The only outstanding piece of architecture was a large wall in squares N–O/14. Kathleen Kenyon seems to be correct in assuming that this wall actually belongs to stratum XV and is a part of building 3160.

The massive city wall of the Early Bronze Age levels also went out of use. Above it were found the remains of weak fortifications. As was mentioned above, the excavators' opinion that the round altar continued to exist in stratum XIV seems unlikely. Instead of the altar, locus 4009, ascribed to stratum XII-B, which is dated to the Middle Bronze Age I, should be added to the plan.

The only traces of any continuity are found in temple 4040, although almost nothing remained of its original plan. In its center was a small irregularly shaped room (4 by 5.5 meters). The space between this room and the walls of the original temple was filled with rubble. The southern wall of the room opened onto a raised niche for which the original altar served as a foundation. Near the middle of the room stood a large stone (about 1.75 by 1.25 meters), with a small depression resembling a cup mark in the center. Only two ceramic finds from this room have been published: a regular Middle Bronze Age II crater (*Megiddo II*, Plate 15:16) and a high decorated base of a chalice or censer (*ibid.*, Plate 15:23). The fenestrated axhead mentioned above (*ibid.*, Plate 182:3) places this later reconstruction of temple 4040 in the Middle Bronze Age I or beginning of Middle Bronze Age II-A.

The sacred precinct retained its tradition of sanctity from the Early Bronze Age to the Middle Bronze Age, though the plans of the later temples were entirely different from the earlier ones.

Opposite page: Ivory panels from the hoard from palace VII–A; This page, below: Figure of deity of bronze gilded with gold — stratum VII or VI; Right: Ivories from the hoard of palace VII–A.

Stratum XIII. Two phases of building were distinguished in stratum XIII. It was sub-divided into XIII-B and XIII-A. This stratum was also reached in area AA, the site of the city's gates on the north side of the mound. From this period onward the information from area BB is supplemented by finds from area AA.

Area BB. The buildings of stratum XIII in area BB are of much better construction than those of the preceding stratum, although the plans are very fragmentary. A group of rooms and other structures uncovered in the western part of the area were surrounded by narrow lanes on the north, south, and west. Similar structures were discovered in the eastern end of the area. Beyond these a new city wall was built, slightly to the west of the Early Bronze Age wall. The new wall was of mud brick on stone foundations, with offsets at regular intervals. A row of rooms opened onto a paved lane which ran parallel to the wall.

On the plans of strata XIII to IX, the sacred precinct is shown as empty of all architectural remains. (Only in stratum VIII does a new temple appear on this traditionally holy site.) Scattered fragments of floors and pavements are found in the area from strata XIII to IX. In strata XII and IX, stelae were found standing in the area and in strata XII and XI bronze statuettes were discovered on some of the pavements. In the opinion of I. Dunayevsky, these are all the remains of a bamah (High Place), which was raised gradually from stratum to stratum, much like the bamah beside the temple in Nahariya. It is also possible that a temple was built somewhere in the vicinity of the bamah. This would explain the phenomenon of the persistence of the sanctity of the area as the site of sacred buildings in the long period from strata XIII to IX during which no temples were built there. However, it has also been suggested that the stratum VIII temple was founded in an earlier stratum.

Area AA. In this area a section of a wall, 1.8 meters thick, similar to the wall found in area BB, was discovered together with the earliest city gate found at Megiddo. It was tentatively attributed to stratum XIII, though this is not certain. Like the wall, the gate was built of mud brick on a stone foundation. It was a pedestrian gate and consisted of two narrow entrances set at right angles, defended by two towers projecting on either face of the wall. A stairwell leading to an

upper story was found intact within the inner tower. From the outside the gate was approached by a flight of steps built against an outer wall 3 meters thick, which was strengthened by a glacis. East of the gate, a drainage channel ran beneath the wall in the direction of the steps.

The lower half of an inscribed Egyptian statuette and two Egyptian stelae found in the temple platform of stratum VII belong, in all likelihood, to stratum XIII. The inscription on the statuette mentions the name of Thuthotep, who, according to J. Wilson, should be identified with a high official under Senusert III (mid-nineteenth century), whose grave was discovered in Egypt. Thuthotep's tomb inscription contains a title that can identify him as the governor of Egyptian holdings in Asia. It can therefore be assumed that Canaan at this time was under Egyptian rule and the seat of the local governor was in Megiddo.

Stratum XII. Strata XII–X date to the Middle Bronze Age II-B (eighteenth to mid-seventeenth centuries). The plans of these strata differ wholly from that of stratum XIII. From strata XII to VII-A (twelfth century) there is, however, a continuity in the general architectural design of the major buildings and other structures. This indicates that, during this long period, no serious changes or interruptions troubled the settlement at Megiddo. Only the city wall built in stratum XIII continued in use in stratum XII as well, but its thickness was doubled by a skillfully built addition. The broaden-

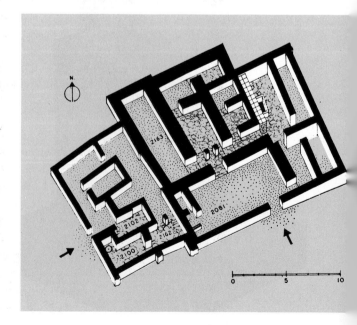

*Opposite page: Public building (2072)—
11th century B.C.; This page: Decorated
Philistine jug: musician and animal
procession — stratum VI–A.*

ing and mooring of the wall toward the slope in this and the next stratum is possibly due to the construction of a rampart and glacis typical of the Hyksos period. The doubling of the wall was evident in both areas AA and BB. Also found in both these areas was a street running parallel to the wall about 12.5 meters from it. A row of houses built against the city wall were entered from the street side. In area AA a row of three houses was completely excavated. They were all built on a similar plan and consisted of a central courtyard enclosed by rooms. The westernmost house contained ten rooms and had a cistern in the middle of the courtyard.

In area BB large and spacious buildings were uncovered that were clearly public structures connected with the sacred area. At the west end of this area was a large building with thick walls that

Schumacher had partly excavated. A number of large stone slabs of different sizes, all placed upright at the same level, were found near the site of the ancient altar. The excavators seem to be correct in suggesting that these stones were connected with the ritual of the sacred precinct and are similar to stelae.

These stelae, the remains of the floors, the figurines, and the temenos wall, all found in the vicinity of the sacred precinct, are strong support for Dunayevsky's conclusion (p. 842) that this was the site of a High Place and that the large structures discovered nearby were temples or other buildings connected in some way with the sacred area.

Stratum XI. This stratum is almost identical with the preceding one with the exception of a stone wall discovered in area AA. The stone foundations of this wall were excavated. The wall, more than 1.5 meters thick, had a row of insets, each 1.5 meters long, on its inner face. Outside the wall was a glacis, which was backed up against the exterior line of the stone wall about .5 meter above the top of the surviving stone foundations. This construction, which indicates that the glacis was now the primary defense system, is typical of the fortifications of the Hyksos period. The thin stone wall served merely as a support or revetment for the superstructure of earth or *terre pisée,* which was piled on the stone foundations with the aid of the insets. The open space between the houses and the wall may have been part of this rampart. The wall apparently continued in use until the end of the Bronze Age, even though it is not shown in the plans of the later strata.

Stratum X. In this stratum the first of a series of palaces is built near the gate in area AA. The building stood at the east end of a row of residential houses near the gate. It is outstanding in its size and the strong construction of the walls.

The palace was enlarged in stratum IX, reached its greatest extent in stratum VIII, and was reduced in size in strata VII-B–VII-A. The identification of this building as a palace is proved beyond question by the rich hoards of jewelry and carved ivories found there in strata VIII and VII-A. It is similar in its basic plan to the other private residences —a large inner courtyard surrounded in the majority of cases by rooms on all sides—and it

The water tunnel of Megiddo.

remained unchanged throughout its existence. The great city gate seems also to have been built in this stratum. It appears on the plans only from stratum IX, but the excavators suggest that it originated in stratum X. The gate is of the type in use from the Hyksos period to the end of the Late Bronze Age. It consisted of a straight passageway about 6 meters wide. Three sets of piers projecting from the inner walls of the gate reduced the width of the passageway to 3 meters (still leaving ample space for chariots) and formed two guard chambers within the passageway proper. The entire structure of the gate covered an area of approximately 11 by 18 meters. The walls of the gate were built of rough stone and rubble faced on the outside with courses of carefully hewn stone blocks, well smoothed and tightly fitted together. Between the fourth and the fifth courses of stone blocks were found remains of carbonized wooden beams, which served to reinforce and bind the stone courses.

Stratum IX. This stratum dates from the second half of the sixteenth century to the first half of the fifteenth century B.C. (the beginning of the Late Bronze Age). The palace in area AA shows clear signs of renovation. It was enlarged, and a thick wall was added on its north and east sides.

The remains of several superimposed floors, separated from one another by 30 centimeters of dirt and rubble, were found in the center of the sacred area in area BB. According to the excavators, some of these floors may belong to earlier strata. In the middle of the floors was a group of flat stone slabs with rounded ends (plano-convex slabs, in the terminology of the excavators), which clearly resemble the stelae of stratum XII.

The residential quarter in the eastern end of area BB did not undergo any important changes in this stratum. One of the buildings, consisting of a central courtyard surrounded by rooms on all four sides, was completely preserved. It was bounded by narrow streets on three sides.

Decorated bichrome ware, which appears here for the first time in stratum X, is found in quantity only in stratum IX.

Stratum VIII. This stratum follows immediately upon the destruction of stratum IX (probably at the hands of Thutmose III — see above) and dates from the second half of the fifteenth century to the first half of the fourteenth century (the Amarna Age). Despite Thutmose's conquest and destruction of the previous stratum, no signs of decline are evident in stratum VIII. In fact, this is one of the periods of the greatest material wealth of Canaanite Megiddo.

The palace was greatly enlarged (to 50 meters in length) and was enclosed by a 2-meter-thick wall. Rooms of different sizes surrounded the spacious, lime-plastered central courtyard. The two western halls are joined by a wide gate, which was supported by two basalt pillars. East of the halls was a room paved with sea shells and a square basin in its center. In the excavator's opinion, this room served as an ablution chamber, which continued in use during stratum VII-B as well.

A rich treasure, including ivory plaques, gold vessels, jewelry and gold and lapis lazuli beads, was found in the palace. This treasure, which was hidden beneath the floor of one of the smaller rooms in the north end of the palace (room 3100), is a clear indication of the great wealth of the kings of Megiddo in the Amarna Age.

The fragment of an Akkadian clay tablet found in the vicinity of the gate, at the foot of the Chicago expedition's camp, most probably belongs to stratum VIII. On the tablet is inscribed a passage from the Gilgamesh Epic. This is the first inscription of this type found in Israel, and it is striking evidence of the many and varied cultural influences exerted on Megiddo in this era.

Area BB. The fortified sanctuary, built on the site of the earlier altars, first appears in the plan of stratum VIII but its construction may be earlier. This building consisted of a single large room (9.6 by 11.5 meters) with the entrance facing north. A niche was cut in the south wall, directly opposite the doorway, which was flanked by towers on both sides. A column base found between the two towers in stratum VII-B suggests that there was a similar row of columns between the towers of the stratum VIII sanctuary. The walls of the sanctuary are 3 meters thick, and even thicker in some places — an indication that the building had more than one story. The tower to the east of the entrance apparently served as a staircase.

This structure is a special type of a fortified temple. It is similar to the temple found at Shechem, which E. Sellin dated to the fourteenth century B.C. and G. E. Wright to the Middle Bronze Age II. Wright has accordingly suggested that the fortified sanctuary at Megiddo was first built in stratum X but according to Claire Epstein it was built in stratum XII. The remains of floors found in the sacred precinct of stratum IX could thus be foundations of the sanctuary, and the stelae could be related to an earlier stratum. This, however, is rather difficult to prove on the basis of the Chicago expedition's reports (but see B. Mazar in the bibliography). The

group of houses east of the sanctuary underwent no noticeable changes in stratum VIII. In this area were found several buildings with the typical central courtyard surrounded by rooms.

Stratum VII-B. This stratum marks Megiddo's last great period of material wealth in the Bronze Age. The city did not undergo any important architectural changes. The palace is somewhat smaller, and its massive walls have disappeared. The central courtyard and the ablution chamber with the sea-shell floor of stratum VIII still remain in use. Room 3103 in the northwest corner of the palace was identified by the excavators as a household shrine because of the raised platform along its western wall. This, however, seems doubtful.

The basic plan of the fortified sanctuary remained unchanged in stratum VII-B. In various places its walls were repaired with large hewn stones, and the niche was replaced by a 1.1-meter-high plastered altar that extended the entire length of the south wall. A number of stone slabs and basins were found on the floor of the temple. Between the remains of the palaces of stratum VII-B and stratum VII-A was a thick layer of debris.   Y. AHARONI

THE IRON AGE

Stratum VII-A is the earliest level that can be ascribed with any certainty to the Iron Age. The layer of debris and the clear signs of destruction separating the architectural remains of VII-B and VII-A, especially in the palace, indicate that these were two separate strata of occupation. It seems, however, that the same or at least very similar inhabitants occupied both levels, since some of the public buildings of VII-B (most notably the sanctuary) were re-used in VII-A.

Stratum VII-A. The date of stratum VII-A was determined by cartouches of Ramses III and Ramses VI. The cartouche of the former was found on one of the carved ivories discovered in the "treasury" (see below) and of the latter on a bronze pedestal of a statue from locus 1832 in area CC. Although the pedestal was discovered beneath a wall belonging to stratum VII-B, the excavators suggest that it was deliberately buried there by the inhabitants of VII-A.

Opposite page: Selection of pottery, mostly ritual vessels, from locus 2081. IA–I; This page, top: Incense stand with bowl. IA–I; Bottom: Bronze stand. IA–I.

According to R. Lamon, the great subterranean water system was also dug at this time, but Y. Yadin's excavations in 1960, 1966, and 1967 have shown that this system is to be ascribed to the period of the Israelite Monarchy (see below).

AREA AA (THE PALACE AREA). The inhabitants of VII-A continued to use the VII-B palace even though a considerable part of it was buried under a 1.5-meter-thick layer of debris. The excavators point out that the plan of the palace in stratum VII-A was altered to a greater extent than is evident from the published plans. The destruction of the palace in VII-B was so extensive that it was found easier in VII-A to level the ruins and rebuild on top of them rather than clear them away. The major change in the VII-A palace was the addition of a structure consisting of three broad rooms in the west wing of the palace. The rooms were built in a row, and their doorways were placed on the long axis. Because the floor of this structure was lower than those of the rest of the VII-A palace, and the inner face of the walls was built of orthostats, not found on the outside surface, the excavators concluded that the foundations of this building had been dug deep into the debris of the previous level. B. Mazar has attempted to ascribe these three rooms to stratum VII-B on the assumption that they were not part of the cellar of the VII-A building. The published plans and cross sections of the area, however, show that the excavators' original conclusion was correct, and the new building was actually the reconstruction of a similar structure in the western wing of the VII-B palace.

Plan of Megiddo in the days of Solomon (stratum VA–IV B). 2156: Gate. 6008: Casemate wall. 6000: Northern Palace-fort. 1 A: Colonnaded building. 1723: Southern Palace–fort. 1482: Administration building. 629: Gallery.

The days of Ahab (Stratum IV–A): 500 B: Gate. 325: Offset-inset wall. 338: Governor's palace. 407: North stable complex. 1576: South stable complex. 925: Water shaft. 1000: Tunnel. 1007: Wall blocking water passage.

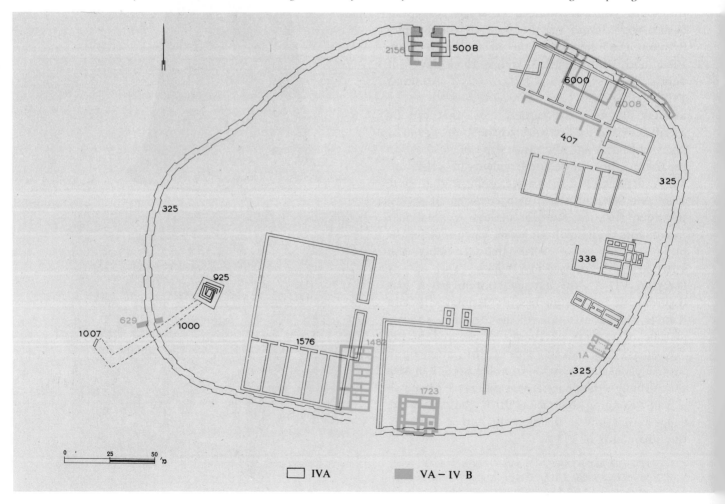

IVA   VA – IV B

This building was called the treasury by the excavators because of the cache of ivories found in it. Its tripartite plan and northern orientation (cf. Hazor) indicate that it may have been a small sanctuary attached to the palace. The cache of ivories, mostly plaques, constitutes the largest and richest collection of Canaanite carved ivory yet discovered.

The cartouche of Ramses III found on an ivory plaque is clear proof that the treasury and its hoard of ivories were in existence at the time of this pharaoh. The richness of the carved ivories, however, and the diversity of their styles (including motifs in a definite Hittite style from the time of the Hittite Empire) indicate that the treasury and its treasure originated before the reign of Ramses III. It can be assumed that the majority of these ivories actually belong to the VII-B palace. Many of the plaques were used originally as inlay panel decoration for palace furniture.

Some potsherds characteristic of the Late Bronze Age (among them fragments of Mycenaean III-B ware, were found in the area of the VII-A palace. These had been brought to the surface during construction work carried out in stratum VII-B and in fact come from stratum VII-B. The city gate of the earlier periods was reused in this stratum without any apparent changes.

AREA BB (THE TEMPLE AREA). Although the VII-A temple is similar on the whole to the VII-B temple, and in fact was built upon its ruins, it nevertheless shows some important differences. The VII-A structure is very poorly constructed. The walls are built of rubble and are only about half the width of those of the VII-B temple. In the south wall, a holy-of-holies niche was added. The niche was supported by a buttress added on the outside because the temple wall was too thin to contain it. A bema ("platform") built of stone and mud stood in front of the niche. The platform is wider in its center, opposite the niche. Worshippers ascended it by a stairway in the southeast corner. Several long stone blocks found on the floor of the temple were assumed by the excavators to belong to the lower part of the stairway. The photographs of the structure, however, show that the bottom of the staircase was complete. These stone blocks may have been small stelae that stood in the niche, similar to those discovered in the sanctuaries of Hazor (q.v.).

Many of the stratum VII-B buildings in the area of the temple continued in use in VII-A. A large new building (2090), consisting of a central court enclosed by rooms on three sides, was erected to the east of the temple in stratum VII-A.

AREA CC. The upper strata of area CC were excavated, for the most part, before the 1935 expedition, but apart from one schematic plan the results of the excavations have not yet been

Below: Walls of northern palace 6000. Note offsets–insets wall (325) above northern tier of rooms. Traces of earlier strata are seen beneath the building, in upper left; Bottom: Typical casemate west of palace 6000. Note entrance at lower left.

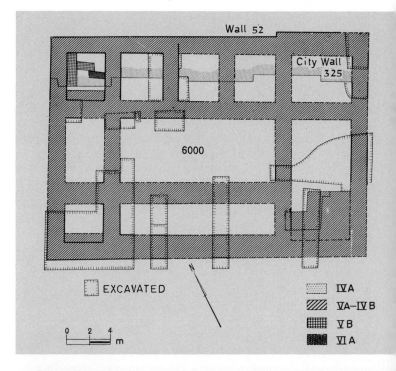

849

published. On this plan the buildings of strata VII-B and VII-A are shown together, and the locus numbers of VII-B are enclosed in brackets. It is therefore difficult to obtain a clear picture of the building in this area. None the less, the plans of the individual buildings (courts and rooms following no discernible plan) and the numerous ovens in the courts, indicate that this was essentially a residential area.

AREA DD. The results of the excavations have not been adequately published for this area as well. The single plan published presents an overall picture similar to that in area AA—a poor attempt at reconstructing the large and impressive buildings of earlier periods.

END OF STRATUM VII–A. The settlement of stratum VII-A was brought to an end by a sudden and total destruction. This is evidenced not only by the fact that the following stratum (VI-B) is totally unlike stratum VII-A but also by the signs of devastation wrought upon the VII-A buildings and by the numerous objects (e.g., the ivories and pottery from the VII-A sanctuary) found strewn over the floors of this level.

If the pedestal bearing the cartouche of Ramses VI does indeed belong to stratum VII-A then the end of this stratum can be dated to approximately 1130 B.C.

Stratum VI-B. Building remains of stratum VI-B were uncovered in several areas (mainly in area AA). The buildings were of very poor construction, and the city seems to have been unfortified. The sacred area which had an almost uninterrupted tradition of temples and bamahs throughout the Bronze Age and beginning of the Iron Age now showed no trace whatsoever of a temple. This demonstrates that the settlement at Megiddo suffered a sharp decline in stratum VI-B and that a new and different group of people occupied the site.

Stratum VI-A. In contrast to stratum VI-B, this level showed evidence of new and extensive building activity. Public buildings and some fortifications are found. The structures in this level are generally built of baked brick set partly on stone foundations. Remains of buildings were uncovered in all areas of the excavation. Area AA is of particular interest.

AREA AA. The center of this area was occupied by a large public building (2072), consisting of two long courtyards, each having a row of rooms on one side. The two units adjoined a common courtyard built to the north. A staircase in the

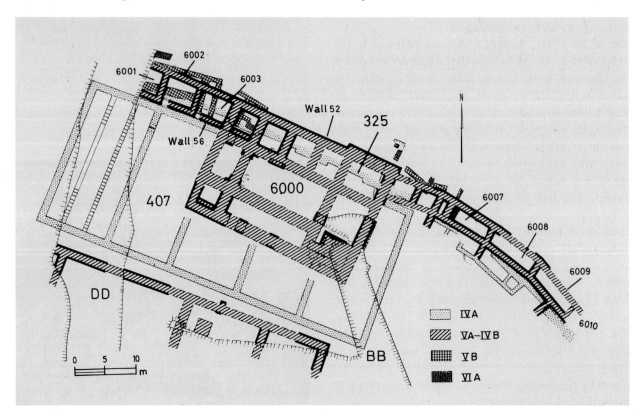

northwest corner indicates that the building, or at least part of it, was two stories high. Late Philistine pottery found in this stratum (including a decorated "beer jug" found in the building) and the huge size of the structure suggest that it may have been used by the Philistine ruler in the last half of the eleventh century B.C. (B. Mazar). It should be noted that it was built near the site of the earlier palaces, but directly above the stratum VII gate. This gate was replaced by a new small gate of only two chambers built just east of the site of the earlier gate. Gates of this new type became the standard gate in the Iron Age II. It also may be "Philistine" in style, for similar gates appear in typical fortifications from the same period in Anatolia and the Aegean.

The ceramic remains of stratum VI-A are typical of the eleventh century B.C. The VII-A city was destroyed by a great conflagration, which may perhaps be ascribed to the Davidic conquests.

Stratum V-B. The buildings of stratum V-B, erected shortly after the destruction of the previous settlement, are very poorly built and indicate a period of decline in comparison to VI-A. In area AA, modest dwellings replaced the large buildings (2072 and 3021) of the previous level. The houses were built of rubble and sun-dried brick. Some of the walls were coated with a mud plaster made from the same clay used for the bricks.

The city gate of level VI-A did not, apparently, exist in V-b. Indeed it seems that the city was entirely unfortified during this period. On the site of the VI-A gate and the line of fortifications are the outer walls of private dwellings, built adjacent to one another. This settlement, most probably dating to the Davidic period, is the first Israelite occupation of Megiddo. The relatively haphazard construction of the houses and the absence of fortifications indicate that V-B was settled before the Israelites began the centralized planning of the royal cities.

Strata V-A–IV-B and IV-A. The upper levels of Megiddo were the most extensively excavated by the various expeditions. Large areas of the mound were laid bare, with layer after layer being removed during many seasons of excavations by different directors. As a result, not only was the general chronology of the later strata and the relative stratigraphy of the entire mound very

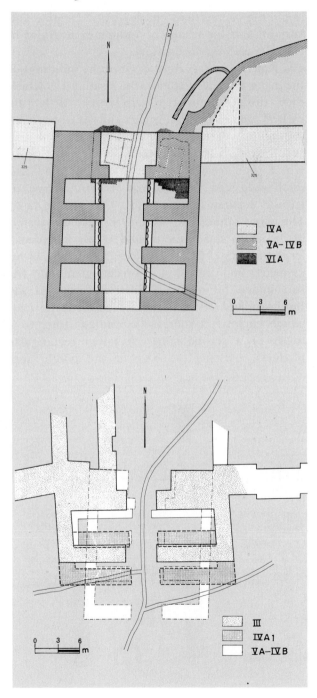

Opposite page: Plan of palace 6000 and adjacent casemates (6001–6003, 6007–6009). Note portions of earlier strata beneath casemates on both sides of the palace; This page: Development of the city gate in the Iron Age strata.

poorly understood, but it was difficult to attribute the various buildings to their proper levels. The studies of J. W. Crowfoot, W. F. Albright and G. E. Wright have contributed much to clarifying the situation. Y. Yadin's excavations in 1960, 1966, 1967 (with the assistance of I. Dunayevsky), and again in 1969, 1970, and 1971, were very valuable in identifying Solomon's level and establishing the correct stratigraphy of the stables and the water system. The main results of the American expedition, the corrections made by Albright and Wright, and the results of Yadin's excavations in 1960–70 are described below.

The American excavators ascribed the buildings of the major Israelite settlement to stratum IV, which they divided into two sub-layers: IV-B (the earlier) and IV-A. Albright and Wright have shown, however, that the buildings of V-A and IV-B belonged in fact to one and the same level, which they termed stratum V-A–IVB. They also established that the buildings of IV-A formed an entirely separate level.

The major buildings of V-A–IV-B were uncovered in the south end of the mound. These included a large building (1723, the palace) measuring 23 by 21 meters and consisting of a rectangular court (A) surrounded by rooms of different sizes. At the southeast end of the structure was a room (M), which enclosed a staircase ascending either to a tower or a second story. A raised rectangular platform, perhaps the base of the porch, was

attached to the northeast corner of the building. The foundations of the building were built of large, irregularly hewn stones sunk deep into the ground. The outer surface of the walls was largely of drafted ashlar masonry in alternating headers and stretchers. Drafted blocks also formed the upper foundations of the walls. These were not visible from the outside. In several places, especially at the corners, the stones were laid in headers extending the entire width of the wall.

The building was surrounded by a large court with a lime and plaster floor. The walls of the court were built of alternating piers of dressed stone and rubble. A large, well-built gatelike structure stood at the northeast corner of the court. It consisted of two pairs of chambers, and its foundations were aligned with the axis of "palace" 1723. Nearby were uncovered two large proto-Aeolic capitals (2.4 meters long). The capitals were not found in situ. The gatelike structure showed clear signs that it had been blocked at a later stage of its existence. Some of the dressed stones in this structure bore mason's marks similar to those on stones from "palace" 1723.

After the destruction of the "palace" (1723), an offset-inset wall (325, see below) was built over its southern end. This wall, ascribed by the American excavators to stratum IV-A, and attributed by them to Solomon, was the main cause of their stratigraphic problems and their difficulty in distinguishing between strata IV-A and VI-B. The excavators assumed that both the offset-inset wall and the stables adjoining it (see below) were built by Solomon and belonged to stratum IV-A. They were then confronted with the remains of the imposing public buildings of the earlier stratum IV-B. These were also clearly Israelite in origin.

As a result, the excavators had no choice but to assume that the "palace" (1723) was built by David as an isolated fort, and that this fort was completely destroyed by Solomon when he built his offset-inset wall and the stables. Another possibility suggested by the excavators was that Solomon built the "palace" himself before he finished planning the entire city, and tore it down when it became evident that it stood in the way of his projected city wall.

Another building (1482) was discovered west of the "palace" (1723). It consisted of two identical wings on the north and south sides of a rectangular court.

629

N

▨ ⅤA–ⅣB
▦ ⅤB
▨ ⅥA

0   1   2   3
|___|___|___|
        m

The walls of this building were parallel to those of the "palace". Because its west end lay directly beneath one of the stables, it too was ascribed to stratum IV-B, but it was noted by the excavators, however, that part of the structure continued in use during IV-A as well. The gate in area AA (see below) was assigned to stratum IV-A.

As long as further study and investigation was limited solely to the evidence then available, the conclusions of the excavators were unavoidable, and indeed these were generally accepted until the excavations in 1960 and the following years (Yadin).

Stratum IV-A. In stratum IV-A a number of large public buildings were uncovered. Among these were two stable compounds — one in the north (stable 407) and one in the south (1576) and the offset-inset wall (325). According to the excavators, the great city gate of six chambers and two towers (gate 2156) belonged to the offset-inset wall. All these structure were ascribed to Solomon.

A large, well-built structure (338) was found near the southeast corner of the northern stable compound alongside unit 364. It had a large courtyard (313) on its west side. All that has remained of this building today is a flat raised platform of regularly spaced piers of ashlar masonry, laid in alternate courses of headers and stretchers with large unhewn stones between them. The corners of the building are exceptionally well-constructed. The upper courses of one corner were made of stones dressed smooth with no bosses, and the lower course consisted of drafted stone with the upper margin the widest. This method of construction is one of the characteristics of the period of the monarchy at Megiddo, Samaria, and Hazor. In the vicinity of the building were found five proto-Aeolic capitals (one was discovered by Schumacher and two by Fisher), similar to those found at Samaria. Fisher attributed the capitals to the "Astarte Temple" which Schumacher had discovered in a later level. Unfortunately nothing remains of this temple today. The excavators ascribed building 338, and its proto-Aeolic capitals, to the Solomonic period.

Near building 338 Fisher uncovered three horned altars of limestone and a large number of objects of a cultic nature. Guy, who also excavated in the vicinity of the building, suggested that it was the residence of the officer commanding the eastern sector of Megiddo (i.e., not the official who lived in the western palace). The excavators were of the opinion that the cult objects found by Fisher belonged to a nearby building, which they assigned to stratum V. Although the connection between the building and the cult objects is not clear, the excavators were certainly correct in concluding that the building was contemporary with the offset-inset wall and the nearby stables.

YADIN'S EXCAVATIONS 1960–1970

The excavation was begun in the northeastern section, due east of Schumacher's trench and the American expedition's area DD. Since the offset-inset wall was very well preserved in this part of the mound, it was possible to examine here Yadin's theory that this wall was not built by Solomon. This theory was based on the fact that at both Hazor and Gezer Solomon had built casemate walls, while at Megiddo the wall attributed to him was a solid offset-inset wall.

In the section excavated, the offset-inset wall proved to have been built on top of the foundations of a fortress or palace constructed partly of ashlar blocks. This building (6000, according to Yadin's enumeration) also lay beneath the foundations of unit 407/1 of the north stable compound. Moreover, both east and west of this palace were found casemate walls, and above them was built the offset-inset wall. It thus became apparent that the stable compounds (the supposed stables of Solomon), the offset-inset wall, and building 338

Opposite page: Plan of gallery 629, showing it cutting through structures of stratum VI–A and the skimpier remains of stratum V–B; Below: Stable complex.

Above: Proto-Aeolic capital; Below: Seal impression: Shema servant of Jeroboam, from Schumacher's excavations; Opposite page: Area D. Plan of stratum III. Note large open-court buildings near the gate.

were all post-Solomonic, and could be assigned to stratum IV-A — the period of the Omrid dynasty. The palace 6000, the casemate wall, and the "palace" 1723 to the south, all belong to stratum V-A–IV-B (the time of Solomon). Painstaking sections made under the palace and the casemate wall proved conclusively its attribution to stratum V-A–IV-B when the clear remains of strata V-B and VI-A were found under them. The plain of the palace 6000 closely resembles that of the Neo-Hittite–Phoenician *Bit-Hilani*.

Once this important stratigraphic distinction was established, it was possible to assign gate 2156 (the massive gate of six chambers and two towers) to the casemate fortifications built by Solomon (V-A–IV-B). This, in turn, solved the knotty problem of the two later Iron Age gates, 500-B and 500, the remains of which had been discovered by the American excavators above gate 2156. The earlier gate (500-B) was a large structure of four chambers (two on each side). The later gate (500) had two chambers (one on each side). The American excavators had assigned both of these gates to stratum III (the 2156 gate being ascribed to the offset-inset wall of stratum IV-A on the assumption that the construction of gate 500-B

began in stratum III, but its plan was altered before its completion, and it was replaced by the smaller gate 500. The latter could not be assigned to stratum II since the settlement was unfortified at that time. With gate 2156 now securely attached to the Solomonic casemate wall of V-A–IV-B, gate 500-B can be assigned to the Omrid offset-inset wall of IV-A. The latest gate, 500, is now ascribed to stratum III.

The Megiddo Water System. The 1960–1967 excavations also clarified the problematic chronology of the city's water system. The two main elements in question were gallery 629 and the subterranean water system.

On the southwest side of the mound, the American expedition uncovered a curious structure which they called gallery 629. This gallery was a narrow passageway (slightly more than 1 meter wide) leading down the southwest slope of the mound to a spring flowing from a small cave at the foot of the mound. The walls of the passageway were built of ashlars laid in courses of headers and stretchers. The American excavators correctly assumed that this passage was part of the city's water system. Stratigraphically the passageway lay beneath the offset-inset wall (325), which the American excavators attributed to Solomon. Therefore, they assumed that the gallery was built before Solomon. They could not, however, attribute this imposing structure to the levels immediately beneath the offset-inset wall, because of the poor quality of their building remains. The excavators thus assigned the gallery to stratum VII-A — the time of Ramses III.

The subterranean water system consists of a vertical shaft (925) and a nearly horizontal tunnel (1000) cut underground. The upper section of the shaft was dug through the debris of previous settlements and was faced with a stone wall. The lower section of the shaft was cut into bedrock. The tunnel was cut from the bottom of the shaft, through bedrock to the cave containing the spring at the foot of the mound (the same spring to which the gallery descended from the outside). This huge engineering achievement served to convey water from the spring through the tunnel to the shaft inside the city wall. Thus in times of siege the inhabitants could safely draw water from inside the city. As a finishing touch to this great project, a stone wall was built to block the mouth of the cave. The water supply was thus accessible only from within the city, and a besieging enemy was prevented from poisoning or otherwise contaminating it.

On the basis of the early dating of the gallery, the dates of the later strata through which the upper part of the shaft was dug, and some ceramic remains within the cave (the latest of which were sherds ascribed to stratum VII-A), the American excavators reached the conclusion that the shaft could not have been dug before the thirteenth century B.C. After finally dating the construction of the shaft and tunnel to the twelfth century, the excavators then ascribed the gallery to a period prior to the completion of the subterranean system, on the assumption that the gallery was rendered obsolete once the tunnel began functioning.

Since the 1960 excavation has shown that the offset-inset wall (325) clearly dates to post-Solomonic times, the gallery could be attributed to the Solomonic period. And in fact, a sounding made during the 1966 excavation revealed 1. the foundation trench of the gallery, which was dug into the debris of previous strata, cut through houses of strata VI-A and V-B; 2. one of the stones of the gallery bore a mason's mark identical with those of the Solomonic buildings.

The gallery can therefore be dated prior to the construction of the offset-inset wall (325), but following stratum VI-A–V-B — i.e., to Solomonic times (V-A–IV-B).

Although the exact date of the construction of the subterranean system still demands further study and excavation, it can be ascribed approximately to the period of the Israelite Monarchy — definitely post-Solomonic but probably no later than the Omrid dynasty (stratum IV-A, the stables and the offset-inset wall). The subsequent discovery of a similar water system of Hazor (q.v.) from the time of Ahab is further support for this conclusion.

Stratum IV-A was thus built during the period of Omrid rule (the second quarter of the ninth century B.C.). Since the remains of the stables (recent attempts by J. Pritchard to interpret the stables as storehouses are not entirely convincing) show clear evidence of later renovations and additions, it is reasonable to assume that the occupation of this level continued with some interruption until the Assyrian conquest in 733 B.C.

Stratum III. The building remains of stratum III attest to clear Assyrian influence both in style and plan. The orientation of the buildings is completely unlike that of the previous level. Private dwellings are numerous and spacious. The streets are straight and intersect at right angles.

Two large buildings (1052 and 1369) constructed to the west of the city gate clearly exemplify this Assyrian influence. Both consist of a large spacious

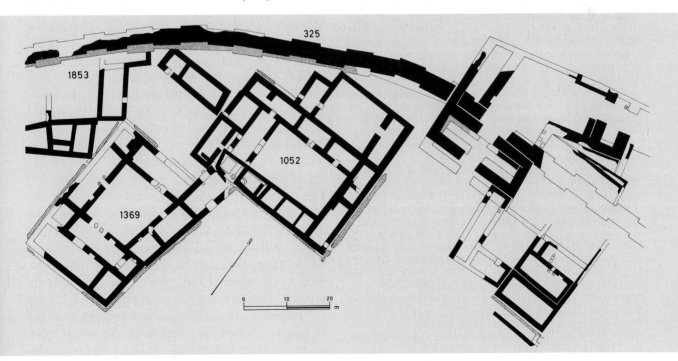

courtyard enclosed by rooms on all four sides.

The gate of stratum III (500) consisted of two chambers. The offset-inset wall (325) built in the previous level continued in use during this level as well.

The city was at this time the capital of the Assyrian province.

Stratum II. This city was an open settlement with no fortifications. The major architectural addition was a fortress built partly on the ruins of the offset-inset wall. This level can perhaps be dated to the time of Josiah, and its destruction ascribed to his defeat by Pharaoh Necho in 609 B.C.

Stratum I. This level too was unfortified. The finds indicate that it dates mainly to the Persian period.   Y. YADIN

BIBLIOGRAPHY

Identification: Estori ha-Parḥi, *Kaftor va-Feraḥ,* Berlin, 1852, 47b (Hebrew) • Robinson, *Biblical Researches* 2, 329, f.
Excavations: G. Schumacher, *Tell el-Mutesellim* 1, Leipzig, 1908 • C. Watzinger, *Tell el-Mutesellim* 2, Leipzig, 1929 • P. L. O. Guy, *New Light from Armageddon,* Chicago, 1931 • C. S. Fisher, *The Excavation of Armageddon,* Chicago, 1929 • P. L. O. Guy–R. M. Engberg, *Megiddo Tombs,* Chicago, 1938 • R. M. Engberg, *Notes on the Chalcolithic and Early Bronze Age Pottery of Megiddo,* Chicago, 1934 • H. May, *Material Remains of the Megiddo Cult,* Chicago, 1935 • R. Lamon, *The Megiddo Water System,* Chicago, 1935 • R. Lamon–G. H. Shipton, *Megiddo* 1, Chicago, 1939 • G. M. Shipton, *Notes on the Megiddo Pottery of Strata VI–XX,* Chicago, 1939 • G. Loud, *The Megiddo Ivories,* Chicago, 1939, idem, *Megiddo* 2 Chicago, 1948.
Studies: R. M. Engberg, *BASOR* 78 (1940), 4–7; idem, *BA* 3 (1940), 41–51; 4 (1941), 11–16 • A. Alt, *ZAW NF* 19, (1944), 67–85 (= *Kleine Schriften* 1, 256–73) • W. F. Albright, *BASOR* 62 (1936), 29; 63 (1937), 25; 70 (1940), 7–9; 94 (1944), 12–27 • J. A. Wilson, *AJA* 42 (1938), 333–35 • W. F. Albright, ibid., 53 (1949), 213–15 • G. E. Wright, *BA* 13 (1950), 28–46; idem, *JAOS* 70 (1950), 56–60 • B. Mazar (Maisler), *BASOR* 124 (1951), 21–25 • K. M. Kenyon, *EI* 5 (1958), 51*–60* • M. Dothan, ibid., 38–40 (Hebrew) • Y. Yadin, *BA* 23 (1960), 62–68; idem, *Bimai Bayit Rishon,* Jerusalem, 1962, 66–110 (Hebrew) • K. M. Kenyon, *Bulletin of the Institute of Archaeology,* University of London 4 (1964), 143–56 • C. Epstein, *IEJ* 15 (1965), 204–21 • I. Dunayevsky and A. Kempinski, ibid., 16 (1966), 142 • D. Ussishkin, ibid., 174–86 • Y. Yadin, ibid., 278–80; 17 (1967), 119–21 • B. Mazar, ibid., 18 (1968), 65–97 • K. M. Kenyon, *Levant* 1 (1969), 38–51 • J. B. Pritchard, in: James A. Sanders (ed.), *Near Eastern Archaeology in the Twentieth Century,* New York, 1970, 268–75 • Y. Yadin, *BA* 33 (1970), 66–69; idem, *Hazor, The Schweich Lectures* 1970, London, 1972, 150–64; idem, *IEJ* 22 (1972), 161–64 • D. Ussishikin, ibid. 20 (1970), 213–15; idem, *BA* 36 (1973), 78–105 • Y. Aharoni, *EI* 10 (1971), 53–57 • C. Epstein, ibid. 11 (1973), 54–57 • I. Dunayevsky and A. Kempinski, *ZDPV* 89 (1973) 161–87 • A. Malamat, *The Gaster Festschrift* (= JANES 5), 1973, 267–79 • A. Eitan, *IEJ* 24 (1974) 275–76 • Y. Aharoni, ibid., 13–16 • Y. Yadin, *EI* 12 (1975), 57–62.

MEIRON

IDENTIFICATION. Meiron, not to be confused with Meron of Joshua 11:5, 7, is situated just north of Wadi Meiron along one of the eastern foothills of Mount Meiron or Jebel Jarmuq. Josephus lists a Mero/Meroth as one of the villages fortified by him in A.D. 66 (*Life* 188; *War* II, 573). It is alternately listed as Ameroth and Berothe(?), one of the border settlements of Tetracomia or Upper Galilee (*War* III, 40). Rabbinic sources preserve the form Meiron (Tosephta, *Demai* 4, 13) and place the ministry of Rabbi Simeon bar Yochai there. His grave and that of his son Eliezer are reputed to be in Meiron. Although some scholars have preferred to locate the Meroth of Josephus at Marun er-Ras far to the north, such a thesis seems untenable in light of recent excavations.

Meiron's closest neighbor is Khirbet Shema' (q.v.), barely 1 kilometer to the south, identified as Teqo'a of Galilee and probably a suburb of Meiron in the first centuries A.D. Both sites made use of the spring of Meiron, probably to be identified as 'Ein Hatra. Meiron is also one of the villages mentioned in the list of priestly courses (I Chronicles 24, Mishnah, *Ta'anit* 4:2, Tosephta, *Demai* 4, 13) as the seat of the family Jehoiarib. Like Khirbet Shema' and Gush Ḥalav, it is well known in the Talmudic period for its production of olive oil (Palestinian Talmud, *Shevi'it* 9, 2). By late medieval times Meiron had become an important pilgrimage center, its sanctity deriving from the mystical traditions of Bar Yochai, the festival of Lag ba-Omer and the centrality of Safad (9 kilometers [5.5 miles] to the east) in the development of Lurianic mysticism.   E. M. MEYERS

THE SYNAGOGUE

The ruins of a synagogue on the site were frequently examined and described during the nineteenth and beginning of the twentieth centuries. C. Wilson cleared the remains in 1868.

The synagogue stands on a terrace cut out of the rock in the northeastern part of the hill, near its summit. The building is rectangular (about 27 by 13.5 meters) and is oriented to the south, toward Jerusalem. Except for a section of the facade, part of the cornice, and several column bases, no other

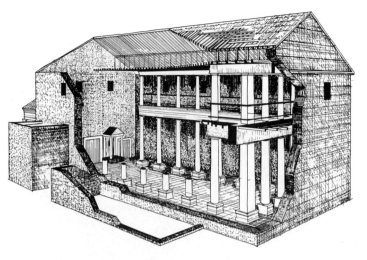

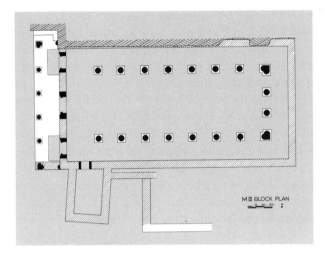

M III BLOCK PLAN

Counterclockwise: Schematic ground plan of Meiron synagogue; Facade of Meiron synagogue, looking north; Reconstruction of Meiron synagogue, looking southwest. Note annex at left and Ark of the Law on south wall.

part of the building has survived. The vertical rock of the terrace formed the west wall of the building. Of the north and east walls, only traces have been preserved. About two thirds of the facade of the synagogue, built of dressed stones, is still standing in position up to the height of the lintels. It contained three entrances, a wide high opening in the center flanked by two narrower and lower ones. The doorposts of the entrances and the lintels have molded profiles with three fasciae. The middle lintel extends beyond the entrance on both sides. The interior of the building was divided into a nave and two aisles by two rows of columns of eight columns each. At the northern end there was probably a transverse row of four columns. Traces of plaster on the west wall indicate that the walls were coated with plaster on the inside. The leveled rock floor was apparently paved with stone slabs. Near the eastern end a retaining wall was erected, and a fill was added in order to maintain the level of the floor. The area in front of

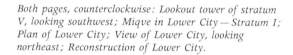

Both pages, counterclockwise: Lookout tower of stratum V, looking southwest; Miqve in Lower City — Stratum I; Plan of Lower City; View of Lower City, looking northeast; Reconstruction of Lower City.

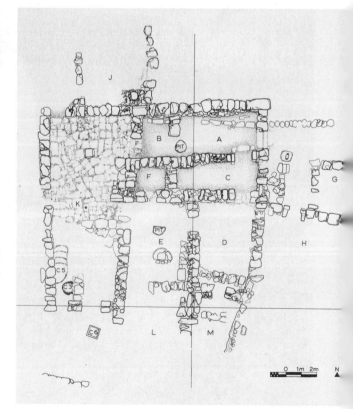

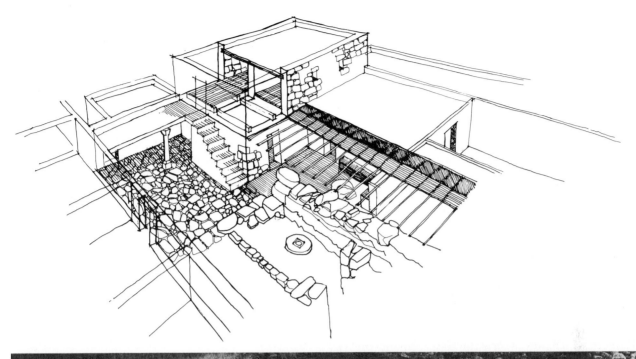

the facade was also leveled. On the west side of the facade stood a stone-cut bench. The synagogue was approached by way of a stone-cut staircase.

The synagogue is the largest of its kind thus far discovered in the Galilee. Its style of construction shows that it belongs to the early type of synagogues (third–fourth centuries A.D.). The traveler Rabbi Shmuel, son of Rabbi Shimon, who visited the synagogue in the thirteenth century, tells of seeing an inscription there which read, "Made by Shalom son of Levi." There is, however, disagreement as to whether this information is true. E. L. Sukenik suggested that the report was corrupted and did not refer to the synagogue of Meiron.

D. BARAG

EXCAVATIONS

Excavations in the area around the synagogue began only in 1971 as part of the joint expedition to Khirbet Shema' under the auspices of the American Schools of Oriental Research and the W. F. Albright Institute of Archaeological Research in Jerusalem. The 1971 and 1972 excavations were carried out in conjunction with the work at Khirbet Shema'. Two further expeditions were fielded in 1974 and 1975. The four seasons of work were supervised by E. M. Meyers, director, J. F. Strange, associate director, and Carol L. Meyers, field archaeologist.

The excavations were concentrated in the following areas: a block of shops and courtyards in the lowermost section of the town (M–I); a patrician house on one of the middle terraces (M–II); the debris laid against the eastern wall of the synagogue (M–III); a large tower on one of the middle terraces (M–IV); and soundings in the west and north, including several cisterns and one tomb. Since much of the ancient town is covered by modern buildings and roads around the tomb of Bar Yochai, it is difficult to determine the size and extent of the ancient settlement. However, an estimate of about 150–200 dunams seems fairly certain.

Digging along the northeast corner of the synagogue, the excavation team discovered the original foundations of the east wall and was thus able to correct the drawings of Kohl and Watzinger. Unfortunately, massive robbing and rebuilding in the medieval period has left all of this area disturbed. In the southeast corner, however, an annex building adjoining the synagogue was excavated to bedrock and provided sealed deposits, which allow the establishment of a late third-century A.D. date for the erection of the synagogue and annex. A cistern dug alongside this building corroborates the dating evidence from the annex.

Excavations in the rectangular tower in field V, which is still standing to a height of 6 meters at some points, indicated that the fortification(?) there was built in the Middle Roman period (second century A.D.) and rebuilt in the Early Arab period (eighth–ninth centuries A.D.). In none of the five excavated sections was there any evidence to link this structure with Josephus' purported fortifications of Mero(th). A circular limestone kiln (diameter 4 to 4.7 meters) of the medieval period was cleared in this area. Inside the northeast corner, a small trench yielded clear stratified material of the Late Hellenistic period, indicating that there was at least a small settlement already at that time.

In the lower city, fragments of a first-century building were found to underlie the major building there, which was constructed in the second century A.D. In at least several rooms, the main period of occupation was quite considerable, with substantial alterations and renewals of floors occurring from time to time. Probably built sometime after the Bar Kokhba War, the building complex was in use until Constantius II, or around A.D. 360. The main purpose of the complex seems to have been industrial. In at least one area (room E) a full workshop was recovered, including an intact workbench made of stone and a circular stone platform probably intended for the making of barrels for Meiron's well-known trade in olive oil. Dating to the period prior to Bar Kokhba was a well-preserved *miqve*, with its plastered walls and pure water storage area intact.

Three cisterns were excavated, associated with the late third- and fourth-century occupation. The single tomb cleared indicated that secondary burial was the rule, with the possible use of wooden ossuaries in loculi. A charnel house with more than a hundred disarticulated skeletons was also excavated. The chronological range of the tombs was Late Hellenistic to Late Roman.

Four seasons of excavations have produced the

Tel Mevorakh. Decorated chalices and goblets from the LBA sanctuary.

question of Meiron's apparent abandonment around A.D. 360, a fact well established by the coins. Whereas nearby Khirbet Shema' flourished into the fifth century, the inhabitants of Meiron appear to have left more than fifty years earlier, perhaps due to the increased demands of taxation under Constantius II. Until the Arab conquest, only scattered remains are to be found. From around 750–1000 and 1000–1399, however, two final phases of occupation are attested.   E. M. MEYERS

BIBLIOGRAPHY

The Site: S. Klein, *Sefer ha-Yishuv*, 106 (Hebrew) • Y. Aharoni, *The Settlement of the Israelite Tribes in Upper Galilee*, Jerusalem, 1957, 95–98 (Hebrew) • J. Garstang, Joshua–Judges, London, 1931, 101–02, 191 ff. • Abel, *GP* 2, 385.
The Synagogue: E. L. Sukenik, *Ma'asaf-Zion* 2 (1927), 109–11 (Hebrew) • Kohl–Watzinger, Synagogen, 80–88, Pl. 11 • Goodenough, *Jewish Symbols* 1, 200 f.; 12, 42.
Later Excavations: E. M. Meyers and J.F. Strange, *IEJ* 22 (1972), 176; 24 (1974), 279–80 • Carol L. Meyers, E. M. Meyers and J. F. Strange, *BASOR* 214 (1974), 2–25 • A. D. Rittenspach, *ibid.* 215 (1974), 19–29.

Meṣad Ḥashavyahu, below: The ostracon; Opposite page: General plan.

MEṢAD ḤASHAVYAHU

IDENTIFICATION. A fortress now called Meṣad Ḥashavyahu and dating to the end of the Israelite period, was discovered approximately 1.7 kilometers south of Yavneh-Yam (Minet-Rubin, map reference 120146). The remains of the fortress were investigated in excavations conducted in 1960 by J. Naveh on behalf of the Department of Antiquities and the Israel Exploration Society. It was found to contain an abundance of East Greek pottery dating to the last third of the seventh century B.C. as well as several Hebrew ostraca.

The ancient name of the fortress is unknown, and the modern name for the site was taken from one of the ostraca which mentions a certain "Ḥashavyahu ben Ya..."

EXCAVATIONS

The fortress covers an area of 6 dunams, and its form follows the natural contour of the *kurkar* hill on which it stands. The fortress is L-shaped and composed of two rectangles: a larger rectangle (4 dunams) containing a courtyard and rooms adjacent to the wall, and a smaller rectangle (2 dunams) consisting of three rows of houses flanking two streets. The wall (3.2 meters wide) of the fortress was built of bricks on a stone foundation with buttresses along its facade (projecting about .7 meter from the wall). The gate complex, including the guardrooms and towers, were built of dressed *kurkar* stone.

The excavations uncovered the southern wing of the gate and the buildings adjacent to it. Six test pits were also made within the fortress area. Each pit showed the same picture: a floor and, below it, either the natural *kurkar* bedrock or the sand fill used in leveling the area. No structural changes were distinguished in the fortress. All the evidence found indicates that the fortress was in existence for a very short period only.

The pottery found on the floors included the local ware common in the seventh century B.C. together with coarse bowls and jars, which until the excavations were considered to be of Persian date. The site must therefore be considered to have been occupied during the final decades of the seventh century B.C. Included among the finds was Greek pottery originating from the eastern islands of Greece and Asia Minor (East Greek pottery). Much of this pottery was decorated in the Middle Wild Goat style dated to 630–600 B.C. Only two sherds of this East Greek pottery have been previously found in Israel (at Ashkelon). At Meṣad Ḥashavyahu, it appeared in large quantities and included ordinary household ware such as amphorae, cooking pots, lamps, and cups. On the basis of this pottery the excavator concluded that the site was occupied by settlers of Greek origin, probably mercenaries, who preferred to use their own pottery, to which they were accustomed. Herodotus (II, 152, 154) relates that Pharaoh Psamtek I (664–610 B.C.), the founder of the Twenty-Sixth Dynasty, hired Greek and Carian mercenaries. It seems likely that other contemporary rulers used Greek mercenaries as well and that the soldiers stationed at Meṣad Ḥashavyahu were in Josiah's employ.

From the fact that the ostraca are written in biblical Hebrew, and from their contents and the names mentioned, e.g., Ḥashavyahu, Hoshayahu, Obadiahu, it is clear that the site was under Judean control. Not only did Josiah apparently control the north and south of the country, but he also (II Chronicles 34:6) expanded his rule westward.

Pieces of a Hebrew ostracon of fourteen lines were discovered inside the guardroom and on the paved square. It is the letter of a worker employed in the hravest, who complains that his garment was confiscated. He pleads his innocence and entreats the governor to return his property. Five other ostraca and a stone weight of four shekels (44.82 grams) with the sign ער were found in the vicinity of the gate. The same sign is also found on an ostracon next to the inscription "weighed four [shekels of] silver." On two other ostraca the number 4 was indicated by four vertical strokes (IIII). It thus appears that four shekels was a common unit of weight at Meṣad Ḥashavyahu.

The fortress was apparently abandoned during Pharaoh Necho's campaign in 609 B.C., the same year that Necho defeated Josiah at Megiddo.

J. NAVEH

BIBLIOGRAPHY

J. Naveh, *IEJ* 10 (1960), 129–39; 12 (1962), 27–32; 89–113; 14 (1964), 158–59 • F. M. Cross Jr., *BASOR* 165 (1962), 42–46 • S. Yeivin, *Bibliotheca Orientalis* 19 (1962), 3–10 • I. S. Shifman, *Epigrafika Wostoka* 16 (1963), 21–28 • J. D. Amusin–M. L. Heltzer, *IEJ* 14 (1964), 148–57 • S. Talmon, *BASOR* 176 (1964), 29–38 • H. Donner and W. Röllig, *Kanaanäische und Aramäische Inschriften*, 1, 2, Wiesbaden, 1962/4, No. 200 • H. Tadmor, *BA* 29 (1966), 102.

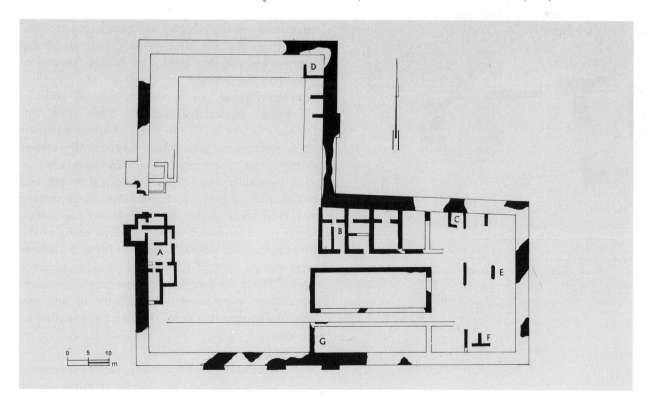

MEŞER

IDENTIFICATION. Meşer is a Chalcolithic site, situated in the lands of kibbutz Meşer, about 12 kilometers (8.5 miles) east of Ḥederah (map reference 155204). The ancient site is about 1 acre in area and lies on a rocky hill partly covered with a thin layer of soil. Settlement was concentrated in the thickest part of this layer. In 1956 and 1957, two seasons of excavations were carried out on behalf of the Department of Antiquities and directed by M. Dothan. Five areas were excavated, and in three of them, B, C, and D, were found three layers with building remains from the Chalcolithic period. Tumuli of the same period were built over the remains of the last settlement.

EXCAVATIONS

Stratum III is the earliest layer. The most important building of this stratum was found in area B. This is a two-room house built on stone foundations (outer dimensions: 13 by 6 meters) with the entrance in the long wall. The pottery found in the house belongs essentially to the Ghassulian

AREA B

STRATUM II

STRATUM III

0   5
            m

culture. Typical vessels are the V-shaped ("flower pot") bowl, the cornet, and the churn, and the common decorations are red slip, painted bands, and incisions. The flint industry consists of adzes, small axes, and a few fan scrapers. The stone vessels include bowls decorated with triangles incised on the rims.

Stratum II is characterized by apsidal houses. One house measures 5 by 11 meters and had a partition wall separating its rounded end from the rest of the building. In the floor of another house, a burial pit for domestic animals, contained, among others, the complete skeleton of a dog. Some funnel-shaped silos were dug in the floor and lined with stone slabs. The finds from this stratum still continue the Ghassulian tradition, but new elements are also present. Bowls of the cream-ware type, cornets, and churns are found, as is also gray-burnished ware, especially carinated bowls with knob-like projections on the carination Metal tools were used along with flint saws and chisels. Outstanding are five copper adzes, which apparently served to cut water cisterns in the rock (see below).

Stratum I is distinguished by rectangular broad houses. One two-room house had raised platforms near the wall, probably for sleeping. Ghassulian features are fewer here, but still present are gray-burnished ware and an increased amount of red-burnished ware. A high loop-handle jug is noteworthy among the new vessels, and band slip appears for the first time. Flat blades (knives) of flint were also found.

Pits were found cut in the rock in all areas of excavation (especially area C). They were apparently in use in all the strata. Narrow channels led to some of the pits, which undoubtedly served as rainwater reservoirs. Other pits were used as silos, especially one with a cylindrical mouth and bell-shaped bottom which contained large storage jars. Near some of the pits were found cup marks. Meşer was abandoned during the first phase of the Late Chalcolithic period. Remains of this settlement were mostly covered with tumuli made of unhewn stones. What the purpose of these tumuli was and when they were erected is difficult to say, but they are inseparable from the latest occupation of the site.

CONCLUSION

Meşer is a Chalcolithic site whose lack of sources of water was solved by the storing of rainwater in cisterns dug close to the settlement. It is so far the oldest settlement known to have stored water in unplastered pits. Stratum III belongs to the Ghassulian culture. The finds closely resemble the Northern Negev culture, which is an offshoot of Ghassulian IV. Thus stratum III at Meşer can be ascribed to approximately the fourth millennium B.C., and strata II–I to the initial stage of the Late Chalcolithic period, which can be dated to the third millennium B.C. This stage is characterized by apsidal houses and red- and gray-burnished ware. Meşer is stratigraphically important because the early phase of the Late Chalcolithic is clearly attested here, and it provides a link between the Ghassulian and the Late Chalcolithic, in which some features of the Early Bronze Age I are already evident. M. DOTHAN

BIBLIOGRAPHY

M. Dothan, *IEJ* 7 (1957), 217–28; 9 (1959), 13–29 • For the date of the site: M. Dothan, *IEJ* 6 (1956), 112–14.

Opposite page: Area B. Two apsidal buildings (stratum II) above a rectangular building (stratum III); This page, below: Pithos; Right, top: Red-burnished bowl — stratum I; bottom: Stone-lined silo.

MEVORAKH, TEL

LOCATION AND REMAINS. Tel Mevorakh (Tell Mubarak) is a small mound situated in the Sharon Plain, on the southern bank of Naḥal Taninim.

In 1923, a mausoleum built of stone from the third century A.D. was discovered at the eastern foot of the mound. In it were found a number of marble sarcophagi, two of them (now in the Rockefeller Museum) decorated with reliefs, one depicting the war between the Greeks and the Amazons.

Several years ago, a tenth-century B.C. shaft tomb was accidentally discovered in a field near the northeastern foot of the mound. The tomb contained some seventy pottery vessels, including red-burnished Phoenician and Cypro-Phoenician ware.

EXCAVATIONS

Four seasons of excavations, designed as student-training excavations of the Institute of Archaeology of the Hebrew University, were conducted at Tel Mevorakh during 1973–76 and were directed by E. Stern.

In the first season of excavations, a trial trench (40 by 10 meters) was dug at the western end of the northern slope. The excavation area was greatly enlarged in the second and third seasons and extended to the center of the mound and the east side. At the end of the third season the stratigraphy of the mound could be quite clearly established.

The first settlement was founded on the low natural hill in the Middle Bronze Age II–A. No fortifications were uncovered from this level.

After the destruction of this settlement a *terre pisée* rampart, about 30 meters square, was heaped up above it in the Middle Bronze Age II–B. The outer face of the rampart was steep, sloping from the highest point at the edge of the mound toward the inner side, and thus creating a crater. The inner slope was strengthened by a series of stone supporting walls. Several infant burial jars of the Middle Bronze Age II–B, discovered near the rampart's present surface and evidently dating from the period of its use, were most valuable in fixing the date of the rampart. On one of the jar handles was a Hyksos seal impression. The rampart was constructed of a hard-packed core covered with rather loose layers of sand, *khamra* and *kurkar*, brought from the surrounding hills. With them were brought many stone implements, including a few obsidian tools.

In the third season of excavations, the north section in the *terre pisée* rampart was deepened in order to examine more closely the form of the natural hill. It became clear that both the slope of the hill and the *terre pisée* rampart are very steeply sloped and end in a layer of black soil peculiar to the beds of rivers or marshes. It can therefore be concluded that, at least on this side, the Middle Bronze Age II–B fortress reached a water obstacle.

Still unsolved is the problem of the eastern border of the Middle Bronze Age II–B fort. Two squares opened in the third season in the eastern slope revealed the remains of buildings of this period but no trace of a rampart. This side may have been fortified by a different method, perhaps by a brick wall now eroded, but this assumption must await further excavations.

In the first season, it could already be concluded that the rampart served as a fortress for a small unit of soldiers, and was part of the defense system of the large nearby Middle Bronze Age town of Tell Burgah, which lies several kilometers upstream of the Crocodile River.

The area excavated inside the mound was quite limited, but nevertheless four different strata the of

Middle Bronze Age could be distinguished, the upper stratum belonging to the Middle Bronze Age II–C and the next two to the Middle Bronze Age II–B. The floor of the lowest stratum was not reached, and the small amount of pottery did not permit exact dating. The walls of the two upper strata were found leaning against the inner side of the rampart and actually supporting it. Of the third stratum, only a small section of a well-paved stone floor attached to a heavy wall was cleared, and its relation to the rampart was not determined. On the floors of strata 2 and 3 was found a large quantity of Middle Bronze Age imported Cypriot ware — a quite rare occurrence in Israel.

Above these strata four phases of the Late Bronze Age were uncovered. In the upper phase, a rectangular podium was found filled to a height of about 1 meter with homogeneous red-brick material. It was bounded on the west, south, and east by a stone wall more than 1 meter wide. On the north, it leans against the Middle Bronze Age II rampart. South of the podium was part of a courtyard with its floor made of a thick beaten lime. Evidently the building for which this podium served as a base was completely razed by the Israelites (see below), and possibly even the upper part of the podium itself was cut during later construction activity. Even so, there can be no doubt that it should be regarded as a large and important building. Only on the eastern side of the excavation area were some floors of this phase preserved. All of them were covered with sherds of pithoi.

Below the podium were the remains of another large building, of which parts of two rooms with stone pavements have survived. This building extends below the unexcavated area.

The third phase of the Late Bronze Age also contained the remains of a large building, occupying the entire excavated area. Its form, interior installations, and especially the finds leave no doubt but that it should be interpreted as a sanctuary. On the long side the building leans against the inner side of the Middle Bronze Age II rampart (as at Hazor, area C), but, between them there was a narrow passageway(?) paved with beaten lime.

Almost all of the sanctuary hall was cleared (except for its northeast corner). It measures 10 by 5 meters and is oriented east–west. The floor and walls were all coated with beaten lime plaster. In

Opposite page: Stone sarcophagus from 3rd century A.D. mausoleum showing scene of war between the Greeks and the Amazons; This page, below: Inner side of Persian casemate wall. Note typical construction method; Bottom: Two phases of Persian building, looking north.

867

Both pages, clockwise from bottom left: "Bes Vase" of the Persian period; Clay figurine of the Persian period. Note details of the throne; Group of Phoenician and Cypro–Phoenician vessels, from 10th century B.C. *tomb.*

the northwest corner stood a rectangular plastered platform (about 1 by 1.5 meters and about 1 meter high). Five steps led up to it from the east. On the lime floor in the corner of the platform was the round imprint of a small (wooden?) column, which may have supported a canopy. A plastered bench ran along the western (short) side of the hall, and in front of it near the center of the room stood two plastered installations whose functions are still obscure. The long northern wall was cleared along its whole length. Immediately to the east of the platform was a long low plastered bench running up to the northeast corner and then turning along the part of the eastern wall that was excavated. The bench thus extended more than 8 meters. In the center of the hall stood a large round stone, which may have served as a column base. The floor of the sanctuary slopes toward the south, on which side was found a drain running against another plastered bench. Because of the slope, the southern wall was destroyed except for a small section in the southwest corner. (The sanctuary entrance may have been on this side.) The finds in the sanctuary include two Mitannian-style cylinder seals, two faience disks, two cups, one of alabaster and the other of clay, a pair of bronze cymbals, a bronze knife, a javelin, arrowheads, and a ring decorated with a palmette. There were also many imported Cypriot vessels of the white-slip type (milk bowls and one cup) and many base ring and

monochrome bowls. Among the finds were of
special interest were some juts like cypriote
bowls, and cups, and especially decorated cadness
and goblets. The nth, that of the type of not
practiced here was the discovery of a beautiful
bronze snake, about 30 centimeters long, which
closely resembles the bronze snakes found in
contemporary sanctuaries at Timna and Hazor.
South of the main hall was a stone-paved courtyard which extended below the above-stated area.
Another wide courtyard on the west was plastered with large well beaten stones. This floor was
partly robbed in antiquity, and its borders on the
south and west are not known.
At first impression, the finds indicate a date in
the fifteenth-thirteenth centuries B.C. (two phases
were distinguished). The sanctuary and its courtyards occupied almost the entire area of the site in
the Late Bronze Age. This entire compound is
subsequently interpreted by the excavator as a
wayside sanctuary — the first of its kind to be
discovered in Israel. (The closest mounds are Dor
and Tel Zeror some 10–12 kilometers from Tel
Mevorakh.)

The removal of the floor of the courtyard revealed
a thick layer of debris over the whole area with no
building remains. This layer dated to the early
part of the Late Bronze Age and since it continued
"streaming" below the sanctuary, it can be assumed that there was another building there.

Above the Late Bronze Age strata, a four-room
house from the Israelite period was found. It
contained two building stages, both dating to the
tenth century B.C. The plan of this stratum is of
interest. A large building was surrounded by a
broad courtyard with a floor made of a thick layer
of beaten lime, and the whole complex was
encircled by a wall 1.5 meters wide. The pottery
includes local red-burnished ware and ordinary
pottery, as well as imported Cypriot vessels,
among them Cypro-Phoenician, bichrome, and
White Painted ware. This complex has been tentatively identified as an administrative center,
official storehouse, or the like.

Above the Israelite stratum are three phases of the
Persian period. The lowest stage is represented
only by a series of deep pits, filled with ashes,
bones, and pottery, including Attic and Cypriot
ware. On one of the local sherds found in a pit
were rows of stamped rosettes much in the manner
of the Judean stamps. From the second stage, a
building was found on the western part of the
mound. In the upper stage of the Persian period,
the entire mound was occupied by what seems to
have been a single large building. Since the last
two stages were encircled by a casemate wall, they
are again interpreted as an administrative center
or large estate.

Above the Persian level were some scattered walls,
apparently belonging to the Hellenistic period.

Both pages, counterclockwise from left: Mitannian–style cylinder seal, from the sanctuary; Bronze snake, from the sanctuary; LBA I sanctuary, west side. Note platform with five steps in corner; Decorated pottery goblet, from the sanctuary; Scarab bearing the name of Thutmose III.

Despite the many Roman and Byzantine finds collected on the mound, it is clear that no structures from these periods were built on its summit. All building activity during these periods was limited to the surroundings. A large wall, the purpose of which is not yet clear, was found at the base of the northern side of the mound.

At the beginning of the excavation the entire surface of the site was densely covered by numerous graves of the Arab period. In one case, three superimposed graves were found. Most of them are of the normal cist type, but two or three were unusual infant jar burials.　　　E. STERN

BIBLIOGRAPHY

Conder–Kitchener, *SWP* 2, 34 • *BBSAJ* 5 (1924), 55–56, Pl. IV; 6 (1924), 77, Pls. V–VI • *BPM* 1 (1924), 55–56, Pl. IV • E. Stern, *IEJ* 23 (1973), 256–57; 24 (1974), 266–68, 26 (1976), 49–50; 199–200.

MINḤA, HORVAT

IDENTIFICATION. Ḥorvat Minḥa (Munḥata) is situated in the Jordan Valley near Kibbutz Gesher, about 15 kilometers (9 miles) south of the Sea of Galilee (map reference 201233), 215 meters below sea level. The site lies at the edge of a terrace, on the bank of the Tabor Valley (Wadi Bira).

EXCAVATIONS

Trial soundings carried out at the site by N. Zori were followed by systematic excavations during two seasons, at the end of 1962 and in the summer of 1963, on behalf of the French Archaeological Mission in Israel and the Department of Antiquities, under the direction of J. Perrot with the assistance of N. Zori. An area of about 800 square meters was excavated and six strata with a total thickness of 2–3 meters were distinguished. The strata are listed here from the bottom up.

Stratum 6. This represents the first occupation layer resting on virgin soil. Carbonized organic remains were found on stone floors, as well as bone fragments and untypical flint flakes.

Stratum 5. A thick wall was cleared for a length of more than 8 meters. It is built of greenish unbaked bricks set on two or three courses of big stones.

Stratum 4. A rectangular structure was uncovered (about 4 by 5 meters) with plastered floors and walls built of a single row of stones, set in two or three courses. Near the wall was a plastered floor. In the center of the structure is a shallow depression with a fireplace provided with stone-built edges. The floor had been renewed several times. The finds in this stratum included limestone bowls, querns, pestles, and numerous flint implements, about half of them arrowheads, javelin heads with sharp edges, and sickle blades with finely denticulated edges.

Stratum 3. A large, nearly circular structure was excavated (diameter 20 meters) with a central courtyard paved with pebbles (sockets of posts— which may have supported the roof—were also discovered). The courtyard was surrounded by rooms. The walls were apparently built of bricks on stone foundations. Aside from implements which did not differ typologically from those of the preceding strata, many fired potsherds were

found, some of them molded. Kitchen middens (bones of cattle, goat, sheep, and pig) are frequent in this stratum.

Stratum 2. In this layer were found oval pits (depth 1.5 meters, diameter 3.5 meters) used as dwelling pits and silos, some of them containing small bricks (15 by 8 centimeters). When these pits were dug out, the main walls of stratum 3 were demolished in some places. Finds include abundant light-colored handmade pottery, semi-globular bowls, deep bowls with elongated knob handles near the rim, high-footed cups, globular pots with short neck and small loop handles descending from the neck to the shoulder, hole-mouth jars, and globular juglets with high, flaring rims or bow rims. Most of the pottery is only slightly burnished. A fine burnish appears on the red ware and on the so-called dark-faced burnished ware. Incised or painted decoration or a combination of the two are common. The incised herringbone pattern, set between parallel lines, appears under the rim or on the lower part of the neck and as a zigzag pattern on the body of the vessel. Painted decoration (lines or zigzag pattern) also appears in

Opposite page, left: Pottery vessel of the "Sha'ar ha-Golan" type; Bottom: Buildings of strata 2A and 2B; This page, left: Figurines of the "Sha'ar ha-Golan" type; Below: Figurine from stratum 2B.

addition to burnish. In this stratum were also found clay figurines of men (of the Sha'ar ha-Golan type) and animals, anthropomorphic pebbles, painted or incised pebbles, etc.

Stratum 1. This layer contained a very badly preserved stone structure and oval-shaped(?) houses. An abundance of pottery was found, including some gray-burnished ware, carinated bowls, deep bowls, and store jars decorated with thumb indented bands beneath the rim, horizontal handles, etc.

CONCLUSIONS

Strata 6, V, and 4 resemble the Pre-Pottery Neolithic B at Jericho and have analogies in their flint industry and architecture. It is possible that settlement at Minḥa was established at the same time as the beginning of the Pre-Pottery Neolithic B at Jericho. Tel 'Ali (q.v.) and perhaps also Ḥamadiya (as shown by the survey conducted by N. Zori) may also have been contemporary with Minḥa (they lie only 10 kilometers [6 miles] to its north and south). In the light of this evidence it can be assumed that there was a marked tendency toward permanent settlement in this region and perhaps also in the entire country (see also Abu-Gosh, Ashkelon, Wadi Beida), a tendency which represents a break with the Natufian tradition.

Stratum 3 at Minḥa was probably occupied immediately after the previous layer. Even if the inhabitants did not yet use pottery — an issue not yet sufficiently clarified — the conditions necessary for its production already existed. This stratum represents a part of the cultural phase appearing outside of Palestine in the lowest stratum of Byblos (Néolithique ancien) and found in this country only on a very small scale. At that time Jericho was abandoned, and the settlement at Minḥa seems to have been of very short duration. To this period may probably also be ascribed the sites ha-Goshrim and Giv'at ha-Parsah. The meager finds at these sites probably reflect a cultural decline.

In stratum II new and clear evidence is found that allows us to establish definitely to which cultures belong such sites as Sha'ar ha-Golan, Tel 'Ali, Hazorea, Tuleilat Batashi, Gharuba, and Jericho (Pottery Neolithic A and B). The differences occurring in the finds from these sites can be disregarded, and they can be considered as belonging to one and the same period. There are no signs of the development or persistence of the earlier,

original culture, but there is evidence of the penetration of a new, foreign culture. The evidence for this new culture are the pit dwellings, the scarcity of arrowheads in the flint industry, the pottery described above attesting to links with Upper Mesopotamia, and several new ways of representing men and animals. It can be assumed that this culture was brought to Palestine by the semi-nomads living on the borders of the Syrian-Arab Desert from the Transjordan Heights to Carchemish and Diar-Baker. The clear relationship between this new culture of Palestine and that of Néolithique moyen at Byblos is of great value in establishing the stratigraphy and chronology.

Although the culture represented in stratum 2 of Minḥa, in Pottery Neolithic Jericho A and B, and in some other sites predates the Ghassulian and the Beersheba culture, it, in fact, represents its beginning, for they differ only in that the latter culture has introduced the use of metal. Minḥa was abandoned at that time, but occupation in the region continued. A larger and more important settlement was established in Neve Ur, 2 kilometers to the south, on the southern slope of the Tabor Valley. The finds collected on its surface are identical with those discovered in the lowest stratum of Khirbet esh-Shunah (see also Central Jordan Valley) situated exactly opposite on the other bank of the Jordan.

Stratum 1 at Minḥa can be compared with stratum 2 at Khirbet esh-Shunah and strata XVI–XVII at Beth-Shean. This last occupation layer marks the final desertion of the site. Other villages too were abandoned in this period, but new settlements or already existing settlements took their place, those sites offering better conditions both for defense and for water supply. It appears that the insecurity of the inhabitants increased, as is attested by the appearance of strong walls on nearly all sites at the beginning of Bronze Age. Ḥorvat Minḥa furnishes new evidence for the continuity of settlement in this country from the sixth to the fourth millennia B.C. The excavation of the lower strata (6 to 3) will throw new light on the earliest phases of cultural and agricultural life in Israel.   J. PERROT–N. ZORI

BIBLIOGRAPHY

J. Perrot, *Syria* 41 (1965), 323–45: 43 (1966), 49–63: *idem, IEJ* 15 (1965), 248–49: 16 (1966), 269–71: *idem, RB* 74 (1967), 63–67: *idem, Bible et Terre Sainte* 93 (1967), 4–16: *idem, Qadmoniot* 2 (1969), 52–56 (Hebrew).

MINYA, KHIRBET EL-

IDENTIFICATION. Khirbet el-Minya is located on the shore of the Sea of Galilee about 14 kilometers (8.5 miles) north of Tiberias, and immediately south of the rocky promontory known as Tell el 'Oreimeh (ancient Kinneret). It is in the rich Gennesar or al-Ghuwayer Plain, which has been occupied probably since ancient times, as is indicated by caves along the cliffs to the southwest and by pottery recovered in various places in the plain and along the mountain borders to the north and west. This area, unfortunately, has not yet been studied in a systematic manner.

Attention was attracted to the large mound known as Khirbet el-Minya in the second half of the nineteenth century, when scholars and pilgrims began to traverse Palestine in the search for identifiable biblical sites. The explorations culminated in *The Survey of Western Palestine* (1, London, 1881, p. 369), in which Minya was identified as Caphar Nahum, an interpretation which was as often accepted as rejected by scholars until the discovery of Capernaum farther north and the actual excavation of the main part of the site of Minya.

EXCAVATIONS

In 1932, excavations were begun by A. E. Mader and continued for five seasons until 1939, under the successive direction of Mader, A. M. Schneider, and O. Puttrich–Reignard. The excavations were sponsored by the Görres-Gesellschaft, the Verein vom Heiligen Lande, the Deutsche Forschungsgemeinschaft, and the Islamic section of the Berlin Museums. The work of the German archaeologists revealed the existence of an almost square (73 by 67 meters) building with round corner towers and a semicircular tower in the middle of each wall, except for the east wall where there was a monumental domed gateway. Aside from a single narrow trench, the center of this square was not excavated, on the probably correct assumption that it contained merely a courtyard. Along the exterior walls, the excavation uncovered a mosque, a throne room, and a group of five rooms with mosaic floors in geometric

Plan of the palace.

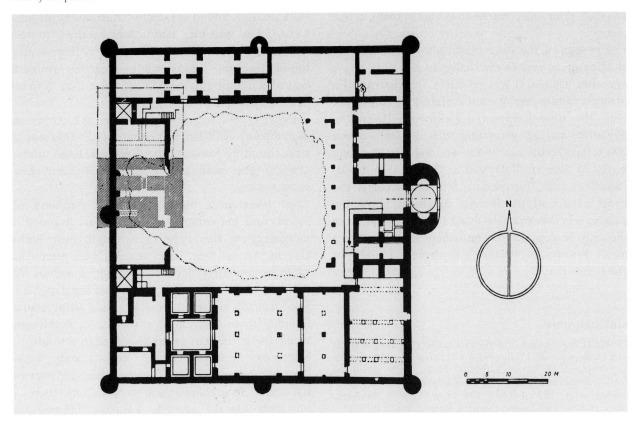

design. These were all situated on the south side. The north side contained the residential wing. The purpose of the rooms on the east and southwest could not be determined. The west side was left unexcavated for the most part. These discoveries indicated clearly that Minya was the site of a palace and a mosque. An inscription found in secondary use, which mentioned the name of al-Walid (705–715), dated its construction to the Umayyad period.

A sounding was made in the west part of the palace by O. Grabar and J. Perrot in 1959 on behalf of the Horace H. Rackham Fund for Research, University of Michigan. This sounding established the stratigraphy of the site. It was found that there was a second major occupation of Minya in Mameluke times, when Minya became a major halt on the caravan route from Egypt to Syria. Later, a khan of the same name, which still exists today, was built to the north, and the palace area was then occupied by only a few miserable houses. The sounding also uncovered a mosaic floor in a large vaulted hall in the west side, indicating the existence of official rooms on this side as well as in the south parts of the palace. Unfortunately the excavations ended before the original floor was reached in more than a few places.

The results of the excavations show that Khirbet el-Minya was built in the Umayyad period in a rich agricultural area. It was probably the chateau of a princely landowner. It must certainly be connected with the now-disappeared bathhouse (from the Byzantine period, according to B. Ravani), about 200 meters to the northwest, and belongs to a long series of known Umayyad settlements in Syria, Palestine, and Transjordan. Still unknown is the exact nature of the interior arrangement of the palace, whether the palace and the bathhouse were the only features of the settlement and whether a major Roman or Byzantine settlement existed in the same area.

O. GRABAR

BIBLIOGRAPHY

O. Puttrich–Reignard, *Palästinahefte des Deutschen Vereins vom Heiligen Lande*, 17–20, (1939) • A. M. Schneider, *Annales archéologiques de Syrie*, 2 (1952), 23–45, with additional bibliography on the work of German archaeologists • O. Grabar, et al., *IEJ* 10 (1960), 226–43 • K. A. C. Creswell, *Early Muslim Architecture*, 1, part 2, Oxford, 1969, 381–89.

MONASTERIES

HISTORY. The first Christian monks appeared in Palestine at the beginning of the fourth century A.D. They lived mainly in the Judean Desert, in the Negev and in the Sinai Desert. Many of them were attracted by the holy places connected with the life of Jesus, such as Jerusalem, Bethlehem, etc.

Hermits withdrew from the world and dwelt isolated in caves near a source of water. In the course of time, friends and disciples joined them, and thus groups of such solitaries were assembled. The founder of such a group, who was revered as a saint, became their spiritual father and teacher. Cells were erected near his cave, or further caves were adapted as habitations. A community of monks of this type is known as a laura (λαύρα). It is composed of a number of cave cells grouped around a main cave or a central building (a church). This system flourished in the wilderness and particularly in Palestine.

In A.D. 334, Saint Chariton established the first laura at Faran (near Jerusalem) and later set up two others at Jericho and Souka. In A.D. 473, Saint Euthymius founded a famous laura in the Kidron Valley. His disciple, Saint Saba, retired to the Judean Desert where he lived as a hermit and founded several lauras and monasteries. A laura was also founded by Saint Gerasimos near Jericho (A.D. 475).

Another type of monastery is known as a cenobium (Κοινόβιον) "life led in community." This was a large building consisting of several fixed units. Cenobia were established mainly in cities and their surroundings.

Saint Hilarion (a disciple of Saint Anthony of Egypt) and his companion Epiphanius founded a monastery of this type in A.D. 330 near Beth-Govrin. At that time, two convents were established in Jerusalem and on the Mount of Olives by Melania, a noble Roman matron, and her daughter, also named Melania. In A.D. 387, Saint Paula founded three convents for women in Bethlehem where the hermit Cassianus also lived in solitude.

Numerous monasteries are known only from literary sources, while for many other monasteries uncovered in archaeological explorations, there is no such literary record. Valuable information regarding monasteries of the fourth century is found in an account written by the nun Etheria, who visited many such sites during a pilgrimage to Palestine. Of special importance for the study of monasteries in Palestine are the writings of Cyril of Scythopolis on the fathers of Christian monasticism in Palestine from the fourth to the sixth centuries. Many monasteries of the fifth century are known from the account of the life of Peter the Iberian, who spread the doctrine of the Monophysites in Palestine.

On the basis of the writings of the Church Fathers and other sources, lists were drawn up of the monasteries in Palestine, as for example, the short list of Couret and the alphabetical list of S. Vailhé, which enumerate 137 monasteries.

O. Meinardus, *Liber Annus* 15 (1964–65), 220–50; 16 (1965–66), 328–56 • A. Ovadiah, *Corpus of the Byzantine Churches in the Holy Land*, Bonn, 1970.

The Monastery Building. Just as the way of life of the monks was governed by fixed rules, so too were monasteries generally built according to a fixed plan, but nevertheless they did not differ substantially from other large buildings of the same period. The main entrance led into an inner court—an open space in the center of the monastery—with colonnades and benches where the monks walked or rested. In the court, there was a cistern or a pool. From the court, a corridor led to the church (or chapel). Other corridors gave access to the cells inhabited by the monks. On the other side of the courtyard was the refectory, and next to it the kitchen and cooking facilities, storerooms, etc. The monasteries had drainage channels and reservoirs for storing water. Monasteries in agricultural regions also had irrigation installations. Opposite the entrance to the court or in one of its corners was a bell tower, two or three stories high. The monks treated the bodies of their deceased companions with great respect, and buried them under the floor of the church or in caves near the monastery. Where a monastery had been founded by a monk who was considered a saint, the cells of the monks were grouped around his tomb, which was generally a domed structure.

Most of the monastery was paved with mosaics or small stone flag set in various patterns. The floor of the church was always paved with beautiful colored mosaics in assorted designs. The colors most frequently used were white, black, blue, red, and pink. Dedicatory or memorial inscriptions set in the floor sometimes indicated the foundation date of the monastery or the duration of its existence.

Communities of hermits lived mainly in the Judean Desert, in the area of Bethlehem and Jerusalem, in the Negev and the Sinai Desert, in the Beth-Shean Valley and on Mount Carmel. The plans of monastic buildings varied according to the local conditions. In the Judean Desert, which was favored by the hermits, monasteries were founded in the fifth and sixth centuries A.D. near caves that served as monks' cells. Although such monasteries were situated in the arid desert region, they were not far from the Jordan Valley, from which they received food and water, and not far also from the cities of Jerusalem and Bethlehem and from Jericho and the towns of Transjordan. In more remote places, they drew their water from ponds and brooks.

In the Sinai Peninsula the hermits settled in the mountainous region of the south, wherever they found a source of water enabling them to grow food. Eventually, as other monks joined them, communities of hermits were established that were self-supporting both economically (agriculture) and in defense — the monastery was built as a fortress with tower-flanked walls.

The monks also engaged in agriculture in the fertile region of Bethlehem, a fact which influenced the plan of their monasteries. A type of building developed there which resembled a farm, with agricultural installations, such as winepresses, oil presses, storehouses, and workshops for manufacturing tools. Also in the fertile, well-watered Beth-Shean Valley, the monasteries were kinds of farms with wine-and oil-presses and an economy based on agriculture.

THE SITES

Khirbet Abu Ghunnein lies about 3 kilometers (2 miles) northeast of Bethlehem (map reference 171125). In 1952, V. Corbo cleared there the remains of a small walled monastery built on a rectangular plan (24.75 by 18.4 meters). In its center is a court containing a cistern. On the north side stands an oblong church (16.7 by 5.1 meters) with an interior apse (diameter 2.25 meters). The bema was enclosed by a chancel screen and was reached by two steps. In the Arab period, the hall was divided into three sections. The mosaic floor of the church — largely destroyed — was decorated with floral motifs.

West of the court were two rooms, one of them oblong, paved with white coarse mosaic, and the other a small room with the remains of a floor of pounded earth. The southeastern part of the monastery has been mostly destroyed.

Corbo considers these the remains of the Photinus-Marinus Monastery, founded in the fifth century by the brothers Marinus and Lukas, disciples of Euthymius.

V. Corbo, *Gli Scavi di Kh. Siyar el-Ghanam e i Monasteri dei Dintorni,* Jerusalem, 1955, 141–45.

Khirbet Abu Ghunnein.

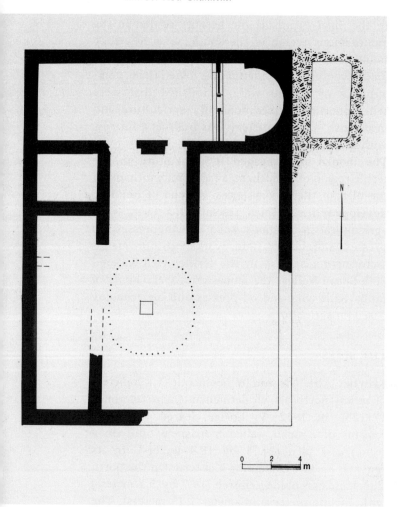

0 2 4
m

Tell Basul. In Tell Basul, about 1 kilometer west of Beth-Shean (map reference 195212), N. Zori, on behalf of the Department of Antiquities, cleared in 1961–62 the remains of a monastery of the fourth or beginning of the fifth century A.D.

The spacious court of the monastery is paved with a beautiful mosaic inlaid with Greek inscriptions. Around the court are seven rooms, including a chapel whose floor was paved with a mosaic decorated with ovals, each one depicted as a bunch of acanthus leaves, bound together with a V-shaped leaf. Each oval contains faunal motifs such as a gazelle, rabbit, cat, lamb, hen, and ducks as well as floral motifs, such as a pomegranate, olive, etc. At the entrance to the chapel the pavement is decorated with a fruit tree flanked by peacocks.

The other six rooms are paved with mosaics in geometric patterns. Also cleared were another eight rooms with floors of stone, mud, and pounded earth.

Ḥadashot Archaeologiot 3 (1962), 20–21 (Hebrew) • N. Zori, in: *The Beth-Shean Valley,* Jerusalem, 1962, 190 (Hebrew); *idem, IEJ* 24 (1974), 227.

Beth ha-Shittah. The remains of a monastery were excavated in October, 1952, by Y. Aharoni, on behalf of the Department of Antiquities, near Kibbutz Beth ha-Shittah (map reference 191217). The monastery consisted of eight rooms built around a square central court paved with basalt stones. The rooms contained agricultural installations, a wine-press, millstones, etc. Two rooms, paved with coarse mosaics, served as chapels. In the center of the pavement of the first room was a large red cross surrounded by twenty-two intersecting circles and two large concentric circles. In the corners of the mosaic were four small crosses inscribed in circles and enclosed in square frames. The mosaic pavement of the second chapel was divided into seventy small squares containing geometric patterns, crosses, Greek letters representing the initials of the Holy Names, and sayings such as "Jesus, the Anointed One, Son of God, is the Savior."

The monks engaged in agriculture in this monastery-farm which was in existence during the fifth and sixth centuries A.D.

Y. Aharoni, *BIES* 18 (1954), 209–15 (Hebrew).

Bir el-Qutt is situated about 2 kilometers (1 mile) northeast of Bethlehem (map reference 170125).

The remains of a monastery of the sixth century A.D. were cleared there from December, 1952, to June, 1953, by V. Corbo. The monastery is built on a rectangular plan (35 by 30 meters), with the entrance on the east side. A narrow corridor leads to a large central court, surrounded on all sides by colonnades and decorated with geometric patterns. Georgian inscriptions found in the court contain the names of five persons. Northeast of the court is an oblong church (about 19 by 7.5 meters) with an interior apse. Its mosaic pavement is largely destroyed. On the southwest side of the church are two doorways, one leading to a chapel, which probably also served as a place of burial. The other doorway led to a kind of passage paved with white mosaics, which was linked on its east side to the central court and on its south side to a rectangular hall, probably the refectory. The refectory was well preserved, with six pillars supporting the ceiling. Its floor was paved with a colored mosaic in a geometric design. A Georgian dedicatory inscription of five lines was found in the floor set in a *tabula ansata*. It mentions three names.

A doorway in the west end of the south wall led to a room that had benches and a basin, and was paved with a mosaic in floral patterns. It was probably the kitchen. South of this room were two rooms with wine- and oilpresses. South of the court were four more rooms, the southernmost of which was a stable.

The monks buried their dead inside the monastery, as is evidenced by an underground cave dug into the rock north of the court, near the entrance to the chapel.

The inscriptions attest to the fact that the monastery was founded by Georgians and dedicated to Saint Theodore.

V. Corbo, *op. cit.*, 112–39.

Khirbet ed-Deir. The remains of a building complex belonging to a Byzantine monastery were cleared at Khirbet ed-Deir and 'Ein al-M'amudiyeh near Hebron by A. M. Stève in 1946, on behalf of the French Biblical School.

At Khirbet ed-Deir, a nearly square structure (12.5 by 10.45 meters) was uncovered, with thick outer walls (.9 meter) built of large dressed blocks (.65–.9 meter long and .45 meter high). The building comprised two symmetrical wings linked by a long narrow corridor (1.78 meters wide)

Below: Bir el-Qutt; Bottom: Beth ha-Shittah.

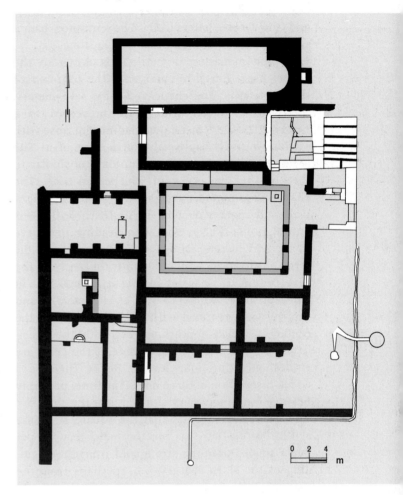

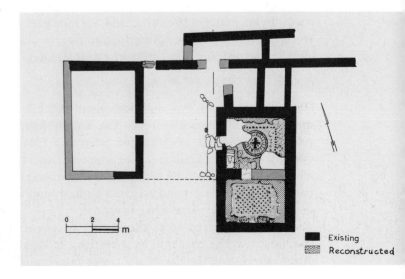

Existing
Reconstructed

paved with white mosaic. Each wing has two chambers (the southern ones, 3.7 by 3.4 meters, and the northern ones, 4.45 by 3.7 meters).

The lintel of the entrance to the monastery consists of a monumental stone block (2.12 by .75 by .6 meters) showing in its center a circle with a cross and the Greek letters AΩ. The entrance had a wooden door in addition to a rolling stone.

From the monastery a path leads down to the chapel near 'Ein al-M'mudiyeh ("the fountain of the baptism"). The chapel (6.65 by 3.15 meters, the walls .9 meter wide were preserved to a height of 2.4–2.75 meters) has an interior apse with a window and a baptismal font in front of it. The style of construction of this building is similar to that of the monastery of Khirbet ed-Deir. The chapel was entered through a door in its northern wall, and another door in the southern wall opens onto a tunnel (8.8 meters long) leading to a cave (3 by 2.15 meters) whose eastern side was in the form of an apse. A pit dug into the rock of the cave provided the water for the baptismal font in the baptistery. A lintel (3 by 1 by .6 meters) found nearby was decorated with a *tabula ansata* in the center of which appears a cross with the Greek letters IC XC AΩ. On either side of the cross are circles enclosing four leaves. Below them is a Greek inscription of three lines. The lintel probably belonged to a monastery situated near the chapel.

The excavator suggests that the square structure at Khirbet ed-Deir was not the monastery proper but a small Byzantine stronghold from the beginning of the sixth century A.D. (perhaps from the time of Justinian), guarding the chapel and the monastery, which were far removed from the main roads. In his opinion, the chapel and the monastery are connected with the Christian tradition of the "wilderness of Saint John the Baptist near Hebron."

C. Kopp, *RB* 53 (1946), 547–58; A. M. Stève, *ibid.*, 559–75.

'Ein el Jedide. In 'Ein el-Jedide, about 1.5 kilometers (1 mile) southwest of 'Ein Karem (map reference 164129) R. W. Hamilton cleared in 1934, on behalf of the Mandatory Government Department of Antiquities, the remains of a monastery comprising five rooms and a chapel built around a court paved with coarse white mosaic.

The court is entered from the south, and to its southeast was the chapel (5 by 4 meters). In front of the entrance to the chapel is a Greek inscription of five lines, partly destroyed, mentioning Holy Fathers, the presbyters and the deacon and "those whose names the Lord knoweth." The chapel has an interior apse flanked by two rectangular recesses and to the west of it was an unpaved rectangular-shaped room (6 by 4.5 meters).

Two rectangular rooms north of the court contained a winepress. From the eastern room the pressed grape juice flowed through an earthenware pipe set in the west wall and passed into a vat in the next room. West of the court is long narrow rectangular room (7 by 5 meters).

This monastery is probably to be dated to the sixth century A.D.

R. W. Hamilton, *QDAP* 4 (1935), 111–17.

Giv'at Ram (Sheikh Badr), Jerusalem. A church and monastery of the fifth century A.D. were cleared in July–August, 1949, in Sheikh Badr under the direction of M. Avi-Yonah on behalf of the Israel Exploration Society and the Department of Antiquities.

The church is a basilica (17.5 by 14 meters) with an external apse (diameter 4.5 meters), a nave (6 meters wide) and two aisles. Only in the southern aisle were remains of the mosaic pavement preserved. West of the church is a paved court leading to a group of monks' cells. Two cells that were cleared are paved with mosaics. South of the church are two courts with white mosaic pavements and a chapel (7.5 meters by 4 meters) paved with a mosaic in a floral pattern and containing a Greek inscription of three lines which reads: "O Lord, God of Saint George, remember the donor!"

Two plastered shaft tombs were discovered north of the church and to their east was a crypt containing bones.

It can be assumed that this monastery was the *gerocomion* (old people's home), dedicated to Saint George, that was built by the Empress Eudocia at the entrance to Jerusalem in the mid-fifth century A.D.

M. Avi-Yonah, *BJPES* 15 (1950), 19–24 (Hebrew).

Khirbet Juhzum lies about 6 kilometers (4 miles) east of Bethlehem (map reference 176123). In February, 1954, V. Corbo carried out soundings in a monastery there from the sixth century. A long room (20 by 6 meters) paved with a colored mosaic in geometric patterns and two superimposed floors were cleared. North of this room was a dormitory paved with white mosaic and containing stone pallets. In a small room on the east, paved with a colored mosaic laid in geometric patterns, a stone monument was found carved on one side with a Greek inscription of six lines. On the other side is a bas-relief showing two peacocks with a cross between them set between two columns.

Corbo believed that this was the monastery of Marcianus.

V. Corbo, *op. cit.*, 156–63.

Jericho. The Nestorian Hermitage. In 1933, D. C. Baramki, on behalf of the Mandatory Government Department of Antiquities, uncovered the remains of a Nestorian hermitage, 4 kilometers (2 miles) east of Jericho near the road to the Allenby Bridge.

A large dwelling chamber and a small adjoining chapel were cleared. The walls are built of sun-dried bricks coated with several layers of plaster. The chapel is paved with a colored mosaic. In its center is a Syriac inscription framed in a black circle, mentioning the names of the builders. The excavator dates this monastery to the ninth century A.D.

D. C. Baramki–St. N. Stephan, *QDAP* 4 (1935), 81–86.

Jerusalem. In September, 1932, a tomb was discovered about 100 meters west of the YMCA building in Jerusalem. J. H. Illife examined the site on behalf of the Mandatory Government Department of Antiquities and uncovered part of the remains of a monastery. Several rooms paved

This page, counterclockwise from left: Khirbet ed-Deir — Baptismal font; Khirbet ed-Deir — Entrance and rolling stone; Khirbet ed-Deir.

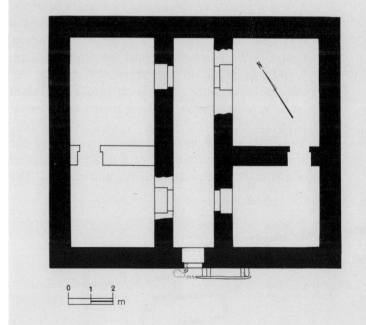

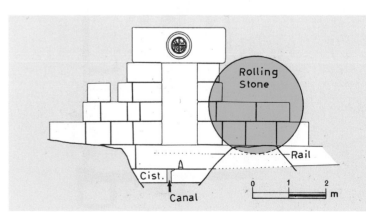

with mosaics and plastered cisterns were cleared. A large number of tombs of monks were found east of the building. Among the finds is a Greek inscription of four lines carved on a tombstone and mentioning "Samuel, bishop of the Georgians and of the monastery purchased near the Tower of David." This inscription is evidence that the building was a Georgian monastery, built at the end of the fifth century A.D. and continuing in use until the seventh century.

J. H. Illife, *QADP* 4 (1934), 70–80.

Khan el-Aḥmar. In 1927, D. J. Chitty and A. H. M. Jones, on behalf of the British School of Archaeology in Jerusalem, cleared the remains of a monastery in Khan el-Aḥmar, 13 kilometers (8 miles) southwest of Jericho (map reference 181134). This monastery is mentioned in literary sources, which relate that from A.D. 425 to 427 Euthymius and Domitianus lived in a cave in the Judean Desert and, after being joined by other hermits, founded a laura. In the years 479 to 482, the deacon Fidus turned this laura into a cenobium and erected a church, a strong tower, and monks' cells.

The parts of the building cleared show that the monastery was surrounded by a wall and consisted of a church, living cells, a tower, and cisterns. The

Khan al-Aḥmar.

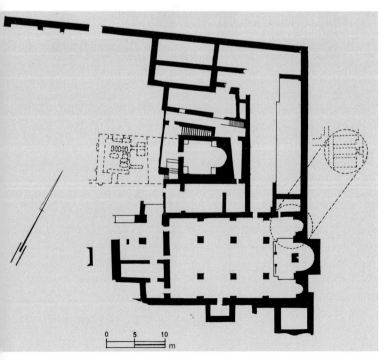

church, a basilica with three apses, was paved with a mosaic in geometric designs. The court in front of the church has a coarse mosaic pavement. There is evidence that the monastery was re-established in the seventh century and continued to exist until its destruction by Saladin or Baybars.

D. J. Chitty–A. H. M. Jones, *PEFQSt* 1928, 175–78 • E. Hanbury Hankim, *ibid.,* 1929, 98–103.

Khirbet el-Makhrum. Khirbet el-Makhrum lies about 6 kilometers (4 miles) east of Bethlehem and about 4 kilometers (2 miles) east of the monastery of Siyar el-Ghanam (map reference 175123). In a survey carried out in 1950 V. Corbo found the remains of a monastery built on a rectangular plan (about 50 by 33 meters) and having two entrances, one in the north and one in the east. The northern entrance leads through a passage to a flagstone courtyard with a cistern. Around the courtyard there are several rooms, and in its southern part were found the remains of an oven were also found. The remains of a church attached to the monastery. The eastern entrance leads to a small court paved with a coarse white mosaic, along two sides of which are chambers and benches. Two doors lead from the court to a small room on the north side and to a long room nearby. South of the court are two chambers flanking a narrow corridor with a mosaic pavement in which a Greek inscription of eight lines is laid which mentions "Our holy father Eglon the hegumen [abbot]." At the end of the passage there is an oblong room (22 by 6 meters) with rows of pillars along two of its walls.

On the basis of topographic indications in the writings of Cyril of Scythopolis, Corbo identified this building with the monastery of Saint Theodosius.

V. Corbo, *op. cit.,* 151–55.

Khirbet el-Mird (Hyrcania, Castellion). At Khirbet el-Mird, about 8 kilometers (5 miles) west of the Dead Sea (map reference 184125), ruins were discovered which are attributed to the Castellion Monastery (or Marda in Aramaic, both names meaning "stronghold, fortress"). This monastery was built in A.D. 492 by Saint Saba on the site of the Herodian fortress of Hyrcania. It reached the height of its prosperity in the sixth century A.D.

The monastery consists of a church, several rooms, and a large court. The church, which lay on the south side of the court, has two entrances. One entrance, in the western facade, leads to the rooms west of the court. A room preserved on the south was probably the diaconicon. Its floor is paved with a colored mosaic surrounded by a border of various kinds of guilloche. In the western corner of the southern slope, a cave was found, which was probably a burial place of the monks. On its walls are paintings depicting holy subjects (most probably of later date). On a stone (35 by 26 centimeters), a graffito in Greek reads "The Lord remember his servant, the monk Adriaos."

In 1952–53, Bible translations and other documents (letters and contracts) were discovered in the cave. They were written in Greek, Christo-Palestinian Aramaic, and Arabic from the fifth to the eighth centuries A.D., and they attest that monks continued to inhabit the site during that time.

A. E. Mader, *JPOS* 9 (1929), 122–35 • J. T. Milik, *RB* 60 (1953), 526–39 • G. R. H. Wright–J. T. Milik, *Biblica* 42 (1961), 1–27.

Ruhama (Khirbet Jammana).

In 1958, excavations were conducted in Khirbet Jammama (on the grounds of Kibbutz Ruḥama, map reference 120100) on behalf of the Department of Antiquities under the direction of R. Gofna. The remains of a monastery from the sixth century A.D. were cleared. The building comprises an enclosed court, surrounded by a chapel, seven rooms and halls as well as two tombs. The court paved with a white coarse mosaic has a cistern in its center and an open plastered drainage channel, in which a covered pottery pipe was laid.

The small chapel lying east of the courtyard was linked on its west side to the large hall (10 by 4 meters), and on its east side it had an interior apse. The parts of the mosaic that survived show beautiful geometric patterns. A white mosaic floor, decorated with three black crosses, was cleared in the northwestern corner of the building. A two-chambered tomb, built of fine ashlar stones, was discovered in the northern part of the court. Another tomb was found south of the building. A square opening gives access to an arched entrance, from which a narrow vaulted passage leads to a door built of dressed stones. From there, three steps descend to the burial hall, consisting of an anteroom and three burial chambers, oriented from east to west. The walls and floor of the anteroom were coated with white plaster. About twenty skeletons were found in this tomb (mainly in the northern burial chamber) laid one above the other in different directions.

R. Gofna, *RB* 67 (1960), 402–03.

Sde Naḥum.

In the years 1955–56, N. Zori, on behalf of the Department of Antiquities, excavated the remains of a monastery at Sde Naḥum. The building complex consists of small rooms and a church grouped around a spacious court.

The church (11.8 by 6.2 meters) contains an exterior apse and a bema, which occupy the entire width of the nave. The mosaic pavement shows a decoration of intertwined lines forming lozenges. Of the mosaic pavement of the nave, the southeast and northwest corners as well as fragments of the border are preserved. The border is formed of an outer band of vine tendrils and an inner narrower band of wavy lines. Between the bands are round medallions (twenty of the seventy medallions are extant), in which animals and fowls are represented.

A large hall is attached to the church on the north side. In the hall the border of a mosaic floor has survived, formed of intertwined geometric patterns. The center of the floor was ornamented with three concentric circles and intertwined geometric patterns. In the west side of the floor a flower vase is seen.

A mosaic pavement with a pattern of squares was cleared in another room northwest of the church.

Sha'ar ha-'Aliyah.

In 1951, excavations were conducted by M. Dothan of the Department of Antiquities near Sha'ar ha-'Aliyah at the southwestern entrance to Haifa (map reference 146247). The remains of a monastery from the sixth century were cleared. The narrow nave (8 by 2.35 meters) is divided broadwise into two parts by a stone partition. The two aisles (8 by 5 meters) were separated from the nave by high walls (which make it impossible for the structure to be a church). West of the building there was a broad court. In the southern aisle, a mosaic floor was cleared, ornamented with circles which intersect and form four ellipsoid figures in each circle, which also surrounded a smaller circle with floral motifs. The field is enclosed by a border composed of three bands. The outer band shows crosslets, the middle one palmettes and floral motifs, and the innermost band contains a meander pattern.

Below: Sha'ar ha-Aliyah — Plan; Bottom: Sha'ar ha-Aliyah. Inscription in mosaic pavement: "This is the place of lucky days".

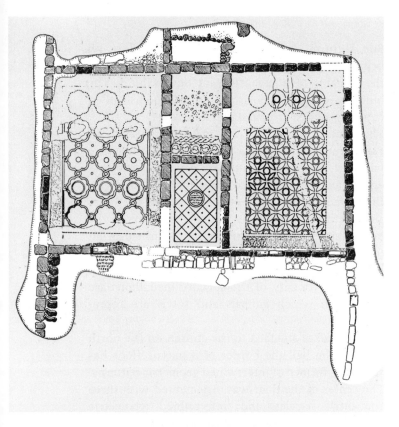

In front of the centrance to the northern aisle is a fragmentary Greek inscription which probably mentions the builders of the monastery. A mosaic floor was cleared in the north aisle. It contains a pattern of small and large circles, each consisting of eight equal circular segments. Stylized birds and flowers are represented inside these circles, and in the spaces between the circles appear floral motifs.

A mosaic floor preserved in the western part of the nave shows a plain ornament consisting of a field of rhomboids within a black border. In the eastern section was a Greek inscription in a double circle, which reads "This is the place of lucky days."

M. Dothan, *BIES* 18 (1953), 216–22 (Hebrew); *idem, IEJ* 5 (1955), 96–102.

Siyar el-Ghanam. In 1934, C. Guarmani conducted excavations at Siyar el-Ghanam, situated 2 kilometers east of Bethlehem (map reference 172124) and uncovered part of the remains of the monastery. In 1951–52, a Franciscan mission under the direction of V. Corbo cleared the entire complex.

The monastery is built on a rectangular plan (80 by 42 meters). Two stages of construction were distinguished: an early stage dating to the end of the fourth or beginning of the fifth century and a later stage from the sixth to the eighth centuries.

To the early stage belong the remains of the church, of which only the apse had survived, and also several rooms in the southern part of the monastery. The building that was cleared dates mainly from the later stage. The monastery was entered from the south by way of a flight of six stairs (6 meters wide), which led to a court paved with large flagstones. Scattered all over the surface were numerous architectural remains belonging to a church, with an exterior polygonal apse, among them a large lintel decorated with crosses.

Near the church was a long room paved with small stones, with three steps in its southern corner and two doorways leading to a small room to the east.

South of this room was a court surrounded by several small rooms, one of which (on the east) was an animal pen as is indicated by the stone troughs found in it.

The central and northern parts of the monastery were almost totally destroyed, but the western wing is well preserved. This area consisted of several rooms containing finely constructed wine-presses. A long narrow room with an oven may have been the bakery. In a small adjoining room paved with colored mosaic were two Greek inscriptions that read: "God help!" and "The Lord protect us from any evil!" Basalt querns were also uncovered. The monastery contained several cisterns and a well-built drainage system. Corbo identifies these remains with the Monastery of the Shepherds.   R. COHEN

V. Corbo, *Gli Scavi di Kh. Siyar el Ghanam e i Monasteri dei Dintorni,* Jerusalem, 1955.

Siyar el-Ghanam.

BIBLIOGRAPHY

O. Meinardus, *Liber Annus,* 15 (1964–65), 220–50; idem, ibid. 16 (1965–66), 328–56 • A. Ovadiah, *Corpus of the Byzantine Churches in the Holy Land,* Bonn (1970) • V. Corbo, *Gli Scavi di Kh. Siyar el-Ghanam e i Monasteri dei Dintorni,* Jerusalem (1955), 141–45 • *Ḥadashot Archaeologiot* 3 (1962), 20–21 (Hebrew) • N. Zori, in: *The Beth-Shean Valley,* Jerusalem, (1962), 190 (Hebrew); *idem, IEJ* 24 (1974) 227 • Y. Aharoni, *BIES* 18 (1954), 209–15 (Hebrew) • C. Kopp, *RB* 53 (1946), 547–58 • A. M. Steve, *ibid.,* 559–75 • R. W. Hamilton, *QDAP* 4 (1935), 111–17 • M. Avi-Yonah, *BJPES* 15 (1950), 19–24 (Hebrew) • D. C. Baramki–St. N. Stephan, *QDAP* 4 (1935), 81–86 • J. H. Illife, *ibid.,* 70–80 • D. J. Chitty–A. H. M. Jones, *PEFQSt* (1928), 175–78 • E. Hanbury Hankin, *ibid.,* (1929), 98–103 • A. E. Mader, *JPOS* 9 (1929), 122–35 • J. T. Milik, *RB* 60 (1953), 526–39 • G. R. H. Wright–J. T. Milik, *Biblica* 42 (1961), 1–27 • R. Gofna, *RB* 67 (1960), 402–04 • M. Dothan, *BIES* 18 (1953), 216–22 (Hebrew); *idem, IEJ* (1955), 96–102.

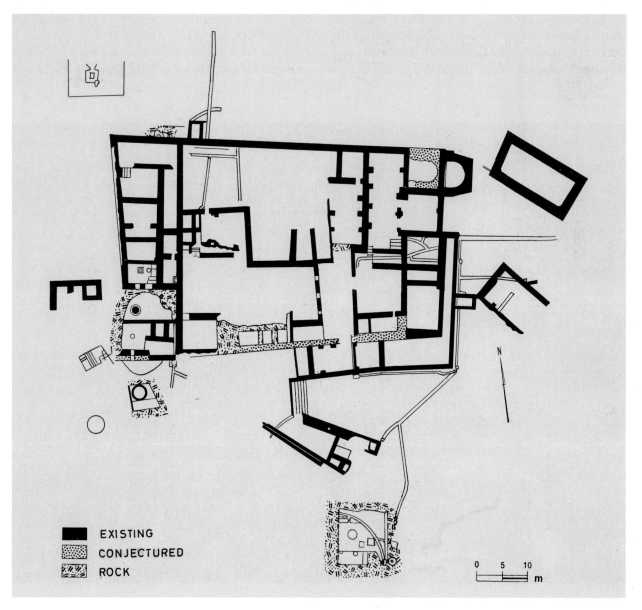

EXISTING
CONJECTURED
ROCK

0   5   10
m

N

MONTFORT

IDENTIFICATION. Montfort, the castle known in Arabic as Qal'at el-Qurein ("the stronghold of the small horn"), was built by the Crusaders on the southern bank of the Kezib Brook (Wadi Qurein), 300 meters above sea level, 180 meters above the bed of the brook, and about 12 kilometers (7.5 miles) from the sea.

The stronghold was built far from any Crusader roads of importance, and its strategic value was therefore limited. Two roads connected it with the centers of Crusader settlement, one turning southwest to M'alia (Chateau du Roi), the other running down the valley of the Kezib Brook toward Khirbet Manawat, and continuing to Acre. Both roads were of local importance only. Although the castle stands on a height, it commands a limited area only. It was built in the twelfth century for the purpose of defending the tract of land in the Kezib Valley belonging to the fief of M'alia, to which the castle of Montfort also belonged in that period.

In the thirteenth century, the castle was enlarged and its builders, the Knights of the Teutonic Order, designated it as the location of their treasury and archives. The site was indeed suitable for such a purpose, having natural defenses and being out of reach of the brigands who infested the main roads.

The castle is built on a steep rock ridge, running east–west and extending from the Kezib Brook in the north to a narrow ravine in the south. The northern and southern slopes of the ridge are extremely steep, while that on the west is terraced. On the east the ridge is joined to the top of the mountain by a narrow saddle. The slope that is terraced from east to west enabled the builders to construct the castle on several different levels, one

General view.

886

above the other, thus increasing its strength and securing its defense in depth.

HISTORY

The site was already occupied in the Roman-Byzantine period, as is evidenced by stones from that period that were re-used in the Crusader buildings. In the excavations several Roman coins and other objects from that period were found.

When the Crusaders built the castle in the middle of the twelfth century, it was called Castellum Novum Regis. In 1187 the Muslims captured Montfort, but it was reconquered by the Crusaders in 1192 and restored to the domain of the lords of the Chateau du Roi, which was a fief of the Courtenay family. When M'alia was sold to the Order of the Teutonic Knights in 1220, the castle itself remained in the hands of the Courtenays. In 1228, Guillaume de Mandelée sold the castle — known as Montfort in the thirteenth century — to the Order of the Teutonic Knights who began to

enlarge it. With the help of contributions, the head of the order, Hermann von Salza, completed its construction, and it was named Starkenberg by its German lords. In 1229, the lordship of the Christians over Montfort was recognized in the peace treaty concluded between the Emperor Frederick II and the Sultan al-Kamil.

By virtue of the economic importance of the castle and the fact that the treasury of the Teutonic Knights was kept there, the treasurer of the order always served as governor (castellan) of Montfort.

In 1266, Baybars besieged the castle, but was forced to lift the siege after a difficult campaign. In June, 1271, he renewed the attack and after a siege of one week succeeded in breaching the southern wall and penetrating the castle. The Teutonic Knights continued the fight by barricading themselves in the keep, but after a short while they surrendered and were granted safe retreat to Acre (Accho-or-'Akka).

Plan and section.

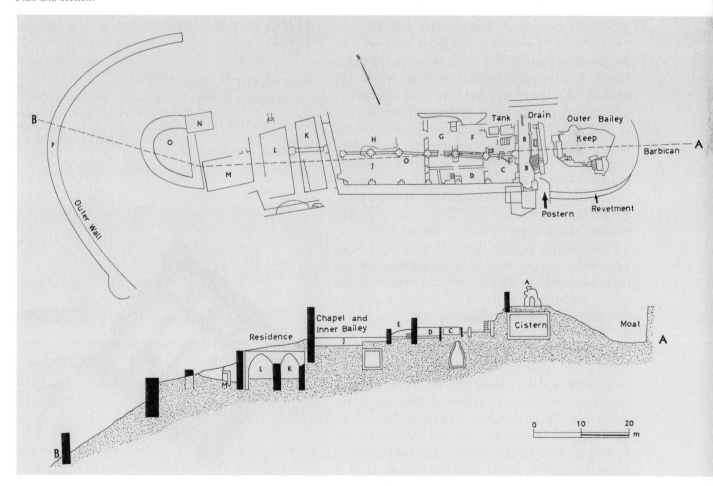

EXCAVATIONS

In 1926, an expedition on behalf of the Metropolitan Museum in New York excavated the site under the direction of W. L. Calver and B. Dean.

The Castle. The outer defense lines of the castle consisted of a curtain wall with square towers, built around the mountain ridge. On the narrow saddle joining the ridge to the top of the mountain, two deep moats were cut into the rock and a strong wall erected behind. On this side, which was the most accessible but also the highest part of the castle, the keep was erected. The inner area of the castle was divided into five main sections as follows (from west to east):

1. THE CEREMONIAL HALL. A large, square hall (length of a side 20 meters), it was used for ceremonies and meetings of the Teutonic Order. The hall was roofed with polygonal vaults, supported by octagonal pillars. The thickness of the eastern wall, the only surviving one, reached 2 meters. The other walls and the vaults of the castle have collapsed. West of this hall was the governor's residence. Beneath the hall of ceremonies were two vaulted dungeons, and west of them was a square tower, the only one in the castle which is preserved to its complete height (18 meters). This tower was provided with embrasures directed toward the valley of the Kezib Brook.

2. THE CHAPEL (8 by 23 meters) situated on the eastern side of the hall of ceremonies, is divided into two aisles and a nave by two rows of octagonal columns, four in each row. Inside the area of the chapel, there was a round cistern. Fragments of stained glass found on the floor were probably remains of the windows in the southern wall.

3. THE INNER BAILEY, north of the chapel, is an open area serving both as a passageway to the main hall and the chapel, and also separated the public buildings on the west from the area of dwellings and workshops on the east.

4. THE DWELLING AND WORKSHOP AREA, east of the chapel, is divided into two parts by a row of four pillars. The southern part contained two rooms and a kitchen, and in the north there were two workshops of armorers. Near the workshops and the kitchen is a winepress. East of the dwelling area is a small paved area with a staircase leading up to the keep. Pottery jars and fragments of bottles were found in the kitchen, and parts of weapons and armor in the workshops.

5. THE KEEP. Of the oval-shaped keep, part of its southern wall, which is built of large stones, and a section of the western wall have survived. The stones are re-used from a building that had existed on the site in the Roman-Byzantine period. In the floor of the keep there was a large cistern.

The only gateway of the castle was built on the southern slope of the ridge and has been completely demolished. The castle had an extensive network of sewers.

At the foot of the castle, on the southern bank of the Kezib Brook, is a large, two-storied Crusader building. This was the main building of the farm supplying food to the castle. It also served for the defense of the approach to the castle and its water supply, the Kezib Brook, which at this spot carries water throughout the year.

On the ground floor of this building, there were stables and storerooms. A stairway on the western side of the building led to the upper floor, roofed by a polygonal vault still extant. In the bed of the brook were the remains of a dam which raised the level of the water and directed it to a channel leading to a mill built on the slope above the brook.

M. BENVENISTI

BIBLIOGRAPHY

Conder–Kitchener, *SWP* 1, 186–90 • Guérin, *Galilee* 2, 129–32 • B. Dean, *A Crusaders' Fortress in Palestine, Bulletin Metropolitan Museum*, New York, 1927 • E. W. G. Masterman, *PEQ* 60 (1928), 91–97 • M. Benvenisti, *The Crusaders in the Holy Land*, Jerusalem, 1970, 331–37.

Tel Mor. Fortress.

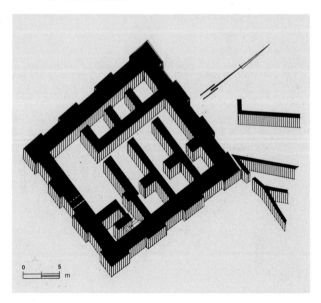

MOR, TEL

IDENTIFICATION. Tel Mor (in Arabic Tell Mura, Tell Kheidar) is situated on the northern bank of Naḥal Lachish (Wadi Sukreir) on the ancient Via Maris, about 1 kilometer (.5 mile) from the sea and 7 kilometers (4 miles) northwest of the ancient city of Ashdod. The mound covers an area of about 6 dunams and rises about 17 meters above the surroundings. The city that once flourished here was supported by the port that served the kingdom of Ashdod and was situated at the source of a perennial stream. According to some authorities, this was the site of the estuary town of Ashdod-Yam, and with its abandonment in the tenth century B.C., its name was transfered to Minet Isdud, the present Ashdod-Yam.

EXCAVATIONS

In conjunction with the construction of the new port in Ashdod, excavations of the site were undertaken on behalf of the Department of Antiquities and financed by the Ashdod Development Corporation. In the autumn of 1959 and the spring of 1960, two seasons of excavations were directed by M. Dothan, assisted by I. Dunayevsky and S. Moskowitz. Twelve strata of settlement (7 meters deep) were distinguished in the course of the excavations. The upper eight strata (area A), covering an area of about 100 square meters, were excavated almost in their entirety and the four lower layers (area B) only in part. Due to erosion, the area of the upper strata was much smaller than that of the lower ones.

The earliest remains (stratum 12) date from the end of the Middle Bronze Age, about the sixteenth century B.C. In a deep depression in a courtyard, pottery, mostly cultic vessels, was uncovered, which point to trade with Egypt. Monochrome Cypriot pottery and red-on-red ware were also discovered. Strata 11–10, dating from the sixteenth and fifteenth centuries B.C., clearly reflect a period of flourishing trade and commercial relations with both Egypt and Cyprus and the Phoenician coast. In stratum 11 miniature offering vessels were found together with many vessels of bichrome ware (Tell el-'Ajjul pottery, q.v.). Stratum 9 was the first level that could be excavated over an extensive area, and thereafter building remains could be examined and more detailed information could be obtained on the city as a whole. Stratum 9, which is dated to the fourteenth century B.C., the days of the Eighteenth Dynasty in Egypt, contained buildings attesting to the city's function as a fort on the Via Maris and to its role as a harbor city. Thick brick walls of the main building on the site (21 by 11 meters) still stand to a height of 1.2 meters. The building, which was of at least two stories, consisted of three long halls and twelve smaller rooms. The main find here were store jars, indicating that the building undoubtedly served as the central storehouse of the port. In this stratum was found a tomb of stone slabs arranged in the form of a gable and containing a skeleton accompanied by funerary offerings. The pottery was for the most part Cypriot. The settlement of stratum 9 was destroyed at the end of the fourteenth century B.C. (perhaps by Pharaoh Seti I).

The following settlements, strata 8–7 date from the end of the fourteenth and the thirteenth centuries B.C. The main building of these towns was a square fortress built of bricks (23 by 23 meters), whose outer walls were constructed with alternating salients and recesses. The interior was symmetrically arranged, like Egyptian buildings of that period. Judging from the thickness of the walls (2.5 meters) and the staircase, the fortress consisted of several stories. A considerable amount of Egyptian, Mycenaean, and Cypriot pottery was uncovered in these layers. On a jug handle were incised markings in Cypriot-Minoan script. The fortress of stratum 7, which probably dates to the time of Ramses II, was completely razed by fire. The thickness of the destroyed layer was 1.5 meters. The city was apparently destroyed in the second half of the thirteenth century, perhaps in a punitive action by Pharaoh Merneptah against the rebellious cities of the Shephelah. It is, however, difficult to believe that the Egyptians would totally demolish one of their strongest forts on the Via Maris, which was vital for maintaining its control of the Canaanite coast. It is more plausible to attribute this destruction to the Israelite tribes, who in that period devastated the coastal plain, although they failed to settle it.

On the ruins of the great fortress of stratum 8 was built a small *migdol* (fort), which was also in use in strata 6 and 5. The *migdol* was a solid, square building (11 by 11 meters) consisting of two rooms with 4-meter-thick walls and of at least two stories, which were reached by a ramp. Also uncovered were houses and workshops with furnaces and clay pipes for smelting and casting copper. On the basis of the finds in these two layers it can be inferred that, after the Israelite conquest, the Canaanite inhabitants resettled the area in the beginning of the twelfth century B.C. Most of the pottery consisted of types common at the end of the Late Bronze Age, including local imitations of Cypriot ware. Egyptian pottery and scarabs may indicate that an Egyptian governor still resided in the fortress in the time of Ramses III. The settlement of stratum 5 continued down to the first half of the twelfth century, when the city passed into the hands of the Philistines.

The two Philistine strata 4 and 3 contained remains of a small open settlement, chiefly small agricultural structures, courts, and silos. Aside from finds that are typical of the beginning of the Iron Age, the excavators also discovered decorated Philistine pottery, such as jars and beer jugs. The city of stratum 3 was conquered at the beginning of the tenth century, perhaps by David on one of his expeditions against the Philistines, or in a campaign of Pharaoh Siamon against Philistia.

After the destruction of the city, the site was abandoned for several generations until it was resettled in the eighth century B.C. (stratum 2). This is the topmost stratum on the summit of the mound. Two parallel brick walls were found, which may have belonged to the casemate wall of the city fortress. It was possibly built by King Uzziah (II Chronicles 26:6) and destroyed by Sargon II, the Assyrian king who, according to his own testimony, subdued Ashdod-Yam and turned the kingdom of Ashdod (and Tel Mor within its territory) into an Assyrian province. Tel Mor was abandoned and the port of Ashdod transferred to the site later known by the Greek name of Ἄζωτος παράλιος, which is identified with Minet Isdud (Ashdod-Yam).

Stratum 1 belongs to the occupation of Tel Mor in the Hellenistic period. A large public building was uncovered on the eastern slope of the mound, as well as an installation for the extraction of purple dye from murex shells. Several plastered pools connected by pipes stood near a cistern, which contained thousands of shells. Judging from the hundreds of pottery vessels in the cistern, this industry began in about 300 B.C. and ceased in the second half of the second century A.D. In the Roman-Byzantine period there was only a poor agricultural settlement on the site.

THE STRATIGRAPHY AND CHRONOLOGY OF TEL MOR

STRATUM	PERIOD
1	Hellenistic period (4th–2nd centuries B.C.)
2	Iron Age II-B (8th century B.C.)
3	Iron Age I-B–II-A (second half of 11th and beginning of 10th century B.C.)
4	Iron Age I-B (second half of 12th and first of 11th century B.C.)
5	Iron Age I-A (first half of 12th century B.C.)
6	Transition from Bronze Age to Iron Age (end of 13th and first half of 12th century B.C.)
7	Late Bronze Age II-B (13th century B.C.)
8	Late Bronze Age II-B (13th century B.C.)
9	Late Bronze Age II-A (14th century B.C.)
10	Late Bronze Age I-A (15th century B.C.)
11	Late Bronze Age I-A (16th century B.C.)
12	End of Middle Bronze Age II-B (approximately 1600 B.C.)

M. DOTHAN

BIBLIOGRAPHY

M. Dothan, *BIES* 24 (1960), 120–32 (Hebrew); *idem, IEJ* 9 (1959), 271–72; 10 (1960), 123–25; 23 (1973), 1–17.

NA'ARAN

IDENTIFICATION. Na'aran is mentioned in the Bible as Naarah (Joshua 16:7) on the border of Ephraim, before Jericho, and as Naaran in the territory of Ephraim (I Chronicles 7:28). Josephus tells of a village named Neara in the valley of Jericho, whose waters were diverted by Herod's son Archelaus for his new city, Archelais (*Antiquities*, XVII, 340). A midrash (*Lamentation Rabbah* 45a, ed. Buber) mentions the enmity existing between Na'aran and neighboring Jericho. Eusebius (Onomasticon 136, 24) describes the village of Noorath as a Jewish settlement about five miles from Jericho. The Jews of the town are still mentioned in sources from the fifth century A.D. (*Life of Saint Chariton*) and from the sixth century (Palladius, *Historia Lausiaca*, 48). The identification with the Arab village of 'Ein Duk (which preserves the name Duk, the citadel famous from Hasmonaean times) was established by the distance given in Eusebius' Onomasticon, and its description in the Bible. The discovery of remains of a synagogue on the site confirmed this identification.

THE SYNAGOGUE

In September, 1918, a shell fired by the Turks at the British fort in Wadi e-Naimah exploded, and a mosaic floor was exposed by the blast. R. Engelbach and E. J. H. MacKay, two English archaeologists serving with the British Army, examined the site in 1919 and copied one of the inscriptions. In the same year, the Dominican Fathers L. J. Vincent and M. J. Lagrange recorded some of the remains— part of the nave and the figure of a lion in the mosaic with an inscription by its side. In 1921, Vincent and B. Carrière continued excavating the synagogue. Parts of the mosaic and the plan of the building were first published by E. L. Sukenik in his book on Beth Alpha. In 1961, P. Benoit found in the Dominican archives Vincent's article about the site, which he published posthumously.

The synagogue in Na'aran includes an adjoining courtyard surrounded by a wall. The entrance to the courtyard was on the north, on which side the wall followed an irregular course (apparently because of the limited area available to the builders). The northern part of the courtyard is paved with small stones up to a wall surrounding an open space in the center of which was a square pool (near a cistern?). In the northwestern corner of the courtyard, a kind of loggia was found (2.65 meters wide), with two pillars in the facade. The courtyard is L-shaped, the short arm (8.7 meters wide) running east–west, and the long arm (10.25 meters wide) north–south. South of the pool was the entrance to the narthex, which was also L–shaped. The short arm of the narthex (10.2 by 3.58 meters) runs north–south, while the long arm (17.4 by 3.65 meters) runs along the facade of the synagogue.

The narthex is paved with a white mosaic laid in a black frame. On the floor facing the middle entrance to the hall of the synagogue was a rectangular mosaic, in which a stylized menorah was depicted surrounded by various geometric motifs. At the foot of the menorah are shown three "hills," reminiscent of the symbolic decoration found at the foot of crosses. The base of the menorah is decorated with a simple guilloche, which continues up as the middle branch to the horizontal bar on the upper end of the menorah. The other branches are in the form of four semi-circular bands, with a white strip separating them. The mosaic within the semicircles forming the branches is laid in graded shades. Between the central branch and the rounded branches are two rhomboid-shaped designs. The menorah terminates in a straight line, above which stand elliptical "lamps" topped by triangles representing flames. The menorah has twelve such lamps, and in this respect differs from all the known depictions of menorahs. Above the menorah was an Aramaic inscription which reads "Remembered be for good, the priest Phinehas son of Justa, who gave the price of the mosaic and the laver." Beneath this inscription, on either side of the menorah, was another inscription: "Remembered be for good, Rebekah wife of Phinehas."

The hall of the synagogue was entered through three doorways, of which the middle was the widest. The thresholds of the eastern and middle openings have survived. The hall, 14.94 meters wide, had a basilical shape and was divided by six pillars or columns into a nave and two aisles. A 19-meter-long section of the hall was preserved. However, its exact length cannot be determined, since the southern end is destroyed. Vincent was of the opinion that its length was 21.94 meters.

This page, below: Plan of the synagogue; Bottom: Inscription in the mosaic pavement; Opposite page: Mosaic pavement.

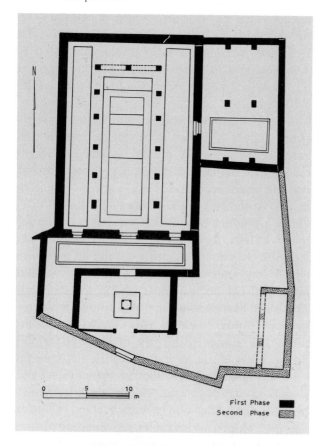

Quite possibly there may have been an apse in the southern destroyed wall. The reconstruction suggested by Vincent in 1921 (ending in a straight wall, with a single column between the rows of columns) is based on what was known at that time of plans of synagogues, but this has been invalidated by subsequent discoveries.

The entire hall was paved with mosaics, considerable portions of which were preserved. The mosaics in the aisles and the intercolumnar spaces are laid in diverse geometric patterns. There are also a few images of birds and animals in the intercolumnar spaces. In the hall, near the main entrance, were preserved the images of two gazelles on a background of flowers. The gazelle on the right side and the front legs of the gazelle on the left were mutilated and repaired in antiquity. However, the craftsman who did the repair was considerably less proficient than the original artist. The floor of the nave is one complete mosaic carpet, surrounded by a broad border. North of the border, parallel to the axis of the floor, is an Aramaic inscription: "Remembered be for good Ḥalifu daughter of Rabbi Safra who contributed [donated] to this holy place, *Amen.*"

The field within the border is divided into three sections. The northern half is decorated with a hexagonal pattern, with the two ends of the hexagons rounded. The hexagons are bounded by bands of guilloche, lotus flowers facing alternately inward and outward, and lines in graded shades of color. In the half circles that fill the spaces between the rounded ends of the hexagons and the border are depicted various fruits (figs, apples, grapes, carobs, and others). The hexagons and the inner circles enclose images of animals, most of which are obliterated, and only a few can still be identified. There are fifteen hexagons arranged in rows of three and eight circles arranged in four rows of two each. The objects preserved intact include a bird in a cage (in the first row on the south) and a fruit basket (in the second two). Among the other objects that can be identified are an octopus, cock, lion, bull, and others. In the circular medallions are a peacock and a fledgling as well as another bird.

The southern half of the mosaic pavement is divided into two panels. In the northern panel is a zodiac set in a square frame (length of a side 4.05 meters) and in the corners appear the four seasons of the year. The figure of autumn, the "season [Tish]re," is preserved in the form of a woman with a staff and shofar in her hand, and a duck next to her. It should be noted that this figure was placed in the wrong corner, near the zodiac signs of the "season *Nisan*" (spring — Pisces, Aries, and Taurus) while the figure of the "season *Nisan*" was placed near the zodiac signs of the "season *Tishre*" (autumn). The "season *Tammuz*" (summer) was totally obliterated. The figure symbolizing the "season *Nisan*" (spring) holds a long staff in her hand, and by her side are three ears of corn. Of the figure of the "season *Tebeth*" (here written טיבית) only a staff and bird were preserved. Inside this square was a circle (3.5 meters in diameter), and surrounding it was sign of Libra (*Me'oz-* (*Me'oznayim*; here written מוזניים) represented by an elaborately clad man holding scales in his hand. *Betulah* (Virgo) is depicted as a young girl with veiled face and hands raised in prayer. The signs of *Aryeh* (Leo) follow in the figure of a lion with raised tail, *Sartan* (Cancer), *(Teo)mim* (Gemini), which is entirely obliterated, *Shor* (Taurus) (an ox shown in profile), *Taleh* (Aries) represented by a fat-tailed lamb, *Dagim* (Pisces) represented by two fish strung up on a rope.

The rest of the zodiac signs have been completely obliterated, but the inscriptions are preserved for the most part. In the center of the circle (1.6 meters in diameter), Helios the sun-god is depicted in his chariot. His head is surrounded by a rayed halo, his garment is star studded, and he holds a whip. Above the two wheels of the chariot are four horses, two facing left and two facing right.

In the third section of the mosaic is depicted a paneled Ark of the Law flanked by seven-branched menorahs on either side. Each menorah has a stepped base, a central branch decorated with circles, and side branches of white and colored squares. The branches end in bars, with lotus-shaped lamps above them. Lamps in the shape of canthari hang down from the outer branches of the menorah.

Beneath the two menorahs are two lions with the figure of a man between them (destroyed). The face of the man is turned toward the viewer and his hands are raised in prayer. Above this figure to the right is an inscription: "Danie[l] *Shalom*, and below this "Remembered be for go[od], Samuel." Between the figures of the man and the lion at the

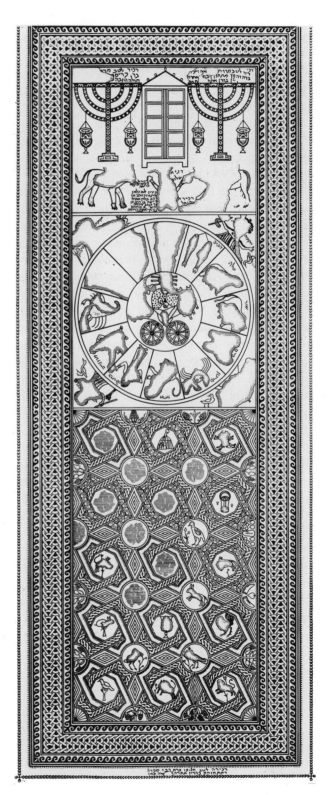

left appears the inscription "Remembered be for good, the *parnas* Benjamin, son of Jose. Remembered be for good every one who donates and contributes or who gave to this holy place gold, silver, or other valuable objects, who brought their share, *Amen*" (translation and restoration: S. Klein).

Above the menorahs, to the right, is the inscription "Remembered be for good, Maruth... Ketina, and Jacob his son who donated to this place, *Amen*," and to the left: "Remembered be for good, Mar... son of Chrospedah who brought their share to this holy place, *Amen*."

DATE AND EVALUATION

Na'aran was the first synagogue of the late type to be excavated (see Synagogues). For this reason, and because of the long delay in publishing the results of the excavation and the piecemeal manner of publication, the place was not correctly evaluated, and various hypotheses as to its date were put forth. From excavations at other sites, the synagogue at Na'aran can now be dated with certainty to the sixth century A.D. Since traces of human images have been preserved, it can be classified with the synagogues of the Beth Alpha and Ma'on type. It was undoubtedly a basilical structure and apparently had an apse which faced south, as the site is situated north of Jerusalem, on the border of Ephraim. The biblical scene (Daniel in the lions' den), the depictions of the Ark of the Law and the menorahs, and the geometric patterns, all point to the fact that the freedom of expression so evident at Gerasa, Beth Alpha, and Hammath Tiberias had ceased to exist. The figurative drawings on the floor were certainly defaced by fanatic Jews, who were careful, however, to preserve the Hebrew letters. It can therefore be concluded that the movement opposing the representation of all figures and images had been revived and had become widespread.

M. AVI-YONAH

BIBLIOGRAPHY

L. H. Vincent, *RB* 28 (1919), 532–63; 30 (1921), 422 f. • E. L. Sukenik, *The Synagogue of Beth Alpha*, Jerusalem, 1932, *passim* • S. Klein, *Sefer ha-Yishuv*, 1, Jerusalem, 1939, 109–10 (Hebrew) • Sukenik, *Ancient Synagogues*, 28–34; *idem*, *Rabinowitz Bulletin* 1 (1949), 9–11 • Goodenough, *Jewish Symbols* 1, 253–57; 3, 642–47 • L. H. Vincent, *RB* 68 (1961), 163–73 • P. Benoit, *ibid.*, 174–77.

NAGILA, TEL

IDENTIFICATION. Tel Nagila is situated in the inner coastal plain about 28 kilometers (17.5 miles) east of Gaza (map reference 127101). The mound is in the shape of a rectangle with rounded corners and covers an area of about 40 dunams, rising about 7 meters above the surrounding area. It lies on a low natural hill on the left bank of Naḥal Shiqma. Prior to its excavation, it had been assumed that the site should be identified with Gath of the Philistines, but since no Iron Age I remains were found in the excavations, this identification had to be abandoned.

EXCAVATIONS

Two seasons of excavations were carried out at Tel Nagila in 1962 and 1963 on behalf of the Institute for Mediterranean Studies, founded by R. A. Mitchell. The excavations were directed by Ruth Amiran assisted by A. Eitan. Four areas were excavated on the mound itself (A, B, C, F) in addition to one area and two tombs on the lower southern ridges of the mound (G, DT-1 and DT-2). In the main area, the center of the mound (area A), fourteen strata were distinguished down to bedrock, with a maximum accumulation of 3.5 meters. These strata represent the history of Tel Nagila, which was occupied with interruptions from the Chalcolithic period to the end of the Mameluke period (about A.D. 1500).

Stratum XIV — Chalcolithic. A round pit with patches of ashes around it as well as a small amount of pottery were found in a small area on virgin soil and bedrock (area A).

Strata XIII–XII — Early Bronze Age II–III. Both strata were reached in a limited area in the center of the mound. The architectural remains consisted of a large house (at least 5 meters long), a rectangular house with stone benches running along its walls, and a section of a curved wall, perhaps of an apsidal structure. South of the mound, on the slope descending toward Naḥal Shiqma, was found a small tomb cut in the rock, containing a group of pottery vessels of the late Early Bronze Age II.

Strata XI–VII — Middle Bronze Age II–B–C. After a long gap of six or seven hundred years, a city of the Middle Bronze Age was established on the site. This city seems to have enjoyed the main, if not the only, period of prosperity in the history of Tel Nagila. A residential quarter and parts of two public buildings in the center of the city (area A), an elaborate fortification system in areas C and F, and a tomb (DT-2) south of the site belong to this period. As was proved in trial soundings, the settlement in this period was not confined to the walled city on the mound proper, but spread outside it on the northern and southern plateaus, as well as on the eastern slope, directly above the river. Little information was obtained on the two lower strata (XI and X). The three upper strata (IX, VIII, VII) are similar in plan and character, with only slight changes from one stratum to the next: walls are re-used, sometimes repaired, and floors are raised, new walls were added, and others removed. The plan shows parts of four blocks of houses opening onto two parallel streets. Intersecting streets or lanes at right angles, enclosing the blocks, are also indicated. The streets are about 1.5 meters wide and are paved with pebbles and potsherds laid in beaten whitish clay. The houses are built close

together, having party walls, either a back wall common to two rows of dwellings or side or front walls connecting adjoining houses. In some cases a flight of several steps leads down to the house from the street. Generally rectangular in shape, the houses seem to be composed of one or two small rooms (averaging 2 by 3 meters), opening onto a courtyard (averaging 3 by 5 meters). One side of the courtyard is sometimes roofed, as is indicated by stone bases for wooden posts. These roofed sheds are often paved with flagstones, but the floors of most rooms and courtyards are of beaten earth. The lower parts of the walls are generally built of rough fieldstones, and the upper structures are of sun-dried brick.

Typical installations in these houses are clay ovens (the one complete specimen has openings on the top and on the side), benches of clay or stone, small round depressions in the floors (to hold vessels), and round silos. It may be assumed that the layout of the excavated area is representative of the general town plan, which seems to have been oriented to conform with the rectangular shape of the settlement. In the immediate vicinity

The mound and areas of excavation.

Area A—strata I-VIII.

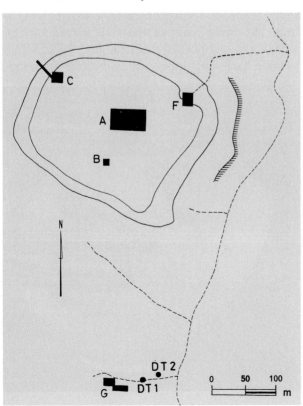

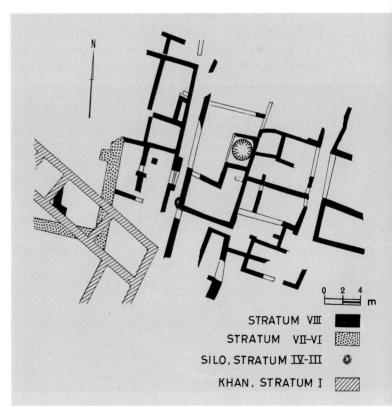

STRATUM VIII

STRATUM VII-VI

SILO, STRATUM IV-III

KHAN, STRATUM I

Right: Fragmentary inscription in proto-Canaanite script — end of the MBA or beginning of the LBA; Below: Scarabs from tomb D2. 1. Hathor head. 2.–3. Scroll designs — end of the MBA; Bottom: Two views of a Bichrome crater — LBA I.

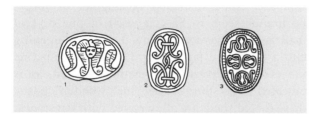

of this residential quarter were uncovered parts of two large buildings, possibly of a public function. Their walls, 1.5 meters wide, are much thicker than usual. Their complete plan has not yet been established.

The finds include, besides the pottery, ostrich eggshells used as vessels, bone inlays from wooden toilet boxes, faience and alabaster bottles, scarabs, and a cylinder seal. Some bronze implements were also found. Of special interest is a vessel in the shape of a bull, found in one of the public buildings, and a potsherd with a fragmentary inscription, incised before firing, containing signs in the alphabetic Proto-Canaanite script.

FORTIFICATIONS OF THE CITY. The fortifications and the manner of their construction were examined in a section cut in the northwest slope (area C) extending from the top of the slope to the foot of the mound. An elaborate construction composed of four components was uncovered: 1. an earthen core-embankment; 2. a brick wall; 3. a glacis; 4. a fosse. First, the core-embankment of earth was piled up around the entire mound. Then, a sun-dried brick wall, 2.3–2.5 meters wide, was erected on the inner slope of the embankment. In the final stage, a glacis was constructed. Large quantities of earth and crushed chalk were thrown and beaten against the wall and over the whole slope, creating a hard even surface. In section this glacis shows alternating layers of the assorted fill material used. The thickness of the glacis at its junction with the brick wall is about 3.5 meters, its top being horizontal for about 2.5 meters. The brick wall originally rose above the top of the glacis. Some of its upper courses are preserved. Thus, the lower part of the wall served on the outside as a supporting wall for the glacis, while its inner face and upper part were free standing

The floors adjacent to the wall on its interior face are 1.5 meters lower than the top of the glacis outside.

A tower was partly uncovered in this area, its floor covered with a thick layer of ashes. Another fragment of this brick wall was uncovered in a section in area F, where traces of conflagration and fallen bricks are further evidence of the last destruction of the Middle Bronze Age II city (to be dated possibly to Aḥmose, about 1550 B.C.). However, there is no indication in which of the Middle Bronze Age strata these fortifications were erected.

TOMB DT-2. This tomb, cut in the rock, was found near the Early Bronze Age tomb mentioned above. It consists of three chambers in a row connected by passageways. The tomb contained the skeletal remains of about fifty individuals, the bones lying in disorder, but some of the skulls were found placed carefully along the walls and in the corners. The accompanying funerary objects included, besides about 150 local pottery vessels of various types, a red-on-black Cypriot jug, forty-eight scarabs, faience and alabaster Egyptian vessels, some bronzes, and an ostrich eggshell.

Strata VI and V — Late Bronze Age. Stratum VI, which represents the Late Bronze Age I, was encountered mainly in the section in area F where a pavement of flagstones was found lying on top of the ruined Middle Bronze Age II city wall. On it was found a bichrome krater, decorated with a bull, bird, and ibex. It is not unlikely that the uppermost public building uncovered in area A (and assigned above to the Middle Bronze Age II) may prove to belong to this Late Bronze Age I stratum. Stratum V, representing the Late Bronze Age II, is attested mainly by pottery, which includes Cypriot and Mycenaean sherds, as well as local painted ware.

Stratum IV — Iron Age II-B; Stratum III — Iron Age II-C. Stratum IV is represented by fragments of walls and floors, as well as large pits in areas A and C, some of them lined with stones. All belong to Iron Age II-B. Stratum III is represented on the mound proper only by pottery.

IRON AGE II-C SETTLEMENT OUTSIDE THE MOUND (AREA G). This area is located about 200 meters south of the mound, near Naḥal Shiqma. Two buildings were unearthed here immediately beneath the surface. One of them, which was almost wholly cleared, consists of rooms arranged on two sides of a courtyard. Numerous pottery vessels, many of them intact, lay on the floors of the rooms. The second building, whose function is not clear, consists of one large room (15 by 2

HISTORY OF TEL NAGILA.

STRATUM	PERIOD	BUILDINGS AND FINDS
Ia–b	Mameluke period	Khan
II	Hellenistic (?)-Roman Byzantine periods	Fragment of a wall, pottery
III	Iron Age II-C	Pottery on the mound (settlement outside the mound)
IV	Iron Age II-B	Pits; fragments of walls and floors
V	Late Bronze Age II	Pottery
VI	Late Bronze Age I	Fragments of buildings in area F. Large public building in area A (?)
VII–XI	Middle Bronze Age II-B–C	City, houses, public buildings, defense system, tomb outside the mound
XII–XIII	Early Bronze Age II–III	Parts of buildings; tomb outside the mound
XIV	Chalcolithic period	Pit; ashes and pottery on virgin soil

meters) with thick walls. Among the meager finds here was a footbath. The pottery from both buildings dates from the first half of the seventh century B.C. In the area between these buildings and the mound, further walls of this period are visible. It appears that during the existence of this settlement, which was probably an open settlement of short duration, the mound proper was not occupied.

Stratum II—Hellenistic, Roman, and Byzantine Periods. Hellenistic pottery was found on the surface of the mound and in the excavated areas. In area A was discovered a section of a building consisting of two walls forming a corner with pottery from the Roman-Byzantine period. Although no occupation layers from these periods were found, they are included in the table, since it can be assumed that some settlement of these periods may yet be discovered in other areas of the mound.

Stratum I—Mameluke Period. To this stratum belongs a large khan extending over more than one third of the area of the mound (the sides measure 104, 91, 95, 83 meters). There were apparently no other buildings on the mound during that period. The khan consists of rows of rooms surrounding a very large courtyard. It is not known whether there were any constructions in the courtyard.

Excavations have so far uncovered several rooms on both sides of the northeastern corner of the building as well as some remains in the vicinity of the entrance gate on the eastern side. The corners and doorposts are built of dressed stones, and the other parts of the walls of rough stones.

In the rooms situated on both sides of the entrance, evidence of two building stages was noted. The finds were not numerous, consisting of a few vessels discovered in situ and many sherds. Although the khan is dated to the Mameluke period, there is no reference to its existence in the written sources of the period or in later ones.

RUTH AMIRAN—A. EITAN

BIBLIOGRAPHY

Y. Aharoni and Ruth Amiran, *BIES* 17 (1953), 53–54 (Hebrew) • S. Bülow and R. A. Mitchell, *IEJ* 11 (1961), 101–10 • R. Gophna, *Yediot* 27 (1963), 173–80 (Hebrew) • Aharoni, *LB*, 250 • Ruth Amiran and A. Eitan, *IEJ* 13 (1963), 143–44; 333–34; 14 (1964), 219–31; *idem*, *Yediot* 28 (1964), 193–203 (Hebrew); *idem*; *Archaeology* 18 (1965), 113–23 • G. E. Wright, *BA* 29 (1966), 70–86; *idem*, *HTR* 64 (1971), 437–48 • A. F. Rainey, *EI* 12 (1975), 75* • Michal Artzy et al., *IEJ* 25 (1975), 129–34.

NAḤAL OREN

IDENTIFICATION. The prehistoric site of Naḥal Oren is situated on the northern bank of the Oren Valley, on the western slope of Mount Carmel about 46–51 meters above sea level. It lies at the point where the valley and the coastal plain merge. The site consists of a cave and a slope descending to the bank of the valley bed. At the widest spot in the valley are three prehistoric sites: the Abu Uṣba Cave in the south and Naḥal Oren and the Ornit shelter in the north.

There is a well about 200 meters from the site of Naḥal Oren. Like the other major prehistoric sites on Mount Carmel, the location of the site of Naḥal Oren was probably due to a combination of various ecological and economic factors, their proximity to the sea, the coastal plain, the valleys, and the mountain area.

The cave and terrace in front of it.

Because of Mount Carmel's sharp slope to the west, the coastal plain enjoyed warm weather and the growth of vegetation in the middle of the winter. This caused early seasonal wanderings.

EXCAVATIONS

M. Stekelis conducted excavations in the Oren Cave in 1942, and found there remains of the Natufian industry. Between 1954 and 1960, an additional series of excavations was carried out by M. Stekelis and financed by the Haifa municipality. A large area of the Pre-Pottery Neolithic B, Pre-Pottery Neolithic A, and the Natufian was explored. A Kebaran layer was reached in a small section of the excavations (Stekelis, Yisraeli, 1963). In the years 1969–71, a third series of excavations took place, directed by T. Noy and E. Higgs, and largely financed by the British Museum. This series aimed at a broad spectrum of finds, particularly from the biological world, and was also part of a general economic study of the prehistoric period undertaken in the Carmel area (Finzi-Vita, Higgs, 1970). In these excavations, several cultural layers were examined (Noy, Legge & Higgs, 1973):

Layers 9 and 8 — Kebaran phase.

Upper layer 8, lower layer 7 — Geometric Kebaran phase.

Upper layer 7 and layer 6 — Middle Natufian.

Layer 5 — Late Natufian.

Layer 4 — Thin layer of indistinct culture.

Layers 3 and 2 — Pre-Pottery Neolithic A.

Layer 1 — Pre-Pottery Neolithic B.

At Naḥal Oren are found the Epipaleolithic, Natufian, and early Neolithic periods.

The site was occupied from 18000–7000 B.C., i.e., for more than ten thousand years. Thanks to the technical methods, especially the flotation method, employed in the latest excavations, finds were made in great numbers. More than 55 percent of the microliths were found in the flotation, as were 85 percent of the small bones. Seeds were recovered only by means of this method.

Layer 9. Kebaran. The layer covers the entire slope. The soil is red, with small and medium-sized pebbles. In square 100, a wall built on the rock was uncovered. The Carbon-14 date for the layer is 18250 B.C. ($\pm$ 300). The main cultural finds are flint tools (see next page, Table I). There are also Mousterian tools, washed down from the upper rock shelter, some of which were reused. The tools are mostly small. The outstanding

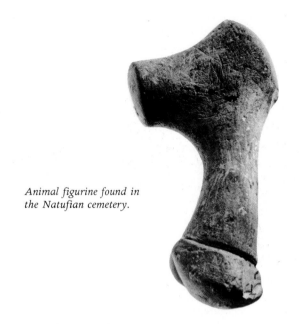

Animal figurine found in the Natufian cemetery.

group are the microliths, of which the fine, steep, and inverse retouch are the most common. The backed retouch microlith is very frequent. The group of obliquely retouched black bladelets is large, as is that of obliquely truncated bladelets.

Layer 8. Kebaran. This layer also covers the entire slope, and here too small and medium-sized pebbles are found. The main finds are flint tools, but there are fewer types than in the previous industry. There is an enormous concentration of the microlith group (74 percent), of which the outstanding group is the obliquely truncated backed bladelets. There is use of core rejuvenated flake for microliths, which are relatively small, as are the few geometric microliths.

The two Kebaran layers are of the Non-Geometric Kebaran culture. Stratigraphically, they fit the end of this phase. Geographically, their distribution is mainly in the Mediterranean and Sub-Mediterranean climate.

Economy. In layer 9 there is much evidence of deer hunting, while in layer 8 the gazelle is more prominent, although the deer remains important. Pig, cattle, and goat are also found. From the presence of fowl and fish we can assume that the coastal plain environment was also exploited. The assemblage in this part of the Carmel is varied, as the flotation finds indicate.

Upper Layer 8 and Lower Layer 7. These layers extend over the entire slope. Several large stones are found, but the chief finds are the flint tools. These are tiny, especially the microliths, and the

Minḥa, Ḥorvat. Pottery figurine of fertility goddess; Neolithic period.

geometric microliths are minuscule. The composition of the assemblage differs from the previous ones. The microliths make up 50 percent, with the geometric microliths forming the major sub-group —27 percent. The main geometric forms are triangles and lunates. The narrow carinated scraper and the truncated burin are typical of this cultural phase. A few sickle blades and several in microburin technique are also found.

This cultural phase may be called Kebaran Geometric B. It is unique and not yet well studied, as compared to the Kebaran Geometric A phase. The geometric tools of the latter are mainly trapezoids and rectangles. The two Geometric Kebaran phases have not previously been found together at any one site. They may well be contemporaneous.

Judging from the tool forms and the composition of the tool groups, these layers appear to be a transition phase between the Kebaran Non-Geometric and the Natufian.

The economy shows a great similarity to the economic structure of the previous layer (see Tables II and III).

Upper Layer 7 and Layer 6. These two layers are Middle Natufian. They cover the entire slope. In layer 7 there are only a few pebbles and stones, while in layer 6 they are numerous. Layer 6 contains protrusions originating from the dwellings and burials of layer 5. No buildings or living quarters were found. The dwellings were apparently in the cave and the cave mouth. Many flint, stone, and bone tools were found, together with art objects and ornaments.

The stone tools are made mainly from local limestone, and some are from basalt. The latter are polishers, made of conical pieces of basalt. The limestone tools include roughly chiseled bowls, deeply hollowed mortars, small mortars, and small cups.

The flint tools are varied, the flint industry being based largely on the long, narrow blade. The two main groups of tools are the microliths and the geometric microliths (Table I), which together make up about 46 percent. In comparison to the earlier industries, however, this is a considerable decrease. The lunates in this stage are numerous. They are medium-sized and show Heluan retouch and considerable use of micro-burin technique. The blades are fine and elongated. The retouch and denticulation and the truncated pieces of basalt

are very characteristic of this layer. There are also sickle blades, borers, denticulation, etc.

The bone tools are mainly points with a very few spatulae, harpoons, and sickle handles.

Many of the art objects were found in the cemetery. They had probably been placed near the burials. Made of bone and stone, they are mainly animal and fowl heads. The bone carvings were later polished. Two objects are engraved on both sides, and additional engravings are found on pieces of bone and stones. The ornaments were made of *Dentalium* and *Cardium* shells, stone, and bone.

THE BURIALS. The cemetery was explored in the second series of excavations and probably belongs to this phase. It was found on the lower part of the slope. The area excavated was 16 by 5 meters. In the center of the cemetery is a large hearth, built of big, flat, smoothed, and polished limestones, and containing a large quantity of ashes. Around the hearth about fifty skeletons were unearthed. The majority of the graves contained single burials, but in some cases two persons were buried in the same grave. The body was laid on the side in a flexed position in a shallow burial pit, the head pointed toward the north. Beneath the head, and sometimes on top of it, were placed flat stones. Near several of the skeletons hollow mortars, about 70 centimeters long, are stuck into the ground. They seem to have been both tombstones and cult objects. Small mortars were also found near some of the skeletons. Several small circular structures built of small stones were discovered in the cemetery. Nothing was found inside or around these structures that could indicate their purpose. Near some burials there were ash hearths, shells, upright stones, and art objects. The cemetery seems to have continued in use over a long period of time.

THE FIRST NATUFIAN layer of Nahal Oren belongs to the Middle Natufian phase. Finds that are typical of el-Wad B-2 (Garrod, 1937) and the Yonim Cave (Bar-Yosef, 1970), sites belonging to the Early Natufian phase, are missing at Nahal Oren. Consequently it seems that the art that was believed to belong to the early Natufian phase actually dates from the Middle Natufian. The Natufian layers of Nahal Oren have many parallels as, for example, el-Wad B-1, Kebara, etc.

Layer 5. Upper Natufian; this is a thick layer covering the entire slope. There are many indica-

TABLE I. PERCENTAGES OF GROUPS OF TOOLS FROM THE KEBARAN AND NATUFIAN LAYERS						
	IX	VIII	VII LOWER	VII UPPER	VI	V
Scrapers	4.92	3.51	5.88	2.80	5.22	4.80
Carinated scrapers	10.66	11.70	14.70	5.60	6.96	2.40
Burins	8.20	3.51	9.66	7.84	11.48	10.82
Flakes	4.10	4.68	6.30	5.60	3.48	4.80
Blades	1.64	1.71	4.62	2.24	6.09	6.00
Truncated pieces	—	—	0.84	—	6.09	3.60
Sickle blades	—	—	0.84	—	1.74	3.60
Microliths	58.61	71.92	23.75	45.80	28.71	37.58
Geometric microliths	5.30	2.34	27.37	25.08	17.40	15.60
Microburin technique	1.64	—	2.10	—	6.09	—
Notched	4.10	—	—	2.24	4.35	7.20
Diverse	—	—	3.80	2.80	2.61	3.60
Total	100.0	100.0	100.0	100.0	100.0	100.0
(Truncated backed bladelets)	14.76	29.41	6.72	8.96	7.76	4.60

TABLE II. PERCENTAGES OF SPECIES IDENTIFIED ACCORDING TO LAYER								
	PIG	ROE DEER	FALLOW DEER	RED DEER	CATTLE	GAZELLE	GOAT	SAMPLE SIZE
Layer 1	4.4	1.6	1.0	0	2.4	76.7	13.9	537
Layer 2 / Layer 3	3.5	1.2	0.9	0	1.5	87.3	5.5	317
Layer 4	3.3	0.9	2.1	0.4	0.9	88.0	4.4	170
Layer 5	3.8	0.8	2.2	0	11.6	81.5	0.1	1359
Layer 6	2.1	0	9.9	0	5.4	82.6	0	113
Layer 7	3.2	0.5	14.9	0.7	3.5	76.5	0	855
Layer 8	0.6	0.5	19.9	0.5	4.0	73.9	0.6	159
Layer 9	Analysis incomplete; suggests fallow deer rising to 30–40 percent.							

TABLE III. DISTRIBUTION OF CARBONIZED SEEDS ACCORDING TO LAYER				
	PPN B	PPN A	NATUFIAN	KEBARAN
T. dicoccum	2	1	—	3
cf.Hordeum sp.	1	—	—	1
Vicia sp.	2	1	5	2
Viciae	3	3	6	25
Ficus	—	—	—	4
Vitis	—	—	1	2
Quercus	2	—	—	—
Olea	1	—	—	—
Carob	2	—	—	—
Punica	1	—	—	—
Lens	1	—	—	—
Graminae	6	4	4	7
Others	1	12	9	20
Totals	23	21	25	64

Below: Natufian burial; Bottom: Natufian structures.

tions, such as houses, dwelling pits, burial sites, etc., that at this time the inhabitants began to live on the slope itself.

The walls of the dwellings on the slopes are built of local limestone. The long mortars of the earlier layer are also used as building material. Small, circular structures of stones and hearths containing ashes are also found.

The stone tools resemble those of the previous layer, but the use of long mortars has ceased.

The flint tools are varied, with the microliths still forming the major group. The use of Heluan retouch is less pronounced. The lunates are small. Sickle blades and truncated pieces are also found in great numbers (Table I).

The bone tools consist of points, several harpoons, spatulae, and a few sickle handles.

Art objects in this phase are sparse, consisting mainly of engravings on stone and basalt.

There is no cemetery belonging to this phase, but individual burials are found in the dwellings. The body was laid in a pit and covered with stones and earth. Above each skeleton were traces of ashes.

The Natufian types are mainly Mediterranean gracile.

Gazelle hunting is of prime importance, accounting for more than 82 percent of the bones found. It is possible that there was some kind of control of this animal. Pig, cattle, and a few deer were also hunted. Many land shells, fish, and small animal bones were found, indicating intensive exploration of the ecological surroundings. The assemblage was probably from nearby mountains and the coastal plain. A few seeds were found (Table III).

Layer 4. A thin layer, perhaps sterile, or belonging to the end of the Natufian or the Proto-Neolithic phase.

Layer 3. Pre-Pottery Neolithic A. The remains of this layer are numerous and furnish a clear image of a complete settlement. Sixteen round or oval houses were unearthed standing on four terraces. The terraces were 3–4 meters wide, and their width determined the width of the houses. The area of each house was about 15 square meters, with walls .6–.8 meter wide and preserved to a height of about 1 meter. The houses were built of large rough stones, found in abundance on the slope. Some of them were constructed against rocks and were therefore preserved in their entirety. The floors are made of *terre pisée* and have hearths built of small stones. Flat stones with small cups, or small, shallow mortars, were found on the floors. Stone bowls, grindstones, querns, and numerous flint implements were also found. Two floors could be distinguished in many houses. In some cases the floor had simply been raised, while in others the plan of the house had been changed. How the houses were roofed could not be ascertained.

FLINT INDUSTRY. A rich and varied assortment of flint implements was uncovered at Naḥal Oren. Some of them continue the technical tradition of the preceding period: the burins — 17 percent; scrapers — 13 percent, awls, flakes, retouched blades and microliths — 16 percent. New groups of implements also made their appearance in this phase. The bifacial (adzes, axes, picks, and chisels) — 6.7 percent. The Tahunian ax, with cutting edge made by transversal blow, is characteristic of the Pre-Pottery Neolithic industries. There are polished

axes of limestone and basalt and a few polished flint axes. The arrowheads (1.2 percent) are small and simple, with straight base and notches; they form a very small group. Most of the sickle blades (7 percent) are short, but there is a new group of elongated sickle blades which includes ventral-dorsal retouch on one edge. All the sickle blades have a luster from prolonged use. Apart from the new group of tools, there are borers (4.5 percent), notches (4.7 percent), and a new type of bifacial waste.

Stone bowls and small cups were made of limestone. The bowls are mostly small and medium-sized and only a few are large. The large ones are generally polished and finely finished. The bowls have rounded bases and simple rims. Shallow cup marks on flat stones are found in every dwelling, their depth and diameter reaching a few centimeters only. It is not clear whether they served as small mortars.

Querns are made mostly from a large limestone block, in the center of which is an oval concave grinding surface. Oval-shaped upper grindstones are common. There are a few pestles but no mortars. There is very little use of basalt. Several obsidian blades were uncovered.

Bone implements are scarce and are mostly awls.

Objects of art are very rare. A figurine of a female, found in house 16, was schematically engraved on small pebbles, the lines of the head and the body being emphasized. In the upper part of the slope,

Both pages, counterclockwise from left, top: Schematic figurine — Pre-Pottery Neolithic A; Small Natufian mortar; Two small bowls — Pre-Pottery Neolithic A; Flint axes — Pre-Pottery Neolithic A; Natufian flint tools.

Both pages, right to left: Arrowheads — early phase of Pre-Pottery Neolithic B; Elongated sickle blades and tanged arrowheads — middle phase of Pre-Pottery Neolithic B; Polished limestone axe;
Below: Rectangular building — Pre-Pottery Neolithic B. In the building's background, large bowl hewn out of rock — Pre-Pottery Neolithic A.

a large bowl was found carved on flattened rock. It is possible that this was a large public court. No building was found that could have been an altar or public gathering place.

Very few burials were uncovered, and these were generally located beneath the house floor. A new burial custom is the removal of the lower jaw.

ECONOMY. The finds suggest similarities to the previous culture. Gazelle ''hunting'' has increased, as has the number of goat bones. Pigs, deer, and some cattle were still hunted (Table II). A few seeds of varied kinds were found. Numerous querns may indicate the intensive use of cereal.

The site was used as a base camp for long periods of the year. Its economic territory was very large. The population size has not been established, since the houses could have served for a small family or for one person only (Flannery, 1972). The planning of the settlement on a very steep slope, and the quality of the building suggests advancements in technology and social organization. The crowding of houses is known in the Neolithic period of the Near East.

Layer 1. Pre-Pottery Neolithic B. As the last settlement on the surface of the terrace in front of the cave, this layer was damaged and partly destroyed by erosion and human activities. Two cultural stages can be distinguished, an early stage and a possible middle stage.

EARLY STAGE. Rectangular and semicircular houses built of local limestone belong to this

phase. In one of the houses, a wall of 80 centimeters built in a foundation trench is preserved. The floors of the houses are of *terre pisée,* and also apparently of lime.

The flint tools both continue the Pre-Pottery Neolithic A and exhibit new developments. High-quality flint is used. The tools were made on elongated blades. The sickle blades (7.9 percent) are mainly elongated, sometimes with fine serration, and have a heavy luster. The bifacial (11 percent) are the same as in the previous culture, but have a wide transversal blow. The arrowheads (4.9 percent) are still simple but show development, having a small tang and notches.

Four skeletons were found in one of the buildings. Two are without their lower jaw, and the other two are intact. The absence of the lower jaw or of the entire skull is also found in other burials.

MIDDLE STAGE. Some architectural remains were found. A large building, made of limestone with its floor paved with valley pebbles, is situated in the center of the slope. It may have been a public building.

New types of tools, especially arrowheads, appear in this phase. They are large, with a tang and barbs. They are made of special flint, colored. The sickle blades are elongated. Some have a small tang. The other tools are similar to the previous phase.

Both Pre-Pottery phases include a large number of limestone and basalt querns, grindstones, and bowls. The querns here are made of basalt for the

first time. A few small obsidian blades and small axes made of a green or black soft stone are also found. There are also some ornaments, mostly made of *Dentalium* shells, rounded chips of shells and bone, and also stone.

The finds of animal bones indicated economic changes. Though the gazelle is still frequently hunted, the goat bones now become very prominent (14 percent). It is possible that the goat was domesticated. Pig and cattle were still hunted, as were many small animals. Seeds were gathered and indicate a wide use of vegetables and fruits.

It seems that also in this phase the site was a base camp for only a few families. The economic territory of the site was large.

The site at Naḥal Oren represents prehistoric phases ranging from intensive food gathering to the beginnings of agriculture.　　TAMAR NOY

BIBLIOGRAPHY

Excavations: M. Stekelis, *BASOR* 86 (1942), 2–10: *idem, QDAP* 11 (1944), 115–18 • M. Stekelis and T. Yisraeli, *IEJ* 13 (1963), 1–12 • T. Noy, A. J. Legge and E. S. Higgs, *Proceedings of the Prehistoric Society* 39 (1973), 75–92.
Studies: D. A. E. Garrod and D. M. A. Bate: *The Stone Age of Mount Carmel* I, Oxford, 1937 • J. G. Echegary: *Excavaciones en la terraza de El Khiam* 1, Madrid, 1964 • J. Perrot, *Supplément au Dictionnaire de la Bible* 8 (1968), 286–446 • O. Bar-Yosef, *The Epipaleolithic Culture of Palestine,* Jerusalem, 1970 (Ph. d. Thesis) • O. Bar-Yosef and E. Tchernov, *JEJ* 20 (1970), 141–50 • C. Finzi-Vita and E. S. Higgs, *Proceedings of the Prehistoric Society* 36 (1970), 1–3 • K. V. Flannery, *The Origins of the Village as a Settlement Type,* ed. P. J. Ucko et al. (1972), 23–54 • F. Hours et al., *L'Anthropologie* 77 (1973), 437–96.

NAHARIYA

SITES. The ancient settlement of Nahariya was situated mainly on the mound on the southern bank of the outlet of the Ga'aton Brook. Since most of its area today is covered with modern houses, no systematic excavations have been conducted on the mound, and its dimensions are unknown. A trench dug at random on the mound, however, revealed that occupation was concentrated on the acropolis, which was first settled in the Middle Bronze Age II. The mound also contained remains from the end of the Iron Age and the Persian period. During these periods, the settlement may have been connected with a small port at the outlet of the Ga'aton Brook. In the *kurkar* hills along the Nahariya coast, where the important Roman road ran from Acre to Achzib and Antioch, additional remains were found from the Hellenistic to the Byzantine periods. These included remnants of buildings, mosaic pavements (among them one of a church), installations, such as pottery kilns, and burials. Z. Goldman and N. Zori examined several of these sites, and in 1941, M. Avi-Yonah excavated a cemetery at Khirbet Itayim dating from the first century B.C. to the Arab period. He uncovered three rock-hewn graves, one of them the tomb of a Greek priest of Tyrian origin of the second century A.D. with wall paintings and Greek inscriptions. In another section of the cemetery, excavated by Yael Israeli and D. Barag, were found large quantities of pottery and glassware, mainly from the second–third centuries A.D. In 1972–74 the Byzantine church was excavated by G. Edelstein.

About 900 meters north of the mound of Nahariya, close to the shore, is a small mound about 40 meters in diameter and situated about 3 meters above the surrounding area. The mound was excavated by I. Ben-Dor and M. Dothan, who uncovered a cultic site with a temple and a bamah (High-Place).

The Temple. The temple was excavated in 1947 by the Mandatory Government Department of

Antiquities, under the direction of I. Ben-Dor. A single structure was found on the site. This was a broad house oriented to the east. It consisted of a large rectangular hall (10.7 by 6.2 meters), flanked by two smaller rooms on its short sides, and additional small rooms in the northeastern corner of the structure. The walls are built of partly hewn stones, .75–1 meter wide, and preserved in some places to a height of 1.15 meters.

Two strata (actually two construction phases) were distinguished. Seven floors were uncovered in the hall (1), floors 7–5 belonging to the early stratum and floors 4–1 to the later stratum. Another earlier phase, antedating the edifice, was also discerned. All the floors of the hall had stone bases, on which stood wooden columns, which apparently supported the ceiling. The two chambers (1-A and 2) were constructed during the later stratum, at which time chamber 2 served as a kitchen. In the early stratum the structure contained silos and a floor. There are signs that sacrifices were offered on the spot.

THE FINDS. Most of the finds came from a rubbish

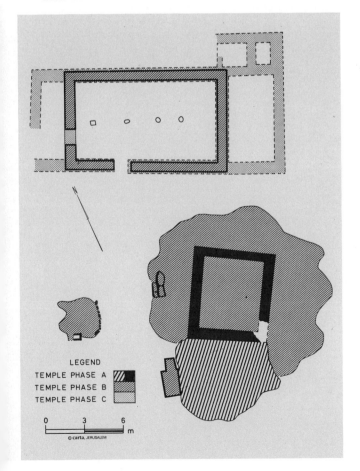

LEGEND
TEMPLE PHASE A
TEMPLE PHASE B
TEMPLE PHASE C

0   3   6
m
© carta, JERUSALEM

Opposite page: General view of the late phase of the temple, seen from the northeast; This page, left: The temples and High Place — General plan of the three phases; Above: Statuette of female deity (modern cast from ancient mold).

heap outside the building, and little was found on the floors themselves. Most of the objects were of a ritual character. Among the pottery was a large number of miniature offering vessels including small bowls with seven tiny cups, and incense burners of various shapes. Several of the latter were double-tiered and had windows and handles. Two metal statuettes were also found, as were a clay statuette and clay figurines of doves, which were apparently set on the cultic vessels. Among the Middle Bronze Age II-B sherds were rims and handles of jars (including hole-mouth jars) and juglets. Several complete vessels were also found:

carinated bowls with disk bases, juglets of the Tell el-Yahudiyeh type, and lamps with one or four wicks. The decoration is mainly pattern combing and occasionally projecting lines in a herringbone pattern. There were also beads, "Canaanite" flint tools, and a bronze ax.

CHRONOLOGY. The major part of the finds dates to the Middle Bronze Age II-B (Hyksos period). Some of the pottery, however, is to be attributed to Middle Bronze Age II-A, and several vessels from the upper stratum may be dated to the beginning of the Late Bronze Age. It is clear, from

This page, below: Pottery vessels of seven cups; Bottom: Pottery vessles of seven cups, in situ; Right: Giv'at Sharett. Glass vessel in pottery sarcophagus — from burial cave; Opposite page: Giv'at Katzenelson. Dog and cock in mosaic pavement of church of the 6th century A.D.

the important finds discovered under the structure's foundations, that this was a cult site even before the construction of the Hyksos building. This building, also of a cultic nature, was apparently constructed in this isolated and remote region, because of the nearby spring.

The Bamah. Further excavations were conducted during three seasons in 1954–55, under the auspices of the Department of Antiquities and directed by M. Dothan with the assistance of Helene Kantor and I. Dunayevsky. These excavations were concentrated in the southern part of the site, adjacent to the temple which was cleared in 1947. In this sector an earlier temple and a bamah were discovered. Three strata (A–C) containing five phases (1–5) were distinguished.

STRATUM A. The early temple is a square structure (6 by 6 meters), partly preserved to a height of .8 meter. Attached to its southern side was an irregularly shaped level space (approximately 6 meters in diameter) composed of pebbles and rubble. Most of the finds from this sector

and its vicinity were of a ritual nature, and provide evidence that the area served as a High Place adjoining the early temple.

STRATUM B. Early in this stratum the large temple in the northern part of the site was constructed (see above). In its initial phase (4) it contained a single hall. At that time the early bamah was enlarged (its diameter now reaching 14 meters) to incorporate the foundations of the early temple. Stone stairs on the western side led to the center of the bamah. Between the bamah and the temple was a court in which a rectangular stone pillar was found, possibly the remains of a pair of pillars which had originally stood at the entrance of the sacred area. In the same area was a pavement with a stone container sunk into it. This was probably an altar.

STRATUM C. In this stratum the bamah was raised and reduced in size, and a rectangular structure was erected in its center. The northern temple then underwent expansion, and chambers were added on its eastern and western sides. In the last phase (5) of this stratum, the rectangular structure was buried under a pile of stones marking the center of the bamah.

THE FINDS. Most of the finds date to the Middle Bronze Age II-B. Their cultic nature is clear in all the strata, and they show little modification between strata. A large amount of pottery was brought to the bamah, some of it miniature vessels, such as small bowls, juglets, jars, and the like— all symbolic offerings. The bowls with seven small cups are particularly numerous. These apparently served as libation vessels. Less frequent are the lamps, among them lamps with seven wicks. The pottery also included cooking pots, found mostly in the court, mixed with animal bones (mainly of goats).

Also found were hundreds of beads (some animal-shaped), bronze, silver, and gold jewelry, several weapons, and pottery figurines of animals (including monkeys). Of particular interest are metal figurines, generally depicting females, some of which were found in jars on the altar and others

on the bamah. These figurines fall into two groups —thin silver plaques, schematically shaped in chased and wrought techniques, and silver and bronze figurines cast in a mold. With the second group was found a stone mold of a naked female figure wearing a conical headgear with a pair of horns projecting from her head. This may have been a mold for casting figurines of Ashrath-Yam ("Asherah of the Sea"), the chief goddess of Ugarit and of seafarers. The statuettes represent a local style, in which the influence of the art of the Phoenician coastal towns, notably Byblos and Ugarit, can be recognized. The late ceramic material of stratum C included Cypriot ware, indicating that the site ceased to exist during the second half of the sixteenth century B.C.

SUMMARY

The strata uncovered in the two excavations can be correlated as follows:

1954/5 EXCAVATIONS	1947 EXCAVATIONS
Stratum A, Phase 5	Inside the *kurkar* under floor 7
Stratum B, Phases 4 3	Floors 7–5
Stratum C, Phases 2 1	Floors 4–1

The sacred area in Nahariya contained a temple and bamah alongside it. When the early temple ceased functioning, a bamah was built on its site, and a new temple was erected to the north of it. The offerings found on the bamah were apparently brought in worship of the goddess Asherah-of-the-Sea. During the period of Hyksos rule, the practice of the cult at the bamah was especially active, and it continued throughout the Late Bronze Age. The sacred precinct in Nahariya with its closed temple and adjacent open bamah has thrown light on similar contemporary sites at Megiddo, Gezer, Byblos, etc. Bamahs of this type, perhaps in a rural version, are found in the country in the Israelite period until the days of Josiah.

M. DOTHAN

BIBLIOGRAPHY

M. Avi-Yonah, *BJPES* 8 (1940), 91–94 • I. Ben-Dor, *EI* 1 (1940), 17–28; M. Avnimelech, *BJPES* 10 (1942), 39–46 (all Hebrew) • I. Ben-Dor, *QDAP* 14 (1950), 1–41 • J. Waechter, *ibid.*, 42–43 • M. Dothan, *EI* 4 (1955), 41–46 (Hebrew); *idem, IEJ* 6 (1956), 14–25; *idem*, in: *Western Galilee and the Coast of Galilee*, Jerusalem, 1965, 63–75 (Hebrew) • D. Barag, *Qadmoniot* 4 (1971), 96–98 (Hebrew) • G. Edelstein and C. Dauphine, *ibid.*, 8 (1975), 128–32 (Hebrew) • M. Barasch, *IEJ* 24 (1974), 222–26.

NAṢBEH, TELL EN-

IDENTIFICATION. Tell en-Naṣbeh, situated 12 kilometers (7.5 miles) north of Jerusalem, is generally identified with biblical Mizpah, an identification suggested by A. Raboission in 1897 and by C. R. Conder independently in 1898. Some scholars, however, reject this identification, preferring to locate Mizpah at Nabi Samwil about 8 kilometers (5 miles) northwest of Jerusalem, and suggest identifying Tell en-Naṣbeh with other sites such as Ataroth-Addar (W. F. Albright).

HISTORY

At the end of the fourth and beginning of the third millennium B.C., the site was occupied by a small settlement. It was subsequently deserted for a long period of time, and occupation was renewed in about 1100 B.C. The settlement existed thereafter nearly continuously until the fourth century B.C.

Mizpah was founded during the period of Israelite settlement by the tribe of Benjamin, near the northern border of its territory. When the Israelite tribes prepared for battle against Gibeah of Benjamin, they first assembled at Mizpah (Judges 20:1 ff.). It was one of the scenes of activity of the prophet Samuel (I Samuel 7:16–17). After the division of the monarchy the city's importance increased due to its proximity to the northern border of Judah and it was fortified by King Asa (I Kings 15:17–22; see also below). After the destruction of Jerusalem by Nabuchadnezzar, Gedaliah, the son of Ahikam who was appointed governor of Judah, established his residence there, and there he was also murdered (II Kings 25:22–25; Jeremiah 40–41). At the time of the return from Babylonian Exile, the city was the capital of the district of Mizpah (Nehemiah 3:7). Judas Maccabaeus assembled his army there against Gorgias (I Maccabee 3:46).

THE SITE

The site lies on a hill surrounded by deep valleys on three sides and connected with the mountain on the north by a saddle. Its area within the great wall reaches 32 dunams and is roughly oval in shape, the maximum length reaching 265 meters and the width 160 meters. The highest point on the mound is 784 meters above sea level, and the lowest is 770 meters.

The main importance of Mizpah lay in its position on the main mountain road (crossing the watershed), which passed at its foot to the east. The city acquired additional importance when the northern border of the Judean kingdom was established in its vicinity, and it was invested with a defensive role. Although the fortifications of the city and its private dwellings were well preserved, the site as a whole was badly eroded, like other sites in the mountainous region. The accumulation of ruins made the stratigraphic investigation difficult and at times even impossible, so that the conclusions of the excavators were largely based. on typological considerations.

The site was excavated under the direction of W. F. Badè, on behalf of the Pacific Institute of Religion in Berkeley, California, during five campaigns between 1926 and 1935. The site was almost completely bared, and tombs from various periods were also discovered both on the mound and in the surroundings. Due to the untimely death of Badè — who had published only preliminary reports — the publication of the results of the excavations was completed by two of his assistants, C. C. McCown and J. C. Wampler.

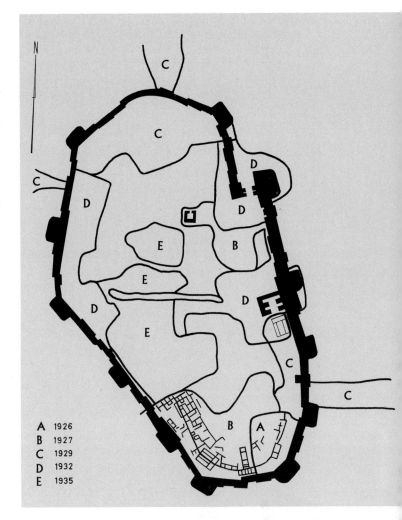

A 1926
B 1927
C 1929
D 1932
E 1935

Below: City gate, seen from the north; Right: General plan of the mound showing the progress of the excavations during the five seasons.

Below: The gate. 1. Wall. 2. East tower. 3. Drainage channel. 4. Entrance 5. Benches. 6. West tower; Bottom: Early gate and adjacent four-room house.

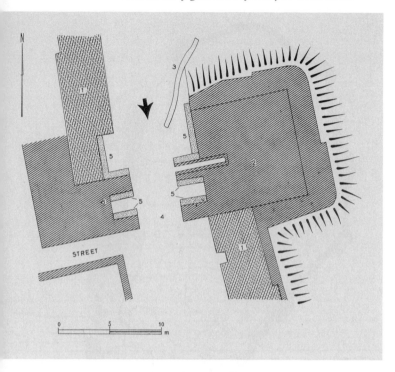

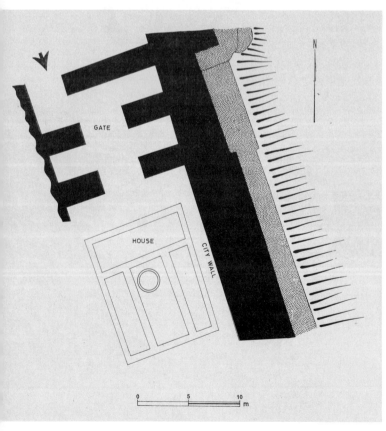

EXCAVATIONS

End of Chalcolithic Period–Beginning of Early Bronze Age. No architectural remains whatsoever were discovered on the mound from these periods. The only evidence of occupation were the sherds found scattered over the surface of the site and in the caves. Some twenty caves were discovered, a few on the mound itself and the majority at its foot and on the hills to its north. They contained an abundance of objects, especially caves 5 and 6. Many caves were used for burials only, but some, like cave 9, served as dwellings. Several caves, initially used as dwellings, were later converted into burial caves. If indeed there was a settlement on the mound in that period, it was probably one of tents and huts of which no remains have survived. A similar situation is also found at other contemporary settlements in Palestine (Jericho, 'Ai Tell el-Far'a [North]), namely, a relative abundance of finds and a nearly complete lack of building remains. Finds from the Ghassulian phase of the Chalcolithic period were discovered in cave 68. Most of the other finds are from Early Bronze Age I, while some isolated objects can be ascribed to Early Bronze Age II.

Iron Age. After an interruption of about two thousand years, the site was re-occupied at the beginning of the Iron Age, in the eleventh century B.C. From the early stage of occupation only a section of a city wall, two towers, and the remains of several private houses were found. The early wall was uncovered mainly in the southern part of the mound, and its complete plan cannot be determined. It was about 1 meter thick on the average and 2.5 meters thick in one spot. It is difficult to distinguish it from walls of houses built against the wall. Some scholars consider these walls the remains of a casemate wall, but they should more likely be interpreted as private houses built against the city wall. The two towers, in the west and northwest parts of the mound, have the form of a rectangle, divided into two rooms. The towers are attached to the early wall, and it is impossible to determine whether they indeed belong to the wall, in which case they can indicate its course.

THE GREAT TOWN WALL. The main architectural remains on the mound are of the great wall, which was uncovered for its entire length of 660 meters. It is constructed of salients and recesses, and incorporates nine–ten towers. On the outer face it reached 12–14 meters in height, and 8–10 meters on the inner face. It is 4 meters thick on the average and 6–9 meters thick together with the towers. The towers are all strengthened by a glacis, and in many sections of the wall by buttresses, retaining walls, or a glacis. The wall is built of rubble, the stones only slightly chipped, set in clay mortar with the interstices between them filled with gravel and small stones. The wall was coated thickly with plaster up to a height of 4.5–5 meters, to prevent the enemy from scaling it. Three sections of a 2–5 meter wide fosse were uncovered, the only Iron Age fosse found so far in excavations in Palestine, but it could not be ascertained whether or not it surrounded the whole city.

The wall was not constructed in a continuous line, but in sections, some of which were not linked together. This discovery, together with the fact that the quality of its construction is not uniform, indicates that the wall was erected by groups of corvée laborers, who were compelled to fulfill set quotas of work imposed on them. The opinion that the wall was built during the strife between Baasha and Asa at the beginning of the ninth century B.C. seems justified. After Baasha was attacked by the Aramaeans, he abandoned the siege of Ramah in Judah: "Then king Asa made a proclamation throughout all Judah; none was exempted: and they took away the stones of Ramah, and the timber thereof, wherewith Baasha had builded; and king Asa built with them Geba of Benjamin, and Mizpah" (I Kings 15:22).

THE GATES. The city gate at Tell en-Naşbeh is the best preserved gateway uncovered in excavations in Palestine. It consists of two pairs of piers 4.2 meters apart, and judging from the surviving remnants, it was 2.2 meters high. The gate was closed by a two-winged door set between the two outer piers. Sockets were found in the threshold. In the doorjamb of the eastern pier was a slot for the bar of the gate (inserted when the door was open), and in the doorjamb of the west pier was a hole (in which the end of the bar was fitted when the door was closed). It could not be ascertained whether or how the gate was roofed (by vaulted stone roofing or horizontal beams). Although this was a gate of direct access, the usual principle of access in a right angle was retained: whoever ap-

proached the gate from the east had to make a left turn, thus exposing his right flank to the defenders upon the wall.

There was an open square (8 by 9 meters) in front of the gate on the outside and another on the inside. Along the square outside the gate and in the guard chambers between the piers, benches were built. The two squares and the gateway were drained by a covered channel.

Below: Israelite houses and cisterns beneath them;
Bottom: Plan and section of tomb 5 — 9th century B.C.

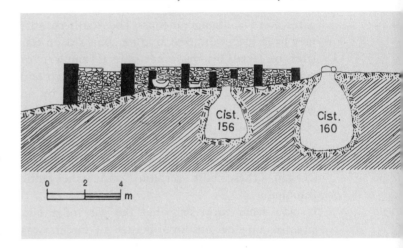

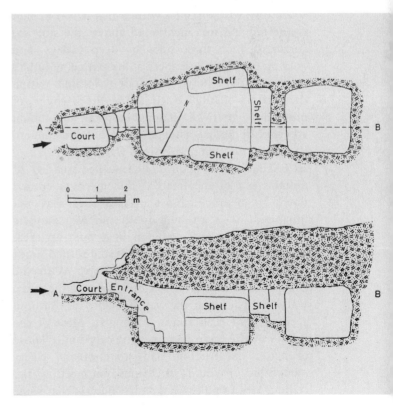

About 60 meters south of the city gate is a structure resembling a gate, built against the wall. It consists of two pairs of piers, in front of which is a wall guarding the entrance. This was a gate with indirect access, in which anyone entering had to make two right-angled turns. It resembles in plan the other gateway with the exception of the defensive wall. In workmanship, its construction is superior to all other buildings in the city. Its eastern wall was linked with the town wall, and the tower east of the defensive wall was probably a gate tower like the tower in the other gate.

It is difficult to determine whether these two gates were contemporaneous. The southern gate may have been built first, and for some reason was later replaced by the other gate (Wampler), or perhaps the southern gate was in use for a certain period of time, and after it was damaged by an enemy, the other was constructed (McCown).

Near the early gate was a cigar-shaped stone pillar, a *massebah* like the one (with a basin nearby) found in the town gate of Tell el-Far'a (North) — these both certainly had some cultic function.

It may seem surprising that the gate of a city situated on the northern border of Judah was erected on its northern extremity and not in the south toward the region with which it was mainly connected. As was mentioned above, the site was surrounded on three sides by deep valleys, and only on the north was there a link with a mountain ridge. That the town was indeed located within the territory of Judah is attested by the discovery of numerous *lamelekh* stamps, typical of Judah, whereas in Bethel, situated only 5 kilometers to the north, no such impressions were found.

HOUSES. About one third of the walled area (10–12 dunams out of the total 32 dunams) was eroded down to bedrock. Most of this area was not inhabited, as is attested by the almost complete absence of cisterns, common in a built-up area. The remaining area was very densely settled, most of the houses being built in groups. With the exception of a few houses built against the town wall, the space near the wall was left free, forming a convenient road running along it. Most of the houses of the town were very poorly built. Those of better construction had stone pillars, either monolithic or built of drums, supporting the ceiling. Strong pillars and stairs indicate that some

of the buildings were two-storied. Three exceptional examples are four-room houses. These are rectangular in shape and consisted of three rectangular rooms forming a square block, and a fourth room across the width of the building. The middle of the three rooms was a courtyard and the three others were dwelling chambers. These three buildings are similar in the outstanding quality of their construction and size (12–13 by 10 meters). Built against the wall, at a distance from the main group of buildings, they may have had a public function of some kind and perhaps were storehouses (for the collection of taxes in kind) or military structures.

The inhabited area of 20 dunams was occupied by about 1,000 persons, the density of population in ancient settlements being usually estimated at an average of fifty persons to a dunam.

WATER SUPPLY. Southeast of the mound is a small spring which may be completely dry in summer time. The city however was not wholly dependent on this spring for its water supply, the most striking evidence for this being the location of the gate in the opposite direction. Most of the water used by the inhabitants was provided by cisterns. During the excavations, fifty-three cisterns were discovered and cleared, all of them private ones and small in comparison with those of other sites.

SMALL FINDS. One of the richest and most complete collections of Israelite pottery was found on the mound and in the nearby tombs (especially the four large tombs 5, 29, 32, 54). The epigraphic finds included seven incised potsherds, stone weights, numerous impressions — sixty-eight *lamelekh* seal impressions — and several private seals, the most beautiful of which is the seal of "Jaazaniah servant of the king." In the opinion of Badè, Jaazaniah was one of the officials of Gedaliah, son of Ahikam, and is identical with Jaazaniah, the captain of the forces mentioned in both II Kings 25:23 and Jeremiah 40:8, but this identification is not absolutely certain. On the seal is carved the image of a cock, the earliest known representation of this bird in Palestine. Other finds include a short dedicatory inscription in Neo-Babylonian, a cylinder seal, and numerous scarabs.

This site was also occupied during the Persian period, but building remains attributable to this period are scarce, consisting mainly of some rooms

Nahariya. Pair of peacocks flanking amphora, detail of mosaic floor of the Byzantine church.

Left: Seal: "Of Jaazaniah servant of the king";
Below: Cylinder seal and impression — from tomb 54 — IA I.

built above the Israelite wall. The excavators also ascribed to the Persian period a thinner wall built on the early destroyed wall. Pottery and other small finds were discovered on the surface of the site and in pits, but not usually in a clear stratigraphic context. D. von Bothmer dated about thirty fragments of Attic pottery to the years 540–420 B.C. Among the imported ware was an East Greek Clazomenian vessel, unique in Palestine, dating from 540–530 B.C. From this period numerous stamped seal impressions were found on pottery reading *Yhd* and *Yršlm* and about thirty *Mṣh* (another five were discovered in Gibeon, Ramat Raḥel, and Jericho). Some scholars considered *Mṣh* an abbreviation for Mizpah, but this opinion is not convincing. In the inscription deciphered by N. Avigad, the name is written in full, *Mwṣh*, and this most probably was intended to refer to Moṣah, a locality west of Jerusalem.

Wampler dated the settlement of the Persian period to 587–400 B.C., after which time, he believed, it was abandoned. However, the opinion of W. F. Albright and G. E. Wright that occupation continued there also during the first half of the fourth century B.C. seems more likely. Some sherds and coins found on the surface of the site and in the tombs in the vicinity belong to later settlements from the Hellenistic, Roman, and Byzantine periods at nearby Khirbet 'Atara and Khirbet Shweikha.

SUMMARY

Remains of two separate periods were found at Mizpah, from the end of the fourth and the beginning of the third millennium B.C. and from the end of the second and first two thirds of the first millennium B.C. The chief importance of the excavations lies in the baring of the Israelite town. Mizpah is the only Israelite town to have been almost entirely cleared, enabling us to obtain a full picture of the type of settlement, its fortifications, buildings, burials, and implements.

M. BROSHI

BIBLIOGRAPHY

For the Identification: Z. Kallai, *Enc. Miqr.* 5, 237–42 (includes bibliography) (Hebrew) • J. Muilenburg, in: C. C. McCown, *Tell en-Nasbeh* 1, Berkeley–New Haven, 1947, 13–49; idem, *Studia Theologica Scandinavicorum* 8 (1954–55), 25–42 • A. Malamat, *JNES* 9 (1950), 222 f.
Excavation Report: J. C. Wampler, *BASOR* 82 (1941), 25–43 • C. C. McCown–J. C. Wampler et al., *Tell en-Nasbeh* 1–2, Berkeley–New Haven, 1947.
The Finds: W. F. Albright, *JNES* 7 (1948), 202 ff. • G. E. Wright, *AJA* 52 (1948), 470–72 • O. Tufnell, *PEQ*, 1948, 145–50 • Trude Dothan, *The Philistines and Their Material Culture*, Jerusalem, 1967, 44 (Hebrew) • K. Branigan, *IEJ* 16 (1968), 206–08 • Stern, *Material Culture*, 34–35.
Inscriptions: N. Avigad, *BIES* 17 (1953), 95–97 (Hebrew); idem, *IEJ* 8 (1958), 113–19 • F. M. Cross, Jr., *BASOR* 193 (1969), 19–20.

NAZARETH

HISTORY. Nazareth is mentioned for the first time in the New Testament as the city where Jesus was raised and educated (Matthew 2:23, Luke 2:39, 51). According to Luke 1:26 and 2:4, Mary and Joseph lived in Nazareth even before Jesus' birth. Jesus later preached in the local synagogue, but was not sympathetically received by the inhabitants, who wanted to cast him from the hill on which the city stood (Matthew 13:57–58; Luke 4:16–30). Jesus' disciples, nevertheless, were known as Nazarenes, after the name of that city.

In non-Christian sources, Nazareth is first mentioned in an inscription in the synagogue of Caesarea, which lists twenty-four priestly families that settled in Galilee. In *Kerevoth* (hymns) from the seventh century A.D., Nazareth appears as the home of the priestly family of Hofzaz (Aphses) (I Chronicles 24:15). In the fourth century, Nazareth was still a small Jewish village (Eusebius, Onomasticon 138:24). The building of a church (which was originally a synagogue) is noted in the sixth century. In 614, the Jews in the mountains of Nazareth helped the Persians conquer the Galilee. During the Crusades, the Christian city suffered at the hands of the Muslims. While Crusader rule lasted, Nazareth was the seat of an archbishop, and a magnificent church in twelfth-century style was built there. The city changed hands several times in the thirteenth century, until the Sultan Baybars ordered its destruction in 1263. Nazareth remained in ruins until the seventeenth century.

EXCAVATIONS

Systematic excavations have been carried out in Nazareth, mainly by the Franciscans near the Church of the Annunciation. In addition, about twenty-five graves accidentally uncovered in the

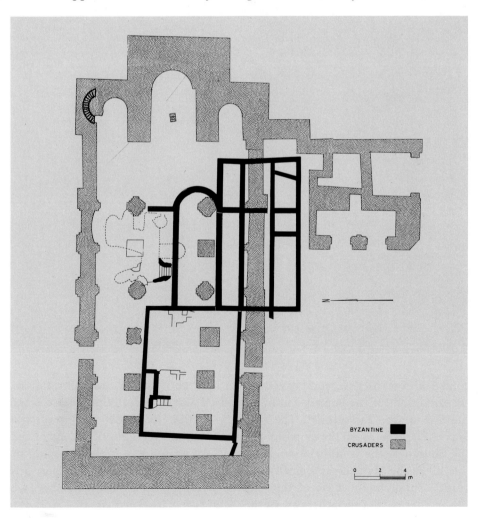

BYZANTINE
CRUSADERS

0 2 4
m

General plan of the Church of the Annunciation.

This page: View of the excavations in the area of the Church of the Annunciation. In center, stylobate of the Byzantine church; Opposite page: Crusader capitals: left, Doubting Thomas and other apostles; right the decapitation of James.

course of construction work have thrown light on the necropolis of the Roman–Byzantine period and the size of the early town. The majority of the graves are situated on the slopes of the hill west of the Church of the Annunciation, and some are on the hill to the east, across a small valley. Only one grave is built in the style of the Israelite period. The greater part of the others are of the loculi type,

and a few are vaulted. Two graves of the loculi type found intact contained lamps, pottery, glass vessels, and beads — objects usually found together with coins of the first–fourth centuries A.D. In a grave on the property of Les Dames de Nazareth, the door, a rolling stone, has survived. The burial chamber, which has loculi in the walls, served as the storeroom of a house during the

Middle Ages. A list of these graves was prepared by C. Kopp.

The plan of a Crusader church found on the grounds of St. Joseph's Church had been reconstructed by P. Viaud. Beneath its floor was a water reservoir hewn out of the rock and at a still lower level, a granary cave and a pit. Potsherds from the Israelite, Hellenistic, Roman, and Byzantine periods and the Middle Ages were also found.

Excavations were conducted in the Church of the Annunciation situated on a small hill surrounded by ancient graves south of St. Joseph's Church. The cave, known as the Grotto of the Annunciation, has been considered a holy site for centuries, and many buildings have sprung up around it. In 1899, B. Vlaminck reconstructed the plan of the Crusader basilica, which had been almost completely destroyed, and uncovered several sections of a Byzantine mosaic near the Grotto of the Annunciation. North of the Crusader church wall, Viaud discovered five capitals made of soft stone, on which episodes from the lives of the Apostles were carved by twelfth-century sculptors from northern France. The grotto was incorporated into the Church of the Annuniciation as a place of worship. Steps leading down to the grotto were added, and a small bema was erected inside. The whole complex constitutes a unique structure.

In 1955, excavations were conducted on the same site under the direction of B. Bagatti of the Franciscan Institute for Biblical Research. The excavations were extended over the entire area of the Crusader church and in the area to the north, where the bishop's palace had once stood, and later the Franciscan monastery. About 5 meters below the level of the Crusader building were found the remains of a church with three wings, a pronaos, and a small monastery. The monastery was situated south of the church and projected beyond the boundaries of the Crusader building. The early building closely resembles other buildings of the fourth and fifth centuries A.D., e.g., the Church of Gethsemane. The church contained several mosaic floors, of which only fragments have survived, but sufficient, however, to note several repairs. Since only some of the mosaics — which are all of equal size — have a cross, it is assumed that the church was built in the first half of the fifth century, when the decree of Theodosius was published (427) forbidding the representation of the cross on floors. The stylobate, which was raised above the mosaic floor and was .9 meter wide, consisted of a double row of stones arranged in diagonal courses, held together by iron cramps. The other walls of the perimeter were built of only one row of stones laid in diagonal courses and only .6 meter wide. The floor of the nave was laid at a different level from that of the northern aisle. The Grotto of the Annunciation continued to serve as a place of worship instead of the northern aisle until the new church was built. It was therefore impossible to examine it. Architectural elements not found in situ — e.g., capitals decorated with crosses on all four faces — helped to clarify the plan of the Byzantine church.

In the excavations in 1955, it was found that the ground below the surface was riddled with cavities and hollows: pear-shaped granaries, vaulted cells for storing wine and oil jars, pits, and small wells. Several oil presses were found at surface level. In the rock-cut cavities, it was possible to detect traces of houses. Some uniform depressions apparently held the foundations of walls. The remains of these structures vanished when the bishop's palace was built. In several granaries, pottery from the Israelite period was found — sherds of jars with two handles and a short spout — indicating that the granaries were no longer in use in later times. Since Roman and especially Byzantine sherds were found in most of the cells, it seems that these rooms were buried under earth during the construction of the medieval buildings. The cells are similar to others discovered beneath St. Joseph's Church and the Franciscan friary, and it can therefore be concluded that the early town extended up to the present-day site of these two churches. The boundaries of the ancient graves also confirm this assumption.

During the construction of the new Church of the Annunciation, the mosaic floors were removed to be re-laid on new foundations, making possible the investigation of the ground below. In the nave of the Byzantine church was a pool hewn in the rock with seven steps leading down to the botton. A row of symbols on the plastered walls is considered by the excavators as belonging to Christians of Jewish origin: small plants, boats, a checkered net, three pointed crosses. Dressed stones with traces of colored plaster, which were preserved in the pool, bore various graffiti, such as the letters *IH* (abbreviation of Jesus' name), the name Sysinius, and fragments of invocations of God. Beneath the floor of the southern aisle were sherds of the third and fourth centuries A.D. and small coins attributed to the end of the fourth and the beginning of the

fifth centuries. The stones used to strengthen the bed of the mosaic floors still bore traces of plaster. Under the floor of the small monastery was a layer of fill about 2 meters thick, containing about eighty stones that belonged to an older building: column bases, capitals without leaves, moldings, ends of arches, jambs of doors and windows, and other dressed stones. From the comparison of these stones with remains of other buildings, it may be concluded that the method of building and even the measurements are similar to those of the Galilean synagogues, especially at Khirbet el-'Amed and E-Dikkeh (see Synagogues), and the early building should perhaps be attributed to the construction period of these synagogues. Many stones were still coated with white plaster and preserved graffiti drawn in charcoal, or with a stylus. These graffiti display several crosses, the words **XE MAPIA**, which refer to the passage in Luke on the Annunciation, a boat, usually connected with Jesus in Christian theology, the names Leon and Sarah, fragments of an invocation of God, and the figure of a man holding in his right hand a cross-headed staff. The structure was an early church dating from before the time of Constantine and was built on the plan of a synagogue.

While deep foundations for the columns of the new church were being dug, the opportunity was taken to examine several caves hewn in the rocky ground below. In one cave situated south of the Crusader church, pottery, metal objects, and a scarab from the Hyksos period were found. Several objects from the same period were found in another cave, mostly hidden under Byzantine and medieval walls. In a third cave, the finds were mixed and the form of the cave was similar to that of the Bronze Age graves at Megiddo. This cave is clear evidence that Nazareth was settled in the Middle Bronze Age.

B. BAGATTI

BIBLIOGRAPHY

B. Vlaminck, *A Report of the Recent Excavations and Explorations Conducted at the Sanctuary of Nazareth,* Washington, 1900 • P. Viaud, *Nazareth et ses deux Eglises de L'Annonciation et de Saint-Joseph,* Paris, 1910 • E. T. Richmond, *QDAP* 1 (1932), 53–54 • C. Kopp, *JPOS* 18 (1938), 187–228 • M. Barash, *EI* 7 (1964), 125–34 (Hebrew) • idem, *IEJ* 13 (1963), 145 • B. Bagatti, *Gli scavi di Nazaret,* 1: dalle origini al secolo XII, Jerusalem, 1967, English translation by E. Hoade, Jerusalem, 1969 • E. Testa, *Nazaret giudeo-cristiana,* Jerusalem, 1969 • B. Bagatti, *Liber Annuus* 21 (1971), 5–32 • J. Prawer, *IEJ* 24 (1974), 241–51.

NEBO, MOUNT

IDENTIFICATION. The mountainous area bordered in the north by Wadi 'Uyun Musa and in the south by Wadi el-Afrit Judeidah Knisa Ḥeri is called Nebo to this day. The highest peak is Jebel Naba. South of it stands the hill of Khirbet el-Mukhaiyet, which is generally identified as the town of Nebo. The hill of Siyagha to the west is traditionally associated with the death of Moses and his memory. Nearby is the hill known in the Byzantine period as *Agri specula* ("watchtower of the field"), which is close to the "field of Zophim" ("field of sentries") appearing in the story of Balak (Numbers 23:14). The memory of Moses is associated not only with the northern stream, 'Uyun Musa, but also with the southern Wadi el-

Afrit, mentioned in the description of the struggle over the body of Moses in the Epistle of Jude (verse 9). These references show clearly that the memory of Moses was not forgotten there despite centuries of changes.

Although no monumental remains are found on Jebel Naba itself, megalithic structures are known in the area: dolmens, stone circles, monoliths, and menhirs. Also visible are stone fences, apparently the boundaries of fields, ancient roads marked by large stones, strong bridges, oil presses, and other rock-cut installations. These remains all point to the presence of man thousands of years ago. Two pottery assemblages were discovered in two caves — one east of Wadi 'Uyun Musa on the flank of Wadi Abu e Namleh, and the other at the foot of Khirbet el-Mukhaiyet near 'Ein-Judeidah. The vessels from the first cave date from the Middle Bronze Age II, and the second

Mount Nebo. Mosaic in the baptistery.

group is attributed to the Early Bronze Age III.

EXPLORATION OF THE SITE

A building near Wadi 'Uyun Musa was examined by N. Glueck who judged it to be a Nabataean fort enclosed by a defense wall. Sherds dating to the Iron Age I–II were found in the ruins, as well as a statue of a goddess, apparently Astarte, holding in her hand a cylindrical object, perhaps a fertility symbol.

In 1933, 1935, and 1937, the Franciscan Biblical School in Jerusalem conducted excavations on the hill of Siyagha, under the direction of S. J. Saller. A rectangular building with an east–west orientation was exposed (external measurements 15.83 by 17.76 meters), as well as a monastery complex. The outer walls of the monastery are made of drafted stone blocks with bosses about 2 meters above the line of the podium. This line passes to the north

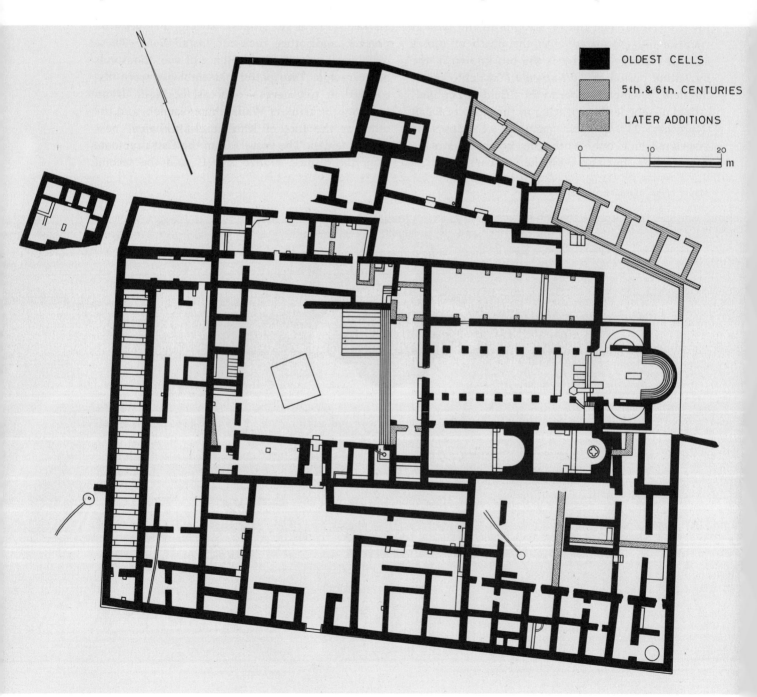

OLDEST CELLS

5th. & 6th. CENTURIES

LATER ADDITIONS

and east, where the ground slopes steeply above the wall of stone blocks, and on the north it is hidden behind a wide buttress. Inside the buildings, which underwent modifications in a later period, there were three well-preserved apses. Above the foundations of the buildings, there were engaged columns of the apse walls. The stones of the apses are smoothed, and their margins are simple and differ from one another. Aside from the margins, double bases were also found scattered in the ruins, which indicate the manner in which the apses were joined. Although no Roman pottery was discovered in the excavations (which were very limited in the interior of the building), several finds from the ruins belong to this period — among them the foot of a lion in colored marble, margins, and a small metal relief, apparently of the Mother Goddess. Several fragments of Samaritan inscriptions were found, which were at first attributed to the fifth century A.D. T. Milik,

however, ascribed them on paleographic ground to the first centuries A.D. His opinion receives support from the fact that there is no mention of the town's conquest by the Samaritans in the fifth century, whereas there is proof of continuous occupation by the monks. This large building is undoubtedly the first monumental evidence of a memorial to Moses in the area. It was a holy site even before the construction of the building, and in the opinion of E. Zolli, it was surrounded by a fence *(siyyag)* and therefore was called Siyagha.

At the time Egeria visited the mountain (about A.D. 395), the monks had already converted the trefoil-apse building into a church, where they exhibited their "relic" — the empty grave of Moses. Several Talmudic stories concerning the discovery of a sanctuary dedicated to Moses may have been taken from Egeria. In A.D. 430 or 480, at the time of a visit by Peter the Iberian, the monks were no longer content with the tradition associating it with

Both pages, counterclockwise from left: General plan; Chapel of Theotocus; Church of Procopius; Inscription in the church of Procopius.

the story of Moses, and adopted a legend according to which Moses was seen by a young shepherd following which the inhabitants of Mount Nebo built the sanctuary. This was the period when bodies of saints used to reveal themselves at frequent intervals.

In the fourth century, the monks built small cells north of the first building, and later erected a large church of small stones west of the building in such a way that the early building became the apse of the church. Still later, large monasteries connected to each other were constructed from the same materials, as well as a chapel in honor of the Holy Virgin, the Church of the Baptism, and several adjoining rooms. The largest monastic establishment in all of Palestine was completely bared here. As works of art, the fourth-century mosaic floors of the first building are outstanding. They contain representations of birds laid without the use of light and shadow, as was usual in tapestries. The mosaics of the sixth and seventh centuries in the other rooms are equally fine. The mosaic in the Virgin's chapel shows depictions of the sanctuary with two courtyards the altar with the eternal light and the holy of holies, as seen from the east gate.

In the basilica and the Virgin's chapel, four large columns supported the ceiling, replacing the fence which at first had formed a partition between the worshippers and the priests. Since the monastery was in existence only till the ninth century, this change, carried out under the influence of the iconoclastic movement, is one of the first changes of which there is proof.

There were common graves in the church and monastery. The dead were laid in deep pits strengthened by masonry. Stone slabs covered the graves and were set on a rim surrounding the grave. The central slab contained a hole by which the slab could be easily lifted to permit burials. In its later form, the monastery was an integrated complex of buildings, but its interior is divided into separate components, which communicated with each other through one opening only. It is not known whether the internal layout was planned by considerations of space (like the monastery of Saint Theodosius) or of function. The second alternative seems more likely because certain installations — e.g., two ovens — were concentrated in only one part of the monastery.

The Hill of Khirbet Mukhaiyet, on which the town of Nebo stood, was excavated by the Franciscan friars only in its upper level. Three churches from the sixth and seventh centuries were found, with pictorial mosaic pavements and another church, the earliest, paved only with flat stones. The mosaics depict scenes from daily life: vintage, hunting, grazing, fishing, and shipping. There are also allegorical pictures of animals against a background of water or trees, and also symbolic depictions, such as a lion and an ox eating straw together (based on the vision of Isaiah 11:7), and two bullocks sacrificed on the altar (based on Psalm 51:19). A figure unique to this site, which occurs twice in different forms, is Earth personified by a woman with fruit in her lap, two boys offering baskets of fruit. This is reminiscent of the ceremony of the first fruits which, in Christian ritual, developed various forms. Altogether, the mosaics show thirty-six persons, thirty men and six women. Of the fourteen inscriptions laid in the mosaics, thirteen are in Greek and one is in Christian-Palestinian-Aramaic. They mention thirty-six people, of whom seven were priests, and of the others eighteen are men and ten are women. Pictured in the mosaics are thirty-eight mammals, thirty birds, twenty water creatures, and seven fishes.

During the paving of a road, the corner of the early elliptical-shaped fortification wall that surrounded the hill was uncovered. It was built of large stone blocks with bosses. Sherds were found from the Iron Age, the Hellenistic and Roman periods, and especially from the Byzantine period. Among the coins found, one was of Alexander Jannaeus, and one of Aretas IV Philopater.

On the hill west and north of the site tombs with loculi and others with arcosolia were found. One loculus contained Rhodian lamps and pyriform juglets.

Numerous tombs and caves of the Israelite, Hellenistic, Roman, and Byzantine periods were explored on the hills east of Khirbet Mukhaiyet by J. Ripamonti from 1962 to 1966.   B. BAGATTI

BIBLIOGRAPHY

S. J. Saller, *The Memorial of Moses on Mount Nebo,* 1, 2, Jerusaelm, 1941 • H. Schneider, *ibid.,* 3, Jerusalem, 1950 • S. J. Saller and B. Bagatti, *The Town of Nebo,* Jerusalem, 1949 • S. J. Saller, *Liber Annuus* 16 (1966), 165–298; 17 (1967), 5–64 • S. Yonik, *ibid.,* 162–221 • V. Corbo, *ibid.,* 241–58, 20 (1970), 273–98.

NESSANA (Niṣana)

IDENTIFICATION. Nessana, a settlement in the Negev, 52 kilometers (32 miles) southwest of Beersheba, was in existence from the Hellenistic period to the Early Arabic period. The site was discovered by U. J. Seetzen in 1897, who mistakenly called it Eboda. E. Robinson visited the site in 1838. A. Musil, C. L. Woolley, and T. E. Lawrence prepared plans of the ruins. In 1916,

during World War I, many ancient remains were discovered there. The Colt Expedition excavated the site in 1935–36, 1936–37. The ancient name (written Νεσᾶνα) is mentioned in papyri (see below). The Arabic name is Auja el-Khafir.

HISTORY

The settlement was founded by the Nabataeans in the Hellenistic period, in the second half of the second century B.C. The oldest building on the site is a fort (25 by 27 meters) with round towers at the corners and a strong retaining wall on the south side. Near the foundations of the fort were

Byzantine fort. 1. North Church. 2. Fort. 3. South Church. 4. The city.

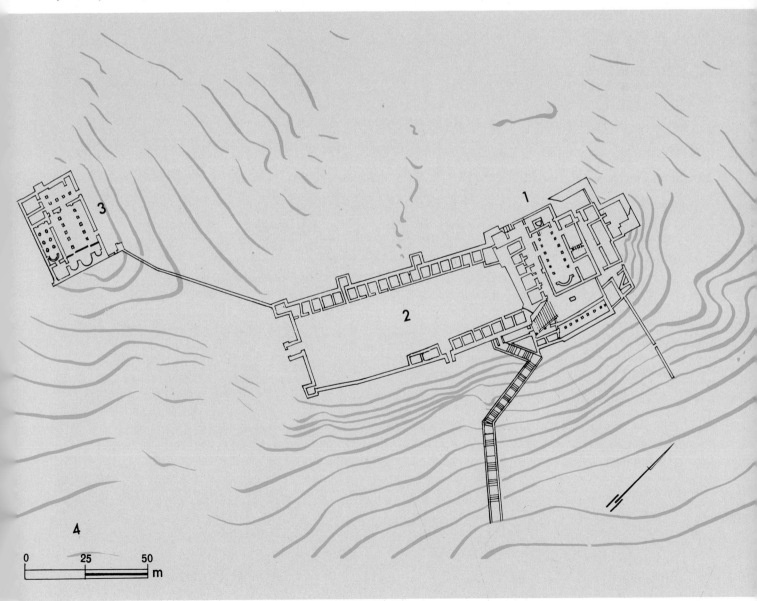

discovered stones with diagonal Nabataean dressing and a typical Nabataean capital. From the pottery and glass finds, it is evident that Nessana flourished in the first century B.C. and the first century A.D. During the second–fourth centuries A.D., the city suffered a decline when trade with Elath was diverted from the Gaza route to a new route to Damascus, built by Trajan.

In the first quarter of the fifth century, a large fort (35 by 85 meters) was erected, which consisted entirely of a casemate wall, with towers in the corners and at the middle of each side. The fort was built for stationing the Theodosian Numerus—''the most loyal.'' At first, seven rooms were built along the length of the western wall of the fort, and another twenty rooms were later added. The center of the courtyard was a wide square. A flight of steps led from the fort down to the city.

Opposite page: Papyrus in Arabic and Greek — 7th century A.D. *This page: Papyrus No. 6 describing the deeds of Saint George — 7th–8th centuries* A.D.

The army occupied the fort till about 600 A.D. It was later annexed to the church and became part of the monastery. At the foot of the fort was established a settlement, which flourished economically until the Arab conquest and continued to exist till the beginning of the eighth century. In the fifth century, a church dedicated to Saints Sergius and Bacchus was built north of the fort. The church, constructed on the foundations of the Hellenistic fort, had an internal apse, very narrow aisles (2.25 meters), and a nave (5.5 meters wide). The church, 10.7 meters wide, was originally 17 meters long, but was lengthened to 21 meters by the addition of a narthex. The early church apparently had a narrow atrium to the west, and was surrounded by long, narrow courtyards on the south and east. Beyond the southern courtyard was a martyrium of two rooms dedicated to Saints Stephen and Sergius. At the beginning of the seventh century, the atrium was converted into a baptistery, several rooms were added to the martyrium, and a small chapel was built on the north side. The church was then paved in a checkered pattern of small colored pieces of marble (opus sectile). Sometime later, a courtyard and hall were added on its north side and a hall on the east. Thus the building on the summit of the acropolis was eventually doubled in area. Steps were also built descending from the fort to the city, and a deep well was dug at the northern end of the acropolis. At the beginning of the seventh century, another church dedicated to Saint Mary was built on another hill south of the acropolis. This church (20.8 by 14.1 meters) is a basilica with three internal apses, a narrow atrium and a narthex, and an additional chapel on the south, also with an apse, nave, and aisles.

At the end of the sixth and beginning of the seventh centuries, the Gaza-Elath route was re-opened, the Negev was protected by garrison troups, and Nessana underwent an economic and religious revival. At that time, many buildings were erected: 116 houses for a population of about 1,500, as is evident from the poll-tax roll of the inhabitants during the years 587–589 A.D.

The finds include a large number of architectural remains carved out of soft rock, in geometric designs — in the style found throughout the Negev. Among the ornaments, the most notable are amphorae, rosettes, intertwining vines, etc. There were also reliefs in ivory and bone in Coptic style, wooden vessels including pen cases, cloth of Egyptian type, baskets, mirrors, leather goods, 146 coins (two Ptolemaic, seven Nabataean, one Jewish [Hyrcanus or Jannaeus], four Roman, and the remainder Byzantine). The glass vessels were late Hellenistic and Early Roman, Late Roman from Syria (the majority), and Early Arab. Among the pottery, the most important are three Rhodian handles and twenty handles from Cos. The pottery included terra sigilatta and stamped Byzantine vessels, as well as painted or glazed ware, and many others of Late Roman, Byzantine, and Early Arab types. The inscriptions (altogether 152) are almost all in Greek, and their dates range from 464 to 630 A.D. They include dedications, tombstones, and graffiti. The majority of the names are Arabic. About ten Nabataean inscriptions were also discovered, mostly lists of names. The papyri — the most important discovery in Nessana — were found mainly in rooms near the two churches. Among the literary papyri, eleven are books or fragments of them: a Greek dictionary of the Aeneid of Virgil, part of the Aeneid, the life of Saint George, and portions of several religious works. The archives include 195 documents from the years 512–689 A.D., among them contracts, deeds of marriage and divorce, of property and inheritance, and of sale, debit, and receipt, the accounts of a camel-mounted cavalry unit, an apportionment of taxes among villages, receipts of tax payments, letters concerning church affairs, requests, instructions given by the Arab governors for payments in silver, grain, or oil, written in Arabic and Greek; instructions for providing road guides, a census roll, complaints of high taxes, lists of fields and harvest yields, commercial accounts, bills of date-sellers, etc.

M. AVI-YONAH

BIBLIOGRAPHY

Surveys: Musil, *Arabia Petraea* 1, 88–109 • C. L. Wooley and T. E. Lawrence, *The Wilderness of Zin* (= *APEF* 3), London, 1914, 115–21 • P. H. Haenster, *Das Heilige Land* 60 (1916), 155 ff.; 61 (1916), 198 ff.; 62 (1917), 12 ff. • K. Wultzinger, in: T. Wiegand, *SINAI*, Berlin–Leipzig, 1921, 99–109 • A. Alt, *Die griechischen Inschriften der Palaestina Tertia*, Berlin–Leipzig, 1921, 37–43.
Excavations: H. D. Colt et al., *Excavations at Nessana* 1, London, 1962 • L. Casson and E. L. Hettich, *Excavations at Nessana* 2, *Literary Papyri*, Princeton, 1950 • C. J. Kraemer, *Excavations at Nessana* 3, *Non-Literary Papyri*, Princeton, 1958.

CHRONOLOGICAL TABLES

The Prehistoric Periods in Palestine

PERIOD	CULTURE	ICE AGE IN EUROPE	GEOLOGICAL EPOCH	APPROXIMATE DATES
Lower Paleolithic	Abbevillian	Mindel	Middle Pleistocene (Quaternary)	500,000
	Lower and Middle Acheulian	Mindel-Riss		to
	Upper Acheulian	Riss		120,000
Middle Paleolithic	Micoquian, "pre-Aurignacian"	Riss-Würm	Upper Pleistocene (Quaternary)	80,000
	Yabrudian	Würm I		
		Würm II		
Upper Paleolithic	Phase I "Emireh"	Würm III		35,000
	Phase II			
	Phase III–V Aurignacian			
Epipaleolithic (Mesolithic)	Phase VI Kebaran			15,000
		Würm IV		
	Natufian	Post glacial	Holocene	8,000
Pre-pottery Neolithic	Phase A			
	Phase B			
Pottery Neolithic				5,500
Chalcolithic	Early phase			4,000 to
	Ghassulian phase			3,150

The Archaeological Periods in Palestine

Paleolithic (Old Stone Age)	25,000–10,000 BC	*Iron Age*		*Roman Period*	
Mesolithic (Middle Stone Age)	10,000–7500	Iron Age IA	1200–1150	Roman I (Herodian)	37 BC–AD 70
Neolithic (New Stone Age)	7500–4000	Iron Age IB	1150–1000	Roman II	AD 70–180
Chalcolithic	4000–3150			Roman III	180–324
		Iron Age IIA	1000–900		
Bronze Age		Iron Age IIB	900–800	*Byzantine Period*	
Early Bronze Age I A–C	3150–2850	Iron Age IIC	800–586	Byzantine I	324–451
Early Bronze Age II	2850–2650			Byzantine II	451–640
Early Bronze Age III	2650–2350	*Babylonian and Persian Periods*	586–332		
Early Bronze Age IV (IIIA)	2350–2200			*Early Arab Period*	640–1099
Middle Bronze Age I	2200–2000	*Hellenistic Period*			
Middle Bronze Age IIA	2000–1750	Hellenistic I	332–152	*Crusader Period*	1099–1291
Middle Bronze Age IIB	1750–1550	Hellenistic II (Hasmonaean)	152–37		
Late Bronze Age I	1550–1400				
Late Bronze Age IIA	1400–1300				
Late Bronze Age IIB	1300–1200				

Selected List of Kings

Egypt

Pre-Dynastic Period
4th and 3rd millennium
Proto-Dynastic Period

Ist Dynasty	c. 3100–2890 BC Narmer	
IInd Dynasty	c. 2890–2686	
IIIrd Dynasty	c. 2686–2613	

Old Kingdom

IVth Dynasty	c. 2613–2494	
	Snefru	
	Khufu	
	Khafre	
Vth Dynasty	c. 2494–2345	
VIth Dynasty	c. 2345–2181	
	Pepi I	

First Intermediate Period
VIIth Dynasty-Xth Dynasty
Middle Kingdom

XIth Dynasty	c. 2133–1991
XIIth Dynasty	c. 1991–1786
Amenemhet I	1991–1962
Senusert I	1971–1928
Amenemhet II	1929–1895
Senusert II	1897–1878
Senusert III	1878–1843
Amenemhet III	1842–1797
Amenemhet IV	1798–1970
Sebeknefrure	1789–1786

Second Intermediate Period — the Hyksos Period
XIII–XVIIth Dynasties
New Kingdom

XVIIIth Dynasty	1567–1320
Ahmose	1570–1546
Amenhotep I	1546–1526
Thutmose I	1525–1512
Thutmose II	c. 1512–1504
Hatshepsut	1503–1482
Thutmose III	1504–1450
Amenhotep II	1450–1425
Thutmose IV	1425–1417
Amenhotep III	1417–1379
Amenhotep IV (Akhenaton)	1379–1362 BC
Smenkhkere	1364–1361
Tutankhamon	1361–1352
Eye	1352–1348
Haremhab	1348–1320
XIXth Dynasty	1320–1200
Ramses I	1320–1318
Seti I	1318–1304
Ramses II	1304–1237
Merneptah	1236–1223
Seti II	1216–1210
XXth Dynasty	1200–1085
Ramses III	1198–1166
Ramses IV–XI	1166–1085

End of New Kingdom

XXIst Dynasty	1085–935
XXIInd Dynasty	935–730
Shishak I	935–914
Osorkon II	914–874
XXIIIrd Dynasty	817–740
XXIVth Dynasty	730–709
XXVth Dynasty (Nubian or Ethiopian)	750–656
Shabaka	716–695
Taharka	689–664
XXVIth Dynasty	664–525
Psamtik I	664–610
Necho II	610–595
Psamtik II	595–589
Psamtik III	526–525
XXVIIth Dynasty (Persian)	505–404
Cambyses	525–522
Darius I	521–486
Xerxes	486–466
Artaxerxes	465–424
Darius II	424–404
XXVIIIth–XXXth Dynasties	404–343

Assyria

Shalmaneser I	1274–1245 BC
Tiglath-Pileser I	1115–1077
Ashurnasirpal I	1049–1031
Shalmaneser II	1030–1019
Tiglath-Pileser II	966–935
Adadnirari II	911–891
Ashurnasirpal II	883–859
Shalmaneser III	858–824
Adadnirari III	810–783
Shalmaneser IV	782–772
Tiglath-Pileser III	745–727
Shalmaneser V	726–722
Sargon II	721–705
Sennacherib	704–681
Esarhaddon	680–669
Ashurbanipal	668–631

Neo-Babylonian Kingdom

Nabopolassar	626–605 BC
Nebuchadnezzar II	605–562
Amel-Marduk	562–560
Nabunaid	556–539
Nergal Sarussur	560–556

Persia

Cyrus	559–530 BC
Cambyses	530–522
Darius I	522–486
Xerxes	486–464
Artaxerxes I	464–423
Darius II	423–404
Artaxerxes II	404–359
Artaxerxes III	359–338
Arses (Xerxes II)	338–336
Darius III	336–331

The Kings of Judah and Israel

THE UNITED KINGDOM

Saul	ca. 1020–1004 BC
David	1004–965
Solomon	965–928

JUDAH		ISRAEL	
Rehoboam	928–911	Jeroboam	928–907
Abijam	911–908	Nadab	907–906
Asa	908–867	Baasha	906–883
Jehoshaphat	867–846	Elah	883–882
Jehoram	846–843	Zimri	882
Ahaziah	843–842	Omri	882–871
Athaliah	842–836	Ahab	871–852
Joash	836–798	Ahaziah	852–851
Amaziah	798–769	Jehoram	851–842
Uzziah	769–733	Jehu	842–814
Jotham	758–743	Jehoahaz	814–800
Ahaz	733–727	Jehoash	800–784
Hezekiah	727–698	Jeroboam	784–748
Manasseh	698–642	Zechariah	748
Amon	641–640	Shallum	748
Josiah	640–609	Menahem	747–737
Jehoahaz	609	Pekahiah	737–735
Jehoiakim	609–598	Pekah	735–733
Jehoiachin	597	Hoshea	733–724
Zedekiah	596–586		

The Hasmoneans

Jonathan	152–142 BC
Simeon	142–134
John Hyrcanus	134–104
Aristobulus	104–103
Alexander Jannaeus	103–76
Salome Alexandra	76–67
Aristobulus II	67–63
Hyrcanus II	63–40
Matthias Antigonus	40–37

The Herodians

Herod (the Elder)	37–4 BC
Archelaus	4 BC–AD 6
Herod Antipas	4 BC–AD 39
Philip	4 BC–AD 34
Herod Agrippa I	AD 37–44
Agrippa II	53–100(?)

The Procurators

Coponius	c. AD 6–9
M. Ambibulus	9–12
Annius Rufus	12–15
Valerius Gratus	15–26
Pontius Pilatus	26–36
Marcellus	36–37
Cuspius Fadus	41–46
Tiberius Alexander	46–48
Ventidius Cumanus	48–52
Antonius Felix	52–60
Porcius Festus	60–62
Albinus	62–64
Gessius Florus	64–66

Seleucid Kings

Seleucus I Nicator	311–281 BC
Antiochus I Soter	281–261
Antiochus II Theos	261–246
Seleucus II Callinicus	246–225
Seleucus III Soter	225–223
Antiochus III the Great	223–187
Seleucus IV Philopator	187–175
Antiochus IV Epiphanes	175–164
Antiochus V Eupator	163–162
Demetrius I Soter	162–150
Alexander Balas	150–145
Demetrius II Nicator	145–140
Antiochus VI Epiphanes	145–138
Antiochus VII Sidetes	138–129
Demetrius II Nicator	129–125
Cleopatra Thea	126
Cleopatra Thea and Antiochus VIII Grypus	125–121
Seleucus V	125
Antiochus VII Grypus	121–96
Antiochus IX Cyzicenus	115–95
Seleucus VI Epiphanes Nicator	96–95
Demetrius III Philopator	95–88
Antiochus X Eusebes	95–83
Antiochus XI Philadelphus	94
Philip I Philadelphus	94–83
Antiochus XII Dionysus	87–84
Antiochus XIII	69–64
Philip II	67–65

The Ptolemies

Ptolemy I Soter	304–282 BC
Ptolemy II Philadelphus	285–246
Ptolemy III Euergetes	246–221
Ptolemy IV Philopator	221–204
Ptolemy V Epiphanes	204–180
Ptolemy VI Philometor	180–145
Ptolemy VII Neos Philopator	145–144
Ptolemy VIII Euergetes II	145–116
Ptolemy IX Soter II	116–107
Ptolemy X Alexander I	107–88
Ptolemy IX Soter II (restored)	88–81
Ptolemy XI Alexander II	80 BC
Ptolemy XII Neos Dionysos	80–51
Cleopatra VII Philopator	51–30
Ptolemy XIII	51–47
Ptolemy XIV	47–44
Ptolemy XV	44–30

Overlapping dates usually indicate co-regencies.

Roman and Byzantine Emperors

Augustus	27 B.C.–A.D. 14	Septimius Severus	193–211	Aurelian	270–275	Valens	364–378
Tiberius	A.D. 14–37	Geta	211–212	Tacitus	275–276	Theodosius I	378–395
Gaius Caligula	37–41	Caracalla	211–217	Probus	276–282	Arcadius	383–408
Claudius	41–54	Macrinus	217–218	Carus	282–283	Honorius	383–423
Nero	54–68	Diadumenianus	218	Carinus	283–284	Theodosius II	402–450
Balba	68–69	Elagabalus	218–222	Numerianus	283–284	Valentinian III	425–455
Otho	69	Alexander Severus	222–235	Diocletian	284–305	Marcian	450–457
Vitellius	69	Maximian I	235–238	Maximianus Herculius	286–305	Leo I	457–474
Vespasian	69–79	Gordianus I	238	Constantius I	293–306	Anthemius	467–472
Titus	79–81	Gordianus II	238	Galerius	293–311	Zeno	474–491
Domitian	81–96	Balbinus	238	Severus	306–307	Anastasius I	491–518
Nerva	96–98	Pupienus	238	Maxentius	306–312	Justin I	518–527
Trajan	98–117	Gordianus III	238–244	Licinius	308–324	Justinian I	527–565
Hadrian	117–138	Philip Senior	244–249	Maximinus II	308–313	Justin II	565–578
Antoninus Pius	138–161	Philip Junior	247–249	Constantine the Great	308–337	Tiberius II	578–582
Marcus Aurelius	161–180	Trajanus Decius	249–251	Constantius II	337–361	Tiberius Maurice	582–602
Lucius Verus	161–169	Trebonianus Gallus	251–253	Constans	337–350	Focas	602–610
Commodus	180–192	Hostilianus	251	Julian	361–363	Heraclius	610–641
Pertinax	193	Volusian	251–253	Jovian	363–364	Constans II	641–668
Didius Julianus	193	Valerian	253–260	Valentinian I	363–375		
Pescennius Niger	193–194	Gallienus	253–268	Gratian	367–383		
Clodius Albinus	193–197	Claudius Gothicus	268–270	Valentinian II	375–392		

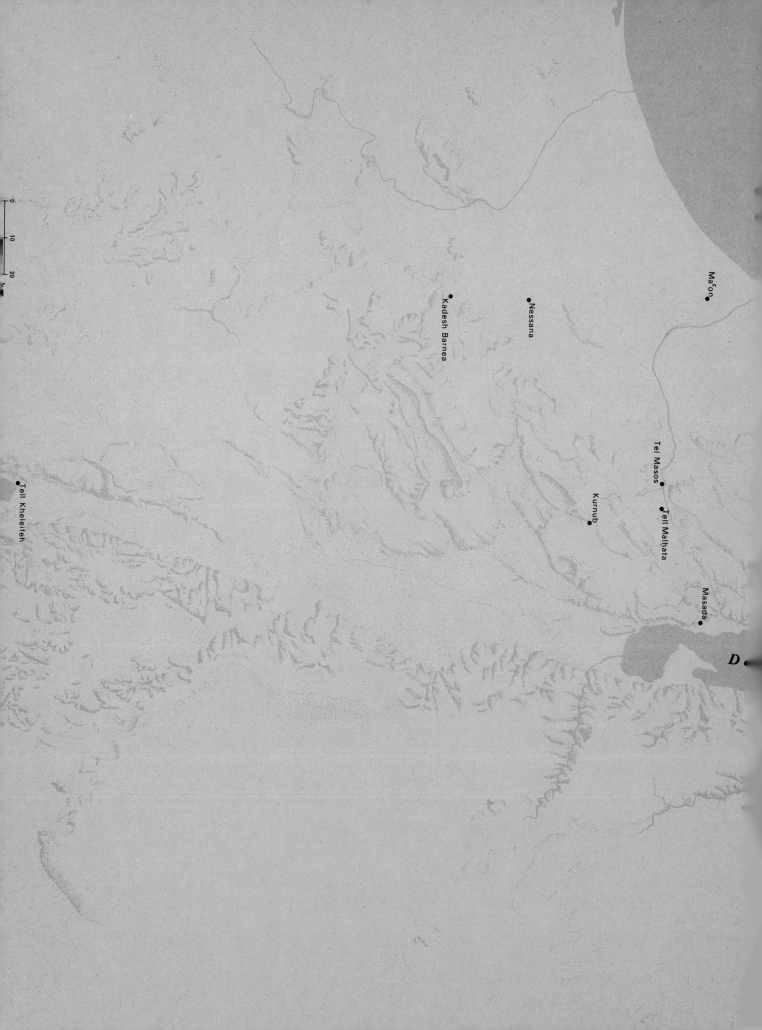

0
10
20
km

Maʿon

Nessana

Kadesh Barnea

Tel Masos

Kurnub

Tell Malhata

Tell Kheleifeh

Masada

D